"James Voiss, in *Rethinking Christian Forgiveness: Theological, Philosophical, and Psychological Explorations*, has compiled the most ambitious project of integrating the philosophy, psychology, and theology of forgiveness that exists today. It zeroes in on fundamental points. I would urge philosophers, psychologists, and theologians—particularly Christian theologians—who are setting out on a scholarly odyssey to understand forgiveness to begin at this scholarly jumping-off point for a thought-provoking, stimulating, surprising, and nondoctrinaire exploration of forgiveness."

> —Everett L. Worthington, Jr.
> Director, Counseling Psychology Program
> Virginia Commonwealth University
> Author (with Stephen J. Sandage) of *Forgiveness and Spirituality in Psychotherapy: A Relational Approach*

"James Voiss has written a very important book on Christian forgiveness. The depth and breadth of his approach are outstanding. I wholeheartedly recommend this book to all those struggling with the meaning of Christian forgiveness."

> —Charles E. Curran
> Perkins School of Theology
> Southern Methodist University

"In this text James Voiss combines exhaustive phenomenological analysis with insightful relevant commentary on practical spiritual life to answer the question 'Is there a distinctive Christian forgiveness?' In a patient and thorough dialogue with philosophers, psychologists, and theologians, he reinterprets forgiveness as far more than a virtuous act. The symbol 'forgiveness' offers entry into the Christian interpretation of the essential relationship between God and human beings and human beings among themselves. Christians are called not simply to receive forgiveness but, as followers of Jesus, to gradually internalize an active reconciling Spirit after the pattern of Jesus and thus contribute to the rule of God in history. This may be the definitive theological study of forgiveness to date. All theologians and those attentive to spirituality should have it on their shelves."

> —Roger Haight, SJ
> Director of the PhD Program
> Union Theological Seminary

# Rethinking Christian Forgiveness

## Theological, Philosophical, and Psychological Explorations

*James K. Voiss, SJ*

A Michael Glazier Book

**LITURGICAL PRESS**
Collegeville, Minnesota

www.litpress.org

A Michael Glazier Book published by Liturgical Press

Cover design by Stefan Killen Design. Cover photo © Thinkstock.

1    2    3    4    5    6    7    8    9

**Library of Congress Cataloging-in-Publication Data**

Voiss, James K.
    Rethinking Christian forgiveness : theological, philosophical, and psychological explorations / James K. Voiss, SJ.
        pages   cm
        "A Michael Glazier book."
        Includes bibliographical references.
        ISBN 978-0-8146-8060-5 — ISBN 978-0-8146-8061-2 (ebook)
    1. Forgiveness—Religious aspects—Christianity.   I. Title.
    BV4647.F55V65   2015
    234'.5—dc23                                         2014042573

To the many friends, companions, and guides who have helped me explore the landscape of Christian forgiveness . . .

*Especially,*

Jim Wyse, SJ +
Laura MacMullin
Jim Barlow
David Donovan, SJ +
Thomas Moran

*. . . with gratitude.*

# Contents

# Acknowledgments

The questions addressed in this book have deep roots in the soil of my life. Over the course of more than thirty-five years as a Jesuit I have wrestled with what it means to forgive, what Christian discipleship calls forth from us in forgiving, how to preach about so mysterious and difficult a phenomenon in a way that connects to real life, and how to incarnate the reality of forgiveness in addressing my own experiences of hurt and alienation. The struggle for understanding and integration has been a journey shared with many, many others. Along the way, the parishioners of Sacred Hearts Parish in Malden, Massachusetts; St. Bavo Parish in Mishawaka, Indiana; and St. Francis Xavier College Church Parish in St. Louis, Missouri, have journeyed with me. Their faith, their struggles, and their support over the course of my exploration of forgiveness have given them a special place in my heart. Without the experience of their companionship and the many lessons they have taught me, this book might never have come to be.

Many others have also played vital roles in bringing this book to publication. While my thinking about forgiveness had been percolating for many years, it took the push of one of my brothers in the Society of Jesus to get me to write. Without fellow Jesuit Bob Fabing's encouragement, it might never have occurred to me to take on this project. His initial push began a movement that rapidly gained momentum. Extended conversations over coffee with Matthew Mancini and Paul Lynch, colleagues from Saint Louis University, helped me to begin sketching out the ideas that gradually formed themselves into the chapters of this book. John Padberg, SJ, my former rector, long-time editor of the Institute of Jesuit Sources, and good friend, and Matt, Paul, Ron Mercier, SJ, Dan Finucane, and Tim Grosch generously gave of their time and shared their wisdom in critiquing the manuscript as it took shape. Tim, in particular, bears special mention for his meticulous reading and thoughtful comments on the various drafts of each chapter. I am deeply indebted to each of them for their generosity and interest in this project.

Pat Lee, SJ, my former provincial, made it possible for me to get a jump start on the actual writing of this book by supporting a year's sabbatical. And once underway, I was moved along by the constant encouragement (and occasional good-natured prodding) provided by dear friends Juliet Mousseau, RSCJ, Tom Reilly, and Laura Finucane, as well as the continuing interest of my Jesuit brothers in the communities of Seattle University and Gonzaga University where I spent that sabbatical year.

Finally, and by no means least in this process, I owe a great debt of thanks to the editorial staff at Liturgical Press. Hans Christoffersen supported and advocated for the proposal of this book project before the first chapter had been written. His enthusiastic response and interest—as well as his great patience with the sometimes-snail's-pace of my writing—helped to keep this project alive. Lauren L. Murphy has shepherded the manuscript through the process of publication with great skill. Linda Maloney provided careful critical feedback and textual editing to get the manuscript into its proper form. To them, and to all of the other women and men at Liturgical Press who have had a hand in bringing this book to print, I am deeply grateful.

# Introduction

## Naming the Question

*C*hristian Forgiveness. Is there such a thing? Ask any Christian and you are likely to receive an astonished, "Of course!" in reply. Forgiveness runs as a unifying theme throughout the Christian narrative. It holds the Christian story together. From the beginning of his public ministry and his announcement of the advent of the Kingdom of God until the moment of his death on the cross, Jesus offered forgiveness to those he met. Sometimes this is made explicit, as in the case of the penitent woman (Luke 7:36-50) or the healing of the paralytic (Mark 2:1-12 *parr.*). At other times the word "forgiveness" might not even be used, but the dynamism of forgiveness is clear. For example, Jesus' response to the woman caught in adultery (John 8:2-11) and his poignant interrogation of Peter at the Sea of Tiberias after the resurrection (John 21:1-19) never use the word "forgiveness," yet forgiveness is clearly at issue in each case.

Beyond these individual encounters, the teaching of Jesus is suffused with concern that his followers learn and practice forgiveness themselves. In the Sermon on the Mount (Matthew 5–7) Jesus exhorts his audience to "turn the other cheek" (Matt 5:39) and to "love your enemies" (Matt 5:44). The parable of the Prodigal Son (Luke 15:11-32) illustrates the extent of the forgiveness to which Jesus' followers are called, while the parable of the ungrateful servant (Matt 18:23-35) and Matthew's explanatory addition to the Lord's prayer ("neither will your heavenly Father forgive you if you do not forgive" Matt 6:15) underscore the consequence of the failure to forgive. Those who do not forgive exclude themselves from the Kingdom of God.

It is clear that forgiveness occupied a central place in Jesus' message and his mission. The Christian Scriptures emphasize the importance of forgiveness for Christian discipleship. But does that really answer the question? Is there such a thing as Christian forgiveness?

That is difficult to say. The question itself is somewhat ambiguous. In one way it could be understood to be asking whether Christians are inclined to be forgiving. Do Christians forgive? Such a question can hardly be answered in absolute terms. But if we were to look at the history of Christianity it would not be unreasonable to conclude that, all too often, Christians are not particularly forgiving. Despite the price to be paid for not forgiving (exclusion from the Kingdom of God), Christians have often been inclined to hold others bound in judgment and, on the basis of that reprobation, to persecute and execute rather than to forgive and reconcile. The litany of examples is already notorious: the violence associated with the Arian and Donatist controversies, extirpation of the Albigensians and the Waldensians, witch burnings, Crusades, Inquisitions, and the wars of religion in the wake of the Protestant Reformation. Contrary to the emphasis on forgiveness in the life and message of Jesus and in the church's preaching, Christian history has been marked by notable lapses in its practice. That much is undeniable.

But there is another way of reading the question. It is not unrelated to the first, but it takes us in a different direction. It does not point us, in the first instance, to the record of Christian successes and failures to forgive on the stage of history. Instead, it leads us back to the teaching of Jesus. It asks about his contribution to understanding a human enactment that had been an option long before he came on the scene. The Jewish Scriptures that nourished Jesus' faith contain their own teachings on forgiveness. No doubt other cultures also promote practices one would call "forgiveness." Such practices are vital in any culture, if for no other reason than to maintain social cohesion. But when Jesus promoted and practiced forgiveness, was he advocating anything different from what had gone before? Or was he just reaffirming what he had learned? To put the question slightly differently, is the forgiveness Jesus wanted his followers to practice any different from other approaches to forgiveness? Is there anything distinctive about it? This is an alternative way of reading our initial question.

We have already seen one clue suggesting that there is—or at least *should be*—a difference. The scandal we now experience when looking back at the historical situations named above evinces the recognition (at least in hindsight) that there is a great conflict, often unrecognized at the time, between the stated values of the Gospel and the actual practice of

Christians. When we ask, "is there a *Christian* forgiveness?" we are asking about precisely this difference. We are asking whether there is something distinctive about being Christian that calls for something distinctive about the forgiveness Christians are supposed to practice.

## Challenges

In what follows I propose to explore this question regarding the distinctiveness of Christian forgiveness. "Explore" is the operative word. Forgiveness is a complex subject, far more so than is often imagined. Before we can venture a response to the question of *Christian* forgiveness it will first be necessary to come to some understanding of forgiveness as a basic human phenomenon. This will not be easy. To make any progress we will have to confront many challenges. It will be helpful to name a few of them at the outset.

The first challenge comes in the form of a series of questions: What difference does it make whether the teaching of Jesus differs from a basic human approach to forgiveness? Why should one care? It will take the rest of this work to justify my response. However, an initial comment will help us to get oriented.

In the first instance this question is addressed to Christians. The answer touches on the interrelationship between Christian identity and Christian mission.[1] To put it simply, Christians understand their identity as Christian in terms of their response to the proclamation of the Gospel. As already indicated, that Good News—proclaimed *by* Jesus and, after the resurrection, proclaimed *about* Jesus—includes a commission to extend forgiveness of sin and to promote reconciliation between God and humankind and among all people to the ends of the world. The scope of this mission is universal. Whether or not there is something distinctive about Christian forgiveness, therefore, bears on both the Christian sense of self and the responsibility Christians have for how they engage in the practice of forgiveness, both within the parameters of their faith communities and beyond. It therefore becomes vital to Christian identity and mission to understand the forgiveness Jesus advocated and its relationship to other understandings of forgiveness. A more profound understanding of

---

[1] On the centrality of mission to Christian ecclesial existence, see Roger Haight, "The 'Established' Church as Mission: The Relation of the Church to the Modern World," *The Jurist* 39 (1979): 4–39.

forgiveness, and therefore of what it means to be Christian, is but the first step toward a more credible witness to the Gospel Christians proclaim.

This brings us to another challenge. Forgiveness is not a univocal term. The past thirty years have witnessed a burgeoning interest in forgiveness in philosophy,[2] psychology,[3] and a host of other disciplines. The horrors of the Holocaust and the Cambodian "Killing Fields" in the mid-twentieth century; genocide in Rwanda; "ethnic cleansing" in the Balkans; the lingering impacts of racism, colonialism, sexism, and interreligious/ intercultural clashes; and the continuing erosion of relational bonds in the wake of interpersonal violence and the erosion of families through divorce are among the ruptures fueling that increased interest in forgiveness. Philosophers, psychologists, sociologists, political scientists, and scholars in many other fields have recognized the need to grapple with forgiveness as a response to such upheaval, whether on the micro- or the macro-scale.

One might hope that such interest would lead to consensus on the meaning of forgiveness and its application. This has not been the case. On some points there has been convergence, if not complete agreement. For example, most authors approach forgiveness as a response to moral harm only,[4] although a few argue that it extends beyond the realm of moral harm.[5] But on other points perspectives are more heavily divided. These divisions sometimes occur within a given discipline; at other times they are more in evidence between disciplines.

---

[2] See, for example, Joram Graf Haber, *Forgiveness* (Savage, MD: Rowman & Littlefield, 1991); Jeffrie G. Murphy and Jean Hampton, *Forgiveness and Mercy*, Cambridge Studies in Philosophy and Law (Cambridge: Cambridge University Press, 1988); and Charles L. Griswold, *Forgiveness: A Philosophical Exploration* (Cambridge: Cambridge University Press, 2007) for recent discussions.

[3] Significant collections of essays on various aspects of the current psychological exploration of forgiveness include Robert D. Enright and Joanna North, eds., *Exploring Forgiveness* (Madison: University of Wisconsin Press, 1998); Everett L. Worthington, *Forgiveness: Psychological Theory, Research, and Practice* (New York: Routledge, 2006); and Michael E. McCullough, Kenneth I. Pargament, and Carl E. Thoresen, eds., *Forgiveness: Theory, Research, and Practice* (New York: Guilford Press, 2000).

[4] Haber takes this position in Haber, *Forgiveness*, 39, as does Griswold in Charles L. Griswold, *Forgiveness: A Philosophical Exploration*, xxv, 40.

[5] See, for example, Kim Atkins, "Friendship, Trust, and Forgiveness," *Philosophia: Philosophical Quarterly of Israel* 29, nos. 1–4 (May 2002): 111–32. The question of the relationship of the specifically moral dimension of harm to the admissibility of forgiveness will return as an important issue for articulating a phenomenology of forgiveness prior to theories of moral judgment.

Among the most frequently emerging differences, some argue that forgiveness requires that the one forgiven first repent. Others disagree. Some maintain that forgiveness includes reconciliation or the restoration of relationship. Others see forgiveness and reconciliation as distinct and independent phenomena. Many make the case that forgiveness is and must be a conditional response to a moral harm. If the conditions are fulfilled, one is morally obligated to forgive (or, others say, not!). Others see forgiveness as unconditional. A few raise the question whether forgiveness is even possible!

All of this leads to the second challenge: how to name forgiveness. The emphasis here is on "how," the *process* we will follow in seeking to name forgiveness. To propose and argue for a particular definition, whether a new one or one already formulated, is one possible way of proceeding. It is not the approach I propose to pursue, for many reasons. First, this has been the approach taken—either explicitly or implicitly—in all the discussions I have yet encountered. Each has assumed a definition and, when the nature of the argument called for it, has adduced arguments to justify the preferred definition. Thus far this approach has not produced an understanding of forgiveness that would be shared and found useful for the purposes of each discussion, whether philosophical, psychological, or theological. I do not anticipate that a further contribution to these kinds of discussions will have greater success. Second, to embrace a definition already proposed would not be especially helpful for advancing the question of this book. Rather than lead to the possibility of identifying any difference between a distinctively *Christian* forgiveness and forgiveness as a basic human enactment, it would doom the inquiry from the outset by starting with the assumption of sameness. But third, as I will argue later, underlying the *nomological* (naming) differences lurks a methodological problem: precisely, the unidentified question about "how" to name forgiveness. This methodological problem draws us into the relationship between the concept "forgiveness" and that phenomenon it seeks to name, a relationship that has remained unexplored in the literature. This oversight has led, as I will argue, to misunderstanding what is at stake in forgiveness. If we pursue the course followed by those who have gone before, we will repeat this same mistake. If we want to come to a deeper understanding of forgiveness we will need to take a fresh approach, to look at forgiveness with fresh eyes. Or, to change the metaphor, we will need to relocate the discussion in a new landscape.

It is important to identify one further challenge involved in naming forgiveness. It, too, touches on the issue of *de-finition*. As I will argue later in the book, the very effort to define (*de-finire*) forgiveness has often involved a dynamism counter to the trajectory of forgiveness itself. It has enacted a kind of violence at the level of concept—excluding the validity of experience that does not fit the preferred definition (an act of power and exclusion)—and has done so without proper warrant. This is not merely an academic subtlety. In the interplay between concept and life, this definitional exclusion pits the concept against the experience of those charged with forgiving and issues judgment on that experience.

A third challenge arises when we shift our attention from forgiveness as a basic human enactment to the task of naming, if possible, a distinctively *Christian* forgiveness. In its formal characteristics this third challenge parallels some aspects of the second. Just as there are multiple ways of naming forgiveness, and good arguments supporting those different approaches, there are also many ways of naming what is "Christian." The historical emergence of distinct denominations under the general heading "Christian" has brought with it theological reflection to support the perspective of those adhering to a particular expression of Christian faith. This theological reflection has, in turn, generated vocabularies, interpretations of the Christian sources and of Christian history and, consequently, distinctive idioms for understanding and naming what is Christian. These different idioms do not always or easily translate from one denomination to another. For example, among some Christians the questions "Have you been saved?" and "Have you accepted Jesus Christ as your personal savior?" make perfect sense, while to others they sound at best presumptuous and at worst appear theologically incoherent. This diversity of idioms could, very understandably, lead to different ways of naming forgiveness.

Herein lies the challenge. This Babel of Christian idioms places any claims about "Christian forgiveness" under a cloud of suspicion. One could, with good reason, question whether, under the heading of "Christian," I am in fact attempting to impose my own idiom as normative. If so, I would be engaging in a kind of power-play, something akin to setting out my own *de-finition* of forgiveness to the exclusion of all others. It is important to address this concern at the outset. In point of fact, I will be arguing that Christian forgiveness *is* distinctive and that it does have something to offer to understandings of forgiveness that do not appeal to the claims of Christian faith. I will be doing so, necessarily, from within my own idiom, an understanding of Christianity that has been stamped by my commitment to my own faith community, Roman Catholicism. Consequently, in the exposition of my argument I may well rely more heavily on sources congenial to my own idiom. However, I will strive to characterize the distinctively Christian in ways that will be recognizable to as broad a range of Christians as possible. It will be the responsibility of the reader, from whatever Christian idiom (or none!) to make the good-faith effort to understand the argument on its own terms and to evaluate its translatability into her or his own Christian (or not!) idiom.

These three challenges arise from the content of the questions we will be probing in what follows. There is another challenge, however, that intersects those arising from content but also circumscribes this entire effort. Those who have written on forgiveness have done so, with only rare exceptions, out of the conviction that, at least in the abstract, forgiveness is a positive value. It merits to be understood and put into practice. Frequent reference among those authors to the atrocities of the twentieth and the beginning of the twenty-first centuries underscores the human urgency of fostering forgiveness if we are to overcome the insidious cycles of violence on all scales of human relationship. Yet the very conditions that make forgiveness a matter of real human urgency also testify to the difficulties of promoting the practice of forgiveness convincingly.

One difficulty emerges from the very personal nature of the experience of harm. When we have been harmed, the power behind our responses arises from the feelings evoked. Even if, in our calmer moments, we might affirm the positive value of forgiveness in the abstract, at the moment that harm occurs our convictions of reason may not hold sway in our choice of response. Consequently, even those who espouse the positive value of forgiveness, whether on the basis of faith claims or of reason,[6] may choose (and historically often have chosen) not to enact it.

A further difficulty is an unavoidable consequence of the global climate of discourse in which we find ourselves at this point in history. Instantaneous communications media have brought us into contact with perspectives, values, and cultural norms that differ from our own. The decline of political colonialism (economic colonialism waged by multinational corporations still thrives) and the emergence of developing nations have recast the once-presumptive cultural superiority of the West (and North) as hegemonic cultural violence. As Jean-François Lyotard expressed in his *The Postmodern Condition*,[7] the big stories (metanarratives) by which we

---

[6] I am not supposing that faith and reason are mutually exclusive. Later I will sketch out a way of articulating their relationship. The point here is that one may appeal to either (or both) justification for advocating forgiveness.

[7] Jean-François Lyotard, *The Postmodern Condition: A Report on Knowledge*, trans. Geoff Bennington and Brian Massumi, Theory and History of Literature (Minneapolis: University of Minnesota Press, 1979).

have historically made sense *of* ourselves *to* ourselves no longer command the trust they once did. Discourse within the cultures shaped by the Western (and Northern) intellectual heritage has become fractured.[8] Further, we have come to recognize that *our* metanarratives cannot be presumed to be normative for others from different historical and cultural backgrounds. The expanding global horizon has called into question the standards by which judgments of truth and claims of reason are made. This makes even more challenging both the attempt to talk about forgiveness as a general human phenomenon and the effort to promote an understanding of forgiveness that identifies itself as Christian.

A final challenge to our exploration arises from the relationship of Christianity to the cultural context from within which I am writing. Very simply, Christianity has had a profound impact on the culture of the West. Many of the basic assumptions governing behavior in the Western world, assumptions about right and wrong, moral and immoral, have been shaped by that religious heritage. Even the project of the Enlightenment, which sought to justify truth and values independently of appeals to religious claims, assimilated much of its content from that religious heritage. The influence of Christianity on social values has also been felt in recent researches into forgiveness. As numerous authors have noted, our basic understanding of forgiveness and its conditions has been shaped by our appropriation of ideas and sensibilities arising from the intersection of Christianity with Western culture(s). The challenge, then, will be to try to identify an understanding of the basic human phenomenon of forgiveness that is not governed by the assumptions inculcated into this cultural heritage.

## Method

The challenges indicated above, and others that will emerge as we proceed, impose conditions on our exploration of Christian forgiveness.

---

[8] This phenomenon echoes the diversity of idioms mentioned above within Christianity. The emergence of multiple expressions of Christian self-understanding may well have contributed to the intellectual conditions beneath this fracturing. Within Roman Catholicism a similar dynamic has unfolded since the Second Vatican Council and the shift away from the (assumed) unified philosophical heritage of Thomism. Karl Rahner identified this problem explicitly and sought to address it in his *Foundations of Christian Faith: An Introduction to the Idea of Christianity* (New York: Seabury, 1978), esp. 7.

It is already evident that starting from the postulation of a definition will not get us very far. The diversity of definitions already used in the literature makes it clear that such a process will not succeed. Moreover, any definition we might propose *a priori* would assuredly already be shaped by the influence of Christianity on the concepts we use. Therefore the first condition is that we clarify an understanding of forgiveness as a basic human enactment. We will need to look *beneath* the definitions to the human phenomenon (phenomena!) they are trying to name. This will require us to put all definitions of forgiveness in the dock before the judgment seat of the experience of forgiving itself.

The second condition we will need to respect arises from the emergence of the post-modern and globalized intellectual ethos. When exploring our questions we will need to be attentive to the unidentified presuppositions and their grounding metanarratives operating within the discussions of forgiveness. We will need to bring these to light and subject them to critical examination before embracing or rejecting them.

This is much more easily said than done. To bring the basic human phenomenon of forgiveness into focus, we will need to examine discussions of forgiveness that have no explicit connection to a religious—and particularly a Christian—horizon of meaning. Two disciplines that prove especially helpful in this regard are philosophy and psychology. Although the language of their discussions has been inherited from a culture stamped by Christian sensibility regarding the positive value of forgiveness, both disciplines strive to justify their findings on the basis of publicly accessible criteria: in the case of philosophy, on the basis of the rigorous logic of argument; in psychology, on the basis of the data of human experience.[9]

Both philosophy and psychology strive to approach their inquiries in as presuppositionless a manner as possible. Between these disciplines and between the methodological and conceptual differences of schools within them there are points of convergence in their findings. But there are also places of significant difference, as indicated above. In our efforts to identify the basic human phenomenon of forgiveness that precedes any possible Christian specification we will need to attend to both the convergences and the differences. To do so, part 1 of this exploration must

---

[9] The extent to which either discipline or any of its subdisciplines succeeds in attaining neutrality with respect to concepts and language stamped by the influence of Christianity on Western culture remains an open question. The issue here is their *intent* to do so. This is a starting point for our own efforts.

be largely expository. It will present the most prominent positions in the philosophical and psychological discussions, indicating their points of convergence and their disagreements.

Part 2 will be analytic and constructive. It will probe into the convergences and disagreements identified in part 1. Our purpose here will be to excavate from the different positions those methodological and conceptual elements that lie beneath them. By means of this analysis we will identify both methodological guidelines and conceptual tools for approaching our own understanding of forgiveness as a basic human phenomenon. This will require, in the process, the articulation of a basic understanding of the "human," an understanding articulated in a manner conducive to our specifically theological concerns but one that can be verified and affirmed independently of any theological commitment.

In part 3 we will take up the specifically theological task of this work. We will bring our understanding of forgiveness as a basic human enactment into dialogue with Christianity. We will engage in a process of rereading the Christian sources on forgiveness, especially the gospels. Our purpose will be to uncover and explore the depths of the distinctively Christian understanding of forgiveness in contrast to forgiveness understood as a basic human enactment. To accomplish this task we will also need to explore the interrelationship between this deeper understanding of Christian forgiveness and the larger horizon of meanings belonging to Christianity as a distinctive worldview.

*Part One*

# Surveying the Landscape

*D*espite a few notable exceptions over the centuries, forgiveness was a largely neglected topic in philosophy until the twentieth century. The place of forgiveness in religious instruction may well have contributed to its neglect as a philosophical topic. But the events of the twentieth century brought to light the length and breadth of human capacities for inflicting harm on others. The First and Second World Wars, the Shoah, the dropping of atomic bombs on Japan, and South African apartheid are perhaps the most famous examples, but by no means the only ones. The last century also saw the decline of colonial powers. As formerly colonized peoples gained their own voices and struggled to reestablish their own cultural identities they made it clear that their former colonizers were by no means purely benevolent. Indeed, the uncovering of the exploitation of indigenous peoples in colonized lands confronted colonizers with the way in which their presumed moral and cultural superiority had legitimated—at least in their own eyes—their systematic abuses.

The realizations that we inhabit (and many of us have benefited by) cultural histories of exploitation *and* that the impact of these histories on human relationships will need to be confronted and overcome if human societies are to function peacefully and productively have inspired philosophers in the latter half of the twentieth century to take up a serious examination of forgiveness as a human response to harm. Since the late 1960s the amount of critical philosophical attention directed toward understanding forgiveness has grown dramatically. It is perhaps no great surprise that many of the first efforts to understand forgiveness took up one of the greatest challenges to its possibility: the Shoah.

1

More than any other event in history, the systematic extermination of the Jews under Nazi direction during World War II has cast a shadow that calls forgiveness itself into question. In the face of such horror and wanton destruction of life, is forgiveness even possible? Who can forgive? Who has the authority to forgive when the victim of the crime is dead? To whom can forgiveness even be extended? What would forgiveness mean?

These are among the questions raised so poignantly by Simon Wiesenthal in his short narrative, *The Sunflower*. As a prisoner of the Nazi state during the war, Wiesenthal was summoned to the bedside of a dying German soldier who had brutally murdered several Jews. Bearing the weight of his own guilt, the soldier asked Wiesenthal for forgiveness. Wiesenthal left the soldier in silence. He then poses the question for his readers, "What would you have done?"

Wiesenthal's question directs our attention in a vivid way to the complexity of the issues raised by forgiveness. Since the 1960s philosophers have been grappling with the definition of forgiveness, its conditions, its limits, and the morality of forgiving or not forgiving. Some philosophers have focused their attention on the intelligibility of the concept of forgiveness and its relationship to and distinction from other concepts like pardon, condoning, and amnesty. Others have wrestled with the relationship of forgiving to questions of justice and of legal practice. Still others have been occupied with forgiveness as an interpersonal issue. Often these three levels of discussion transition from one to the other in a given treatment. At present there is no overall consensus in response to the questions these different lines of inquiry have pursued. However, there has been some convergence on many points, and even the places of disagreement can be instructive for our own inquiry.

Over the past fifty years, two distinct discussions have coalesced in the philosophical literature. We can distinguish them in terms of the interplay of their methodologies, the kinds of questions they ask, the interests that drive their questions and, in some cases, the personal experiences that shape the individual philosopher's driving concerns. One line of exploration proceeds in the manner of continental philosophy. Often influenced by ideas derived from Kant and Nietzsche, it also is frequently approached in a manner influenced by the ideas and methods of phenomenology, particularly the works of Edmund Husserl and Martin Heidegger. The philosophers most engaged with this line of exploration are francophone.[1] I shall refer to them as "French-continental."

---

[1] Some American scholars are also engaged in this discussion, among them John Caputo and Richard Kearney. I will include them among the "francophones" because their

The other philosophical approach could be distinguished as "anglophone." It consists primarily of English-speaking philosophers, largely from the North American context. These I shall refer to as "Anglo-American." It is difficult to specify a single methodological orientation among these thinkers; however, loosely stated, there is an inclination to an "analytic" style. This shows itself in the application of logical rigor and definitional precision in order to distill the meanings of individual terms and their distinctions from other related concepts. This latter approach devotes its attention to articulating the conditions under which forgiveness may be morally enacted or, conversely, under which it must morally be withheld.

In part 1 we shall look at both of these lines of thought. We can think of them as representing distinctive movements across the landscape of forgiveness. That is, each approach—French-Continental and Anglo-American (and the argument presented by each philosopher from within each approach)—circumscribes for itself the landscape of forgiveness as it understands the term. It then plots a course across that landscape—a *trajectory*—from experience of relational rupture to forgiveness. Among the philosophers participating in the French-Continental discussions we will find points of agreement and disagreement even as they trace their course across a common conceptual landscape; so, too, among the Anglo-American philosophers. Both agreements and disagreements will be instructive for the questions I want to address in this present exploration. There are also points of agreement and disagreement between the two groups.

In addition to the philosophical approaches represented in the French-Continental and Anglo-American discussions of forgiveness, psychological researchers have begun to devote attention to the topic. Since the 1960s a growing number of psychologists have recognized that, especially for those who have experienced significant personal trauma, forgiveness can be an important part of psychological recovery and the capacity to forgive can serve as an indicator of psychic health. Drawing on philosophical insights and on clinical experience, and reading the data in the light of diverse psychological theories—behavioral, cognitional, developmental, object-relations, and psychoanalytic among them—psychologists have begun to examine the psycho-dynamics of forgiveness and have developed processes to help those wrestling with forgiveness.

---

engagement in this question, it seems to me, has been mediated by their dialogue with these other philosophers whose cultural heritage is, at least partly, French.

In part 1 our task will be to survey the landscape of forgiveness as it has been identified and traversed in these three discussions. This will bring to light issues which we will need to address in part 2, when we attempt to name forgiveness as a basic human enactment and to articulate why forgiveness is so difficult.

# $\mathcal{C}$hapter 1

# French-Continental Landscape

## Preliminaries

$\mathcal{P}$erhaps the philosopher most implicated in French-Continental philosophical discussions of forgiveness is Jacques Derrida (1930–2004). His penetrating analysis of forgiveness stands in relation to his critical engagement with the themes of the gift and of hospitality. Both in content and in method of exploration Derrida has pursued a course of inquiry that has challenged the very possibility of speaking meaningfully of forgiveness at all. Through his analysis he comes to the remarkable conclusion that the idea of forgiveness, when pressed to its limits, is self-contradictory; it is aporetic. As he puts it,

> If there is something to forgive, it would be what in religious language is called mortal sin, the worst, the unforgivable crime or harm. From which comes the aporia, which can be described in its dry and implacable formality, without mercy: forgiveness forgives only the unforgivable. One cannot, or should not, forgive; there is only forgiveness, if there is any, where there is the unforgivable.[1]

The aporia to which Derrida points has posed a challenge to continental reflection on forgiveness. We will therefore need to examine closely the nature of his argument. We will also need to probe the response he has evoked from one of his contemporaries, Paul Ricoeur. What we will discover through our exploration of Derrida's provocative ideas and

---

[1] Jacques Derrida, *On Cosmopolitanism and Forgiveness* (London: Routledge, 2001), 32–33. The reference to "mortal sin" in this passage does not correspond to the Roman Catholic understanding of the term. Mortal sin is not "unforgivable."

through engagement with his interlocutors is that his approach to the question of forgiveness offers useful insights into our own question in terms both of ideas and of a way of questioning the material. But before we turn to Derrida it is important to note that many of his key positions emerged from dialogue with another thinker on the question of forgiveness, Vladimir Jankélévitch. It will therefore be helpful to examine Jankélévitch's ideas before we engage with Derrida.

## Vladimir Jankélévitch

The name Vladimir Jankélévitch (1903–1985), is less well known than that of many other French-speaking philosophers of the twentieth century. Born in Bourges, France, in 1903, to Russian parents, Jankélévitch, despite his extensive publications, was never embraced by the mainstream of the academy in France.[2] In part this was a function of Jankélévitch's independence of thought, expressed in his disinclination to identify with the most prominent trends of philosophy in his day,[3] but in part it was a result of the political situation in France during and following World War II. As a person of Jewish ancestry he was excluded by law from teaching in France from 1941 to 1947.[4] Those experiences, and his awareness of the Nazi program to exterminate Jews, deeply impressed themselves on his philosophical work.

As Andrew Kelly notes in his introduction to *Forgiveness*, "Jankélévitch does not have a strict system of thought in which there is some ultimate beginning point from which all of the other aspects or tenets of his system can be deduced."[5] Nevertheless, his thought does exhibit certain thematic concerns. Many of the themes he identified would become the basis for future philosophical developments among the French-Continental philosophers who took up the question of forgiveness. Three of his themes are especially relevant to our own question because of the echoes they find in Derrida's work: the interrelationship of time, becoming, and resent-

---

[2] See the translator's introduction in Vladimir Jankélévitch, *Forgiveness*, trans. Andrew Kelly (Chicago: University of Chicago Press, 2005), viii–x.

[3] See ibid., x–xii, exp. x, where Kelly quotes from a letter dated January 2, 1958, "now there is room in France only for herds: Marxists, Catholics, existentialists. And I am not from any parish."

[4] See ibid., ix.

[5] Ibid., xiii.

ment; the discussion of the inexcusable and the unforgivable; and the understanding of the gift.

Jankélévitch begins his book, *Forgiveness*, with a discussion of time.[6] He is concerned with the fleeting nature of time, that it can neither be pinned down as an object nor isolated into discrete points. The attempt to do so conceptually arrests the flow of time and thereby distorts its fundamental truth, yet time is always in the process of coming to be through what he calls "futurition."[7]

> Becoming, in the first place, is essentially futurition and, second-arily, preterition. That is, depending on whether one looks toward the future or toward the past, becoming ceaselessly posits a future, and with the same stroke and at the same time it deposits a past behind it. Successively, it makes the future present and makes the present past, and it does this in the same movement and with the same continual renewal.[8]

This characteristic of time is also true of life. The natural dynamism of life moves toward what is becoming, growing from what has been. In both time and life this dynamism entails the passing away of what has been to make way for what is to come. This forward movement of becoming sets up the problematic nature of the experience of harm and the need for forgiveness, for what has been done cannot be undone. The irreversibility of time is foundational to the experience of resentment. When harmed, we are tempted to resentment. Resentment tries to constrain the coming to be of the future by binding one to the past. It holds the becoming back. Forgiving undoes the hold of resentment and allows the futurition to proceed.[9]

Although he does not provide a simple definition of forgiveness, Jankélévitch does point to the chief characteristics that occupy his concern.

> Here are three aspects that are among the most characteristic: True forgiveness is a significant *event* that happens at such and such an instant of historical becoming. True forgiveness, which is at the

---

[6] Kelly (ibid., xv n. 21) cites a letter from Jankélévitch of 8 October 1929, published in his *Une Vie en toutes lettres*, 172–73.

[7] See, for example, Jankélévitch, *Forgiveness*, 14–17, 21–25.

[8] Ibid., 14.

[9] Ibid., 15. See also pp. 19 and 20, where he observes, "Rancor often resembles a lump that becoming has not yet succeeded in dissolving."

margins of all legality, is a *gracious gift* from the offended to the
offender. True forgiveness is a *personal relation* with another person.[10]

Each of these aspects (he will add others later) bears elaboration.

First, the *event* character of forgiveness, as Jankélévitch understands
it, derives from the nature of time as a continuous flow. Events cannot
be anticipated. They are spontaneous, supernatural, and instantaneous.[11]
"Supernatural" in this context does not necessarily indicate a divine intervention. Rather, it points to an origin outside of "natural" human
enactments.[12] As such, second, events are not subject to the dictates
of reason. In this Jankélévitch distances himself from any approach to
forgiveness that would attempt to instrumentalize it or place it at the
service of some other good.[13] Thus forgiveness is a gift: not a calculated
exchange in view of some future gain, but a grace offered without demand
for recompense.[14] Because of its gratuity, its noninstrumentality, and its
spontaneity, forgiveness stands outside the calculations of moral and legal
norms. As Jankélévitch maintains, "forgiveness ceases to be forgiveness
if even a milligram of reasonable motivation comes to justify it."[15] Third,
forgiveness is a response to an offender. It is therefore intrinsically relational. It is extended toward an Other.[16]

This latter point bears some elaboration. In this relationship, *as* a relationship in which forgiveness has been extended, the offended party
renounces all claim to recompense.[17] To put it in other terms, forgiveness,

---

[10] Ibid., 5.

[11] See, for example, ibid., 37, 94, 123.

[12] Jankélévitch's characterization of something beyond "natural" human enactment
in order to get at the "supernatural" quality of forgiveness as an "event" seems to me to
describe well the experience that, at times, forgiving feels beyond one's capacity. Then,
suddenly, it is no longer impossible. On the level of conscious experience the "event" is
beyond my natural abilities. However, Jankélévitch does not delve into the depths of
unconscious processes. I believe that what he describes in terms of "supernatural" and
"event" can also be understood in terms of the eruption into consciousness of a change in
one's disposition with respect to an offender and offense—a change that has transpired
originally at an unconscious level by the realignment of unconscious meanings. I will
take this up in chap. 5.

[13] See Jankélévitch, *Forgiveness*, 5, 9, 42, 53.

[14] Ibid., 10.

[15] Ibid., 113.

[16] Ibid., 10–11, 95, 151–52.

[17] Ibid., 10. The point being made here correlates well with that made by Pamela Hieronymi, "Articulating an Uncompromising Forgiveness," *Philosophy and Phenomenological*

if it is forgiveness, is total, not partial. The notion of a partial forgiveness is incoherent to Jankélévitch.[18] For this reason forgiveness cannot be equated with forgetting, particularly the kind of forgetting that comes with the passage of time. Forgetting would only submerge the event in the unconscious and perpetuate its memory, awaiting a future time to resurface with its rancor over the event.[19] Such an understanding of forgiveness would undo the clear relational dimension of its occurrence. Moreover, *as* relational, forgiveness cannot be mediated by a third party. On this point Jankélévitch is taking aim at any kind of socially or politically proposed or enforced effort to "integrate" the offender and the offended into a larger social whole, a kind of socially enforced forgetting. In such a process of integration

> the offended person stomachs his humiliation, but this is a laborious and difficult process of stomaching. With habituation aiding, he makes *as if* the injury was nothing and did not occur, but he does not make *that* it never took place. He attenuates the memory of it without annihilating its effectivity. The pain of humiliation is always there, but it has passed into latency, has become invisible, has changed into an aftertaste. Such a forgiveness is far too complex, and it has far too many ulterior motives to be forgiveness pure and simple.[20]

The socially sanctioned process of integration does not effect forgiveness, but instead suppresses the pain of the offended party in favor of some larger social "good." But the rancor provoked by the offense remains, buried but still effective in the life of the wounded party, albeit in surreptitious ways. The relational aspect of forgiveness has been overtaken and instrumentalized by a third party. It has ceased to be personal-relational.

The way Jankélévitch presents these three characteristics of forgiveness raises a question: What is the role of personal freedom in granting forgiveness? As an event, arising spontaneously and independently of intellection and calculation, forgiving would appear to be an *a-volitional* occurrence. It does not seem, in Jankélévitch's telling, to have been arrived

---

*Research* 62, no. 3 (May 2001): 529–55, at 551; that the one forgiving also, by that fact, absorbs a cost. See chap. 2.

[18] Jankélévitch, *Forgiveness*, 96, 152.

[19] Ibid., 36–37.

[20] Ibid., 32–33.

at by an "act of will."[21] This also appears to be an implication of his discussion of forgiveness as an event of grace. Forgiveness would seem to have the character of grace, both for the one who is forgiven and for the one who forgives, liberating both for the coming of a future in which resentment does not hold sway. On the other hand, there is a dimension of Jankélévitch's discussion that suggests one can withhold oneself from forgiveness. One can cling to the resentment. This suggests that freedom does play a role. In the framework Jankélévitch provides, however, the role of freedom is ambiguous. This is evident in his rejection of rationally motivated conversion from resentment to forgiveness.

> Forgiveness excludes this well-reflected-upon consent. Forgiveness, like repentance, rather implies an arbitrary event that is always synthetic in comparison with the old life: as opposed to so many apparently sudden conversions, ones that a long and invisible process has in reality been preparing for a long time, the decision to forgive is contingent. It does not mature little by little, does not emanate in any way from the past by an immanent and continual evolution, or does not result from a progressive incubation. . . . This decision is an end that is a beginning.[22]

The ambiguity on this point remains obscure in the text because, where one would expect to find the offended person deciding to forgive, Jankélévitch speaks as though it is forgiveness that acts.[23] This is in contrast to his discussion of the offense, which he treats as an expression of freedom.[24]

---

[21] The use of the term "will" here should not be interpreted as an endorsement of a faculty psychology; I am appealing to the common use of the term.

[22] Jankélévitch, *Forgiveness*, 148.

[23] See, for example, his statements: "Forgiveness, as we shall see, does not deny that the misdeed has been effectively committed, but it behaves *as if* it had not been committed," and "Forgiveness, on the other hand, *decides* to consider the event as null and as not having come to pass, even though it certainly did, alas! come to pass; and come to pass it did only too much!" (ibid., 98; Jankélévitch's emphases). The point is further underscored when, in expanding on the supernaturality of forgiveness, he explains: "The supernaturality of forgiveness consists in this, that my opinion on the subject of the guilty person precisely has not changed; but against this immutable background it is the whole lighting of my relations with the guilty person that is modified, it is the whole orientation of our relations that finds itself inverted, overturned, and overwhelmed!" (ibid., 152). Note the passive construction of the syntax. The one who forgives experiences the event of forgiving as having been enacted within one, not as a matter of one's own "having done."

[24] See, for example, ibid., 158–59. The questions of agency and freedom in the enactment of forgiveness will be a significant concern in later discussions.

Jankélévitch's presentation of forgiveness, expounded within the framework of his understanding of time, has a tone of eschatological openness. That is, forgiveness is open-ended toward an unspecified future. The claim he makes at the beginning of his work, that forgiveness frees the forward movement of futurition for its becoming, receives an even stronger affirmation near the end.

> Forgiveness extends unlimited credit to the guilty person. And the perverted man will grow tired of hating and tormenting the generous man sooner than the generous man will grow tired of forgiving the perverted man. It is of little importance if a burst of rancor must someday challenge the absolution. That which will have lasted for only a time wanted, at the time, to last forever, and for centuries and centuries. It suffices that the sincere intention of forgiving has, at the moment of forgiveness, sincerely and passionately excluded every chronological limitation, just as it suffices that love, even if, in fact, it has to be unfaithful and versatile, wanted to be eternal on the day of the oath. One understands, consequently, why forgiveness can be the founder of a future.[25]

Forgiveness is the foundation of a future in relationship, a nonoppressive relationship, a relationship in which the offenses of the past do not bind the parties involved to the resentment and alienation they occasioned. Rather, forgiveness opens a future in which relationships can be reconstituted and carried forward.

The forgiveness that founds this future refuses to reduce the offender to the offense committed. It acts, instead, as if the offense had not occurred.[26] Moreover, "it forgives all the misdeeds that this guilty person would be able to commit or still will commit."[27] For forgiveness, insofar as it is gracious and supernatural, is a creative act in the order of love.[28] Its internal dynamism is toward the future and toward what is coming to be.

The overall tone of Jankélévitch's presentation has a positive ring to it. Forgiveness becomes a possibility when excuses and intellection have reached their limits. It goes beyond the inexcusable. But in the closing pages of *Forgiveness*, Jankélévitch takes up a theme alluded to earlier in the text: the unforgivable. He distinguishes between the inexcusable and

---

[25] Ibid., 154–55.

[26] Ibid., 98.

[27] Ibid., 154.

[28] See, for example, the contrast between the order of justice and the order of charity in ibid., 94.

the unforgivable when he observes: "If, then, all is not excusable for the excuse, everything is forgivable for forgiveness, all . . . save, of course, the unforgivable, admitting that an unforgivable exists, that is, a crime that is meta-empirically impossible to forgive."[29] The nature of this meta-empirical impossibility is not defined. It appears to be an "impossible possibility." This point is confirmed in the opening lines of the conclusion of *Forgiveness*:

> In one sense, forgiveness extends to infinity. Forgiveness does not ask if the crime is worthy of being forgiven, if the atonement has been sufficient, or if the rancor has continued long enough. . . . Which amounts to saying: there is an inexcusable, but there is not an unforgivable. Forgiveness is there to forgive precisely what no excuse would know how to excuse: for there is no misdeed that is so grave that we cannot in the last resort forgive it.[30]

Forgiveness can overcome all offenses. And yet . . . !

Jankélévitch introduces a tension. Forgiveness, he says, finds its meaning in the repentance of the offender.[31] But the "criminals" do not ask for forgiveness, have not asked because they have not repented. To forgive in the absence of repentance would be to rob forgiveness of its meaning.

There is a sharp change in tone and voice in the conclusion to *Forgiveness*. Jankélévitch appears to have shifted his focus from reflection on the nature and conditions of forgiveness in the abstract to the reality of forgiveness as an issue in response to a specific offense, the Shoah.[32] His reflections in *Forgiveness* on the absence of repentance echo the position he took in 1965, when France was debating the establishment of a statutory limitation on war crimes and crimes against humanity committed during the Nazi era.[33] In his essay Jankélévitch emphasizes the distinctiveness of crimes against humanity—these particular crimes against humanity—in terms of the number of people killed,[34] the pre-

---

[29] Ibid., 93.

[30] Ibid., 156.

[31] Ibid., 157.

[32] He addresses this tension in the introduction to his essay, "Should We Pardon Them?" trans. Ann Hobart, *Critical Inquiry* 22, no. 3 (Spring 1996): 552–72, at 552.

[33] Ibid. That position was later expanded into the essay cited here. It was then developed into a larger form and published as *Pardonner?* (Paris: Le Pavillon, 1971) and was later reprinted as *L'Imprescriptible* (Paris: Éditions du Seuil, 1986).

[34] Jankélévitch, "Should We Pardon Them?" 558, 563.

meditation and planning,[35] the clearly articulated principle that governed the planning, and the genocidal intent. In addition, Germans have, he avers, distanced themselves from the crimes of their parents. They do not feel the "distress and the dereliction of the guilty" that would render a pardon meaningful.[36] Consequently, no one has even asked for pardon. And yet, in practical terms, many have already "pardoned" the Germans in the sense that they have established "normalized" business relationships, a situation Jankélévitch finds abhorrent.[37]

Jankélévitch's opposition to establishing a statute of limitations on Nazi war crimes, although this counters the tone of most of *Forgiveness*, is actually consistent with many of its key themes. To enact a pardon of the kind under discussion would, in his mind, be to support a legalized "forgetting." A statute of limitations would be a rationalized, mediated, instrumentalized gesture toward forgiveness but would not achieve forgiveness itself. Rather, it would be violating the nature of forgiveness. The state would be attempting to function as a mediating party between the offenders and the offended and would be doing so according to a rationality that looks to political and economic advantage. Moreover, it would be making time a basis for forgiveness, a move Jankélévitch has taken great pains to repudiate.

Despite the places in which Jankélévitch's opposition to pardoning war crimes coheres with the larger project spelled out in *Forgiveness*, he recognizes that there is no clear or easy resolution of the tension between his philosophical reflection and his actual political position.[38] *Forgiveness* itself ends on the note of a paradox, or, if one will, an aporia.

> Love is strong like death, but death is strong like love. In truth, love is simultaneously stronger and weaker than death, and it is thus just as strong. This extreme and almost heartrending tension is that of the mad forgiveness that is accorded to the wicked person. Where misdeed flows, grace overflows. Besides—what Saint Paul did not add—where grace overflows, evil overflows in response and submerges this overflowing itself, with an infinite and mysterious outbidding. The mystery of irreducible and inconceivable wickedness is, at the same time, stronger and weaker, weaker and stronger than

[35] Ibid., 563, 564.
[36] Ibid., 567.
[37] Ibid., 566.
[38] Ibid., 553.

love. Likewise, forgiveness is strong like wickedness; but it is not stronger than it.[39]

Vladimir Jankélévitch's discussion of forgiveness brings to the surface many of the issues and tensions that will occupy the continental philosophical discussion after him. His emphasis on forgiveness as an unexpected, spontaneous event, the idea that its morality is not circumscribed in any system of ethics or law but stands above them, and the interpersonal-relational character of forgiveness will remain key concerns for subsequent thinkers. The same is true of his recognition of aporetic elements in forgiveness itself, the tension between the ideal of forgiveness and its practical application, and the forward-looking, eschatological dimension of forgiveness awaiting its completion. These contributions of Jankélévitch's analysis live on, in large part through the way in which they have engaged the figure who has made, perhaps, the most provocative contribution to French-Continental philosophical discussion of forgiveness: Jacques Derrida.

### Jacques Derrida

Jacques Derrida, born in French Algeria in 1930, became over the course of his life one of the most prolific and controversial thinkers of the twentieth century. His contributions to philosophy have had wide-ranging influence in the social sciences as well as in the humanities, not least because of his deconstructive critical methodology. Deconstruction, as practiced by Derrida, brings to light embedded contradictions (aporias) enshrined in the ideas and ideals that have often lain unexamined as foundations on which theories and programs have been built. Once the instability of these foundations has been exposed to critical reflection, many of the supposedly unshakeable positions reliant on them must be rethought.

The purpose behind deconstruction is not disruption for its own sake. Derrida's work seeks to push the limits of understanding, language, and concept for reasons rooted in his ethical concerns. Especially in the realm of political and legal ethics, but also on a personal level, we make judgments about right and wrong on the basis of "established" norms. Whether these be Kantian categorical imperatives, appeals to long-established custom that "must" be right, convictions about natural law, or religious beliefs, these established norms often go unexamined. Even as

[39] Jankélévitch, *Forgiveness*, 164–65.

they present their values as normative and, if one will, as "true," they rely on the concealment of inherent instability in their own formulation to stay in place. As long as the instabilities remain concealed, those who adhere to those systems of moral thought can appeal to them as the basis for their judgments about right and wrong. Ethics becomes a matter of "knowing" the right principle.[40]

Derrida sees both violence and irresponsibility in these systematic approaches to moral judgment.[41] It is violent in that the standards maintain themselves by repressing disruptive voices that might bring the contradictions to light.[42] Irresponsibility results from the fact that one treats ethics as a matter of knowing: I know the laws and apply them (or not). But in that framework there is no real moral decision, only a decision to follow a law or not.[43] Derrida's deconstructive methodology, therefore, has as its purpose to destabilize systems of knowing and deciding so as to throw us back on the need to make responsible decisions. It does so by confronting us with the aporias in our thinking, their undecidability on the basis of any appeal to reasons that might stand above the contradictions,[44] and the necessity, nonetheless, of taking action.[45]

Derrida employs his deconstructive method in analyzing a variety of important themes. For our purposes it will be helpful to examine two that are heavily implicated in his discussion of forgiveness: hospitality and the gift. These will provide us with a greater understanding of the issues

[40] See the discussion in François Raffoul, "Derrida and the Ethics of the Im-Possible," *Research in Phenomenology* 38 (2008): 270–90, at 282.

[41] See ibid., 271, 282.

[42] The argument here arises in the postmodern critique of metanarrative. Metanarratives are frameworks of interpretation that function to suppress "interruptive" voices or ideas that would call the legitimacy of those metanarratives into question. See Jean-François Lyotard, *The Postmodern Condition: A Report on Knowledge* (Minneapolis: University of Minnesota Press, 1984), 31–36; idem, *The Differend: Phrases in Dispute*, trans. Georges Van Den Abbeele, Theory and History of Literature (Minneapolis: University of Minnesota Press, 1988), nos. 160, 200, and 227. See also the discussion of "event" in Lieven Boeve, "Critical Consciousness in the Postmodern Condition: New Opportunities for Theology?" *Marquette University Quarterly* 10, no. 2 (1997): 449–68, at 453; and idem, "Bearing Witness to the Differend: A Model for Theologizing in the Postmodern Context," *Louvain Studies* 20, no. 4 (Winter 1995): 362–79, esp. 370.

[43] To Christian ears this can sound very close to the critique leveled by Jesus against the religious leaders of Jerusalem.

[44] Raffoul, "Derrida and the Ethics of the Im-Possible," 272.

[45] One can detect points of connection with Jankélévitch's analysis.

at stake in his discussion of forgiveness. But before turning to these two issues we will need to take a closer look at deconstruction.

## Deconstruction

As indicated above, Derrida employs deconstruction to disclose the aporetic structures embedded in our concepts. By probing concepts and pushing them to their limits he sharpens the awareness of their inherent instability, thereby destabilizing the security of our common ways of thinking.[46] These aporias present the loci of responsible decision-making. That is, they point us to matters about which we must make decisions, without appeal to any overriding principles that can decide the issue for us. "The aporia is the experience of responsibility. It is only by going through a set of contradictory injunctions, impossible choices, that we make a choice. If I know what I have to do, if I know in advance what has to be done, there is no responsibility."[47] The aporias bring us to a moment of "undecidability" in which our only option is to choose and we must take responsibility for the choices we make.[48]

The deployment of deconstruction provokes us to consider two aspects of the aporetic that bear on our own concerns. The first is that the aporetic brings us to the limits of possibility by disclosing the impossibility of what we name in our concepts. Impossibility ("im-possibility") is not a negative concept for Derrida. "Impossibility does not mean: that which cannot be, but rather: that which *happens* outside of the anticipating conditions of *possibility* of the egological subject, outside of the horizons of expectation proposed by the subject, outside of transcendental horizons of calculability."[49] While the aporias reveal that our desired ethical accomplishments must founder on the shoals of the violence of our ethical calculations, the im-possible opens the space in which our choices become responsible and, as such, potentially moral. The second aspect of the aporetic as it sketches the landscape of our responsible decision-making is that it "*happens*." There is an event quality to our decision-making (especially, as we shall see, in the realms of hospitality, the gift—if that is possible—and forgiveness). By "event" Derrida signals both an occurrence

[46] John D. Caputo, Mark P. Dooley, and Michael J. Scanlon, eds., *Questioning God* (Bloomington: Indiana University Press, 2001), 62.

[47] Ibid., 62.

[48] See Derrida, *On Cosmopolitanism and Forgiveness*, 53–54.

[49] Raffoul, "Derrida and the Ethics of the Im-Possible," 286.

and the condition of our own ignorance of its occurrence. According to Derrida our ignorance, especially in the cases of the gift and forgiveness, is a constitutive condition of the happening itself.[50]

We need to note one final element of Derrida's thought that plays an important role in his discussions of hospitality, the gift, and forgiveness. It is the role of the economic cycle of exchange. Derrida argues with respect to these three themes that their intended referent is made impossible (im-possible) because they are each implicated in a cycle of exchange. Because they are inscribed within an economy, the claims these concepts want to name are subverted. As soon as they appear as what they claim to be, they disappear. Examining this self-deconstructing characteristic of hospitality and the gift *because* of their inscription in an economy of exchange will help us to understand the particularities of Derrida's pronouncements on forgiveness.

## Hospitality

Hospitality occupies a distinctive place in Derrida's concern. Following an insight of Emmanuel Lévinas, Derrida holds that hospitality is not so much a question within ethics as it is the locus of the "ethicity of ethics."[51] "*Ethics*," he states, "*is hospitality*,"[52] for ethics is based on the power and conditions of welcome offered to the other. This is clearly evident in the discussion of immigration and "cities of refuge" in *Cosmopolitanism*.[53] Drawing on an observation by Hannah Arendt, Derrida makes note of "the progressive abolition . . . of a right to asylum" and a "massive influx (*arrivée*) of refugees, which necessitated abandoning the classic recourse to repatriation or naturalization."[54]

These two social "upheavals," arising between the two world wars, significantly reconfigured the status of hospitality in Western Europe, prompting policies that were increasingly inhospitable. This historical

---

[50] See, for example, the discussion of "the gift" between Derrida and Jean-Luc Marion in John D. Caputo and Michael J. Scanlon, eds., *God, the Gift, and Postmodernism* (Bloomington and Indianapolis: Indiana University Press, 1999), 60.

[51] Jacques Derrida, *Adieu to Emmanuel Levinas*, trans. Pascale-Anne Brault and Michael Naas (Stanford, CA: Stanford University Press, 1999), 94; cited in Raffoul, "Derrida and the Ethics of the Im-Possible," 287.

[52] Derrida, *On Cosmopolitanism and Forgiveness*, 17.

[53] Ibid.

[54] Ibid., 6, 7. Derrida is drawing on Hannah Arendt, "The Decline of the Nation-State and the End of the Rights of Man," 267–302, in *The Origins of Totalitarianism* (London: Allen and Unwin, 1967).

reality evokes a question about the nature of hospitality itself. Derrida distinguishes between the idea of hospitality that is unconditional, imposing no conditions on the guest, and the conditional hospitality inscribed within laws (whether politically enacted or simply laws of custom) that allow the host to impose limits on hospitality. The tension arises between these two "laws"—*the* law of hospitality, which is unconditional, and the laws of hospitality that impose conditions.

> Hospitality is culture itself and not simply one ethic amongst others. Insofar as it has to do with the *ethos*, that is, the residence, one's home, the familiar place of dwelling, inasmuch as it is a manner of being there, the manner in which we relate to ourselves and to others, to others as our own or as foreigners, *ethics is hospitality*; ethics is so thoroughly coextensive with the experience of hospitality. But for this very reason, and because being at home with oneself (*l'être-soi chez soi—l'ipséité même*—the other within oneself) supposes a reception or inclusion of the other which one seeks to appropriate, control, and master according to different modalities of violence, there is a history of hospitality, an always possible perversion of *the* law of hospitality (which can appear unconditional), and of the laws which come to limit and condition it in its inscription as law.[55]

The very attempt to extend hospitality enacts violence against hospitality itself and against the one to whom it is extended, because it requires that one make conditional what is, in its purity, unconditional.[56]

> To put it in different terms, absolute hospitality requires that I open up my home and that I give not only to the foreigner (provided with a family name, with the social status of being a foreigner, etc.), but to the absolute, unknown, anonymous other, and that I *give place* to them, and that I let them come, that I let them arrive, and take place in the place I offer them, without asking of them either reciprocity (entering into a pact) or even their names. The law of hospitality commands a break with hospitality by right, with law or justice as rights.[57]

---

[55] Derrida, *On Cosmopolitanism and Forgiveness*, 16–17.

[56] Jacques Derrida, "Foreigner Question," 3–73, in *Of Hospitality: Anne Dufourmantelle Invites Jacques Derrida to Respond*, ed. Jacques Derrida and Anne Dufourmantelle (Stanford, CA: Stanford University Press, 2000), at 15.

[57] Ibid., 25.

This description of absolute hospitality brings to the surface two of the aporetic tensions that permeate hospitality discourse. The first arises in the reference to "reciprocity" and "entering into a pact." Here Derrida gestures to the problem of economic interest and the idea that hospitality can be circumscribed by exchange and still remain hospitality.[58] Once there is an exchange, the hospitality has been compromised in its essential structure. It is no longer hospitable, but legal, a "modality of violence."

The second aporetic tension concerns anonymity. We normally think of hospitality as extended to someone known—or at least someone with whom, as a condition of being able to extend hospitality, we have some acquaintance. But Derrida insists that even the request for a name undermines the integrity of absolute hospitality. It incorporates a symbolic exchange into the interaction. A price has been paid. Hospitality is sundered. Here Derrida's understanding of absolute hospitality hews to the understanding of the "event." It arises as something unexpected, unanticipated, for which one cannot plan.[59] Hospitality, if it happens, occurs as the advent of transcendence in immanence.[60] It is directed toward no *telos*. It simply arrives. The im-possible arrives.

Derrida makes the claim that *the* law of hospitality and the laws of hospitality conflict with one another. At the same time, he observes that the two are indissociable. *The* law of hospitality can only be expressed functionally by means of laws, even though those concrete laws violate *the* law by the conditions in which they exist. Conditional laws of hospitality, on the other hand, can only be laws of hospitality insofar as they reach out to articulate the absolute hospitality in their limited conditionality. Their relationship is aporetic in its structure.[61]

### The Gift

Derrida's deconstructive analysis of hospitality alludes to his concern about inscribing hospitality in an economy of exchange. To guard against such a destruction of hospitality Derrida indicates that absolute hospitality must be anonymous, an event beyond knowing in which I give place to the other without restriction. The concern only alluded to

---

[58] See also reference to economic interest in Derrida, *On Cosmopolitanism and Forgiveness*, 11–12.

[59] Notice the similarity to Jankélévitch's discussion of forgiveness and event, above.

[60] Raffoul, "Derrida and the Ethics of the Im-Possible," 289.

[61] See, for example, the discussion in Derrida, "Foreigner Question," 55.

in the discussion of hospitality plays a more sharply defined role in his discussion of the gift. Here the deconstructive dynamics of exchange take center stage.

As with his discussion of hospitality, the driving interest underlying Derrida's discussion of the gift is ethical. Although in common parlance we speak of giving a gift with great ease, Derrida finds that in the actual practice of "gifting," by the gesture of extending a gift, we commonly impose a kind of obligation on the recipient. Better said, the recipient becomes obligated by the gift, whether we impose the obligation or not. The obligation is often obscured by the language of gift, but it is still enacted in the giving.

Derrida draws attention to this practical reality because, he argues, when a gift is given, by definition there should be no exchange.[62] A gift should not receive repayment. But, as Derrida argues, the very structure of the gift, as enacted in the real world, does involve repayment and therefore undoes its status as gift. That is, the gift is aporetic at the most fundamental level. It is impossible. To demonstrate this aporia, Derrida first draws our attention to the

> conditions of possibility of the gift (that some "one" gives some "thing" to some "one other") [and this] designate[s] simultaneously the conditions of the impossibility of the gift. And already we could translate this into other terms: these conditions of possibility define or produce the annulment, the annihilation, the destruction of the gift.[63]

The annulment arises from the fact that the gift always occurs within the context of a relationship between the giver and the recipient. The giving creates an asymmetrical relationship of debt, whether recognized as such or not. If anything is given back, the gift is no longer gift, but merely a commodity of exchange.[64] Moreover, whether recognized or not, the return payment is an inexorable consequence of the gift because the giving itself is inscribed in time as the basic milieu of (ex)change.

> The temporalization of time (memory, present, anticipation; retention, protention, imminence of the future; "ecstasies," and so forth)

---

[62] Jacques Derrida, *Given Time: 1. Counterfeit Money*, trans. Peggy Kamuf (Chicago: University of Chicago Press, 1992), 7.

[63] Ibid., 12.

[64] Ibid.

always sets in motion the process of a destruction of the gift: through keeping, restitution, reproduction, the anticipatory expectation or apprehension that grasps or comprehends in advance.[65]

We cannot escape the deployment of time or its eradication of the gift.

The argument Derrida is making goes beyond repayment by means of "things." He argues that the economy of exchange can fulfill its circulation symbolically as much as materially.[66] An expression of thanks can undo the gift just as a material repayment can. So, too, argues Derrida, can our knowledge, awareness, or recognition of the gift as gift. The mere recognition of the *appearing* of the gift annuls it as gift.[67] Each of these responses to the appearing contributes to the economic circulation of the gift. This complicates and intensifies the aporia to which Derrida points. If a gift is to be given and not be annulled, the giver must not be aware of having given the gift. The recipient must not be aware of having received the gift.[68] So thorough must this non-awareness be that even forgetting may not be enough to preserve the gift as gift.[69]

The aporetic problems of the gift are clear. The conditions called for by the aspirations of the concept of gift are violated by the effort to enact them. If the gift is possible, something Derrida is always careful to allow, it is so only beyond the im-possibility set by its conditions.[70] That is, for the gift to be possible it would have to be beyond the knowledge of the giver, beyond the knowledge of the recipient, and outside all traces of an economy of exchange.

[65] Ibid., 14.

[66] Ibid., 13.

[67] Ibid., 13–14.

[68] Ibid., 14.

[69] Ibid., 16. Derrida points to the possibility of repressed memories as discussed in psychoanalysis: "For there to be gift, not only must the donor or donee not perceive or receive the gift as such, have no consciousness of it, no memory, no recognition; he or she must also forget it right away [*à l'instant*] and moreover this forgetting must be so radical that it exceeds even the psychoanalytic categoriality of forgetting. This forgetting of the gift must even no longer be forgetting in the sense of repression. It must not give rise to any of the repressions (originary or secondary) that reconstitute debt and exchange by putting in reserve, by keeping or saving up what is forgotten, repressed, or censured. Repression does not destroy or annul anything; it keeps by displacing. Its operation is systemic or topological; it always consists of keeping by exchanging places. And, by keeping the meaning of the gift, repression annuls it in symbolic recognition."

[70] Caputo and Scanlon, *God, the Gift, and Postmodernism*, 59, 72.

> So the gift does not exist as such, if by existence we understand being present and intuitively identified as such. So the gift does not exist and appear as such; it is impossible for the gift to exist and appear as such. But I never concluded that there is no gift. I went on to say that if there is a gift, through this impossibility, it must be the experience of this impossibility, and it should appear as impossible. The event called gift is totally heterogeneous to theoretical identification, to phenomenological identification. That is a point of disagreement. The gift is totally foreign to the horizon of economy, ontology, knowledge, constative statements, and theoretical determination and judgment.[71]

This understanding of the gift and its aporias, at once so foreign to our common ways of thinking and yet so deeply interwoven with them, places it in close proximity to Derrida's analysis of hospitality. First, as in his discussion of hospitality, so too in his analysis of the gift, Derrida draws attention to the ways in which the attempt to enact the gift can become the vehicle of violence toward the other. Second, this violence is integral to the aporetic structure of the gift itself. The gift is an enactment that must occur within an economy of exchange, as is true of the aporia in hospitality. Thus, third, the gift, like hospitality, is impossible. The tension between the purity of the ideal espoused in the concept and the inexorable violation of that ideal in the effort to enact it cannot be bypassed in our normal ways of giving. Further, the purity and its violation are indissociable, as are *the* law of hospitality and the laws that condition its enactment. *If* a gift is to occur, it cannot be at the service of any other objective but must occur within the context of a not-knowing.[72] Derrida brings these themes into his analysis of forgiveness.

### Forgiveness

Derrida's discussion of forgiveness begins with an observation regarding the use of the language of forgiveness. This language has its roots in

---

[71] Ibid., 59.

[72] At this point there appears to be a difference between hospitality and the gift. Derrida emphasizes with respect to hospitality that the one offering it may not know in advance and, in the case of absolute hospitality, may not even impose the condition of knowing the name of the recipient. This is parallel to the discussion of the giver of the gift. It is not clear, however, whether the recipient of hospitality must be ignorant of its deployment as well, whereas the recipient of the gift must.

a particular religious (Judeo-Christian) heritage.[73] Within that heritage it has a particular usage. It is distinctive, but it is also in the process of becoming a globalized language. But since the Second World War this language has been deployed in ways that neither respect that heritage nor, Derrida believes, the intention of forgiveness itself.

> From this [universalization of Abrahamic language of forgiveness]—and this is one of the guiding threads of my seminar on forgiveness (and perjury)—the very dimension of forgiveness tends to efface itself in the course of this globalization, and with it all measure, any conceptual limit. In all the scenes of repentance, confession, forgiveness, or apology which have multiplied on the geopolitical scene since the last war, and in an accelerated fashion in the past few years, one sees not only individuals, but also entire communities, professional corporations, the representatives of ecclesiastical hierarchies, sovereigns, and heads of state ask for "forgiveness."[74]

By over-use and inappropriate use, Derrida believes, the language of forgiveness has been stretched beyond its limits.

Derrida identifies two ways in which forgiveness language has been abused in recent times. The first is in the attempt to inscribe forgiveness within the confines of legal, political, and institutional negotiations of wrongdoing. Forgiveness is actually "heterogeneous" to such contexts.[75] This deployment of forgiveness language is therefore distorting. The second distortion occurs when forgiveness is invoked in the service of some other, presumably "higher" end, for example, when one advocates that individuals or groups forgive so that social harmony might be achieved. He argues:

> I shall risk this proposition: each time forgiveness is at the service of a finality, be it noble and spiritual (atonement or redemption, reconciliation, salvation), each time that it aims to re-establish a normality (social, national, political, psychological) by a work of mourning, by some therapy or ecology of memory, then the "forgiveness" is not pure—nor is its concept. Forgiveness is not, it *should not be*, normal, normative, normalising. It *should* remain exceptional

---

[73] Derrida, *On Cosmopolitanism and Forgiveness*, 27–28.
[74] Ibid., 28.
[75] Ibid., 27.

and extraordinary, in the face of the impossible: as if it interrupted the ordinary course of historical temporality.[76]

Already, early in his discussion of forgiveness, Derrida has signaled some of the key issues that orient the further development of his thinking. The rejection of any finality extrinsic to forgiveness itself points to his concern to avoid economies of exchange. The reference to "the impossible" and the interruptive quality of forgiveness indicates its event character, its unexpected arrival. The idea that forgiveness is not normative or normalizing evokes Derrida's understanding of an ethics beyond the law (a perspective he shares with Jankélévitch and Lévinas). And he hints at the idea that forgiveness is an interpersonal and relational matter (another commonality with Jankélévitch and Lévinas), not something enacted between groups. It is important that we examine each of these in further detail. But before doing so we will need to take a closer look at another set of issues introduced explicitly in the statement above: the notion of a *pure* forgiveness and the related notion of a *pure concept* of forgiveness.

In his approach to *pure* forgiveness Derrida identifies what its pure *concept* would be. He rejects the notion that forgiveness is deployed when addressing common, "venial" offenses. The only point at which forgiveness would be an issue for him is when we are confronted with the unforgivable. He argues: "One cannot, or should not forgive; there is only forgiveness, if there is any, where there is the unforgivable."[77] (Derrida identifies such offenses with what, in religious language, would be called "mortal sin."[78]) This aporetic formulation, forgiveness only of the unforgivable, sets up the contrast between Derrida's approach to forgiveness and that of Jankélévitch.

Derrida takes exception to the conflict he finds in Jankélévitch's discussion of forgiveness. On the one hand Jankélévitch's theoretical formulation, as noted above, suggests a real openness to forgiveness as an unrestricted possibility in response to harm.[79] On the other hand,

---

[76] Ibid., 31–32 (Derrida's emphases).

[77] Ibid., 32.

[78] Ibid. Whether this identification is apt is an open question. In the Catholic Christian context the tradition maintains that mortal sins *are* forgivable. The point Derrida seems to want to make is that only the most serious of offenses—he will mention crimes against humanity—merit the response of forgiveness and that they do so because they are beyond the possibility of forgiveness.

[79] Ibid., 35.

Derrida sees Jankélévitch opposing forgiveness in cases of crimes against humanity in his address regarding forgiving the Germans and in his *L'Imprescriptible.*[80] For Jankélévitch the Shoah is inexpiable.[81] Moreover, those guilty of the crime (or the German people as a whole, whom Jankélévitch appears to hold responsible) have never asked for pardon. They have not expressed repentance. Therefore, he holds, they should not receive pardon.[82]

On this point Derrida recognizes that Jankélévitch is consistent with *one* of two strands of the Abrahamic tradition. One strand of that heritage presents forgiveness as a totally gratuitous, utterly gracious gift. The other strand (evident in Jankélévitch's insistence on repentance) emphasizes a conditional forgiveness.[83] Forgiveness is only extended "proportionate[ly] to the recognition of the fault, to repentance, to the transformation of the sinner who then explicitly asks forgiveness."[84]

Derrida rejects this conditional forgiveness on two grounds. Most immediately, he argues that the one who has repented is no longer the same as who he or she was at the time of the offense. The repentant one is "no longer guilty through and through."[85] Such a one would seem not to need forgiveness. But more fundamentally, Derrida objects to conditional forgiveness because its logic proceeds according to the mode of an economic transaction. According to the logic of Jankélévitch's position, one who cannot repay (with repentance) cannot be (or should not be) forgiven.[86] Forgiveness in this approach is contingent on *human possibility* and is tied to the possibility of imposing punishment on the offender.[87]

> In "L'Imprescriptible," therefore, and not in *Le Pardon*, Jankélévitch places himself in that exchange, in that symmetry between punishing and forgiving: forgiveness will no longer have meaning where the crime has become, like the Shoah, "inexpiable," "irreparable," out of proportion to all human measure. "Forgiveness died in the death camps," he says. Yes. Unless it only becomes possible from

[80] Ibid., 33–34. Whether Derrida is accurate in his reading of Jankélévitch is an open question.

[81] Ibid., 36.

[82] Ibid., 34.

[83] Ibid., 34–35, 44, 51.

[84] Ibid., 34–35.

[85] Ibid., 35. See also 38–39.

[86] Ibid., 36.

[87] Ibid., 37.

the moment that it appears impossible. Its history would begin, on the contrary, with the unforgivable.[88]

Thus Derrida argues for an "impossible" forgiveness, a *pure* forgiveness, one that can only arise as a possibility when one is confronted with what is unforgivable. Such a forgiveness would be outside of human calculation. Pure forgiveness would be unconditional and beyond every possibility of economic exploitation.[89]

Where does such a radical understanding of forgiveness come from? The rationale for Derrida's position becomes clearer if we recall the concerns he has expressed with respect to hospitality and the gift.[90] Once forgiveness enters into awareness as a strategy to be deployed in relationship it becomes part of an economic cycle of exchange. It no longer "gives" anything. It no longer opens a hospitable place. It imposes a debt on the one who is forgiven and becomes part of a calculation of means to achieve an end. Only when the matter requiring forgiveness is beyond our capacity to forgive does forgiveness attain the possibility of purity of expression. Then there can be no repayment. There is no circulation. The enactment is beyond the law and beyond rationality.

The understanding of unconditional forgiveness presented by Derrida parallels his discussions of hospitality and the gift in other respects. First, pure forgiveness stands in an irreducible tension with heterogeneous, conditional reality.[91] On the one hand, if forgiveness is to "appear," then it must submit to conditions.[92] On the other hand, as its aporetic structure reveals, once it appears, forgiveness becomes other than what it is supposed to be. The conditional expression must therefore always keep referring back to the unconditional forgiveness as the basis of its meaning.[93] Second, according to Derrida's analysis it would seem that,

---

[88] Ibid.

[89] Caputo, Dooley, and Scanlon, *Questioning God*, 57; Derrida, *On Cosmopolitanism and Forgiveness*, 41–42.

[90] See, for example, Derrida, *Given Time: 1. Counterfeit Money*, 1, 31, 101, 115, 163: as cited in Horner, *Rethinking God as Gift*, 213–15. Derrida himself makes connections between the gift, hospitality, and forgiveness in numerous places.

[91] See Derrida, *On Cosmopolitanism and Forgiveness*, 44–47; and Caputo, Dooley, and Scanlon, *Questioning God*, 57–58. Derrida discusses the necessary asymmetry between the one who forgives and the one forgiven. Such asymmetry excludes payment.

[92] Derrida, *On Cosmopolitanism and Forgiveness*, 44–45.

[93] Ibid., 45. See also, Caputo, Dooley, and Scanlon, *Questioning God*, 58.

as with the gift and hospitality, forgiveness, too, would have to occur—if it does—outside the realm of knowledge. Once it is recognized, as with the gift, it would lose its status by being drawn into an exchange of recognition, gratitude, dependence. Thus, for Derrida, if forgiveness occurs it would involve a kind of forgetting.[94] Third, if forgiveness occurs, it "arrives." It has the status of an event, beyond our volition. (How such an event would emerge from and take shape within our volitional acts, when not intended as such, is not clear.) And finally, in its unconditionality, forgiveness—if it occurs—extends a welcome to the offender without conditions. The dynamics of forgiveness, therefore, share a deep kinship with those of hospitality.

Jacques Derrida's analyses of the gift, hospitality, and forgiveness have provoked extensive engagement among philosophers, theologians, and social scientists in dialogue with continental philosophy. "Provoked" is the operative term. While some have been roused to embrace his ideas and his deconstructive methodology as an important critical moment in their own works, others have reacted more skeptically. One philosopher who has taken the issues raised by Derrida seriously while also being critical in his reception of them is Paul Ricoeur. His discussion of Derrida's analysis of forgiveness presents a distinctive reception of the problematic issues Derrida raises, while attempting to move beyond the limits imposed by the aporetic impossibilities Derrida defines. Ricoeur's contributions to the continental philosophical discussion of forgiveness will provide us with additional resources for exploring our topic.

### Paul Ricoeur

The writings of Paul Ricoeur (1913–2005) span over fifty years. As a philosopher he combined phenomenological methods of description with careful attention to interpretation (hermeneutics) while exploring themes within a wide range of disciplines, among them psychoanalysis, theology, historiography, literary criticism, the understanding of personal identity, and various subdisciplines within philosophy. As with Jankélévitch and Derrida, so too with Ricoeur: the events of World War II found their way

---

[94] See, for example, Robyn Horner, *Rethinking God as Gift: Marion, Derrida, and the Limits of Phenomenology* (New York: Fordham University Press, 2001), 214 n. 46, citing an observation by Kevin Hart, "Jacques Derrida: The God Effect," 259–80, in *Post-Secular Philosophy: Between Philosophy and Theology*, ed. Phillip Blond (London: Routledge, 1998), at 261.

into his writings. This is evident in his *Memory, History, Forgetting*.[95] The questions Ricoeur takes up in this work are haunted by the horrors of the Nazi regime and of war itself. More broadly, questions about the nature of memory, what it does and does not do, its relationship to history as a form of cultural memory and an archival practice, and the function of forgetting as both a culturally imposed phenomenon and an individual experience drive his inquiry.

Ricoeur's phenomenological description and hermeneutic analysis probe deeply into the structuring dynamics of memory, history, and forgetting by bracketing the subject who remembers, does history, and forgets from the analysis of each phenomenon.[96] As his critic, Alain Badiou, explains, this strategy conveys a sense of objectivity with respect to the analysis. It is only at the end of the work, in the "Epilogue," that Ricoeur takes up the question of forgiving. As he there observes:

> Forgiveness raises a question that in its principle is distinct from the one that, beginning with the preface to this book, has motivated our entire undertaking, namely, the question of the representation of the past on the plane of memory and of history at risk of forgetting. The question now posed concerns an enigma different from that of the present representation of an absent thing bearing the seal of anteriority. It is twofold: on the one hand, it is the enigma of a fault held to paralyze the power to act of the "capable being" that we are; and it is, in reply, the enigma of the possible lifting of this existential incapacity, designated by the term "forgiveness."[97]

The connection between this epilogue on forgiveness and the work as a whole becomes clearer when one considers that, at this point, Ricoeur is moving from examining what remembering, doing history, and forgetting entail to a consideration of what "one" (a human subject) is doing when confronting faults and harms that have arisen in the past (near or far). Faults, as he names them above, deploy a power to hamper us as "capable beings"—whether because we have committed them or have suffered them. Forgiveness, conversely, if it is possible, is what sets our capability free from the constraints of fault.

---

[95] Paul Ricoeur, *Memory, History, Forgetting*, trans. Kathleen Blamey and David Pellauer (Chicago: University of Chicago Press, 2004).

[96] Alain Badiou, "The Subject Supposed to Be a Christian: On Paul Ricoeur's *Memory, History, Forgetting*," *The Bible and Critical Theory* 2, no. 3 (2006): 27.1–27.9, at 27.3.

[97] Ricoeur, *Memory, History, Forgetting*, 457.

In order to probe the possibility of forgiveness, Ricoeur appeals to two "speech acts."[98] The first is the confession of fault. This he will examine in relationship to the capacities and structuring conditions of the "capable being" mentioned above. The second speech act he aligns with "the great sapiential poetry that in the same breath celebrates love and joy. There is forgiveness . . ."[99] These speech acts will provide the paradigm case for his exploration of the possibility of forgiveness. But this exploration, for its part, is presented as an engagement with the problem of the impossibility of forgiveness as spelled out by Derrida. Four Derridean themes in particular will occupy Ricoeur's attention: the impossibility of forgiveness, the impossibility of the gift and the dynamics of market exchange; the unforgivable; and forgiveness as an eschatological hope.

### *The Impossibility of Forgiveness?*

Like Derrida, Ricoeur takes exception to Jankélévitch's insistence in "Should we pardon them?" that one ask for forgiveness.[100] Forgiveness should be unconditional. It should even forgive the unforgivable. Once conditions enter in, the act of forgiveness is inscribed within an economy of exchange. This is the basis of its impossibility. But from the opening paragraph of this epilogue Ricoeur stands apart from Derrida's position while also affirming the problem Derrida has identified regarding the possibility of forgiveness. In setting out his own project, Ricoeur explains: "Forgiveness—if it has a sense, and if it exists—constitutes the horizon common to memory, history, and forgetting. Always in retreat, this horizon slips away from any grasp. It makes forgiving difficult: not easy but not impossible. It places a seal of incompleteness on the entire enterprise."[101]

This opening statement contrasts with Ricoeur's later expression of agreement with Derrida's thesis that "forgiveness is directed toward the unforgivable or it does not exist."[102] To effect this distance between

---

[98] Ibid., 457–58.

[99] Ibid., 458.

[100] Ibid., 478.

[101] Ibid., 457. The language employed here points toward what we will examine as the "eschatological dimension" of forgiving in chap. 6.

[102] Ibid., 468. Richard Kearney notes that Ricoeur is attempting in this epilogue to "give due credence to the strong arguments of Derrida, Jankélévitch and Arendt, while seeking to shift the final emphasis from 'impossible' to 'difficult.'" Richard Kearney,

Derrida's impossibility (or, rather, to bridge the abyss Derrida never tries to cross himself) Ricoeur relocates the terrain on which the analysis will take place. He shifts the argument from an analysis of the concept of forgiveness in its "purity" to "the sign of an 'anthropology of capable being': an anthropology grafted onto a philosophy of religion that says '*you can forgive.*'"[103] In other words, Ricoeur attempts to overcome the "impossibility" of forgiveness by shifting the focus of attention to the one for whom forgiveness can be a real, existential question, the "capable being."

Ricoeur's argument is expansive. It includes a penetrating analysis of guilt and responsibility, both as antecedent conditions to any individual life and as implicated in individual responsible actions. Guilt or fault, he argues, imposes limits on the capable being. Forgiveness—sought and extended—lifts the obstacles of guilt and fault, restoring capability. But to create a space in which the impossible becomes the "merely difficult," Ricoeur must first rethink the problematics of the gift as defined by Derrida, for the dynamics involved in giving and receiving and their implications for the impossibility of the appearing of the gift are paradigmatic for Derrida's analysis of forgiveness.

Ricoeur agrees with Derrida that the gift cannot occur if there is an economic exchange. This analysis also applies to forgiveness. But this poses a conceptual problem. Derrida subsumes forgiveness under the critique of the circularity of the gift and thus pronounces its impossibility. For him, forgiveness becomes a strategy of "equalizing the partners" in the exchange.[104] This eradicates forgiveness as forgiveness in the moment it is recognized. But Ricoeur sees a difficulty with this analysis. Forgiveness does not seek to equalize. In the dynamics of harm and response it is retribution that tries to equalize relations. According to Ricoeur, if we follow Derrida's line of thinking, forgiveness and retribution would have the same functional value in the relationship between offender and offended. This is, of course, absurd. Something must therefore be amiss with the analysis of the impossibility of the gift.

To open up a space for the possibility of gift, and therefore of forgiveness, Ricoeur appeals to Marcel Mauss's work on the gift, from which Derrida drew in formulating his own arguments. He observes: "Mauss does not oppose gift to exchange, but to the market form of exchange,

---

"Forgiveness at the Limit: Impossible or Possible?" *Proceedings of the American Catholic Philosophical Association* 82 (2009): 85–97, at 85.

[103] Kearney, "Forgiveness at the Limit: Impossible or Possible?" 86.

[104] Ricoeur, *Memory, History, Forgetting*, 481.

to calculation and to self-interest."[105] Ricoeur identifies this calculation
and self-interest as the locus of the problem:

> The adversaries argue this way: giving obliges giving back (*do ut des*);
> giving secretly creates inequality by placing the givers in a position
> of condescending superiority; giving ties the beneficiary, placing
> him or her under obligation, the obligation to be grateful; giving
> crushes the beneficiary under the weight of a debt he cannot repay.[106]

While Ricoeur agrees that the dynamics of a market exchange undo the
gift, he opens up the possibility that there are other kinds of giving that are
not governed by such market exchanges and do not enslave the beneficiary
in the manner described. This kind of giving can occur when there is no
reciprocation, or when the gift exceeds the requirements of exchange. In
this latter category Ricoeur mentions acts of superabundant generosity
and acts of love, especially love extended to one's enemies. As he argues,

> The commandment to love one's enemies begins by breaking the rule
> of reciprocity and requiring the extraordinary. Faithful to the gospel
> rhetoric of hyperbole, according to this commandment the only gift
> that is justified is the one given to the enemy, from whom, by hy-
> pothesis, one expects nothing in return. But, precisely, the hypothesis
> is false: what one expects from love is that it will convert the enemy
> into a friend. The potlatch celebrated by Marcel Mauss breaks up the
> order of the market from within through munificence—as does in
> its own fashion the "expense" formulated by Georges Bataille. The
> Gospels do this by giving to the gift a measure of "extravagance" that
> ordinary acts of generosity can only approach from afar.[107]

Ricoeur thus introduces a "nonmarket form of gift" in which the dynamics
are not giving and return, but giving and receiving.[108] The expectation of
return does not exist.

It is clear from this understanding of gift that there is an asymmetrical relationship between the giver and the recipient. Whereas Derrida
finds in this an impetus to repayment and therefore a motive force for
the market economy, Ricoeur sees in the opening that this asymmetry

---

[105] Ricoeur, *Memory, History, Forgetting*, 480.
[106] Ibid., 481.
[107] Ibid., 482.
[108] Ibid.

creates the possibility—very difficult, but still there—of the real enactment of a gift and, by extension, of forgiveness. Indeed, "this asymmetry is constitutive of the forgiveness equation."[109]

Ricoeur has thus set himself a formidable task. He must hold to the unconditional nature of forgiveness (in agreement with Derrida) while opening a space in which the gift of forgiveness is not assimilated to the circulation of market economics. That is, he must preserve the fundamental asymmetry in the relationship of the one who forgives to the one who receives forgiveness.

## The Difficult Possibility of Impossible Forgiveness

The foundational elements for addressing the challenge of opening a space for actual forgiveness are already implied in the shift from "objectivity" in the tone of most of *Memory, History, Forgetting* to the emphasis on the subject in the epilogue. Ricoeur draws our attention immediately to the one for whom forgiveness is a question, and to the existential conditions that shape the emergence of forgiveness as a question. Two of those conditions require special attention.

The first condition is the context of guilt or fault into which every person is born.[110] Every culture has some sort of narrative about this basic reality. Conditions of guilt and fault preexist our own individual existence and shape it, both on the level of corporate or social identity and on the level of personal sense of self.[111] But guilt or fault becomes one's own experience through one's own action. We recognize this because and to the extent that we become aware that we are responsible for our actions.[112] Yet this responsibility, as Ricoeur describes it, is also ambivalent. The action originates with the agent, but the agent is not its total master.

---

[109] Ibid., 483.

[110] Ricoeur discusses the relationship between a primordial and pre-historical loss of innocence and evil and the subsequent emergence of individual evil actions by responsible agents in *Memory, History, Forgetting*, 464–65.

[111] Ricoeur observes (ibid., 459): "The fault is the existentiell presupposition of forgiveness (I am using 'existentiell' in order to emphasize the impossibility of distinguishing here between a trait that is inseparable from the historical condition of the being that we in each case are and a personal and collective experience shaped by a historical culture whose universal character continues to be alleged)."

[112] As Ricoeur observes (ibid., 460): "The experience of fault offers itself as a given to reflection. It gives rise to thought. What is first offered to reflection is the designation of the fundamental structure in which this experience comes to be inscribed. This is the

At this level of depth, self-recognition is indivisibly action and passion, the action of acting badly and the passion of being affected by
one's own action. This is why recognizing the tie between action and
the agent is never without a surprise for consciousness, astonished,
after the action, "no longer being able to dissociate the idea of its
own causation from the memory of the particular act which it has
performed." In this regard, the representation of the act [in memory]
prevents, as it were, the return of the action to the agent.[113]

The one who has acted badly experiences, in the self-recognition and
the inability to undo what has been done, the upsurge of guilt. Integral
to this experience is the affectively charged awareness of oneself as the
originator of the action, but as unable to dispose of its aftermath. Ricoeur
thus explains: "Imputability constitutes in this respect an integral dimension of what I am calling the capable human being. It is in the region of
imputability that fault, guilt, is to be sought."[114]

This experience opens up a twofold abyss in the interior of the one
who offends. On the one hand, it establishes an abyss between innocence
and offense—the innocence of the one offended and the innocence the
agent himself or herself had or felt prior to the act. The agent experiences
affectively a disruption of right relationship to self and to the other. On
the other hand, the commission of an imputable act opens an abyss between the one who committed it and the act itself. The fact that the act
has been committed and stands independently of the agent separates it
from his or her process of becoming. It stands over against the agent as
a historical datum that can bind the sense of self to the past as guilty.
(It will be the purpose of the apology—Ricoeur speaks of "avowal" of
fault—to bridge these abysses.[115])

The second condition that shapes the emergence of forgiveness arises
precisely at the threshold of this second abyss. The act and the agent are
not one. This is crucial to the possibility of forgiveness.

---

structure of the imputability of our actions. There can, in fact, be forgiveness only where
we can accuse someone of something, presume him to be or declare him to be guilty."

[113] Ibid., 462. Ricoeur is citing from Jean Nabert, *Elements for an Ethic*, trans. William
J. Petrek (Evanston, IL: Northwestern University Press, 1969), bk. 1, "The Givens of
Reflection," chap. 1, "The Experience of Fault," 3–15, at 4.

[114] Ibid., 460.

[115] The place of apology in Ricoeur's argument and its relationship to the "unconditional" or "aneconomic" quality of forgiveness will be addressed below.

> Everything, finally, hangs on the possibility of separating the agent
> from the action. This unbinding would mark the inscription, in the
> field of the horizontal disparity between power and act, of the ver-
> tical disparity between the great height of forgiveness and the abyss
> of guilt. The guilty person, rendered capable of beginning again: this
> would be the figure of unbinding that commands all the others.[116]

The "causality" of the act has its roots in the *becoming* of the agent.
Although, as Ricoeur notes, "the tie between fault and self, guilt and
selfhood *seems* indissoluble,"[117] in fact, the person is not reducible to the
act he or she has committed.[118] The person, as a "capable being," possesses
potentialities that come to expression in acts but are not exhausted by
any individual, finite act. He or she has a possible future beyond the
act, a future that need not be bound by the guilt of the past. Thus "this
intimate dissociation [between agent and act] signifies that the capacity
of commitment belonging to the moral subject is not exhausted by its
various inscriptions in the affairs of the world. This dissociation expresses
an act of faith, a credit addressed to the resources of self-regeneration."[119]
The agent who has done wrong has the possibility to become otherwise.

The act of forgiveness, as Ricoeur understands it, unbinds the agent
from the offensive act. It opens up the possibility of a future in which
the past does not impede the possibility of future good or of a future in
relationship with the one who has been harmed.

> Under the sign of forgiveness, the guilty person is to be considered
> capable of something other than his offenses and his faults. He is
> held to be restored to his capacity for acting, and action restored to
> its capacity for continuing. This capacity is signaled in the small acts
> of consideration in which we recognize the *incognito* of forgiveness
> played out on the public stage. And, finally, this restored capacity
> is enlisted by promising as its projects action toward the future.
> The formula for this liberating word, reduced to the bareness of its
> utterance, would be: you are better than your actions.[120]

---

[116] Ricoeur, *Memory, History, Forgetting*, 490.
[117] Ibid., 466.
[118] Ibid., 489–90.
[119] Ibid., 490.
[120] Ibid., 493.

Thus Ricoeur holds out the possibility of a difficult forgiveness that would unbind the offender from the deeds of the past and liberate him or her for a future in restored relationship. Consequently, as in Jankélévitch and Derrida, so also Ricoeur's analysis possesses an eschatological element.[121] Forgiveness is a possibility, but "possessing an irreducibly practical nature, it can be uttered only in the grammar of the optative mood."[122]

## Derridean Challenges to Ricoeur's Proposal

The discerning reader will have noticed certain gaps or lacunae in the presentation of Ricoeur's argument when seen in relationship to the aporias identified by Derrida. These could call into question the status of Ricoeur's reworking of Derrida's analysis of forgiveness. We will need to address these before bringing this discussion to a close. The lacunae are: the discussion of the unforgivable, the role of apology in Ricoeur's analysis of forgiveness, and the pivotal question of the separability of the agent from the act.

Derrida makes the claim that forgiveness, if there is such a thing, can only be of the "unforgivable." Some offenses are of such magnitude and horror as to be "crimes against humanity." These, as Jankélévitch argued, are imprescriptible. One cannot impose a statute of limitations on the prosecution of such crimes. Forgiveness would seem to be out of the question. Yet, if we take Derrida at his word, it is precisely such cases that open the space for the possibility of the impossible: forgiveness in its purest form, without the possibility of advancing political aims and without any economic exchange.

Ricoeur confronts this problem by first noting the issue of imprescriptability. This is a legal issue responding to the demands of justice. The purpose of the prescription of crimes is to establish manageable limits so that claims of debt cannot be prosecuted into the indefinite future. The good operation of society requires foreclosure of questions of debt, whether they be financial, material, or the "debt to society" incurred by criminal action. Social institutions, in order to prosecute crimes and equalize the debt arising from the crime, must maintain the existence of a bond between the agent and the action committed.[123]

---

[121] Ibid., 492; see also 457.
[122] Ibid., 493.
[123] Ibid., 473.

However, social institutions operate on the level of calculable debt. Some crimes are so disproportionate that no calculation of compensation is meaningful. No expiation is possible. Crimes against humanity are among these.

On the level of social institutions such crimes are both imprescriptible and unforgivable. Institutions are not warranted to forgive. That is not their function, according to Ricoeur.[124] The location of forgiveness is in the interpersonal space between persons in relationship. But shifting the locus of the discussion to the interpersonal does not automatically resolve the problem. Ricoeur acknowledges this when he notes three dilemmas with respect to forgiveness. These arise when one considers the paradigmatic context of the enactment of forgiveness, the exchange in which someone acknowledges fault and asks for forgiveness and the offended party grants it.[125] Ricoeur signals these three dilemmas by means of three questions: "Can one forgive someone who does not admit his fault? Must the one who pronounces forgiveness himself have been offended? Can one forgive oneself?"[126] These dilemmas arise in view of both the "unforgivable" nature of the crime and the demand of pure forgiveness that it be unconditional.

The first Ricoeur dispenses with quickly. Respect for the "sense of self of the guilty person" requires that one expect an admission of responsibility. He thus lodges the resolution in the interpersonal relationship and in a positive regard for the person as person. The second dilemma is more problematic. The harm done can continue to ripple out to touch many more than were directly harmed by the action. Is it therefore only the one directly harmed by the initial act who should be asked for forgiveness? What about the further harms? As a correlate question to this second dilemma, he asks: can someone other than the "primary offender" ask for forgiveness? These questions he does not address directly but only highlights their intractability. But the third dilemma, self-forgiveness, he relates to the analysis of height and depth (presented above) as a means of overcoming the aporia of market economics.[127] To grasp the significance of this response we will need to consider Ricoeur's understanding of apology and of the separation of the person from the act.

---

[124] Ibid., 458–59, 488.

[125] Ibid., 478–79.

[126] Ibid., 478, citing Olivier Abel, "Tables du pardon: Géographie des dilemmes et parcours bibliographique," 208–36 in *Le Pardon: Briser la dette et l'oubli* (Paris: Autrement, 1992), at 211–16.

[127] Ricoeur, *Memory, History, Forgetting*, 479.

Paul Ricoeur presents as a paradigmatic case of forgiveness the situation in which the "capable being" who offended expresses regret and asks for forgiveness. The apology is key to his exposition, as it functions in a manner parallel to a promise. In the apology one manifests the desire to distance oneself from the kind of action that produced the harm. In the terms presented above, the apology attempts to bridge the abyss between innocence and the guilty action. One cannot overcome the abyss between the action as now historical reality and one's own history. One cannot surmount the guilt. But in the speech act the person effectuates a promise of self-distancing from the act, insofar as this is in her or his hands to accomplish.[128]

On the level of the request and the granting of forgiveness it would seem that we have returned to the mutuality of exchange that would eradicate the reality of forgiveness. But forgiveness does not just operate on this horizontal plane, as Ricoeur argues. On the vertical plane of the distance between guilt and the unmerited act of forgiveness, the distance is immense.[129] Forgiveness is what effects the separation of the offender from the offensive act—the separation the offender desires but cannot effect alone. Because the forgiveness granted comes from a place so far removed from the abyss of the guilt, it cannot be repaid; it remains outside the market economy. Thus, viewed only from the perspective of the interpersonal dynamics on the horizontal plane, the interaction in the speech act—requesting forgiveness and granting it—may appear to be an economic exchange.[130] However, the difference between what each side brings to the interpersonal encounter is such as to render the encounter an-economic.

According to this analysis it is the act of forgiveness that effects the separation of agent from act in the relation of persons. Ricoeur's discussion of this issue therefore bypasses one of the aporias raised by Derrida, that the repentant person is not in need of forgiveness because he or she is no longer the "same" person.

---

[128] Ibid., 478, 485.

[129] One could make the case that it borders on infinite distance because it is not a matter of degree on a single scale but a matter of kind.

[130] Ricoeur adverts to this appearance when he observes (*Memory, History, Forgetting*, 480): "Now the idea of gift has its own difficulties, which can be divided into two parts. It is important first to recover the reciprocal dimension of the gift in contrast to an initial characterization of it as unilateral. It is then a matter of restoring, at the heart of the relation of exchange, the difference in altitude that distinguishes forgiving from giving, following the essence of exchange."

It is the unbinding that governs all the others. But is it itself possible? Here I concur one last time with Derrida's argument: separating the guilty person from his act, in other words forgiving the guilty person while condemning his action, would be to forgive a subject other than the one who committed the act. The argument is serious and the response difficult. It is to be sought, in my opinion, on the side of a more radical uncoupling than that supposed by the argument between a first subject, the one who committed the wrong, and a second subject, the one who is punished, an uncoupling at the heart of our very power to act—of agency—namely, between the effectuation and the capacity it actualizes. This intimate dissociation signifies that the capacity of commitment belonging to the moral subject is not exhausted by its various inscriptions in the affairs of the world. This dissociation expresses an act of faith, a credit addressed to the resources of self-regeneration.[131]

What makes the distinction between the guilty person and the repentant person real in the relationship is the act of forgiveness itself, not the repentance that moves one to ask for forgiveness.[132] No amount of repentance can undo the historical reality that one has acted badly and is responsible for the action. It is the word of forgiveness that effectuates the separation of the person from the guilt associated with the deed, a separation within the context of that relationship.[133] This separation is effected by the forgiver's act of faith in the better future of the offender. By this means forgiveness "release[s] the agent from his act."[134]

And what of self-forgiveness? Ricoeur recognizes that the dynamics of forgiveness must be understood in terms of the liberation of the guilty self for a future not bound by the guilt of the past. Whether an individual

---

[131] Ricoeur, *Memory, History, Forgetting*, 490. In this formulation Ricoeur anticipates the discussion of the characteristics of forgiving, particularly that it is characterized by hope and that it possesses an intrinsic orientation toward the future—an eschatological orientation. We will examine these characteristics in chaps. 6 and 10.

[132] This becomes especially clear when working within a speech-act theory where the making of the request and the granting of it are explicitly verbal and are understood to be causative of what they express. Later we shall see the limits this paradigm imposes on forgiveness and why, therefore, it cannot be taken as normative.

[133] This will be important later. The individual granting forgiveness liberates the individual within the context of that relationship. The one forgiving does not have the authority to enact that forgiveness on behalf of others.

[134] Ricoeur, *Memory, History, Forgetting*, 489.

can produce such liberation in isolation is not clear from Ricoeur's presentation. The answer would hinge on whether one can unbind oneself from a guilt in which one holds oneself bound. Ricoeur's discussion of forgiveness from within a speech act paradigm sheds no light on this particular question.

## Conclusion

Our foray into the landscape of continental discussions of forgiveness shaped by Jacques Derrida's provocative ideas has brought us, by way of Paul Ricoeur, to the boundary lands between the pure concept of forgiveness and the impossibility of its enactment on the one hand, and the conditions under which the impossible transmutes into the very difficult. This is one prominent line of thought, but largely restricted to those engaged in philosophical approaches shaped by continental philosophy. As we cross over this boundary land in the direction indicated by Paul Ricoeur we come to the realm of Anglo-American moral philosophical reflection. This is the landscape to which we now turn.

# Chapter 2

# Anglo-American Discussions of Forgiveness

### Preliminaries

*T*he Anglo-American moral philosophical discussion of forgiveness operates from within a very different framework from that examined in the previous chapter.[1] As with Ricoeur, this philosophical approach devotes attention to the one who forgives, but the questions that govern this conversation are very different from those central to the continental discussion. Here the topic of forgiveness is securely anchored within the waters of moral philosophy. Questions about the definition of forgiveness are tightly correlated with the conditions governing forgiveness as a moral response to a moral harm. Set within the context of moral philosophy and ethics, the primary agenda is determining when it is or is not morally permissible to forgive.

Herein lies the contrast between the problematic raised by Derrida and the Anglo-American discussions. Derrida's analysis of the aporias of forgiveness renders any conditioning of forgiveness in its expression a betrayal of forgiveness itself. Conditions make "pure" forgiveness impossible. The Anglo-American approach, on the contrary, seeks to articulate the conditions that make forgiveness possible as a moral enactment. Hence the starting points of the two discussions and the rules governing them are quite distinct.

The present chapter will examine four different approaches to forgiveness in the Anglo-American context. The purpose of this examina-

---

[1] Paul Ricoeur, although a native of France, spent much of his later career in the United States. It is perhaps no accident that the concerns of his analysis of forgiveness seek to bridge the gap between the approaches of his continental and American colleagues.

tion is not to set the stage for a choice between French-Continental and Anglo-American approaches; both discussions have valuable insights to contribute to our examination of forgiveness. Nor is it to argue for a choice among the four perspectives we will be exploring; each of them has strengths and limitations. Nor will it suggest that the four positions presented in what follows cover the entire terrain of the Anglo-American discussion; they do not.

The overriding purpose of this chapter is the same as that of the first: to survey the terrain of the discussion so that we can draw from it resources to help us understand and name forgiveness as a basic human phenomenon, independently of any appeals to religious doctrine or belief systems. This will require us to attend to both the ideas being articulated *and* the methods, assumptions, and values embedded in the arguments presented to support those ideas. The four approaches we will be examining have been chosen precisely because each author is explicit about the methodological moves being made and the presuppositions that underlie their respective approaches. This is evident in the way each defines forgiveness as a moral issue, in their discussions of the conditions under which forgiveness may or may not be morally enacted, and especially in the way in which each engages the discussion of resentment (or, more broadly, retributive emotions)[2] as the personal, affective experience that raises forgiveness as an issue.

Before we examine the different perspectives at the heart of this chapter it is important to say a further word about the place of "resentment" in the discussion. Each of the authors we will be examining is aware that resentment has been a central theme in the analysis of retributive emotions and of forgiveness since the resurgence of philosophical interest in forgiveness in the latter part of the twentieth century. Two lines of thought have left their mark on the discussion. The first can be traced back to Friedrich Nietzsche (1844–1900). Against the background of his thought on "the will to power" and the "Übermensch" [super-man], Nietzsche read the experience of resentment, as he called it, *ressentiment* [from the French], as a sign of weakness. It signals the vulnerability of the one affected by it to the impact of the attitudes of others on one's own psyche. The affect shows itself in malicious impulses and a desire for revenge (retribution). Resentment is therefore something to be eschewed,

---

[2] I have adopted the language of "retributive emotions" from Jeffrie G. Murphy. See Jeffrie G. Murphy and Jean Hampton, *Forgiveness and Mercy* (Cambridge: Cambridge University Press, 1988), 2–3 n. 3.

and forgiveness is an issue only for those weak enough to be affected by resentment in the first place.[3]

The second line of thought traces its origins to two sermons given by Bishop Joseph Butler (1692–1752). Recognizing that resentful feelings can arise spontaneously and that they can incline toward an appropriate defense of oneself, Butler argues that not all resentment is wrong. On some occasions and in certain circumstances resentment is the expression of a good impulse worked into our makeup by a good God.[4] Thus Butler's analysis of resentment distinguishes two forms: a spontaneous upsurge on the occasion of an offense, and a "settled anger" that harbors malign thoughts and cultivates negative affections—and possibly actions—against the offender. This latter is the form to be avoided. But both forms need to be overcome. Butler therefore defines forgiveness in terms of the forswearing of resentment.[5]

These two approaches to resentment (Nietzsche's and Butler's) have influenced much of the contemporary philosophical analysis of forgiveness in the Anglo-American context. Nietzsche raises the critical question whether forgiveness might, in certain circumstances, be morally objectionable. Thus contemporary Anglo-American philosophers, concerned with the conditions for forgiveness as a moral action, have grappled with precisely that question.[6] At the same time, recognizing the destructive potential in resentment and that forgiveness is commonly understood to overcome resentment's destructive impulses, philosophers have also delved into analyzing the relationship between forgiveness and resentment, making use of Butler's ideas. This will become apparent in

---

[3] Citing Friedrich Nietzsche, *On the Genealogy of Morality*, trans. Maudemarie Clark and Alan J. Swensen (Indianapolis: Hackett, 1998), Charles Griswold observes "that in §11 Nietzsche refers to the 'instincts of reaction and *ressentiment*' (p. 23); and in §14, tracing how *ressentiment* creates new ideals, he remarks, 'not being to avenge oneself is called not wanting to avenge oneself, perhaps even forgiveness ("for *they* know not what they do—we alone know what *they* do!"). They also talk of "love of one's enemies"—and sweat while doing so' (p. 27). So forgiveness is actually the *expression* rather than the forswearing of *ressentiment*." Charles L. Griswold, *Forgiveness: A Philosophical Exploration* (Cambridge: Cambridge University Press, 2007), 15 n. 21.

[4] Murphy and Hampton, *Forgiveness and Mercy*, 22. For the texts of the two sermons, see Joseph Butler, "Upon Resentment" and "Upon Forgiveness of Injuries," in idem, *Sermons* (New York: Robert Carter & Brothers, 1729).

[5] Murphy and Hampton, *Forgiveness and Mercy*, 15.

[6] This will become evident in the conditions prescribed for the moral enactment of forgiveness in the authors we will be considering.

what follows as we examine the discussions of forgiveness by Jeffrie G. Murphy, Joram Graf Haber, Pamela Hieronymi, and Charles Griswold.

### Jeffrie G. Murphy and Forgoing Resentment

One of the contemporary philosophical voices that has been most influential on the present discussion of forgiveness is that of Jeffrie G. Murphy. He has been researching and publishing on the theme of forgiveness since the early 1980s, moved in part by his engagement with questions of value and affectivity that lie beneath the legal doctrines and structures that govern our common life.[7]

In a collaborative work with the late Jean Hampton of the University of Pittsburgh entitled *Forgiveness and Mercy*, Murphy sketches his own approach to the topic of forgiveness in relation to resentment. Recognizing that much of the language of forgiveness in our culture has been shaped by religious (and particularly Christian) thinking, Murphy sets out to articulate an intentionally *secular* understanding of forgiveness, one that does not appeal to religious doctrines for its justification but that can learn from those sources.[8] This allows him to draw on Bishop Butler's analysis of forgiveness and resentment in articulating his own approach.

Murphy finds support within Butler for the conviction that forgiving is "the sort of thing that one does for a reason."[9] This leaves Murphy with the challenge of identifying what constitute good reasons for forgiving, reasons that would be compelling to secular rationality. To make his case, Murphy's argument draws on three sets of interrelated presuppositions.

The first set of presuppositions is perhaps the most basic. It is the set of fundamental values and convictions underlying the investigation of forgiveness as a moral activity. Among these are the conviction that human beings are of value *in se* and not because of what they might accomplish; the understanding that we are responsible agents and therefore can be held accountable for our actions; and the idea that our responsibility includes the use of our reason and that we can, by that means, come to

---

[7] In his own words, "I am particularly interested in the degree to which certain moral and legal doctrines are rooted in specific *passions* (feelings, emotions) and the degree to which a philosophical examination of those passions will have a bearing on an understanding and evaluation of the doctrines they in part generate and for which these doctrines in part serve as the rationalizations." Murphy and Hampton, *Forgiveness and Mercy*, 2.

[8] See, for example, ibid., 30.

[9] Ibid., 15.

a knowledge of what it is right to do (rational judgment). Thus this first set of presuppositions lays out the landscape of our action, including forgiveness and how we deal with our emotional life, as fundamentally moral. It is the landscape of responsible action.

The second set of presuppositions concerns that dimension of ourselves for which forgiveness can become a problem. For Murphy, forgiveness is primarily about feelings and how we deal with them, not specifically about behaviors.[10] But our feelings are shaped by many influences. As Murphy notes,

> We are all, to a great extent, products of whatever system of so-cialization is operative in our culture. If this socialization process cultivates certain irrational or destructive or self-demeaning emotions within us, we will become prisoners to those emotions—no matter how free we may think ourselves in acting upon them without impediment. Similar harm will be done if our culture seeks to extinguish emotions that are in fact healthy and valuable—a worry later to be explored with respect to resentment and hatred. Thus it must be regarded as a relevant project within social and political and legal philosophy to examine the passions or emotions (such as resentment) in order at least to attempt to deal with the question of the degree to which, if at all, these passions or emotions should be reinforced, channeled in certain directions, or even eliminated where this is possible.[11]

Thus the task of this secular philosophical approach to forgiveness is to understand the conditions within which it is legitimate to forgive and to provide rational support for revising aspects of socialization that foster distorted ways of feeling—and therefore of acting. Conversely, on the basis of reason, the task is to foster those emotions that are appropriate to circumstances and are non-destructive.

The moral focus of the first set of presuppositions and the critical assessment of emotional responses in the second provide the context for the third set. Murphy discusses forgiveness under the heading of "virtue."[12] That is, forgiveness, when engaged in the proper way,[13] expresses a positive

---

[10] Ibid., 21.

[11] Ibid., 9.

[12] See Murphy and Hampton, *Forgiveness and Mercy*, 7, 12, 15, 17.

[13] As we will see below, Murphy identifies conditions that, according to his argument, specify whether forgiving is a reasonable act. In the absence of those conditions

moral value. Better put, when *we* forgive, under the right conditions, we are doing something morally praiseworthy. To restate this in terms of the preceding two sets of presuppositions, when we forgive within the proper conditions we are affirming a positive moral value (the value of persons, the value of one's own worth, the value of the moral order) by a responsible act informed by reason.

These three sets of presuppositions shape Murphy's approach to forgiveness. They establish an intrinsic connection between two fundamental questions. As he explains:

> The question "What is forgiveness?" cannot after all be sharply distinguished from the question "How is forgiveness justified?" As the foregoing cases show, not all instances of ceasing to resent will be ones of forgiveness—for example, forgetting is not. We cannot define forgiveness and *then* ask what moral reasons make it appropriate; because, I suggest, my ceasing to resent will not constitute forgiveness unless it is *done for a moral reason*. Forgiveness is not the overcoming of resentment *simpliciter*; it is rather this: forswearing resentment on moral grounds.[14]

The nature of the connection Murphy draws between these two questions will become clear if we examine more closely his discussion of resentment in relationship to forgiveness and then consider the conditions under which forgiveness would be moral (or not).

### Resentment, Forgiveness, and the Conditions of Forgiveness

As indicated above, Murphy treats forgiveness as a potential response to an affective condition, resentment. He agrees with Butler that this affective condition is not, in and of itself, wrong. In a given instance it might be morally appropriate. In another it might not. The distinction in assessment rests, in Murphy's analysis, on the nature and dynamics of resentment and on the moral content of the occasion that provokes resentful response.

Murphy makes the argument that resentment is a feeling. But it is not *just* a feeling. It is an emotional feeling. "Emotions, unlike such simple

---

forgiveness would not be reasonable. It might also be immoral. Alternatively, when the conditions are fulfilled it might be immoral not to forgive.

[14] Murphy and Hampton, *Forgiveness and Mercy*, 23–24.

sensations as headaches, have a cognitive structure and are thus open, at least in part, to rational evaluation and control."[15] In other words, resentment arises from what we perceive and understand to be taking place or to have taken place. Our cognitional processes are implicated when resentment arises. They are foundational to its occurrence. This also implies that our rational processes can to some degree moderate our perceptions of a situation so as to undo the impetus to resentment.

Of course, not every perception provokes resentment. Resentment is, as Murphy notes, a response to the transgression of a specific value. It arises when one experiences that one's own self has somehow been harmed.[16] The offensive act sends to the offended party a message that the offender somehow regards the offended party in a demeaned or degraded way.[17] Resentment, therefore, is a defensive response, seeking to protect oneself and one's own worth from the harm perceived.[18] In some cases this response (resentment) may be morally justified, in others, not. In either case the fundamental mechanism is the same, an affective response to a perceived threat to the value of my own person. The natural reaction to such a threat is to distance oneself from the offending party and, in some cases, to seek retribution.[19] But the question of forgiveness only arises, for Murphy, if resentment is the appropriate response. This is central to distinguishing forgiveness from other responses to harm, such as excusing or justifying what was done. As Murphy explains,

> We may forgive only what it is initially proper to resent; and, if a person has done nothing wrong or was not responsible for what he did, there is *nothing to resent* (though perhaps much to be sad about). Resentment—and thus forgiveness—is directed toward *responsible wrongdoing;* and therefore, if forgiveness and resentment are to have an arena, it must be where such wrongdoing remains intact—i.e., neither excused nor justified.[20]

---

[15] Ibid., 5 n. 7.

[16] Ibid., 16, 25, 93.

[17] Ibid., 25.

[18] This raises many issues we will not be able to address here, among them: Is resentment only legitimate when my perception is accurate? Who would judge the accuracy of my assessment of the situation? Murphy brushes up against such questions when he considers the case of a friend who restrains someone from his excessive drinking. See ibid., 26.

[19] Ibid., 25.

[20] Ibid., 20. Emphasis in original. I contest this both on the grounds of the nature of the enactment of forgiveness as a response to harm *qua* harm and on the basis of the

This observation adds a further element to Murphy's discussion of resentment, namely, the issue of responsibility. The wrong one resents must have been, according to Murphy, the responsible act of a responsible agent. This condition flows from the three sets of presuppositions mentioned above. In the face of a harm to the fundamental value of a human person (first set) one reacts defensively (affective and cognitive response, second set) to the offender and distances oneself from him or her. The issue of virtue (third set) arises both in the proper moral judgment of the offense and in the forgiveness of the offense under the morally appropriate conditions.

Against the background of this understanding of resentment and its moral implications Murphy identifies forgiveness as "forswearing resentment on moral grounds" (as noted above). Three aspects of this definition bear closer examination. First, to forswear resentment is not to eliminate it entirely. To define forgiveness in terms of the elimination of a feeling would make any claims of "having forgiven" impossible; the reemergence of resentful feelings at a later time would falsify the claim. Rather, in Murphy's discussion, to forswear means to commit oneself to not acting on the basis of resentment and to laboring to overcome the presence of resentful feelings arising from the occasion of harm.[21]

Second, implicit in this definition is an understanding of the offended person as a rational, responsible agent. The decision to forgive emerges from a rational assessment of the situation. It involves volition, but, since forgiveness seeks to overcome an emotion that is not entirely under volitional control, this decision expresses itself as a commitment to oppose the expression of that feeling and to oppose the invocation of that feeling as a justification for future hostility. Exercising oneself in moderating the affective life (Murphy speaks of "passions") is a dimension of forgiveness understood as a virtue.

Third, Murphy prescribes that forgiveness must be for "moral reasons." He understands moral reasons in relation to the promotion of the values identified in the first set of presuppositions discussed above. "Acceptable grounds for forgiveness must be compatible with self-respect, respect for

---

non-objectivity of judgments regarding what it is appropriate to resent. We will return to this question in chap. 5.

[21] See Murphy and Hampton, *Forgiveness and Mercy*, 20–23. It is important to note that Murphy does not delve into the nature of the labor involved in forswearing resentment in any depth or into the implications of that labor for understanding the enactment of forgiving itself. This will be our task in chap. 5.

others as moral agents, and respect for the rules of morality or the moral order."[22] If the granting of forgiveness violates any of these three values, it would be immoral, according to Murphy. Thus to speak of "moral reasons" is a way of naming the formal conditions that must be satisfied if forgiving someone is to be a moral act.

So far, so good. But what do these formal conditions look like in the concrete? To answer this question Murphy examines five reasons commonly used to justify forgiveness: repentance of the offender, good motivations, the suffering of the offender, the humiliation of the offender, and longstanding history of relationship.[23] He argues that it is morally justifiable to forgive someone in "cases where we can draw a distinction between the immoral *act* and the immoral *agent*."[24] If the offender can be separated from the act or at least from the meaning of the act, it is morally permissible to forgive. The kind of separation Murphy intends is most evident in the case of repentance.

> This is surely the clearest way in which a wrongdoer can sever himself from his past wrong. In having a sincere change of heart, he is withdrawing his endorsement from his own immoral past behavior; he is saying, "I no longer stand behind the wrongdoing, and I want to be separated from it. I stand with you in condemning it." Of such a person it cannot be said that he is now conveying the message that he holds me in contempt. Thus I can relate to him now, through forgiveness, without fearing my own acquiescence in immorality or in judgments that I lack worth. I forgive him for what he now is.[25]

"Thus, to the degree that the items on the preceding list represent ways in which an agent can be divorced from his evil act, they represent grounds for forgiveness that are compatible with self-respect and respect for the rules of the moral order."[26] In his examination of these five conditions Murphy comes to the conclusion that each of them "*may* be consistent

---

[22] Murphy and Hampton, *Forgiveness and Mercy*, 24.

[23] Ibid. After introducing the five cases Murphy provides a summary examination of each. In addition to these, Murphy also considers two additional cases based on appeal to motivations strongly associated with Christianity: the desire to reform the sinner and the recognition that we, too, are sinners (p. 30). We will examine these two issues later.

[24] Murphy and Hampton, *Forgiveness and Mercy*, 24. Note the parallel to Ricoeur (chap. 1).

[25] Ibid., 26.

[26] Ibid., 25.

with self-respect, respect for others, and respect for the rules of the moral order."[27]

To summarize, Jeffrie Murphy espouses a conditional forgiveness. Forgiveness is a mode of engagement with resentment arising from a moral harm (a breach of a moral value). It involves a commitment (forswearing), negatively, to avoid acting on the impulses arising from the resentment and, positively, to actively work to overcome the resentful feeling toward the offender arising from the offensive action. This commitment is moral when it is deployed in situations in which the agent is appropriately separated from the action and/or the meaning of the action that offended the moral value. Thus, forgiving engages affective, cognitive, and volitional aspects of the responsible person. When properly exercised, forgiving is a virtuous act.

Murphy's contributions to Anglo-American discussions of forgiveness have garnered much attention, testifying thereby to their important place in the discussion. Each of the remaining philosophers we will be considering has responded appreciatively, but also critically, to Murphy's proposal. In their critical appropriation of and engagement with Murphy's ideas they bring to light further important considerations for the development of an understanding of forgiveness as a basic human phenomenon. One of those critics, the late Joram Graf Haber, proposes an alternative approach that, although consonant with many of Murphy's conclusions, relies on a different set of presuppositions.

### Joram Graf Haber and Forgiveness as a Performative Utterance

Like Jeffrie Murphy, Joram G. Haber worked at the intersection of philosophy and law. He shared Murphy's interest in the ethical implications of the law and legal practice. With many other philosophers he recognized the importance of feelings in moral theory, arguing that an appeal to abstract principles is insufficient to account for the complexity of human experience.[28] Likewise, in view of that complexity, he

---

[27] Ibid., 29. Emphasis added. One point Murphy does not belabor in this work but discusses in detail elsewhere is the tension between supposedly "unconditional forgiveness" and forgiveness conditioned only on the repentance of the offender. See Jeffrie G. Murphy, *Getting Even: Forgiveness and Its Limits* (New York: Oxford University Press, 2003), 36–38, 72, 87–93. We will return to this theme later.

[28] See Joram Graf Haber, *Forgiveness* (Savage, MD: Rowman & Littlefield, 1991), 2. This is where he states: "For my part, I believe that morality cannot be construed within the bounds of principles alone but must also include feelings and attitudes."

acknowledged the difficulty involved in attempts to define forgiveness, an acknowledgment shared by many of his colleagues.[29]

Despite these general areas of agreement, Haber's book, *Forgiveness*, explicitly challenges what he identifies as the prevailing philosophical trends in the discussion of forgiveness. He contests three prominent approaches to the topic: the deontological (determining moral content on the basis of universal principles) and consequentialist (determining morality on the basis of the consequences of an action) and the resurgent discussion among virtue theorists. His assessment suggests that he sees each of them as inadequate because each focuses attention too narrowly. Each reduces the discussion to the terrain on which it stands, thereby missing the complexities of the topic. He explains:

> Over the past fifteen years, there has been increasing interest in the role of feelings as philosophers have returned to the approach of Aristotle—to a study of the virtues with an emphasis not so much on what a moral agent should *do* as on what kind of person a moral agent should *be*. This interest has grown out of a dissatisfaction with the methodological commitment to the primacy of moral principles that has been the hallmark of ethics ever since Kant. Deontologists and consequentialists have tended to de-emphasize a concern with moral "being" in favor of a concentration on moral "doing." These philosophers construe the central question of ethics as asking what we, as responsible moral agents confronting decisions of right and wrong, ought to do. They see it as their task to formulate principles of behavior defining our duties by distinguishing right actions from wrong ones. In contrast, virtue theorists take the central question of ethics as asking, "What kind of person ought we to be?" They see it as their task to identify traits and attitudes reflecting good character and pay careful attention to the role of the affections.[30]

This statement lays out Haber's agenda with respect to the discussion of forgiveness as he sees it. In virtue ethics he identifies an emphasis on the formation of character (what an agent should *be*) to the exclusion of adequate accounts of what an agent should do. This he believes is

---

[29] Ibid., 4. Haber makes explicit reference to the works of William Neblett, "Forgiveness and Ideals," *Mind* 83 (1974); R. J. O'Shaugnessy, "Forgiveness," *Philosophy* 42 (1967): 336–52; and Joanna North, "Wrongdoing and Forgiveness," *Philosophy* 62 (1987): 499–508.

[30] Haber, *Forgiveness*, 2.

inadequate because ethics concerns moral *action*. Questions about the morality of a person's character can only be approached via empirical observation of the person's actions.[31] But since morality of actions involves not only the character of the individual but also the individual's intention (something not accessible to empirical observation), Haber sees this approach to ethics as incoherent.[32] Thus virtue theories cannot provide a basis for judging the moral worth of any action, including the act of forgiving. The deontological and consequentialist approaches emphasize the doing, governed by abstract moral principles that can provide the basis for judgments about right and wrong action. But these principles, as Haber argues, run into problems when they are filtered into the reality of human experience. Abstractions do not translate well into particular circumstances.[33]

Haber's criticisms of the prominent approaches to ethical theory set the stage for his own proposal. He does not reject the importance of virtue, not even as applied to forgiveness. But he sees a flaw in the way the arguments are developed. Similarly, he does not reject the importance of ethical principles, but relating the application of principles to concrete circumstances is a problem that must be overcome on the level of the application of a method. Finally, Haber sets aside the task of defining forgiveness. Instead, he lays out the requisite conditions for enacting it morally.

In order to overcome the limitations he finds in other approaches, Haber proposes first to "delimit" the concept of forgiveness (not define it) by distinguishing it logically from other concepts.[34] He develops a paradigmatic understanding of forgiveness that, like the deontological and consequentialist approaches, adheres to moral principles. He also takes into account the importance of feelings in moral reasoning while overcoming the limitations he sees in virtue theories. Here he focuses particular attention on behavior as the benchmark for assessing the moral status of the act of forgiveness. He thus bypasses the tendency to

---

[31] Ibid., 13–14.

[32] We will say more on this below in presenting Haber's objections to Murphy's analysis of forgiveness.

[33] This point is strikingly similar to Derrida's charge that the purity of the gift, forgiveness, and hospitality are lost when the ideals they name have to be mediated through finite conditions. Haber arrives at this concern for different reasons and by different means, but the parallel is striking.

[34] Haber, *Forgiveness*, 3.

"define" forgiveness in favor of specifying the rules governing its proper enactment.[35]

Haber embarks on his constructive project by examining forgiveness as a "performative utterance" (speech act).[36] That is, he argues that forgiveness is enacted when one states "I forgive you" in accordance with certain rules of discourse. This is not the only mode in which forgiveness can be enacted, but Haber takes it as the paradigm case. As paradigm it contains or enacts in an emblematic manner the rules governing forgiveness. The validity of other cases can then be assessed in relationship to this paradigm.

It is important to note that this approach to understanding forgiveness contrasts sharply with Murphy's. The point of contrast concerns how one arrives at the assessment of forgiveness as a specifically *moral* act. In his introduction Haber explicitly critiques Murphy on two grounds related to virtue ethics. First Haber notes, *contra* virtue ethicists, that virtue can be displayed in morally bad action. The action may not "count" as a virtue in such circumstances, but the characteristics of the virtue may still be present. This raises a problem with Murphy's approach to forgiveness as a state of feeling. It makes no sense to Haber to speak of a morally bad feeling. One cannot deploy feelings in morally good or bad ways. The judgment of morality concerns actions or behaviors, not feelings, and behaviors are to be judged good or bad (moral or immoral) in relationship to some further criterion of value beyond themselves. Second, Haber rejects the notion that forgiveness is an intrinsically value-laden concept. As mentioned above, forgiveness can be enacted for non-moral and immoral reasons or for no reason at all. To define forgiveness in a way that makes its morality part of its "essence" is to distort the concept. Yet this is what he sees Murphy doing when he defines forgiveness in terms of overcoming resentment *for moral reasons*.[37] Haber wants to locate the morality of forgiveness, therefore, not in a feeling state but in a decision by the victim, a decision that operates according to specific rules and is expressed in action.

---

[35] Ibid., 53.

[36] Ibid., 4–5. Paul Ricoeur makes use of speech act theory as well.

[37] Haber, *Forgiveness*, 7, 22. It is important to note that Haber misreads Murphy on the definition of forgiveness as "overcoming" resentment. Murphy also rejects the notion that forgiveness can be defined in terms of "overcoming" resentment. He opts for the term he finds in Butler, "forswearing" resentment. There is a more substantial point of disagreement on the issue of "moral reasons."

*Forgiveness as a "Performative Utterance"*

In laying out his argument for forgiveness as a performative utterance, a speech act that makes real what it expresses, Haber shares many pre-suppositions with Murphy. He agrees that one can discuss forgiveness as a virtue, provided it is enacted for moral reasons and that there are no other considerations that would exclude forgiveness.[38] He also recognizes that forgiveness arises as an issue in the face of resentment. Like Murphy, Haber affirms that resentment is interrelated with cognitive processes. But he goes beyond Murphy when he argues that resentment is based on a *judgment*: "So, resentment is the emotion that reflects the belief that the injury received should not have been intentionally inflicted in the manner done. It is a form of personal protest, that, in the words of Jeffrie Murphy, 'expresses our respect for self, for others, and for morality.'"[39]

This belief arises from our evaluation of the situation. Hence our resentment is based on a cognitive judgment. Haber's emphasis on the aspect of judgment is crucial to his argument about what one is doing when forgiving *and* to his understanding of the moral dimension of forgiveness. He argues that forgiveness occurs through the revision of a judgment on the basis of rational considerations of behaviors displayed by the offender.[40] Thus, for Haber, forgiveness is not measured by "overcoming" feelings but by the reorientation of one's attitude toward the offender when that is done for moral reasons. The reversal of one's moral judgment comes first, according to the logic of Haber's position. Subsequent to that, the attitudinal reorientation includes a decision or willingness to overcome the resentment arising from the harm.[41]

It is important to note that Haber places a great deal of emphasis on the role of behavior in forgiving. This shows itself in the understanding of forgiveness as other than the revision of feelings. But it also shows itself in his paradigm case of forgiveness, the example against which other claimants to the label "forgiveness" must measure themselves. For Haber, forgiveness is an intentional act resulting from a judgment. That

---

[38] Ibid., 7.

[39] Ibid., 36. Haber is citing Murphy, "Forgiveness and Resentment," *Midwest Studies in Philosophy* 7 (1982): 503–16, at 507. Murphy makes the same point in Murphy and Hampton, *Forgiveness and Mercy*, 19, 22, 176; and Murphy, *Getting Even: Forgiveness and Its Limits*, 115.

[40] Haber, *Forgiveness*, 12ff.

[41] Ibid., 40.

act expresses itself paradigmatically through the spoken, "I forgive you."[42] But for that expression to be a performative utterance, certain conditions apply. Haber identifies three kinds of conditions: those necessary if forgiveness is to be enacted at all, the necessary conditions for the proper performance of a speech act, and the relational conditions that must be met (behaviors) if the victim is to have moral grounds to judge that forgiveness is warranted.

### Conditions Necessary for Forgiveness

The first set of conditions, those necessary for forgiveness to arise as an issue at all, reflects the logic of Haber's analysis of forgiveness in relation to cognitive judgment. Someone must have done something that was wrong. Moreover, the agent must have been acting responsibly, that is, the agent is culpable for the action. This action must have caused personal harm to the victim. The victim has recognized this harm and judged it to be a wrong act by a responsible agent and therefore resents it. Unless all these conditions have been fulfilled, according to Haber, forgiveness is not at issue.[43] When the conditions have been fulfilled, and when the injured party has overcome or is willing to overcome resentment arising from the action, then she can forgive. When she expresses forgiveness she affirms the truth of the conditions of the harm and of her revised stance with respect to the resentment.

### Conditions for Performance of a Speech-Act

But how does one "express" forgiveness properly? This is the concern of the second set of conditions, those related to the proper performance of a speech-act (performative utterance). Haber draws these from the work of John L. Austin. They consist of six rules according to which a speech act may legitimately be performed. The first four define conditions necessary for accomplishing the act as such. They are: (1) "There must exist an accepted conventional procedure" that involves the use of conventional

---

[42] Ibid., 53.

[43] This is a summary of Haber's own summary, found at Haber, *Forgiveness*, 40. On this account the absence of any of these conditions renders forgiveness a non-issue. Thus if there is no moral culpability involved by a responsible agent, whatever one may be feeling about the situation, the response—*ex supposito*—cannot qualify as forgiveness. We will examine this issue in part 2.

verbal expressions; (2) the parties engaged in the speech act must be the appropriate persons for the intended speech act; (3) they must fulfill the conditions of the conventional procedure correctly and (4) completely.[44] These four define what is essential to a speech-act as such.

Two further conditions pertain to the one who performs a speech-act. The first of these concerns the integrity of the participants. What they represent in the speech-act must correspond to their actual state and their intentions for future conduct. That is, what they say must honestly represent their awareness of the situation and their intentions for the future. Finally, the participants must conduct themselves in accord with the specifications of the speech-act. According to Austin's presentation, when these conditions have been met, a speech-act has been realized.

Haber's proposal of the paradigm case of forgiveness as a speech act expressed in the terms "I forgive you" follows these conditions. When the victim of the harm chooses to forgive, that forgiveness, if it is not to be dependent on the vagaries of shifts in emotional states, should be expressed (according to Haber) by means of behavior, specifically by means of a performative utterance according to the conditions specified by Austin.[45]

### Conditions of Rational Moral Judgment

In addition to the criteria for identifying a situation in which forgiveness would be an appropriate possible response and for specifying what would constitute a completed paradigmatic enactment of forgiveness (speech-act), Haber also specifies criteria that must be met if the revision of judgment involved in forgiving is to be rational. He is very clear that one ought not to forgive except for morally justified reasons.[46] As he argues, when someone has harmed me I *ought to* feel resentment.

---

[44] Haber, *Forgiveness*, 41, citing John Langshaw Austin, *How to Do Things with Words* (Cambridge, MA: Harvard University Press, 1962), 16.

[45] There are two points to note in this proposal. First, Haber's construction of the paradigm case is consistent with the goal he established at the beginning of the book. He is following a strict logic. The conditions specified provide a behaviorally focused account of forgiveness which can be enacted independently of how one feels at any given moment. Second, however, in setting forth this proposal Haber appears to be blurring the lines between descriptions of what actually happens in an instance of forgiveness and the imposition of his own vision of what *ought to* happen when forgiving. This distinction will become important in part 2.

[46] Haber, *Forgiveness*, 70.

Resentment of the agent for the action is a reflection of a proper respect for my own moral worth as a human person.[47] If the conditions of the harm fall within the scope of the judgments Haber has specified (a responsible agent acted in a manner that was wrong and that caused me harm), then my resentment is morally grounded.[48] Since my resentment is morally grounded, I *ought not to release* that resentment unless I judge that the conditions of my relationship with the agent in respect to the offending action have changed.

What are the moral conditions that can justify forgiving? Fundamentally, they must be reasons that preserve one's self-respect.[49] The preeminent reason Haber identifies—this is, for him the *sine qua non* for forgiveness to be a moral action—is that the offender separate himself or herself from the deed and its meaning.[50] This requires, first, that the offender undergo an interior reassessment of the deed in the form of repentance.[51] This repentance, however, must be expressed both through behavior that demonstrates that the offender wishes not to be identified with the action or its meaning *and* through an explicit apology to the one harmed.[52] (This is in accordance with the conditions of a performative utterance.) Under such conditions the victim of the offense has cognitively accessible data to justify a reorientation of his or her attitude toward the offender. This does not *obligate* the victim to do so, but it provides the material conditions that would make it possible to alter his or her judgment of the offender and therefore to commit to the effort, subsequent to that judgment, to adjust his or her affective orientation toward the offender.

Haber's position resembles that of Murphy when he speaks of the separation between the agent and the action. However, he distinguishes his perspective from Murphy's in two ways that reflect the framework of his argument. First, Haber argues that Murphy treats the separation between the agent and the act as something the victim must effect. This makes sense, given Murphy's understanding of forgiveness in relationship to the modification of feeling. If the victim is able to recognize that the

---

[47] Ibid., 78.

[48] See ibid., 82–83.

[49] Ibid., 90. On p. 89 Haber identifies some reasons he considers inadequate justification for forgiveness—reasons that, however, are commonly invoked.

[50] Ibid., 104–5.

[51] Ibid., 90.

[52] Ibid., 99.

agent is not absolutely identified with the act, then he or she can move toward the modification of feeling in a manner that respects his or her own dignity. Murphy then examines five possible reasons for which one might morally come to the decision to forgive.

Haber rejects both these five reasons presented by Murphy and the justification he provides for them. In Haber's framework, if forgiveness is to be granted it is not the victim who must distance the offender from the action; it is the agent who must do so.[53] He or she must repent of the action that caused the harm. Any other reason adduced for extending forgiveness Haber finds problematic. As he summarizes in concluding his book,

> In the final analysis, I have identified just one good reason we may use to forgive—and that is because the wrongdoer has repented. I have endeavored to show that, if forgiveness is to be valued as a moral response, it must be for a reason that permits the lifting of the victim's resentment. In the absence of repentance, forgiveness betrays a lack of self-respect. It also collapses into condonation of wrongdoing, and it is wrong to condone wrongful behavior.[54]

Thus although both Murphy and Haber place emphasis on the separation of the wrongdoer from the deed as part of the enactment of forgiveness, they understand it very differently. The differences between them reflect the basic presuppositions that guide their inquiries.

### Pamela Hiernoymi and Uncompromising Forgiveness

Pamela Hieronymi presents a third approach to identifying the conditions for the moral enactment of forgiveness. Her argument brings to light aspects of the human experience of forgiving that have not been named by Murphy or Haber. In her article, "Articulating an Uncompromising Forgiveness," she shares some of the same basic assumptions as both Murphy and Haber,[55] but the problem she addresses covers a slightly

---

[53] Ibid., 104.

[54] Ibid., 110. Haber is making an absolute claim here but providing no evidence to support it. Forgiving in the absence of clear evidence of repentance *might* be an indicator of a lack of respect. It might also be an indicator that one's self-respect has other sources than Haber has taken into account. This issue will receive further examination in part 2.

[55] Pamela Hieronymi, "Articulating an Uncompromising Forgiveness," *Philosophy and Phenomenological Research* 62, no. 3 (May 2001): 529–55.

different terrain. As she puts it, any philosophical account of forgiveness must be "articulate" and it must be "uncompromising."[56] These two terms name the two main sets of conditions that she argues must be satisfied if forgiveness is to be a moral enactment. Her use of these terms requires some clarification.

Like Murphy and Haber, Hieronymi approaches the question of forgiveness as an issue in moral philosophy.[57] Also like Murphy and Haber she recognizes the importance of affections, particularly of resentment, in the dynamics of forgiveness. But her own position on forgiveness appears to stand between those of Murphy and Haber with a significant inclination toward Haber's position. She seems to accept the commonly held idea that forgiveness involves "forgoing resentment."[58] A modification of feeling occupies an important place in her account of forgiveness. However, if that modification is to be moral, something more is required. As she explains:

> If both resentment and forgiveness admit of justification, i.e., if one resents or forgives another person thinking one has good reason to, then forgiving will entail more than figuring out how to rid oneself of certain unfortunate affects. Ridding oneself of resentment by taking a specially-designed pill, for example, would not count as forgiveness. Genuine forgiveness must involve some revision in judgment or change in view. An account of forgiveness must therefore *articulate* that revision in judgment or change in view. It must be an articulate account.[59]

Thus Hieronymi aligns with Haber in her strong emphasis on articulated reasons that can justify the decision to forgive.

Hieronymi elaborates: "An account of forgiveness must articulate the revision in judgment or change in view that allows us to overcome our anger or resentment *without compromise*."[60] This "uncompromising" aspect refers to three judgments one must maintain in the midst of the decision to forgive. (Again, this emphasis on judgment places Hieronymi very close to Haber.) These judgments are: (1) that the act was wrong and

---

[56] Ibid., 529.

[57] Ibid.

[58] Ibid. Hieronymi also recognizes that other feeling states arising from "being hurt" could be responded to by forgiveness. See ibid., 529, n. 2.

[59] Hieronymi, "Articulating an Uncompromising Forgiveness," 530.

[60] Ibid., 531. Emphasis supplied.

was a "serious offense, worthy of moral attention," (2) that the offending party is a member of the "moral community who can be expected not to do such things," and (3) that the offended party ought not to have been wronged.[61]

When one judges all these conditions to be in place, one is morally justified in resenting the one who offended, for resentment, according to Hieronymi, is a "protest" against the wrongdoing.[62] The protest is on two levels. Primarily it is a protest that the action should not have happened. But Hieronymi also recognizes in resentment a future-oriented, self-protective aspect. We hold to resentment over time because the offending action represents a threat to our worth, our well-being, our standing in the moral community. She thus elaborates: "I think resentment is best understood as a *protest*. More specifically, *resentment protests a past action that persists as a present threat.*"[63] Because the person has disrespected my moral value in the past, that past action communicates a message about his or her assessment of my worth in the present. This past event, as she puts it, "makes a threatening claim."[64]

Hieronymi is making an important point, one also acknowledged by Murphy and Haber. The event that caused the harm has meaning.[65] It sends a message that endures into the present, at least in the interior life of the person harmed, until that message has in some way been vitiated. But how is that meaning to be altered? If forgiveness is to be uncompromising it must not back away from any of the three judgments made above. Forgiveness must arise from a revision in judgment that would undermine the need for resentment.[66] It must neither condone the offensive action, nor give up on the worth of the offender, nor abandon the judgments regarding the moral status of the act.[67]

Here, once again, Hieronymi inclines to the position of Haber. The solution to the problem does not lie in the victim's revising her or his feelings. The offender would still remain "objectively" guilty of the morally offensive act. The one element that, according to Hieronymi, could justify the revision of one's moral judgment of the offender and thereby

---

[61] Ibid., 530.
[62] Ibid.
[63] Ibid., 546.
[64] Ibid., 548.
[65] Ibid., 546.
[66] Ibid., 535.
[67] Ibid., 542 n. 17.

open the door to morally justified forgiveness is an apology from the offender.[68] If the offender apologizes, this *can* rationally undermine the reasons for resentment and can lead to a revised judgment of the person, for by the apology the offender renounces the deed and the message it communicates—the message that denigrated the victim—thereby identifying himself or herself with the moral community in condemning the offensive action.[69]

In making her case for this position Hieronymi underscores the social dimension of both our identities and our actions.[70] When one is harmed by another the message of the harm is not purely private. The fact that it can linger into the future as a threat highlights its power as a socially significant statement about our worth. It is a threat to our sense of self, precisely insofar as that sense of self draws its own meaning from a relational, social context from which we appropriate the meanings by which we understand our own selves. Identity and social relations, as Hieronymi recognizes, are interwoven. Thus while an *uncompromising* forgiveness must hold to the validity of the moral judgments identified above, an *articulate* forgiveness must be able to explain that the basis for forgiving does not violate one's dignity. The repentance of the offender, followed by an apology, provides a justification for forgiving that satisfies the demands for an uncompromising and articulate forgiveness. It does so in a way that also reflects the intrinsic interconnection of personal identity and social meaning.

> If we understand the event [moral offense] as carrying broader, social meaning, and if we understand one's identity as at least partially constituted by how one is perceived by others, then we can both start to make sense of remorse and start to see why one's repentance and change in heart requires ratification by others.[71]

The recognition of the social character of offense and repentance serves Hieronymi's argument by identifying what forgiveness adds to the repentance of the offender. First, "in accepting the apology, the offended in some way ratifies, or makes real, the offender's change of heart."[72] This

---

[68] Ibid., 545.
[69] Ibid., 548.
[70] Ibid., 550.
[71] Ibid.
[72] Ibid.

"ratification"—the acceptance of the apology—"will leave the original meaning of the event in the past."[73] Through this action the event will acquire a new meaning. Although not "articulated" in the same terms as those used by Haber, this position has similarities to the "performative utterance" theory Haber employs. The interpersonal interaction "effects" what it signifies.[74] In this case, by "ratifying" the apology, forgiveness lends the victim's voice to the offender's in support of his or her reentry into the moral community.

Hieronymi also identifies a second effect of forgiveness. In this she names explicitly a point not addressed by either Murphy or Haber. "With forgiveness, the offended agrees to bear in her own person the cost of the wrongdoing and to incorporate the injury into her own life without further protest and without demand for retribution."[75] As she elaborates, "forgiveness is not *simply* a revision in judgment or a change in view or a wiping clean or a washing away or a making new. Someone will bear the cost in his or her own person. The wrong is less 'let go of' or washed away than it is digested or absorbed."[76]

Thus when we forgive, according to this account, we do more than revise our judgment. If the conditions have been met and if we *choose* to extend forgiveness[77] we confirm the offender's status as a member of the moral community by ratifying his or her change of heart through accepting the apology. We also agree to accept whatever "costs" we have endured or will endure into the future arising from the harm insofar as they are unable to be undone by the repentance (and, where necessary, the restitution) of the offender.

[73] Ibid.

[74] To Catholic ears this language is reminiscent of the sacraments. We will explore this further in part 3.

[75] Hieronymi, "Articulating an Uncompromising Forgiveness," 551. There is an affinity here between Hieronymi's position and Ricoeur's articulation of the "vertical axis." See chap. 1 above.

[76] Hieronymi, "Articulating an Uncompromising Forgiveness," 551 n. 39.

[77] Hieronymi discusses the "elective" quality of forgiveness and its related issues in ibid., 551–52. Among those issues is whether one is morally defective for refusing to forgive if the conditions have been fulfilled. The specific form of the question concerns whether having "reasons" that "rationally require" forgiveness contravenes freedom itself. Her response: "when assessing a person's freedom by asking whether she 'could have done otherwise,' one should not include among the forces that impinge on freedom the reasons on which the person acts."

Hieronymi's discussion of forgiveness covers much the same terrain as those of Murphy and Haber. Casting her discussion in terms of "articulateness" and being "uncompromising" has focused her analysis on adherence to conditions defining the offense as "moral" and providing rational grounds to justify a change in affect. In addition, her argument has underscored the importance, already indicated in Murphy and Haber, of seeing the offense as a *communication*, an expression of a meaning. But Hieronymi has expanded on the implications of this insight by highlighting the interrelationship of personal identity and social frameworks of meaning, thereby indicating a basis for insisting on the social mediation of forgiveness. She has also added a further element, not emphasized in our previous authors: the notion that forgiveness *qua forgiveness* does something *more* than revise a judgment, attitude, and feeling. It also reflects the forgiver's commitment to assume a cost arising from the historical offense.

## Charles Griswold and the Revision of Narrative

The question of the *meaning* of an offense and the relationship of meaning to forgiving occupies a prominent place in Charles Griswold's *Forgiveness: A Philosophical Exploration.*[78] Early in his prologue he identifies two aspirations for his account: that it be "defensible" and that it be a "secular" account.[79] He does not define what he means by "defensible," but as his argument unfolds his intention becomes clear. He argues that "forgiveness is a concept that is governed by norms and conditions."[80] He therefore seeks an account of forgiveness the norms and conditions of which are mutually coherent, consistent, and beyond rational reproach. At the same time this account must be able to encompass not only the paradigm case he will present, but also "less perfect" forms of forgiveness.[81] In other words, he wants to name forgiveness in a way that can be as inclusive as possible of various real-life cases. At the same time he wants to articulate an ideal against which those cases can be measured.

---

[78] Griswold, *Forgiveness: A Philosophical Exploration.*

[79] See, for example, Griswold, *Forgiveness: A Philosophical Exploration*, xiv, xv. Analogous language runs throughout the book.

[80] Charles L. Griswold, "Forgiveness, Secular and Religious: A Reply to My Critics," *Proceedings of the American Catholic Philosophical Association* 82 (2009): 303–13, at 303.

[81] By "less perfect" he intends those cases that might still be called "forgiveness" but that do not conform to all the conditions he will specify by the paradigm.

The second aspect of Griswold's aspiration, to provide a "secular" account of forgiveness, reflects his awareness that much of contemporary language around forgiveness has been shaped by Jewish and Christian sources and traditions. In the face of this heritage he wants to identify an understanding of forgiveness that does not appeal to or rely on religious convictions for its justification.[82] Near the conclusion of his prologue he poses the question that shapes his inquiry:

> How can one accept fully that moral evil has been done and yet see its perpetrator in a way that counts as "reconciliation" in a sense that simultaneously forswears revenge, aspires to give up resentment, and incorporates the injury suffered into a narrative of self that allows the victim and even the offender to flourish?[83]

Several aspects of this way of naming the question bear particular attention. First, it is clear that by posing the question in this way Griswold stands within the general framework of those philosophers we have considered thus far. He approaches the question of forgiveness in relation to the concerns of moral philosophy. He is interested in specifying the morally justifiable conditions for exercising forgiveness in the face of a moral offense. Second, he aligns himself with approaches that treat resentment as central to the subject of forgiveness, while linking the aspiration to give up resentment with the repudiation of revenge. Third, he shares with others the awareness that the victim's evaluation of the perpetrator must undergo change if forgiveness is to occur. But fourth, for forgiveness to occur, the injury arising from the offense must be situated within a revised narrative.[84] That is, forgiveness must be enacted on the basis of a new interpretation of the offender and the injury, a new meaning that opens a way forward in relationship. Finally, Griswold's approach indicates that the narrative is "a narrative of the self." The revision of meaning has a correlation with the self-understanding of the one forgiving.[85]

---

[82] See, for example, Griswold, *Forgiveness: A Philosophical Exploration*, xv, xvii, 2, 113, 123.

[83] Ibid., xxv.

[84] The idea of incorporating the harm into a new narrative can be understood as naming the process that enables one to "absorb" the cost, as identified by Hieronymi. Griswold does not develop this idea.

[85] One further point that will be addressed later is the way Griswold's definition incorporates reconciliation into the understanding of forgiveness. I think this is problematic. There is an integral relation between the two, but I do not believe it has yet been adequately named.

The details of Griswold's account of forgiveness, as suggested above, have much in common with other approaches, but the presentation reflects nuances shaped by his distinctive concerns and by his definition of the task of forgiveness. This appears in his discussion of forgiveness as a virtue, in the place of resentment in his analysis, and in the conditions he sets forth if one is to forgive morally.

Griswold shares with Murphy and Haber the notion that forgiveness is a virtue. He elaborates his understanding of this virtue in contrast to what he calls "perfectionist" accounts of the human ideal, accounts "in which forgiveness has little or no place."[86] Instead, he proposes a non-perfectionist account that takes seriously the vicissitudes of the human condition. Among these he identifies (with Hannah Arendt) the non-reversibility of history,[87] the human capacity for change even within our finitude,[88] the fact that we can act as responsible agents,[89] and the human and social need to address and overcome wrongs.[90] He summarizes this human condition thus:

> Our interdependence as social and sympathizing creatures; our embodiment and our affective character; our vulnerability to each other; our mortality; our standing to demand respectful treatment from one another, as befits creatures of equal dignity, and our obligations to one another; the pervasiveness of suffering—most often unmerited where it is intentionally inflicted—and of pain, violence, and injustice: these are part and parcel of that imperfection. In short, the context is that of creatures such as ourselves, inescapably rooted in a world that is, so to speak, fractured and threatening. Forgiveness is responsive to the demands of a world so understood, and in a way that helps to enable its possessor to live a good life.[91]

Forgiveness, then, is part of enabling fallible, finite human beings to live well in the conditions that circumscribe our personal and social lives.

---

[86] Griswold, *Forgiveness: A Philosophical Exploration*, xxii. See also chap. 1 above.

[87] Griswold, *Forgiveness: A Philosophical Exploration*, xv, citing Hannah Arendt, *The Human Condition* (Chicago: University of Chicago Press, 1958), 237. See also the discussion of this point in Jankélévitch in chap. 1 above.

[88] See Griswold, *Forgiveness: A Philosophical Exploration*, 14.

[89] Ibid., 7.

[90] Ibid., xiv.

[91] Ibid., 14–15.

Like the other authors we have examined, Griswold devotes considerable attention to analyzing resentment and to the place of overcoming resentment in his understanding of forgiveness. But he also argues that there is more to forgiveness than moderating a feeling.

> So forgiveness cannot *simply* be forswearing resentment, even though it does require at least the moderating of resentment. We recognize a different phenomenon, namely that of letting go of resentment for moral reasons, as well as of revenge, without forgetting the wrong that was done, and even in some cases (re) accepting the offender as a friend. This is what we are calling forgiveness.[92]

Thus he agrees with our other authors on the necessity of having moral reasons for forgiving, with Haber and Hieronymi on the importance of remembering the deed, and, as will become clear, on the role of rational judgment.

In contrast to other authors, however, Griswold is more restrictive in naming the "reactive sentiment" to which forgiveness responds. For example, he rejects Norvin Richards' suggestion that forgiveness might also be manifest in letting go of contempt or of disappointment.[93] These sentiments are not appropriately addressed by forgiveness because they do not "[involve] the attribution of responsibility to the wrongdoer, as well as the belief that one has been wrongly injured."[94] In other words, resentment arises from the recognition that someone has done something for which she or he is responsible and has by that act caused harm to the one who now experiences resentment. This characterization is fairly consistent with the views already identified by other authors. Resentment is thus an affective state based on cognition and moral judgment.[95]

---

[92] Ibid., 40.

[93] Ibid., citing Norvin Richards, "Forgiveness," *Ethics* 99, no. 1 (1988): 77–97, at 79. It is unclear whether Griswold would allow that other "reactive sentiments" might meet the specified conditions.

[94] Griswold, *Forgiveness: A Philosophical Exploration*, 40.

[95] Ibid., 26, 42. Griswold disagrees, however, with what he believes is Hieronymi's position on the target of resentment. Citing "Articulating an Uncompromising Forgiveness," 530 ("resentment protests a past action that persists as a present threat"), he argues that Hieronymi sees resentment as directed at the act rather than at the person. This is a plausible reading until one notes that the condition for forgiving is that the offender distance himself or herself from the act. This suggests that Hieronymi understands forgiveness to be extended to the person for the act. How is this reconcilable with the

Griswold's account of the cognitive dimension, however, goes beyond what we have encountered in the other authors. When one experiences a moral harm it is an affront to the self. Griswold agrees with our other authors in affirming that this harmful action contains a message. It communicates a meaning that calls into question the victim's value or worth, thereby provoking resentment as a defense against this message.[96] But Griswold develops this aspect of meaning further by identifying a narrative structure to our way of inhabiting the world and, consequently, our way of understanding and responding to the offense. We tell stories to make sense of ourselves and our world. Thus the offended party seeks to rewrite the story.[97] The retributive impulse attempts to reassert the value of the victim against the meaning of the story in which the offense has taken center stage.[98] But, as Griswold argues, although resentment can engender an impulse toward revenge, the purpose of revenge can never be attained. Revenge "seeks to change the past by punishing the agent," but it cannot do so. "For the past cannot ever be changed."[99]

There is a tension here between the need to rewrite the story of harm in order to reaffirm one's own worth and the (metaphysical) inability to actually change history. The obvious responses to harm are the impulse to seek revenge or, alternatively, to fall into complacency or condonation of the offense. If these are the only two options, the offended party is at an impasse; there can be no resolution of the moral harm. Griswold sees forgiveness as providing the way forward.

> Forgiveness accepts that the past is unchangeable, but asserts that our responses to it are not (and these include our decisions about the future). It denies that the alternatives to vengeful violence are

---

statement quoted above? I believe it is not inconsistent to claim both that resentment is directed at the offender for the act and that it protests the meaning of the act. The two seem to me to be integrally related. I believe that Griswold and Hieronymi are actually much closer in their positions than Griswold states.

[96] Griswold, *Forgiveness: A Philosophical Exploration*, 27, 45.

[97] This theme pervades Griswold's argument. It is underscored in the conditions for a valid apology and in the mutual reinterpretation he specifies for both the offender and the victim if reconciliation is to occur. See, for example, Griswold, *Forgiveness: A Philosophical Exploration*, 28, 30. See also p. 51 for conditions of an apology in relationship to reforming a narrative, and pp. 53–59 for the presentation of the mutual revision of the story required.

[98] Ibid., 27–28.

[99] Ibid., 29.

either condonation or resigned and submissive acceptance. And it claims to express both respect for self and the dead or injured.[100]

The way through the impasse is to forgive. But what is forgiveness? How do we do it? Like our other authors, Griswold holds that there are conditions for forgiving.[101] His response to these questions reflects the framework he has sketched out. With our other authors, Griswold maintains that any act of forgiveness will involve forswearing resentment.[102]

> Keeping in mind our brief discussion of resentment as a quasi-cognitive emotion, I propose that forgiveness requires that resentment for the relevant injury be appropriately moderated *and* that the agent make a further commitment to work toward a frame of mind in which even that resentment is let go. Forswearing the emotion is indeed the ultimate goal.[103]

But if that forswearing is to be a moral act it must be accomplished on a moral basis. It must adhere to the requirements of a moral act, particularly as specified by the immoral act to which it responds. That is, forgiveness can only be appropriately deployed if the victim can affirm that the resentment is no longer warranted.[104]

What would be legitimate grounds for arriving at such a judgment? Griswold is very clear that, just as the offending act was an affront to the dignity of the victim, so the conditions for arriving at a revised judgment must maintain and affirm that dignity.[105] They must be "conditions of a moral nature that may warrant a change of belief about 'the bad person's' character, and therefore warrant that the injured party should emend her view that the wrongdoer is reducible to the agent who did those wrongs."[106] Thus, while holding on to the moral principle that it is wrong to treat someone in the way that I, the victim, have been treated, I can morally forgive *if* something occurs that changes the offender's moral relation to the offense and to me.

---

[100] Ibid.

[101] Ibid., xv.

[102] Ibid., 41, 42.

[103] Ibid., 42.

[104] Ibid., 43.

[105] See the discussion of the origins of resentment and its moral content in Griswold, *Forgiveness: A Philosophical Exploration*, 45–46.

[106] Ibid., 54.

Griswold identifies this change in terms of a transformation in the offender that includes a transformation of the offender's moral relation to the victim. The first part of this change he identifies as "contrition." It includes four elements: a recognition that what was done was wrong and that the offender is responsible for it,[107] a repudiation of that wrongful action,[108] an expression of regret for having done the act,[109] and a commitment to change behavior in the future.[110] In addition to these four aspects of "contrition" Griswold identifies two further conditions that must be met if the necessary transformation is to be judged complete and if, therefore, forgiveness is to be justified. The offender must demonstrate that he or she has understood the offense from the perspective of the offended person.[111] The offender must also construct and communicate a narrative of the offensive event that recasts the offender's relationship to the event in the light of the contrition. As Griswold explains,

> The offender's regretful address would offer some sort of *narrative* accounting for how she came to do wrong, how that wrong-doing does not express the totality of her person, and how she is becoming worthy of approbation. She needs to make herself intelligible by offering up an account that is neither fiction nor excuse making, and that puts the wrong-doing as well as the self that did the wrong in a context. The injured party deserves answers to questions such as "who is this person, such that she could have injured me thus? Such that she warrants forgiveness?"[112]

This account of forgiveness is similar to what we have already seen. It requires an apology as evidence to justify a change in perspective on the offender. It requires that the offender recognize the meaning of the event and repudiate it. But it goes beyond the other accounts in the emphasis it places on fashioning a narrative. Griswold specifies the necessity that the offender's narrative take account of the experience and perspective of the injured party so that the injured party will have evidence to support a revised judgment of the offender.

---

[107] Ibid., 49.
[108] Ibid.
[109] Ibid., 50.
[110] Ibid.
[111] Ibid., 51.
[112] Ibid.

Griswold is very insistent that, even having fulfilled these conditions, the offender has no "right" to be forgiven.[113] The fulfillment of the conditions does not compel the victim to respond. However, *if* the victim is to forgive, he or she must also undergo change. The victim, in view of the steps taken by the offender, has the information necessary to make it possible for him or her to reassess the offender in light of the behaviors and the revised narrative the offender has presented.[114] If this information is to issue in forgiveness, the victim must also change, as Griswold puts it, "seeing the offender and oneself in a new light."[115] That is, the victim, on the basis of this new information, must then refashion his or her own narrative about the event and about the offender in a manner that is consistent with the giving of forgiveness.

## Conclusion

The Anglo-American moral philosophical discussions of forgiveness that we have examined contrast sharply with the problematic at the heart of Derrida's provocation in chapter 1. They take as a given that forgiveness is possible but that it should only be deployed morally. The task, therefore, has been to identify the conditions under which a moral enactment is possible.

Although there are significant disagreements among the philosophers examined in this chapter, they do occupy common terrain as seen in three points. First, they emphasize the importance of resentment and, derivatively, of affections in general. Minimally, the affection of resentment tells us that we have been harmed and sets the stage for engaging the question of forgiveness. Second, they agree on the importance of cognition. The events that evoke a retributive reaction, and therefore raise the possibility of a forgiving response, communicate a meaning. This meaning must be recognized in order for a retributive response to be evoked. Therefore cognition is integral to the dynamics of forgiveness. Third, for forgiveness to be a moral act it must be performed in a manner that respects and upholds the moral order. It must be undertaken according to conditions that are themselves moral. The authors we have examined argue for different ways of naming the requisite conditions for

[113] Ibid., 68–69.
[114] Ibid., 53–59.
[115] Ibid.

a moral enactment of forgiveness, but they agree *that* such conditions are necessary if forgiving is to be moral.

Thus in this chapter the conversation has shifted from the pursuit of a pure concept of forgiveness to identifying the conditions under which it can morally be deployed. Our exploration of the Anglo-American moral philosophical terrain has raised issues that we will need to examine more closely in part 2. But for now we need to turn our attention to a third part of the landscape, the contemporary discussion of forgiveness in psychology.

$\mathcal{C}$hapter 3

# Psychological Approaches to Forgiveness

## Preliminaries

*I*n the first two chapters we examined philosophical discussions of forgiveness. These have followed a progression, one could even say a "trajectory." In chapter 1 we traced a course across the landscape of French-Continental philosophical treatments of forgiveness, from an analysis of the concept of forgiveness in relationship to time (Jankélévitch), to the notion of forgiveness as a pure concept that calls into question any claims about its finite deployment (Derrida), until we arrived at a presentation of forgiveness as a "not impossible, but very difficult" human enactment (Ricoeur). This first chapter moved from abstract conceptual understanding in the direction of the human person ("capable being" in Ricoeur) who must confront the question of forgiveness. Chapter 2 continued the direction of this progression, delving more deeply into the moral dimensions of the practice of forgiving in interpersonal relationships. Drawing on analyses of forgiveness from within the Anglo-American context, we explored the pragmatic conditions for engaging in forgiveness as a specifically moral enactment. This exploration brought into focus the importance of affective life, cognition, and judgment for understanding forgiveness and for assessing the morality of forgiving.

By introducing these aspects of the discussion (affective life, cognition, judgment), chapter 2 has brought us to the boundary lands between philosophy and psychology. It has done so under the rubric of identifying the conditions for forgiveness as a *moral* enactment. In the present chapter our attention will shift. The moral question will still be present, but it will move into the background. In its place, in this chapter, we will explore what psychologists have to say about forgiveness. Their concerns, in contrast to those of the philosophers, lead them to parse the *psycho-dynamic processes* of forgiveness and find ways to help those who have experienced traumatic events to come to forgiveness, when that is therapeutically warranted. This shift in focus will illuminate aspects of forgiveness only glimpsed in the philosophical discussions.

But before we turn to the particulars of the psychological discussion it will be helpful to orient ourselves to the terrain we will be exploring. Just as the philosophical discussions reflect diverse approaches (we focused on the French-Continental and the Anglo-American), so also within psychology there are diverse perspectives and approaches. This diversity reflects the different psychological schools that analyze and theorize about the processes of the human mind. It also reflects different thera-peutic approaches to addressing mental, emotional, and relational diffi-culties. The distinctions between these diverse psychological approaches are not absolute; the theories and therapeutic strategies of one school of psychology will draw upon and modify the insights of another.[1] This is evident in the psychological discussion of forgiveness. Insights into the experience of forgiveness have been contributed by psychologists working from perspectives informed by psychoanalytic, Jungian, object relations, existential, cognitive, developmental, and family systems theories.[2]

This diversity of theoretical and therapeutic perspectives is both an asset and a challenge for our present inquiry. It is an asset because each approach casts into relief those different aspects of forgiveness most relevant to its own concerns. Like light passing through a prism, each discipline refracts the phenomenon of forgiveness into the spectrum its own questions are designed to address. The results of each can comple-ment the findings of the others or, alternatively, can push them to greater refinement. But the diversity can also be a challenge. The diversity of schools of psychological thought and the differences in their presuppo-sitions render a choice among competing approaches unserviceable. That would require a judgment about their relative merits that is beyond the scope of the present work.

---

[1] For example, the work of Robert D. Enright et al. is categorized as "cognitive" in James N. Sells and Terry D. Hargrave, "Forgiveness: A Review of the Theoretical and Empirical Literature," *Journal of Family Therapy* 20 (1998): 21–36, at 26, but is identified as "developmental" in Debra Kaminer, Dan J. Stein, Irene Mbanga, and Nompumelelo Zungu-Dirwayi, "Forgiveness: Toward an Integration of Theoretical Models," *Psychiatry* 63, no. 4 (Winter 2000): 344–57, at 347.

[2] Kaminer et al., "Forgiveness," 347.

For this reason the present chapter will pursue a different manner of exploration than was used in chapters 1 and 2. There we devoted our attention to significant theorists and their contrasting perspectives in order to bring the philosophical issues to the fore. The present chapter will not focus on particular theorists. Instead, it will draw our attention to areas of relative consensus on the landscape of psychological discussions of forgiveness.

Of course, this still leaves a very broad swath of terrain to consider. But dimensions of the philosophical discussions we have encountered already can guide us in focusing our attention. They suggest two areas of contemporary psychological exploration of forgiveness that will be helpful to our efforts to name the human experience of forgiving.

In chapter 2 we noted the importance of cognition for the discussion of forgiveness. It will therefore be valuable for us to consider how cognitive psychological approaches to forgiveness can illuminate what is occurring when we undertake to forgive. So too will those approaches based on developmental theories of psychology. For, as we have seen in the "futuritive" account of Jankélévitch and in the notion of "personal becoming" operative in Ricoeur's thought, there is something of a developmental process implicated in forgiving. Both cognitive and developmental approaches are well represented in the psychological literature on forgiveness.

There is, however, a limitation to these approaches. Cognitive and developmental psychology are helpful for understanding aspects of our conscious states, including our affective responses to perceived harm. But there is another aspect of our psychic life not as well represented in the discussion of forgiveness influenced by these two disciplines: the unconscious. Already in our exploration of the Anglo-American discussion, hints have emerged that there is more at stake in forgiving than what is directly accessible to conscious reflection.

The awareness that, even after a decision to forgive, retributive emotions may resurface signals that a deeper understanding of the human enactment of forgiveness must take account of our unconscious processes. How do unconscious structures and dynamics affect our conscious life? What role might the unconscious play in our ability to forgive? Conversely, how does our conscious life affect the structures and dynamics of the unconscious? These are some of the questions we will need to address, for understanding these dynamics is essential to naming what is at stake when we undertake to forgive. It will therefore be important to examine what present thinking on the structures and dynamics of the unconscious can contribute to our understanding of forgiveness.

The expanse of literature that has been generated since interest in forgiveness began to blossom in psychology covers a wide swath. However, three foci have consistently surfaced in the discussions: the definition of forgiveness, the understanding of our own human agency (freedom) and the factors that condition it when forgiving, and the occasion of the harm that generates the need to forgive (or not). We shall examine each of these themes in turn.

## Defining Forgiveness

At present there is a general consensus among psychological theorists *that* the effort to understand forgiveness must begin with a clear definition of the term. Researchers from across the spectrum of psychological disciplines affirm this basic conviction and the importance of arriving at an understanding that will be broadly accepted.[3] Unfortunately, in almost every case authors lament in the next breath the current lack of consensus.[4] Susan Denham and her colleagues name this problem and indicate the reason for its urgency:

> Forgiveness is a construct in search of a comprehensive definition. Until the crispest possible definition of forgiveness is depicted, both conceptual and methodological problems will proliferate. We have considered many definitions of forgiveness and found points of disagreement. Some explicitly cite behavior—or at least the motivation toward prosocial behavior—as part of forgiveness. Others emphasize the emotional transformations and/or the important motivational

---

[3] See, for example, Michael E. McCullough, Kenneth I. Pargament, and Carl E. Thoresen, eds., *Forgiveness: Theory, Research, and Practice* (New York: Guilford Press, 2000), 9; Everett L. Worthington, Jr., "Initial Questions about the Art and Science of Forgiving," 1–13, in *Handbook of Forgiveness*, ed. Everett L. Worthington, Jr. (New York: Routledge, 2005).

[4] McCullough follows this observation with the hopeful assertion that progress is being made in Michael E. McCullough, Kenneth I. Pargament, and Carl E. Thoresen, "The Psychology of Forgiveness: History, Conceptual Issues, and Overview," 1–14 in *Forgiveness: Theory, Research, and Practice*, at 7–8. Others appear to be less optimistic. For example, see Joshua M. Thomas and Andrew Garrod, "Forgiveness after Genocide? Perspectives from Bosnian Youth," 192–211, in *Before Forgiving: Cautionary Views of Forgiveness in Psychotherapy*, ed. Sharon Lamb and Jeffrie G. Murphy (New York: Oxford University Press, 2002), at 196; Mona Gustafson Affinito, "Forgiveness in Counseling: Caution, Definition, and Application," 88–111, in *Before Forgiving*, at 90.

changes wrought by forgiveness. Still others focus on the cognitive reasoning involved in forgiveness decisions.[5]

This formulation highlights the lack of consensus and the reason why this lack is a problem. The absence of a consensus definition undermines the coordination of conceptual refinements in the analysis of the phenomenon of forgiveness and it fosters methodological confusion.[6] If we do not know what we are dealing with (a feeling? a set of behaviors? changes in motivations?) we will have difficulty understanding what is taking place psychologically and will have difficulty knowing how to proceed therapeutically.

These difficulties are further compounded by another factor. Forgiveness is not the property of academic psychologists. Although it has become a subject of interest for academics, the attempt to arrive at a consensus definition that serves academic purposes runs afoul of the fact that non-academic usage of the term does not fit neatly into the (theoretically determined) vocabulary of scholarly research. Nancy DeCourville and her colleagues point out that

> definitional issues have been acknowledged by researchers . . . who pointed out that there is a tendency for both researchers and laypersons to assume a common understanding of the term "forgiveness." This tendency is a barrier to communicating about and researching forgiveness because people undoubtedly differ in how they define and practice forgiveness. Nonetheless, research has generally employed

[5] Susanne A. Denham et al., "Emotional Development and Forgiveness in Children: Emerging Evidence," 127–42, in *Handbook of Forgiveness*, at 129. Part 2 will implicitly make the argument that the attempt to overcome the definitional conflicts will require a phenomenological analysis of what one is doing when undertaking to forgive. Essentially, it is necessary to return to a descriptive account of the dynamics operating when forgiving if one is to avoid importing one's own theoretical biases into the definition.

[6] McCullough, Pargament, and Thoresen indicate this connection obliquely when they observe, "If considered acceptable to the academic community, such a consensual definition of forgiveness would not only enable researchers to be sure that they are discussing the same phenomenon (forgiveness) when using the same language ('forgiveness') but it would also allow other conceptual features that might otherwise be associated definitionally with forgiveness (e.g., stage-like, developmental course; intentionality; primacy of motivational or affective systems; etc.) to be freed from the moorings of definition and transformed instead into researchable hypotheses about the nature of forgiveness" ("The Psychology of Forgiveness: History, Conceptual Issues, and Overview," 9).

definitions derived by scholars, with seemingly little concern with how forgiveness is actually experienced and defined by laypersons.[7]

In response to the perceived lack of consensus, scholars have been prone to propose their own definitions. This has resulted in a multiplicity of offerings.[8] Why no consensus? Why so many definitional options? Three interrelated factors play a significant role. First, as Nancy DeCourville suggests, there is a gap between the common usages of "forgiveness" and the understandings of the term employed by researchers.[9] The assumption that "forgiveness" is a univocal term is refuted by experience, yet the desire to arrive at a consensus definition persists among researchers. This can lead to the situation in which criteria for establishing a definition of forgiveness that excludes cases embraced by others must be imported from beyond the experience of enacting forgiveness itself.

Second, the interests, theoretical presuppositions, and objectives of the individual researchers impose conditions on what will qualify as an adequate definition of forgiveness.[10] But third, as some researchers

---

[7] Nancy DeCourville, Kathryn Belicki, and Michelle M. Green, "Subjective Experiences of Forgiveness in a Community Sample: Implications for Understanding Forgiveness and Its Consequences," 1–20, in *Women's Reflections on the Complexities of Forgiveness*, ed. Wanda Malcolm, Nancy DeCourville, and Kathryn Belicki (New York: Routledge, 2008), at 2–3. This charge can be applied with some merit to each of the philosophical discussions in chapters 1 and 2. Whenever definitions are used to exclude from consideration cases of forgiveness that others consider relevant, those definitions are subject to the critique implied in DeCourville's observation. This is, perhaps, most evident in Haber's dismissal (Joram Graf Haber, *Forgiveness* [Savage, MD: Rowman & Littlefield, 1991], 33) of forgiveness as a consideration in non-moral harm as "idiosyncratic."

[8] For a partial survey of the distinctive options, see Steven J. Sandage and Ian Williamson, "Forgiveness in Cultural Context," 41–55, in *Handbook of Forgiveness*, at 41.

[9] They observe: "There is research suggesting that laypersons' definitions and experiences of forgiveness are different from how forgiveness is defined in the literature" (DeCourville, Belicki, and Green, "Subjective Experiences of Forgiveness in a Community Sample," 4). This leads them to argue for a less restrictive approach to defining forgiveness. "Our findings argue for broadening existing definitions (at least operational definitions as reflected in measures of forgiveness) to include, as much as possible, the experiences of those who have forgiven, despite the fact that there has been at least one call to narrow the manner in which forgiveness is defined (e.g., "definitional drift," Enright et al., 1998, pp. 50–51)" (ibid., 17).

[10] DeCourville expands on this point when contrasting different areas of research on therapeutic approaches to forgiveness in "Subjective Experiences of Forgiveness in a Community Sample," 2. The influence of distinctive directions of research on defini-

have proposed, there may in fact be many different *kinds* of forgiveness. Some scholars have conceptualized different definitions according to a spectrum; others have proposed a range of models. For example, Sue Walrond-Skinner proposes a typology of six distinct but defective approaches to enacting forgiveness before articulating her own vision of what would be a more complete expression.[11] Worthington presents a schema of definitions distinguished according to the closeness of the victim's relationship to the perpetrator and whether forgiveness is understood as a matter of decision, something that is just experienced, or an (intentional) interpersonal process.[12] Varda Konstam and her associates identify four types of models of forgiveness.[13] These distinctive options reflect the diversities of the experience called "forgiveness" *and* the diversity of interests and theoretical perspectives brought to bear in trying to understand the phenomenon of forgiveness.[14]

tions of forgiveness is reflected as well in the argument for a distinctive definition of forgiveness for children by Denham et al., "Emotional Development and Forgiveness in Children," and in Jennie G. Noll's description of the characteristics of trauma and their implications for forgiving in her "Forgiveness in People Experiencing Trauma," 363–75, in *Handbook of Forgiveness*, as well as in Sue Walrond-Skinner's discussion of family therapy in her "The Function and Role of Forgiveness in Working with Couples and Families: Clearing the Ground," *Journal of Family Therapy* 20 (1998): 3–19. See also Michael E. McCullough and Everett L. Worthington, Jr., "Religion and the Forgiving Personality," *Journal of Personality* 67, no. 6 (1999): 1141–64, at 1142; and Everett L. Worthington, Jr., "More Questions about Forgiveness: Research Agenda for 2005–2015," 557–73, in *Handbook of Forgiveness*.

[11] Walrond-Skinner, "The Function and Role of Forgiveness," 10–13.

[12] Worthington, "More Questions about Forgiveness," 566, diagram 32.2.

[13] Varda Konstam et al., "Forgiveness in Practice: What Mental Health Counselors Are Telling Us," 54–71, in *Before Forgiving*, at 56.

[14] For further examples of this diversity in the literature, see Janice Haaken, "The Good, the Bad, and the Ugly: Psychoanalytic and Cultural Perspectives on Forgiveness," 172–91, in *Before Forgiving*, at 173; Sells and Hargrave, "Forgiveness: A Review of the Theoretical and Empirical Literature"; Everett L. Worthington, Jr., "Initial Questions About the Art and Science of Forgiving," 4 (on the distinction between emotional and decisional forgiveness); June Price Tangney, Angela L. Boone, and Ronda Dearing, "Forgiving the Self: Conceptual Issues and Empirical Findings," 143–58, in *Handbook of Forgiveness*, at 144 (on the distinction between self-forgiveness and forgiveness of others). Thomas and Garrod, "Forgiveness after Genocide? Perspectives from Bosnian Youth," 198, drawing on the works of Enright and Fitzgibbons and of McCullough, Pargament, and Thoresen identify six styles of forgiveness used in assessing their work with genocide survivors.

The persistent lack of a consensus definition has not dampened enthusiasm for the pursuit of a common concept, but it has shifted the emphasis. Rather than seeking to prescribe a definition—a set of prescriptive conceptual boundaries for what does or does not count as forgiveness—some researchers have looked for points of convergence among the different approaches. McCullough and Worthington, for example, have identified "three crucial features" of forgiveness—features that, as described, would accommodate most of the proposed definitions while allowing for diversity.

> First, interpersonal forgiveness occurs in the context of an individual's perception that the action or actions of another person were noxious, harmful, immoral, or unjust. Second, these perceptions typically elicit emotional responses (e.g., anger or fear), motivational responses (e.g., desires to avoid the transgressor or harm the transgressor in kind), cognitive responses (e.g., hostility toward or loss of respect or esteem for the transgressor), or behavioral responses (e.g., avoidance or aggression) that would promote the deterioration of good will toward the offender and social harmony. Third, by forgiving, these negative emotional, motivational, cognitive, or behavioral responses are modulated, so that more prosocial and harmonious interpersonal relations can possibly be resumed. This is a common definition for a construct that is both common and transcendent.[15]

Worthington follows a similar approach in the concluding chapter of *Handbook of Forgiveness*, where he observes that, despite the common claim among psychological researchers that there is no consensus on a definition, there "seems to be a near consensus."[16] And McCullough, Pargament, and Thoresen observe, "the fact that no scholars have offered serious disputations of these distinctions [of forgiveness from other related concepts such as condonation, forgetting, and denying] in recent years suggests that real conceptual progress has been made in understanding forgiveness."[17] As a tentative step toward that consensus, they "propose to define forgiveness as *intraindividual, prosocial change toward a perceived transgressor that is situated within a specific interpersonal context.*"[18]

---

[15] McCullough and Worthington, "Religion and the Forgiving Personality," 1142–43.

[16] Worthington, *Handbook of Forgiveness*, 557.

[17] McCullough, Pargament, and Thoresen, "The Psychology of Forgiveness: History, Conceptual Issues, and Overview," 7–8.

[18] Ibid., 9 (italics in original).

To date, no individual proposed definition has gained universal acceptance. Whether or not any proposal does, the discussion surrounding the pursuit of a consensus is very instructive for the purposes of our own inquiry. It brings to the surface common themes and convictions concerning the phenomenon of forgiveness.

## Convergence on Consensus Understanding

If the pursuit of a consensual definition of forgiveness has not yet achieved resolution in psychological research, many of the discussions do appear to be converging on a common understanding, or at least a common sense of the terrain on which the issues will need to be resolved. As many researchers have observed, the lack of agreement on a definition of what forgiveness *is* stands in contrast to the near unanimity concerning what forgiveness is *not*.[19] Among the concepts most commonly contrasted with forgiveness are condonation, pardon, forgetting, and excusing.[20] Condonation is a stance that gives tacit approval to the offensive action. It is distinguished from forgiving in that forgiveness becomes an issue precisely because one does not approve of an action. Pardon is most commonly identified with the legal dispensation of consequences normally imposed by legal authorities for offenses committed (punishment); it therefore stands outside the realm of interpersonal forgiveness. Forgetting is distinguished from forgiving because it occurs

---

[19] DeCourville, Belicki, and Green, "Subjective Experiences of Forgiveness in a Community Sample," 2; Suzanne Freedman, Robert D. Enright, and Jeanette Knutson, "A Progress Report on the Process Model of Forgiveness," 393–406, in *Handbook of Forgiveness*, at 394.

[20] See, for example, Freedman, Enright, and Knutson, "A Progress Report on the Process Model of Forgiveness," 394; McCullough, Pargament, and Thoresen, *Forgiveness: Theory, Research, and Practice*, 7–8; Sharon Lamb, "Introduction: Reasons to Be Cautious about the Use of Forgiveness in Psychotherapy," 3–14, in *Before Forgiving*, at 7; Robert D. Enright, Suzanne Freedman, and Julio Rique, "The Psychology of Interpersonal Forgiveness," 46–62, in *Exploring Forgiveness*, ed. Robert D. Enright and Joanna North (Madison, WI: University of Wisconsin Press, 1998), at 48. However, even here the agreement is not absolute. For example, Jerome Neu introduces nuance into the discussion of excusing when he argues that the function of excusing, in some cases, may only be to mitigate the significance of the harm, not obviate the need for forgiveness entirely as some theorists have argued. See Jerome Neu, "To Understand All Is to Forgive All—Or Is It?" 17–38, in *Before Forgiving*, at 20. This appears to place Neu on common ground with Murphy's argument regarding possible reasons for forgiving even in the absence of an apology.

passively, not as a function of a conscious decision.[21] One can forget an offense without having forgiven it. Excusing proposes that the action that occasioned the harm was justified on some grounds and therefore (supposedly), does not require forgiveness.[22] Most of the literature shares these common convictions.

One point on which there is significant disagreement is the relationship of forgiving to reconciling. Some approaches to forgiveness see reconciliation (reestablishment of relationships on a level approximating what preceded the rupture) as integral to forgiveness itself.[23] This is a minority position. By far the majority of psychological researchers posit a firm distinction between reconciling and forgiving. They trace the basis for this distinction to the commonly held view that forgiveness as a psychological enactment is possible regardless of the comportment of the offender.[24] Reconciliation, by contrast, requires change by the offender as well.[25]

---

[21] See, for example, Margaret R. Holmgren, "Forgiveness and the Intrinsic Value of Persons," *American Philosophical Quarterly* 30, no. 4 (October 1993): 341–52. Jerome Neu's discussion reflects a more ambivalent assessment of the possible role of forgetting in the process of forgiving. See Neu, "To Understand All Is to Forgive All—Or Is It?" 33.

[22] This notion that a "justified" action that causes harm does not require forgiveness is predicated on the conviction that only morally offensive—that is, by definition, "morally unjustified"—harms are the proper occasion for engaging in forgiveness. This conviction, a commonplace in some philosophical discussions, has a strong representation in some of the psychological literature. However, as will become apparent below, this is not a universal conviction. In proposing a basic understanding of forgiveness as a human enactment I will contest the assumption that, in the absence of a moral harm, forgiveness is not an issue.

[23] This is certainly the case for Griswold, as presented in the preceding chapter. Mona Gustafson Affinito points to a work by Terry Hargrave that subsumes reconciliation and forgiveness under the rubric of "relationship reconstruction." Affinito, "Forgiveness in Counseling: Caution, Definition, and Application," 91; citing Terry D. Hargrave, *Families and Forgiveness: Healing Wounds in the Intergenerational Family* (New York: Bruner/Mazel Publishers, 1994), 79.

[24] Freedman, Enright, and Knutson, "A Progress Report on the Process Model of Forgiveness," 394; Tangney, Boone, and Dearing, "Forgiving the Self: Conceptual Issues and Empirical Findings," 144. For a comparison of psychological and theological perspectives on this issue, see Nathan R. Frise and Mark R. McMinn, "Forgiveness and Reconciliation: The Differing Perspectives of Psychologists and Christian Theologians (Survey)," *Journal of Psychology and Theology* 38, no. 2 (Summer 2010): 83–90.

[25] Keith Yandell puts it very well when he observes, "While the ideal result of forgiveness is reconciliation, it seems plain that the reconciliation of victim and offender cannot, itself, be an essential element in the victim forgiving the offender. Were it so, the offender

### Dynamics of Forgiveness

In addition to the convergence of scholarly perspectives on what forgiveness is not, there is also considerable agreement regarding the dynamics of forgiveness, the things that take place when one is forgiving. These dynamics, although not constituting a definition, do point toward an emerging commonality of understanding. Four aspects of the dynamism of forgiveness that are frequently discussed include affective change (or a commitment to change one's affect), a change of behavior, a reinterpretation of the event of harm (reframing), and the role of personal agency. These four aspects of the dynamics of forgiveness, as treated in the psychological literature, appear to mutually condition each other in the act of forgiveness itself.

The first aspect, affective change or a commitment to affective change, permeates the psychological discussion as it did the Anglo-American philosophical discussion. Denham and colleagues put it very succinctly. "Forgiveness is a transformation of one's affect, cognitive judgments, and motivations toward an offender."[26] As the philosopher Norvin Richards points out, this construal of forgiveness in terms of the modification of feelings is integral to many therapeutic approaches to forgiveness.[27] It also forms the core of much research on forgiveness as psychologists seek ways to measure the reduction in retributive feelings. The language used to describe this affective change often includes phrases like "letting go" of "negative" feelings (such as resentment or desire for revenge) and related concepts.[28] The common conviction is that forgiveness entails as one of

---

could prevent the victim from forgiving by simply refusing to reconcile. It is forgiveness that is an element in reconciliation, not reconciliation that is included in forgiveness. Nor can the offender's rehabilitation properly be the prisoner of the victim's willingness to forgive, though it is rightly prisoner to the offender's remorse and repentance, and possibly to the offender's making restitution and willingness to reconcile. The refusal of an offender to repent should not prevent the victim from forgiving, and the victim's refusal to forgive should not preclude the offender's restoration to rectitude." Keith E. Yandell, "The Metaphysics and Morality of Forgiveness," 35–45, in *Exploring Forgiveness*, at 44. We will examine this issue in greater detail in a later chapter.

[26] Denham et al., "Emotional Development and Forgiveness in Children," 129.

[27] Norvin Richards, "Forgiveness as Therapy," 72–87, in *Before Forgiving*, at 72.

[28] See, for example, Frederick A. DiBlasio, "The Use of a Decision-Based Forgiveness Intervention within Intergenerational Family Therapy," *Journal of Family Therapy* 20 (1998): 77–94, at 78; Sells and Hargrave, "Forgiveness: A Review of the Theoretical and Empirical Literature," 30; Helen Chagigiorgis and Sandra Paivio, "Forgiveness as an Outcome in Emotion-Focused Trauma Therapy," 121–41, in *Women's Reflections on the Complexities of Forgiveness*, ed. Wanda Malcolm, Nancy DeCourville, and Kathryn Belicki (New York:

its constitutive elements a movement in the direction of attenuating (or eliminating) retributive emotions directed toward the offender for the offense.[29] To put this in other terms, forgiving involves an affective trajectory away from retributive emotions.

The second aspect is a change of behavior. This is commonly referred to as the emergence of "prosocial" behaviors, those that promote positive relations.[30] These behaviors are conceived as the opposite of those that would spontaneously arise from the retributive emotions. That is, "by forgiving, these negative emotional, motivational, cognitive, or behavioral responses are modulated, so that more prosocial and harmonious interpersonal relations can possibly be resumed."[31]

Although this aspect is often affirmed in the literature, there is a caveat. It is not always possible or advisable from the perspective of the psychological and physical well-being of a victim to pursue behaviors that would actually reestablish relationship with an offender. In the case of abusive relationships, for example, if prosocial behavior is understood as opening oneself to further abuse, it would certainly be problematic.[32] The issue is how one understands "prosocial behavioral change." One approach bypasses the difficulty. "McCullough and colleagues define the essence of forgiveness as prosocial changes in one's *motivations* toward an offending relationship partner."[33]

---

Routledge,2008), 121; Julie Juola Exline and Anne L. Zell, "Does a Humble Attitude Promote Forgiveness? Challenges, Caveats, and Sex Differences," 235–51, in *Women's Reflections on the Complexities of Forgiveness*, 236; Ann Macaskill, "Just-World Beliefs and Forgiveness in Men and Women," 39–59, in *Women's Reflections on the Complexities of Forgiveness*, at 42; and Everett L. Worthington, Jr., "Initial Questions About the Art and Science of Forgiving," 4.

[29] See, for example, Chagigiorgis and Paivio, "Forgiveness as an Outcome," 123; Marjorie E. Baker, "Self-Forgiveness: An Empowering and Therapeutic Tool for Working with Women in Recovery," in 61–74, in *Women's Reflections on the Complexities of Forgiveness*, ed. Wanda Malcolm, Nancy DeCourville, and Kathryn Belicki (New York: Routledge, 2008), at 63–64; DiBlasio, "The Use of a Decision-Based Forgiveness Intervention"; DeCourville, Belicki, and Green, "Subjective Experiences of Forgiveness in a Community Sample," 8; Denham et al., "Emotional Development and Forgiveness in Children," 129.

[30] For example, see Denham et al., "Emotional Development and Forgiveness in Children," 129; McCullough and Worthington, "Religion and the Forgiving Personality," 1142–43; McCullough, Pargament, and Thoresen, "The Psychology of Forgiveness," 8.

[31] McCullough and Worthington, "Religion and the Forgiving Personality," 1142–43.

[32] Noll, "Forgiveness in People Experiencing Trauma," 364, 366.

[33] McCullough, Pargament, and Thoresen, "The Psychology of Forgiveness," 8. Emphasis added.

This focus on motivational change seems to be trying to name something other than the affective change mentioned above in that it is understood as potentially running counter to one's retributive feelings.[34] The underlying premise is that behaviors—at least responsible, intentional behaviors—arise from motivations and are characterized by those motivations. These motivations can lead one to seek to modify affective responses. They are therefore grounded in psychic processes not entirely under the sway of one's feelings. Prosocial behaviors, in this context, are the external expression of prosocial motivations: those that seek to establish peaceful, harmonious relationships in a social context.[35]

The third common aspect of the psychological discussions of forgiveness focuses on cognitive change. It is the reinterpretation of the event and/or of the offender, "reframing," as it is commonly called.[36] This reframing puts the event or the offender into a larger context, a larger horizon of meanings.[37] The purpose of reframing is to come to a different understanding of the event and of the perpetrator.[38] The victim's understanding of the event changes in that she no longer sees herself *merely* or *primarily* as a victim. She reclaims a larger context for her own sense of meaning and for the meaning of the event. From within that larger

[34] This distinction is supported by Denham and associates when they write: "Some explicitly cite behavior—or at least the motivation toward prosocial behavior—as part of forgiveness. Others emphasize the emotional transformations and/or the important motivational changes wrought by forgiveness. Still others focus on the cognitive reasoning involved in forgiveness decisions," in Denham, et al., "Emotional Development and Forgiveness in Children," 129.

[35] I think the general distinction has merit. However, as presented it does not adequately account for the fact that motivations are also affectively charged, not merely conceptualizations of values that stand opposed to the values embedded in the retributive impulses. A theoretical framework for addressing this phenomenon is needed. Part 2 will present the outlines for such a framework.

[36] See, for example, Macaskill, "Just-World Beliefs and Forgiveness in Men and Women," 42; Mark S. Rye et al., "Religious Perspectives on Forgiveness," 17–40, in *Forgiveness: Theory, Research, and Practice*, at 17–18; Yandell, "The Metaphysics and Morality of Forgiveness," 39–44; Freedman, Enright, and Knutson, "A Progress Report on the Process Model of Forgiveness," 395; Sells and Hargrave, "Forgiveness: A Review of the Theoretical and Empirical Literature," 28.

[37] This notion parallels what Griswold describes in terms of narrative. It also seems to me to be presupposed by the five examples of situations in which forgiving would be morally appropriate. For example, appealing to the good intentions of the offender is a way of reframing the action that offended.

[38] Enright, Freedman, and Rique, "The Psychology of Interpersonal Forgiveness," 54.

and different context of meaning her understanding of the perpetrator can also change, seeing him as something more than the agent who produced the harm.[39]

These three common aspects of the psychological discussion, affective change, prosocial behavior, and reframing, are interrelated. Affective change can foster prosocial behavior and reframing. The dynamics can begin with the affective. However, prosocial change can modify feelings and perspectives, and reframing can lead to revised motivations and behaviors as well as revised feelings. Research can focus on one aspect or another according to the questions being pursued by the researcher, but the current literature suggests that, in the experience of the person who is forgiving, change in one aspect calls forth change in the others in the enactment of forgiveness.[40]

Permeating all three of these aspects is a fourth: personal agency. In all of the psychological discussions, whether explicitly identified or tacitly assumed, the capacity for intentional action is essential. Forgiving is, to some extent, something one can choose.[41] So too are the three different aspects just mentioned. One can choose to try to modify one's feelings. One can choose to foster prosocial behaviors in the face of an offense. One can choose to wrestle with reframing the event and/or the offender within a larger context of meanings, one that makes forgiving a plausible

[39] Murphy gets at this effect through the work of separating the perpetrator from the action in Murphy and Hampton, *Forgiveness and Mercy*, 24. Haber adheres to the same logic but limits the conditions for the separation to the demonstrated repudiation of the event by the offender in Haber, *Forgiveness*, 104–5. So also in Hieronymi, "Articulating an Uncompromising Forgiveness," 548; and in Griswold, *Forgiveness: A Philosophical Exploration*, 49–51.

[40] In Freedman, Enright, and Knutson, "A Progress Report on the Process Model of Forgiveness," the authors advert to this phenomenon. It is implicit in the notion of "phases" in a process as they have articulated it.

[41] See, for example, Freedman, Enright, and Knutson, "A Progress Report on the Process Model of Forgiveness," 403; Denham, et al., "Emotional Development and Forgiveness in Children," 128, 130; Exline and Zell, "Does a Humble Attitude Promote Forgiveness?" 236; Julie Juola Exline and Roy F. Baumeister, "Expressing Forgiveness and Repentance: Benefits and Barriers," 133–55, in *Forgiveness: Theory, Research, and Practice*, at 145; Richard Fitzgibbons, "Anger and the Healing Power of Forgiveness: A Psychiatrist's View," 63–74, in *Exploring Forgiveness*, at 67; Bill Puka, "Forgoing Forgiveness," 136–52, in *Before Forgiving*, at 149. The role of personal agency is expanded to the level of the social group in Sandage and Williamson, "Forgiveness in Cultural Context," 44, 52.

option. Throughout the literature the emphasis on personal agency in forgiving shows itself in the language of "decision."[42]

The commonly shared conviction that we can make choices about forgiving and its various aspects leads us into the vexing question of human freedom. We will return to this topic in more detail later, but for the present we should note that, even though a capacity to choose (freedom) is presupposed in all of these discussions (and in the philosophical discussions as well), it is not assumed that this freedom is absolute. We are responsible for our choices—up to a point. We can choose to modify our feelings, our behaviors, our perceptions of harm producing events—up to a point.[43] But we also have limitations. Our feelings, our motivations (for or against prosocial behavior) and our ways of interpreting the world around us are not entirely at our disposal.[44]

### Factors Affecting Our Freedom to Forgive

We cannot simply "will" our feelings, our motivations, or our perceptions to be different than they are. Therapeutic processes for affective and cognitive modification implicitly recognize this reality. Many factors can co-condition and impede our ability to choose even to seek to be in a different state of mind or heart. Two factors have figured prominently in the psychological discussions of forgiveness: our relational contexts and our psychological developmental status. A third factor is garnering increasing attention: the dynamics and structures of the unconscious.

### *Relational Contexts and Freedom to Forgive*

We have already seen the issue of relational context, at least in an attenuated form, in the Anglo-American analyses of forgiveness. For

---

[42] See, for example, DiBlasio, "The Use of a Decision-Based Forgiveness Intervention within Intergenerational Family Therapy." The language of "decision" likewise pervades Affinito, "Forgiveness in Counseling: Caution, Definition, and Application."

[43] Murphy makes explicit reference to this point in Murphy and Hampton, *Forgiveness and Mercy*, 4 n. 7.

[44] Jerome Neu draws attention to this difficulty when he observes: "There are limits on choosing our emotions and motives," in Jerome Neu, "Rehabilitating Resentment and Choosing What We Feel," *Criminal Justice Ethics* 27, no. 2 (Summer/Fall 2008): 31–37, at 36. Neu offers a perceptive assessment of these complexities throughout the course of this article. The issue of the limitations of our freedom with respect to our feelings arose in the philosophical discussions of forgiveness in relation to the resurfacing of retributive feelings after one has forgiven. See Murphy and Hampton, *Forgiveness and Mercy*, 21.

example, Griswold's argument that a victim of abuse should not forgive an unrepentant abuser for fear of condoning the behavior implicitly invokes relational context in making the argument.[45] Within the psychological discussions, however, the examination of relational context, more broadly understood, has taken on greater prominence than is represented in the philosophical approaches we have considered. The broader understanding in question includes the way in which specific interpersonal relationships affect one's ability to forgive. But it also examines the extent to which the cultural milieu within which one lives and grows can shape how one engages with the question of forgiveness.[46] To put this in other terms, the relationships that impact our lives and the culture within which we live affect our capacity to enact forgiveness. They do so in many ways. For example, our relational context shapes what we recognize as an offense deserving of resentment as a response; it provides us with the conceptual and imaginative resources for reframing a situation; it also furnishes us with socially sanctioned templates or benchmarks for the kinds or degrees of forgiveness to be extended.[47] Our relational context shapes our affective, cognitive, behavioral, and developmental experiences, and therefore our capacity to forgive.

Psychological research has begun to assess the impact of such influences on one's practice of (non-)forgiveness and, consequently, on therapeutic intervention. Sandage and Williamson draw attention to the fact that fundamental norms affecting forgiveness decisions and modes of enacting forgiveness may differ from one culture to the next at a fundamental level. This can have profound importance when identifying appropriate therapeutic strategies for helping someone to forgive. As they observe: "forgiveness interventions that promote forgiving someone else

[45] See, for example, Griswold, *Forgiveness: A Philosophical Exploration*, 51. Murphy gets at a similar issue in his discussion of "self-forgiveness" as a therapeutic issue in cases of morally reprehensible actions such as child abuse. See Jeffrie G. Murphy, *Getting Even: Forgiveness and Its Limits* (New York: Oxford University Press, 2003), 76, 80.

[46] For example, McCullough, Pargament, and Thoresen, "The Psychology of Forgiveness," 7, observe that socio-cultural issues are implicated in one's willingness to forgive. Sandage and Williamson, "Forgiveness in Cultural Context," 48, affirm that some cross-cultural aspects of forgiveness exist but need to be further studied.

[47] The concepts of "degrees of forgiveness" or "kinds of forgiveness" are not universally embraced; their acceptance is contingent on the way one defines forgiveness. The point made here is that in those contexts where the notions are recognized as legitimate they are also correlated with other cultural variants as co-conditioning elements in the movement toward forgiving.

as an individual choice or decision that can be legitimately motivated by personal benefits may represent an individualistic cultural tool but may not fit the worldviews of highly collectivistic groups."[48] In a collectivistic group an individual's decision to forgive might be construed as disloyalty or selfishness by the collective. The collective might exert pressure to dissuade the individual from forgiving. Sandage and Williamson therefore argue that therapists need to recognize the distinctive influences shaping the sensibilities of their clients if they are going to assist them with forgiveness issues. But, as they explain, this is a complex task, for

> Most people live within numerous interpenetrating cultural or re-
> lational systems, which can be a source of the very conflicts that
> raise forgiveness issues. For example, intergenerational acculturation
> differences are a source of conflict in many families and cultural
> groups. Awareness of cultural dynamics of power and control in
> various systems can help prevent the use of forgiveness interventions
> that are ineffective or even harmful.[49]

Any one person can carry within himself or herself several competing systems of value, cognitive paradigms, relational patterns, and personal narratives. These are shaped by personal histories, aspirations, and experiences of power dynamics in relationship with others. All of these elements, often encoded within the shared narrative of a regional culture (the academy, a religious group, military service, etc.) play a role in the negotiation of forgiveness questions.

The points raised by Sandage and Williamson are echoed in the findings of other psychologists and researchers. For example, Roy F. Baumeister and his colleagues identify some of the contextually complicated aspects of forgiveness when they contrast the dynamics of "communal relationships" with those of "exchange relationships," in which forgiveness might be enacted but not explicitly named.

> Communal relationships are defined by a norm of mutual concern
> for each other's needs and wants. Exchange relationships are gov-
> erned by norms of equity and payback, so that each favor should be
> returned or compensated. Exchange relationships may be especially
> fertile grounds for this sort of unstated forgiveness because to release
> the other from a debt or obligation (unilaterally and without getting

---

[48] Sandage and Williamson, "Forgiveness in Cultural Context," 52.
[49] Ibid.

anything) goes against the relationship norms. Even in communal relationships, however, people may occasionally want to influence the other's behavior by using a sense of debt or obligation that may accompany past transgressions ("After all I've sacrificed for you . . ."), even if those people do not privately harbor lingering resentment or hurt.[50]

Within the dynamics just described, power plays an unmistakable role. Here it is the often-hidden coercion of social convention. Rules are in place to govern interactions. Often these kinds of rules are not explicitly recognized, or only become explicit when one senses that they have been transgressed. But such rules give order and structure to social relations and, in the case of exchange relationships, provide the framework and even the motivation for engaging in forgiveness "according to the rules." The desire for future gain or avoiding the psychic stress of conflict influences the manner in which one confronts the question of forgiveness.

But power dynamics also shape other relational contexts in which the question of forgiveness can arise. As indicated above, women and children, and even the elderly—anyone in a dependent relationship—may feel themselves subject to rules of relating that influence their confrontation with the experience of harm and the need to forgive. Sharon Lamb draws attention to the ways in which power dynamics can reshape (and historically have reshaped!) the question of forgiveness in the case of women. She argues that, given the history of the oppression of women, to press for them to give up their anger at the injustices done to them is immoral. Hence, in such relational contexts, forgiveness (especially unilateral forgiveness) is problematic.[51] As she explains: "Concerning women, and particularly women who have been abused, the idea of offering forgiveness toward unrepentant perpetrators in an effort to help a woman free herself from anger is dangerous and plays into deep stereotypes of women's 'essential' nature, stereotypes that have been harmful to

---

[50] Roy F. Baumeister, Julie Juola Exline, and Kristin L. Sommer, "The Victim Role, Grudge Theory, and Two Dimensions of Forgiveness," 79–104, in *Dimensions of Forgiveness: Psychological Research and Theological Perspectives* (Philadelphia & London: Templeton Foundation, 1998), at 89. This brings us back to the questions raised by Derrida's arguments concerning "exchange" and the inscription of forgiving within an "economy." We will return to this issue later.

[51] Sharon Lamb, "Women, Abuse, and Forgiveness: A Special Case," 155–71, in *Before Forgiving*, 165.

women in the past."[52] Similar arguments have been made with respect to the experience of children subjected to abuse.[53] These power dynamics, often so embedded within the values of a cultural system that they can go unrecognized, nonetheless structure relational contexts in ways that influence how one approaches questions of forgiveness.

These findings suggest that relational context can have a profound impact on freedom to forgive. It can support one in enacting forgiveness; it can distort forgiveness into capitulation to an offender and/or the will of a group; and it can suppress forgiveness entirely.

### Psychological Development and Freedom to Forgive

A further aspect of relational context that has achieved some recognition in contemporary psychological literature on forgiveness is age. Research has indicated that the capacities for forgiveness and the inclination toward forgiveness are different at different stages of life. Susanne Denham and her colleagues have argued for the need to understand forgiveness as it emerges within the developmental horizons of children's experience. As they explain: "Any given age has unique emotional, cognitive, and social tasks that determine a child's success in development. By zeroing in on these special tasks, we can pinpoint the nature of forgiveness during childhood and how it may change."[54] Other researchers have found that the elderly have a greater openness to forgiving than adolescents or younger adults.[55]

These findings raise questions regarding forgiveness as a developmental issue. For example, the reference to "the nature of forgiveness during childhood" reflects the suspicion that what it means to forgive might be different at different stages of maturation, development, and social

[52] Ibid., 156.

[53] Sue Walrond-Skinner examines the dynamics of dependence in the development of a child's capacity for forgiveness in her "The Function and Role of Forgiveness." See also Noll, "Forgiveness in People Experiencing Trauma," 366.

[54] Denham et al., "Emotional Development and Forgiveness in Children," 130.

[55] See, for example, Étienne Mullet and Michèle Girard, "Developmental and Cognitive Points of View on Forgiveness," 111–32, in *Forgiveness: Theory, Research, and Practice*, at 218; Sells and Hargrave, "Forgiveness: A Review of the Theoretical and Empirical Literature," 32. Varda Konstam cites other research in support of this same point in Konstam et al., "Forgiveness in Practice," 57.

competence.[56] This would imply that efforts to define forgiveness should take developmental stages into account. But the differences in willingness to forgive at different life-stages also raises questions about our freedom to forgive. To what extent do developmental processes and stages foster or impede the capacity to forgive itself?

This topic of human development has come to occupy an important place in psychological discussions of forgiveness. The term "development" as it is used in these discussions has many distinct but often overlapping applications.[57] For the purposes of our interests, I will highlight two.

In the first sense development can refer to the process of mental or psychic maturation itself. Jean Piaget's groundbreaking work on the development of cognitive abilities in small children revealed that cognitive processes must develop and mature.[58] Lawrence Kohlberg's schematization of stages in moral decision-making likewise confirmed a process of development in our capacity for moral judgment.[59] Their work, and that of later researchers, has contributed to understanding how the mind

[56] Denham and associates identify different studies that support their interest in further research. They draw particular attention to the issue of socialization in the development of forgiveness skills and to the role of the development of forgiveness skills in socialization. See Denham et al., "Emotional Development and Forgiveness in Children," 136–38.

[57] Robert Karen, for example, illustrates the multivalence of the term when he writes: "In the capacity to forgive we see our largeness of heart. And, in struggling to forgive what is most difficult for us to forgive, we reveal our courage, imagination, and potential for growth. The development of forgiveness is, I now think, as clear a marker of general psychological development as there is." Robert Karen, *The Forgiving Self: The Road from Resentment to Connection* (New York: Doubleday Anchor Books, 2001), 9–10. However, Konstam notes: "There is also disagreement in the literature as to whether forgiveness is a necessary part of personal growth and development," in Konstam et al., "Forgiveness in Practice," 55.

[58] See, for example, Jean Piaget, *Genetic Epistemology*, trans. Eleanor Duckworth (New York: Columbia University Press, 1970). For a useful commentary on Piaget's understanding of cognitive development, see Barry J. Wadsworth, *Piaget's Theory of Cognitive Development: An Introduction for Students of Psychology and Education* (New York: David McKay, 1971); Mary Ann Spencer Pulaski, *Understanding Piaget: An Introduction to Children's Cognitive Development* (New York: Harper & Row, 1971).

[59] Kohlberg presents his stages of moral development in Lawrence Kohlberg, Charles Levine, and Alexandra Hewer, *Moral Stages: A Current Formulation and a Response to Critics*, Contributions to Human Development 10 (Basel and New York: Karger, 1983). See also his *The Meaning and Measurement of Moral Development*, The Heinz Werner Lectures 13 (Worcester, MA: Clark University Press, 1981); idem, *The Philosophy of Moral Development: Moral Stages and the Idea of Justice*, Essays on Moral Development 1 (San Francisco: Harper & Row, 1981); idem, *The Psychology of Moral Development: The*

itself constructs and deploys capacities and strategies for dealing with the world by the expansion, self-correction, and use of cognitive abilities.

The second sense of development in contemporary research on forgiveness concerns the process one goes through in enacting forgiveness.[60] Forgiveness itself is not an undifferentiated moment. It is often experienced as the passage through a series of interrelated internal changes that can be identified as a process. Development in this sense refers to the progressive movement of the process from early, less-complete states of efforts at forgiveness to later, more-complete expressions.[61]

These two senses of development are evident in various proposals of therapeutic strategies for helping individuals to forgive.[62] These therapeutic proposals reflect sensitivity to cognitive and moral developmental stages, drawing clients through a progressive series of steps as they move toward forgiveness.

---

*Nature and Validity of Moral Stages*, Essays on Moral Development 2 (San Francisco: Harper & Row, 1984).

[60] This understanding is implied in Sells and Hargrave, "Forgiveness: A Review of the Theoretical and Empirical Literature." It is also clearly manifested in different-stage approaches to forgiving developed by different therapists, most notably the process promoted by Enright and associates. See Robert D. Enright, "Counseling Within the Forgiveness Triad: On Forgiving, Receiving Forgiveness, and Self-Forgiveness," *Counseling & Values,* 40, no. 2 (1996): 107–27; and Enright, Freedman, and Rique, "The Psychology of Interpersonal Forgiveness," 52–55, esp. Table 5.1, p. 53.

[61] See, for example, Denham et al., "Emotional Development and Forgiveness in Children," 129–30; Freedman, Enright, and Knutson, "A Progress Report on the Process Model of Forgiveness," 394; Haaken, "The Good, the Bad, and the Ugly: Psychoanalytic and Cultural Perspectives on Forgiveness," 174; DiBlasio, "The Use of a Decision-Based Forgiveness Intervention," 93; John Gartner, "The Capacity to Forgive: An Object Relations Perspective," *Journal of Religion and Health* 27, no. 4 (Winter 1988): 313–20, at 317.

[62] This has been especially evident, for example, in the work of Robert Enright and his colleagues. See, for example, "Piaget on the Moral Development of Forgiveness: Identity or Reciprocity?" *Human Development* 37, no. 2 (March–April 1994): 63–80; cited in McCullough, Pargament, and Thoresen, "The Psychology of Forgiveness." The influence of Lawrence Kohlberg's research on their project is also widely recognized. See, for example, Sells and Hargrave, "Forgiveness: A Review of the Theoretical and Empirical Literature," 26–28. For a sketch of the process developed by Enright and associates, see Enright, Freedman, and Rique, "The Psychology of Interpersonal Forgiveness," esp. 52–55. Preliminary results of the use of this schema in therapeutic contexts can be found in Freedman, Enright, and Knutson, "A Progress Report on the Process Model of Forgiveness." On the appropriation of Piaget and Kohlberg in forgiveness research in general, see Lamb, "Introduction: Reasons to Be Cautious about the Use of Forgiveness in Psychotherapy," 7.

The recognition that our cognitive abilities and our processes of development shape both our understanding of forgiveness and our enactment of it draws attention to the operations of our conscious cognitive and affective processes when we engage the world. Cognitive therapies help us to understand our conscious life and to refashion it in ways we find healthier and more satisfying, using the data most readily accessible to our consciousness. Developmental approaches operate in a similar mode, but correlate mental states with an articulated understanding (schema) of the movement from less-well-formed psychic functioning to better-formed psychic functioning.

### *The Unconscious and Freedom to Forgive*

But conscious processes are not the whole story when considering our psychic life and its development. Since the time of Sigmund Freud, psychoanalytically-based theories of the human psyche have drawn attention to the unconscious, its dynamics and structures. These lie beneath our conscious processes and shape their functioning in ways that can easily go unrecognized.[63] These dynamics and structures have their own histories of development, unique to each person, but emerging in recognizable forms and patterns that psychoanalytic theorists and, more recently, object relations and attachment theorists have identified.

It is important to say a word about the terms "structures" and "dynamics" as I am using them here. The language of structures in this case does not indicate some sort of physical "thing." It refers to relatively stable patterns of activity in our psychic processes themselves, patterns that undergird, support, and shape our conscious life in a variety of ways. Freud's famous schematization of the mind into the id, ego, and superego does not identify three "things" in the operation of the mind. Rather, it distinguishes three complexes of interrelated, interacting kinds of "movement" (dynamisms). We can identify and distinguish them in terms of the kinds and "directions" (trajectories) of energy they exert in our psychic life. They are stably present in the operation of the psyche, constituting the psychic structures. They are also dynamic; they exhibit "movement" in our psychic processes. The active (dynamic), and often conflictual interaction among them gives structure to much of the drama of the psychic life. Thus "structures" in this sense refers to relatively consistent,

---

[63] Haaken, "The Good, the Bad, and the Ugly: Psychoanalytic and Cultural Perspectives on Forgiveness," 173–75.

stable patterns in the operation of the psyche. "Dynamics" refers to the movements of those patterned energies, the ways in which they operate that disclose those energies as functioning according to consistent patterns (structures).

Psychological research on the structures of the psyche, their development and operation, especially in the fields of object relations and attachment theories, has further deepened understanding of the unconscious and its relationship to conscious life. These theories explore and attempt to articulate how the structures of the unconscious develop in infancy. Although there are different perspectives among theorists, some points have achieved significant consensus. One point of general agreement bears on the relationship between the unconscious and our freedom to forgive. It has to do with the importance of early experiences in the development of the sense of self.

Simply put, the structures of the unconscious emerge and, as it were, assemble themselves in the dynamic process of the differentiation of the self from the other in infancy (this is perhaps better rendered "the differentiation of the other from what only gradually emerges into awareness as a 'self'")[64] and over the course of a history of relations with others.[65] The initial stages of this history occur at a time prior to facility with language. The capacities for conceptual thought and reflective awareness have not yet developed, but the elements of that pre-linguistic history have enduring meaning for the infant and can have a profound impact on adult life. They are affectively charged. Their energy gives shape to some of the foundational structures of the emerging self.[66]

These early, pre-linguistic dynamics and structures do not disappear or lose their force once we acquire the use of language. On the contrary, as Janice Haaken emphasizes, the earlier structural developments provide the

[64] Gartner, "The Capacity to Forgive," 318. See also Julia Kristeva, "The Passion According to Motherhood," 79–94, in *Hatred and Forgiveness*, trans. Jeanine Herman (New York: Columbia University Press, 2010), at 82; and eadem, "The Triple Uprooting of Israel," 213–21, in ibid., 215, as well as the discussion in Gustav Bovensiepen, "Attachment-Dissociation Network: Some Thoughts about Modern Complex Theory," *Journal of Analytic Psychology* 51 (2006): 451–66.

[65] See Lynne Murray, "Intersubjectivity, Object Relations Theory, and Empirical Evidence from Mother-Infant Interactions," *Infant Mental Health Journal* 12, no. 3 (Fall 1991): 219–32; and Bovensiepen, "Attachment-Dissociation Network," 453.

[66] See ibid., 452–54; Joseph Sandler, "Fantasy, Defense, and the Representational World," *Infant Mental Health Journal* 15, no. 1 (Spring 1994): 26–35, at 27–28.

foundations on which later developments are based.[67] In later (linguistically mediated) experience a variety of external factors can also contribute to the store of dynamics and structures that are hidden within the unconscious but still effective in shaping conscious life. Culturally mediated values and interpersonal events can push "to the margins" (into the unconscious) aspects of the conscious life that are seen to be counter to "the operation of conventional codes and normative ideals."[68] (We have already touched on this above in the discussion of relational contexts.)

For the purposes of our interest in the psycho-dynamics of forgiving, research into the unconscious and the development of psychic structures shows us "how responses to conflict are overdetermined by a complex array of associations from the past, specifically those associations formed through early attachments. The emphasis is on the rich generativity of mind and the disjuncture between the imaginary and the 'real' in the interpretation of events."[69] The fact that many of these associations operate at an unconscious (or unthematic) level does not render them any less effective in our conscious life. Indeed, their unrecognized status may contribute to the power they exert on our conscious responses to experience. Thus, when we are confronted with an experience of harm the orientation of our unconscious structures and dynamics may provide powerful resistance to our conscious desire to enact forgiveness.

This is, admittedly, a very basic presentation of the unconscious, its development, and its relationship to conscious processes. Even so, it suggests four points with respect to the importance of the unconscious for understanding forgiveness and the limitations of our freedom to forgive. First, the structures of our psyches undergo a process of development, one that is intrinsically rooted in relationship to the "other." This is the process by which we come to our sense of self.[70] Early experiences in our development are foundational in shaping the dynamics and structures of our sense of self. They continue to exercise an influence on that sense of

---

[67] Thus Haaken observes: "The concept of the dynamic unconscious suggests a realm of mind resistive to the demands of external reality, particularly to demands that conflict with infantile fantasies and desires. The term *infantile* in the psychoanalytic tradition is not necessarily pejorative. Rather, it suggests that advanced psychic structures rest on older, deeper structures of the self." Haaken, "The Good, the Bad, and the Ugly: Psychoanalytic and Cultural Perspectives on Forgiveness," 173–74.

[68] Ibid., 174.

[69] Ibid.

[70] Gartner, "The Capacity to Forgive," 318.

self and on our engagement with the larger world even though, and to some extent because, they are unconscious.

Second, the individuality of each history of development inscribed in the unconscious structures and dynamics operating within each person helps to explain the diversity of interpretations and affective responses to stimuli we can encounter in ourselves and others. It makes sense of the commonly observed phenomenon that two people can undergo the "same" event but interpret and respond to it in radically different ways.

Third, recent research into the unconscious helps to clarify *why* reframing an event can be an effective tool in the process of forgiveness. The relationship between the unconscious and conscious life is not unidirectional. While the unconscious can powerfully shape our conscious life, our conscious experience can also act on and reshape some of the dynamics of the structures in our unconscious. Recasting an event or a person within a different interpretive matrix can help us to disconnect the unconscious associations that can fuel a hostile interpretation of an event and can help us instead to associate more positive affective elements.

But fourth, deeper awareness of the role of the unconscious in our conscious life also suggests the need for caution when advocating that one person forgive another. It reminds us that the meanings of events for the individual who has been harmed cannot be reduced to the publicly accessible "facts."[71] The meanings for that individual may not even be readily accessible to her consciousness, but may instead be bubbling up from the subterranean recesses of the unconscious, shaping a spontaneous response in ways she cannot fully understand. In such circumstances, to press for forgiveness on the basis of what is consciously accessible, counter to the unconscious impulses, may be to enact a kind of soft violence on the psyche of the person involved.

---

[71] Haaken gets at this point when she writes: "I would like to avoid at the outset any pronouncement about whether forgiveness is good or bad, a virtue or a weakness. Rather, I suggest that the function of forgiveness depends on how it operates within a wider arena of human dramas. In other words, without a signifying frame of reference, the term is devoid of useful significance. From a psychodynamic perspective, this frame of reference includes a range of developmental and psychic factors associated with moral conflict." Haaken, "The Good, the Bad, and the Ugly: Psychoanalytic and Cultural Perspectives on Forgiveness," 174. See also her comments on the danger of therapists imposing their own values on the experience of the client, thereby contributing to further repression of unconscious dynamics, in ibid., 179, and the impact of socially constituted and promoted values and beliefs on the way in which a client attempts to work through an injury in ibid., 182.

Thus in the psychological discussions of forgiveness we find a kind of tension with respect to forgiveness and human agency. On the one hand it is taken for granted that we can make decisions for (or against) forgiving others for the harm they have done us. On the other hand there are multiple factors that render that freedom less than absolute. The contexts within which our relationships are lived out and the dynamics of our individual psychic structures can at times energize us to forgive and at other times impose (often unrecognized) obstacles to embracing a forgiving response to harm.

## The Question of Harm

Up to this point our exploration of psychological discussions of forgiveness has taken for granted an understanding of the harm being forgiven. With the discussion of moral harm from our exploration of the Anglo-American philosophical discussion in the background it would be easy to assume that, in this present discussion, "harm" carries the same meaning. However, a closer reading of what has just been presented in the psychological discussions reveals that this is not so. The psychological literature on forgiveness, in fact, exhibits a certain ambivalence with respect to the understanding of "harm." We therefore need to make this ambivalence explicit and to examine what it can tell us about harm and about forgiveness itself before we attempt to tease out an understanding of forgiveness as a basic human enactment.

Much of the psychological language surrounding the harm for which forgiveness is potentially an appropriate response echoes the philosophical discussions. Harm is understood in terms of a moral violation, something for which one can appropriately blame another. In the absence of such moral agency, blame would be inappropriate—so the argument goes—and therefore forgiveness would make no sense. For example, Ann Macaskill has argued that "the term 'forgiveness' does not appropriately describe the adjustments made in response to aversive events outside anyone's control. Rather, it would seem that individuals reduce their anger and come to accept the situations that have occurred."[72] Thus she argues that such situations involve "acceptance" rather than forgiveness since, in these cases, blaming is "illogical."[73] A similar kind of reasoning is present in Holmgren's discussion regarding situations in which one

---

[72] Macaskill, "Just-World Beliefs and Forgiveness in Men and Women," 41.
[73] Ibid., 55.

is "wrongfully harmed,"[74] and the idea that forgiveness is only relevant to moral harm (intentionally perpetrated by a moral agent) is explicitly pressed by Enright and associates when they challenge what they see as "definitional drift" creeping into the understanding of forgiveness.[75] They argue that erosion of the inherent link between forgiveness and moral harm would undermine the concept of forgiveness and its usefulness in therapeutic contexts. Their position on this point aligns with Macaskill's that response to other harms not intentionally generated by moral agents would be better understood in terms of "acceptance."

The focus on moral harm in psychological literature is not always a matter of explicit reflection on the part of those writing about forgiveness. For many it appears to be a matter of available language. The metaphors most commonly used to talk about forgiveness are so permeated by the presumption of moral harm that the language available to psychologists when writing about forgiveness unavoidably reflects this presumption. The language for referring to the agent who effects the harm, for example, includes terms like "wrongdoer," "perpetrator," and "offender," all of which have moral (and legal) overtones.[76] A similar presumption shows up in the way of characterizing the harm as "unfair" or "unjust."[77]

Despite this extensive acceptance of the idea that forgiveness is correlated exclusively with moral harm, other perspectives have been gaining currency. Indeed, Jerome Neu, who works in both philosophy and

---

[74] Margaret R. Holmgren, "Forgiveness and Self-Forgiveness in Psychotherapy," 112–35, in *Before Forgiving*, e.g., 119, 121. The idea permeates the essay. We should note that Holmgren is a philosopher, not a psychologist. However, her essay explicitly addresses itself to the understanding of forgiveness in relationship to harm, albeit from a philosophical perspective.

[75] Enright, Freedman, and Rique, "The Psychology of Interpersonal Forgiveness," 50–51. We shall return to examine this argument in detail in part 2.

[76] See, for example, Karen, *The Forgiving Self*, 23; Denham et al., "Emotional Development and Forgiveness in Children," 130; Freedman, Enright, and Knutson, "A Progress Report on the Process Model of Forgiveness," 393. Freedman et al., use the term "offender" as a synonym in *Handbook of Forgiveness*, 395. Norman S. Care, "Forgiveness and Effective Agency," 215–31, in *Before Forgiving*, at 215; and Walrond-Skinner, "The Function and Role of Forgiveness in Working with Couples and Families," 6.

[77] See, for example, Baker, "Self-Forgiveness: An Empowering and Therapeutic Tool for Working with Women in Recovery," 65; Chagigiorgis and Paivio, "Forgiveness as an Outcome in Emotion-Focused Trauma Therapy," 126; Exline and Zell, "Does a Humble Attitude Promote Forgiveness?" 236; McCullough, Pargament, and Thoresen, "The Psychology of Forgiveness," 8.

psychology, has raised issues that render problematic the exclusive focus on moral harm as the condition for engaging forgiveness. He opens the door to a greater degree of complexity on the question when he observes:

> There are unfortunately many situations—tragic situations—in which the best that one can do is still wrong, has a moral cost that remains to be regretted by the agent and (perhaps) forgiven by the victim. Or, to put it slightly differently, the lesser of two evils may still leave the chosen evil a wrong (an undeserved harm) even while ultimately the right thing to do.[78]

In other words, sometimes the only options available for responsible action are morally problematic, yet we must choose. The morally better choice is the one that would do the lesser moral harm. Does the one who makes such a choice in such conditions require forgiveness? Has she not made the morally responsible choice? However one addresses those specific questions, Neu's scenario introduces into the issue of moral judgment a complexity that is often overlooked. To generalize from the particular situation Neu has raised, we can argue that judgments of the morality or immorality of the harm done rest on a broader range of considerations than the discussions of them sometimes acknowledge.

Some psychologists take the issue of making moral harm the basis for forgiveness further. They argue that forgiveness may be a relevant and legitimate consideration in situations in which the harm done has not been a moral harm (something that should not have been done). Forgiveness, then, can become an issue in any experience of loss (although the examples usually given involve loss in interpersonal relationships arising from someone's choice). For example, Robert Karen observes: "A divorce, even if handled sensitively, even if it comes in later childhood, will likely leave the child feeling somewhat damaged because of the loss of his intact family. The shattering of his external world is reflected in his sense of self—smaller, lacking, less good. There's no escaping such traumas."[79] Even though the divorce might be regarded by an external observer as a legitimate resolution of a bad marriage, even if it is handled in a morally upright manner, for the child the hurt it causes can still be a matter requiring forgiveness. For, as Karen notes, "the legitimate changes of the people we love, like a grown child's moving away or falling in love

---

[78] Neu, "To Understand All Is to Forgive All—Or Is It?" 21.
[79] Karen, *The Forgiving Self*, 47.

with someone else, become not just hurts to be dealt with but the be-ginnings of grudges."[80] The lingering resentment that is the hallmark of such grudges is precisely what forgiveness sets itself to overcome. Thus, from a psychological perspective, these experiences of hurt can become the terrain on which forgiveness needs to be enacted, even in the absence of any ascribable moral fault.[81]

Opening the door to considering non-moral harms as occasions for forgiveness—as some psychologists are doing—changes the landscape of the discussion in two ways. First, it shifts the condition for possibly invoking forgiveness as a legitimate response away from the existence of a (putatively objective?) moral breach toward the cognitive judgment of the person who has experienced the harm. Second, it implicitly (and in some cases explicitly) turns attention to the experience of harm *qua* harm as the necessary and sufficient condition for possibly engaging a forgiveness response. In these emerging approaches the privileged locus of assessment on the suitability of enacting forgiveness in a given circumstance is the way the situation is understood by the one who has experienced the harm. The perception of harm, as harm, and not necessarily the presence of a moral judgment of the harm, is what triggers the possibility that one might respond with forgiveness. In outlining the parameters for forgiving, McCullough and Worthington explain: "interpersonal forgiveness occurs in the context of an individual's perception that the action or actions of another person were noxious, harmful, immoral, or unjust."[82] In their descriptive (rather than definitional) presentation moral harm is implied in the terms "immoral" and "unjust." But these are presented as *possible* kinds of occasions warranting forgiveness, beside two other descriptors (noxious and harmful) that are not morally based.

This more capacious understanding of harm inserts a tension into the discussion of forgiveness. In a way it brings us back to the question of definition. What are we talking about when we discuss forgiveness? Has the definition of forgiveness been watered down to nothing more than "acceptance" of painful situations? Or is something more than mere

---

[80] Ibid., 53.

[81] The psychiatrist Richard Fitzgibbons elaborates a similar case. See Fitzgibbons, "Anger and the Healing Power of Forgiveness," 64–65.

[82] McCullough and Worthington, "Religion and the Forgiving Personality," 1142. A similar perspective is implicit in Michael E. McCullough, et al., "Interpersonal Forgiving in Close Relationships: II. Theoretical Elaboration and Measurement," *Journal of Person-ality and Social Psychology* 75, no. 6 (1998): 1586–1603, at 1587.

acceptance operating in forgiveness? On what basis, if any, is it meaningful to talk about forgiving someone for something that is not morally
blameworthy? And if it is meaningful, where does moral judgment fit
into the discussion? Can the harm that sets the stage for forgiveness as a
possible response really be understood without appeal to moral standards?

Such questions do not admit of easy answers, yet resolving them is
critical to the first part of our quest: the search for a basic understanding
of forgiveness as a human enactment. To address these questions we
will need to dig more deeply into the perspectives beneath the different
understandings of forgiveness and of the harm to which it responds. We
shall take up these questions in part 2.

# Part Two

# Excavations

Our explorations in the landscape of forgiveness have thus far (in part 1) taken us across diverse terrain. Each distinctive discussion—French-Continental Philosophy, Anglo-American Moral Philosophy, and Psychology—has explored the landscape from the perspectives of its own priorities and questions. In the process each has introduced us to aspects of forgiveness that will be important for understanding it as a basic human enactment.

The task we confront now is to dig more deeply into what we have so far explored. Our purpose in doing so will be to name that human enactment. By the end of part 2 we will want to be able to address the question: "What are we doing when we undertake to forgive?"

In order to arrive at an answer to that question we shall begin by revisiting some of the issues raised in part 1, identifying places of agreement and of conflict between the various perspectives we have examined (chap. 4). Understanding what lies beneath those agreements and disagreements—in particular how they disclose points of convergence and divergence in questions, methods, and understanding of the human person confronted with the task of forgiving—will provide us with direction for the next step of our inquiry.

Drawing on the indications that emerge from chapter 4, we shall then undertake the task of constructing a description of the person faced with the question of forgiveness (chap. 5). The question at issue in that chapter will be twofold: examining the nature of the harm that can become an occasion for forgiveness and the nature of the human person such that the event of harm can be experienced *as* harm.

Finally, we shall employ the resources of the analysis in chapter 5 to articulate what one is doing when undertaking to forgive. That is, we shall provide a phenomenological description of forgiveness as a basic human enactment. We shall then test this descriptive account against the problematic issues that surfaced in chapter 4.

Once we have established the viability of this description of forgiveness as a basic human enactment we will have a benchmark against which to assess Christian forgiveness. We will then be able to turn our attention in part 3 to the question of a distinctively Christian forgiveness.

# $\mathcal{C}$hapter 4

# Foundations of Faultlines

## Preliminaries

*I*n part 1 we examined three distinctive approaches to understanding forgiveness: the French-Continental Philosophical, the Anglo-American Philosophical, and the Psychological. As we discovered, there are places of convergence and overlap in many of the discussions, but there are also places of real, profound disagreement. This fact draws our attention to the intriguing truth that there are very clear faultlines in the landscape of forgiveness research. In some of the topics we have examined, the disagreements between authors are so fundamental to their positions they clash like tectonic plates. To concede the issue defining the line of confrontation would be to radically alter how one understands and approaches the meaning of forgiveness itself. Two such faultlines in particular stand out.

The first we can identify in terms of a tension Jacques Derrida names, one woven into the historical fabric of the Judeo-Christian heritage on forgiveness. That heritage presents two contrary visions of forgiveness, one conditional and one unconditional.[1] Derrida privileges the unconditional as "pure" forgiveness.[2] The Anglo-American discussion, by contrast, takes the conditionality of forgiveness for granted. It is diametrically opposed to Derrida's approach.

The course of the faultline does not run as an absolute split between the French-Continental and Anglo-American philosophical discussions; on

---

[1] Jacques Derrida, *On Cosmopolitanism and Forgiveness* (London: Routledge, 2001), 34–35.

[2] We have traced the rationale for this decision in relationship to the larger horizon of Derrida's concerns in chap. 1.

each side of the line we can see gestures toward the other. Paul Ricoeur, for example, feels compelled to draw the "impossible forgiveness" of Derrida into the landscape of conditional forgiveness by arguing for a "very difficult forgiveness." Similarly, some philosophers and some psychologists seem to leave open the possibility of an unconditional (or at least "unilateral") forgiveness.[3] Though this is not exactly the same as Derrida's project, advocates of unilateral forgiveness incline in some respects toward its deeper goals.

The second faultline touches on the morality of forgiveness. Whereas the dominant lines of the first faultline divide the French-Continental and Anglo-American philosophical discussions, the course of the second faultline transects the psychological discussion, leaving some psychologists standing with the Anglo-American philosophers and some opposed. This faultline has to do with the definition of forgiveness in relationship to the moral nature of the harm that evokes the response. Many (not all) Anglo-American philosophers argue that, for forgiveness to be an issue, a real (not imagined or falsely judged, but objective) moral harm must have occurred.[4] If the harm was not a moral one, forgiveness is not an issue. To talk of forgiveness would be a distortion of the concept and an

---

[3] Philosophical support for the possibility of unilateral (sometimes called "unconditional") forgiveness appears in Karen D. Hoffman, "Forgiveness without Apology: Defending Unconditional Forgiveness," *Proceedings of the ACPA* 82 (2009): 135–51; Michele Moody-Adams, "Reply to Griswold, *Forgiveness: A Philosophical Exploration*," *Philosophia* 38 (2010): 429–37; Bernard G. Prusak, "What Are the 'Right Reasons' to Forgive? Critical Reflections on Charles Griswold's *Forgiveness: A Philosophical Exploration*," *Proceedings of the American Catholic Philosophical Association* 82 (2009): 287–95; Kelly Hamilton, "'Hate the Sin but not the Sinner': Forgiveness and Condemnation," *South African Journal of Philosophy* 28, no. 2 (2009): 114–23. Psychological support for unilateral forgiveness appears in Suzanne Freedman, Robert D. Enright, and Jeannette Knutson, "A Progress Report on the Process Model of Forgiveness," 393–406, in *Handbook of Forgiveness*, ed. Everett L. Worthington, Jr. (New York: Routledge, 2005), esp. 393, 400; Étienne Mullet and Michèle Girard, "Developmental and Cognitive Points of View on Forgiveness," 111–32, in *Forgiveness: Theory, Research, and Practice*, ed. Michael E. McCullough, Kenneth I. Pargament, and Carl E. Thoresen (New York: Guilford Press, 2000), at 114, where unconditional forgiveness is seen as the highest expression in a development of the capacity to forgive that is itself grounded in love. See also Harry J. Aponte, "Love, the Spiritual Wellspring of Forgiveness: An Example of Spirituality in Therapy," *Association for Family Therapy and Systemic Practice* 20 (1998): 37–58.

[4] This position is maintained by Jeffrie G. Murphy, Joram Graf Haber, Pamela Hieronymi, and Charles Griswold.

expression of an unacceptable "definitional drift."[5] Many psychologists share this view.[6] Some embrace it in a strong form, absolutely excluding non-moral harm as an issue of forgiveness. Others embrace it in a less definitive manner. They employ language that indicates the acceptance of this understanding as normative. But there are other psychologists who stand opposed to this perspective. They see forgiveness as also extending to non-moral harms, to traumas of various kinds.[7]

These two faultlines pose a serious challenge to our project. We are in search of an understanding of forgiveness as a basic human enactment, one articulated without appeals to any sort of religiously based motivation. The conflicts represented by these faultlines (and some additional issues we will be considering later) indicate that we cannot pursue a course of simple synthesis without running the risk of conceptual incoherence. Alternatively, if we are to sketch out a coherent understanding of forgiveness on the terms we have set for ourselves we must do so in a way that possesses its own integrity. The question is, how?

A closer look at the different positions presented in part 1 suggests a possible way forward. If we look at each of these realms of discourse in isolation from the others, each possesses a kind of integrity in itself. Once we stand on their terrain, within the boundaries they have set for themselves, they exhibit coherence. It is when we stand outside those

---

[5] Robert D. Enright, Suzanne Freedman, and Julio Rique, "The Psychology of Interpersonal Forgiveness," 46–62, in *Exploring Forgiveness*, ed. Robert D. Enright and Joanna North (Madison, WI: University of Wisconsin Press, 1998), at 51.

[6] Among them, ibid., 47, 48; Ann Macaskill, "Just-World Beliefs and Forgiveness in Men and Women," 39–59, in *Women's Reflections on the Complexities of Forgiveness*, ed. Wanda Malcolm, Nancy DeCourville, and Kathryn Belicki (New York: Routledge, 2008), at 42, 55.

[7] These include Paul W. Coleman, "The Process of Forgiveness in Marriage and the Family," 74–94, in *Exploring Forgiveness*, at 88–89; Susanne A. Denham et al., "Emotional Development and Forgiveness in Children: Emerging Evidence," 127–42, in *Handbook of Forgiveness*, ed. Everett L. Worthington, Jr. (New York: Routledge, 2005), at 127–29, who speak of injury and loss as occasions of potential forgiveness without identifying the necessity of moral harm as basis for that experience. Likewise Julie Juola Exline and Anne L. Zell, "Does a Humble Attitude Promote Forgiveness? Challenges, Caveats, and Sex Differences," 235–51, in *Women's Reflections on the Complexities of Forgiveness*, at 236; Julie Juola Exline and Roy F. Baumeister, "Expressing Forgiveness and Repentance: Benefits and Barriers," 133–55, in *Forgiveness: Theory, Research, and Practice*, at 135; and Jennie G. Noll, "Forgiveness in People Experiencing Trauma," 363–75, in *Handbook of Forgiveness*, at 364, 371, who discuss forgiveness in relationship to the experience of trauma.

boundaries and question them from a different location in the landscape of forgiveness that we discover difficulties, what appear to be flaws or limitations. Why is this so? Why this double perspective?

The answer begins to emerge when we examine the ways in which the boundaries of discourse are constructed. Each discourse operates according to presuppositions, values, interpretations of data, and methods of analysis that make sense among those who accept the terms of that discourse. They are shared by the participants in the discussion. The differences in the deeper structures of the elements that ground each discourse also explain the incompatibilities that emerge between them. Even when members of the same community disagree with one another, they do so on the basis of a common ground that is sufficiently shared so that they can understand one another. But when the basic, often unspoken principles and methods of one community are sufficiently alien to the principles and methods of another, or when a group within a community undergoes a sufficiently radical reorientation and realignment of its principles, common understanding breaks down. The ideas of the distinct communities become mutually unintelligible, or at least unpersuasive.[8]

Charles Taylor provides a useful image for understanding this phenomenon: a multistory building. The basement of the building corre-

---

[8] This phenomenon has been observed and analyzed extensively over the past half century. Johannes Baptist Metz, *Christliche Anthropozentrik: Über die Denkform des Thomas von Aquin* (Munich: Kösel, 1962), drawing on and revising Hans Leisegang's work on "Denkformen" (Hans Leisegang, *Denkformen* [Berlin: de Gruyter, 1928], republished in expanded form as Hans Leisegang, *Denkformen* [Berlin: de Gruyter, 1951]), adapted the concept of thoughtform to account for epochal shifts in basic principles governing our understanding of being and our relationship to it. Thomas S. Kuhn, *The Structure of Scientific Revolutions* (Chicago: University of Chicago Press, 1962) provides an account of paradigm changes in scientific research. The basic argument supports the point being made here. Bernard Lonergan's *Insight: A Study of Human Understanding* (London: Darton, Longman, and Todd, 1957) offers a penetrating analysis of the bases of this phenomenon in terms of cognitional theory. He also expands on the significance of fundamental presuppositions for how we pose questions and our methodological assumptions in Bernard Lonergan, "The Transition from a Classicist World-View to Historical-Mindedness," 1–10, in *A Second Collection*, ed. William F. J. Ryan and Bernard J. Tyrrell (Toronto: University of Toronto Press, 1974). More recently Charles Taylor's magisterial *A Secular Age* (Cambridge, MA: Belknap Press of Harvard Univ. Press, 2007) performs a philosophical-historical exegesis of secularity and secularism that illustrates the emergence of modern secularity as a function of profound shifts in the presuppositions governing our thinking about ourselves and our world.

sponds to convictions and attitudes that are so thoroughly taken for granted, so deeply encoded into the metaphors and language we use to make sense of anything, that they are not even recognized as subject to critique,[9] yet they are heavily correlated with later theoretical explanations of "factual matters."[10] Because the "basement" convictions are presumed to be beyond question they provide a methodologically secure warrant for the second-story analysis used to explain and justify the interpretation of the ground-floor "facts."

Taylor's use of this image illustrates an important point. When making an argument or presenting an idea we must justify it on a theoretical

---

[9] Taylor develops this image in chap. 12 of *A Secular Age*, using it to illustrate, in successive layers, the depths of embeddedness of various discourses regarding the nature and emergence of secularity and the manner in which their higher theoretical claims are predicated on other claims taken for granted by a given worldview, but, from another perspective are questionable. He observes: "It turns out that basement and higher floor are intimately linked; that is, that the explanation one gives for the declines registered by 'secularization' relate closely to one's picture of the place of religion today. This is hardly surprising; any explanation in history takes as its background a certain view of the gamut of human motivations, in whose context the particular explanatory theses make sense. For instance, various 'materialist' accounts, for whom religion is always 'superstructure,' its forms always to be explained by, say, economic structures and processes, are in effect denying any independent efficacy to religious aspirations. They are asserting for all time what I have just claimed mainline secularization seems to be saying about the modern age. Thus one very important focus of disagreement, even among those who are together on the ground floor, arises from their respective pictures of the upper story, which must also set them at odds in the historically explanatory basement. This to a large extent underlies the historical disputes I alluded to above" (*A Secular Age*, 433).

[10] Postmodern thought approaches this topic in its critique of "meta-narratives." See, for example, Jean-François Lyotard, *The Postmodern Condition: A Report on Knowledge*, trans. Geoff Bennington and Brian Massumi (Minneapolis: University of Minnesota Press, 1979); idem, *The Differend: Phrases in Dispute*, trans. Georges Van Den Abbeele (Minneapolis: University of Minnesota Press, 1988); Lieven Boeve, *Interrupting Tradition: An Essay on Christian Faith in a Postmodern Context*, Louvain Theological & Pastoral Monographs 30 (Leuven: Peeters, 2003); Stanley J. Grenz and John R. Franke, *Beyond Foundationalism: Shaping Theology in a Postmodern Context* (Louisville: Westminster John Knox, 2001). The emphasis in postmodern thought is on the way meta-narratives occlude questions and insights that might otherwise arise by delegitimating them or limiting the imagination. The discussion therefore is quite critical of meta-narrative. Taylor, by contrast, without denying legitimacy to some of the concerns in that discussion, recognizes that, epistemologically, some sort of foundational narrative will be operative in the "basement" of any common discourse. It is the necessary foundation both for shared understanding and for the "interruption" that is so favored by those critical of meta-narrative.

basis by aligning information in relationship to the matter in question. The choice of information to use, the manner in which we organize it, and the criteria according to which we judge that we have arrived at an adequate demonstration of the point all depend on the range of meanings we take to be established.

The issue of "meanings" is pivotal. The image of the building makes intuitively obvious what, in a more nuanced manner, we can analyze in terms of "matrices of meanings."

The phrase "matrix/matrices of meanings" requires some explanation. Taylor employs the idea of a matrix to name corporately and in their interrelationships the various components/ideas/ influences that interact to produce a given development or shift in awareness.[11] A matrix suggests a flexible but relatively stable set of components that give rise to and/or situate other developments, in this case the emergence of new assumptions or presuppositions that shape our view of the world and our place in it. The interrelationships of the constitutive components can undergo realignment in light of new factors coming into play, thereby producing new effects (understandings).

In what follows I will distinguish three interrelated levels of matrices: *shared matrices of meanings*, which correspond roughly to the common-sense or accepted "truths" on which other understandings are developed; *personal matrices*, which correspond to the "sense of self" of the individual and participate in the shared matrix of one's milieu but are modified in the light of individual experience; and *specific matrices*, which are the relatively stable constellations of meanings one brings together to resolve a cognitive lacuna (answer a question or solve a problem).

When we speak of "meanings" in this context, some further clarifications are in order. First, "meanings" as the term is used here is not restricted to "ideas" or "concepts." Rather, the term embraces the whole range of affective, cognitional, valuational, historical, and relational elements of our conscious and unconscious life and the dynamic interactions we have with them as we construct our understanding of the world and what encounters us in it. Second, meanings do not exist in isolation. The singular term "meaning" is a limit concept. It has a heuristic function in

---

[11] See, for example, Taylor, *A Secular Age*, 61, 149–50, 155, 183, 295, etc. For further detail on this notion of a matrix of meanings, see James K. Voiss, "Thought Forms and Theological Constructs: Toward Grounding the Appeal to Experience in Contemporary Theological Discourse," 241–56, in *Encountering Transcendence*, ed. Lieven Boeve, Hans Beybels, and Stijn van den Bossche (Leuven: Peeters, 2005).

that it directs our attention to a conceptual center of gravity. But that center itself is grasped only in its interrelationship with and distinction from a broad range of other interrelated meanings, a matrix.[12]

Third, as the argument Taylor is making in *A Secular Age* illustrates, meanings are not static or absolutely stable.[13] They can change, develop, shift in their associations. If the association with a particular "meaning" undergoes a radical transformation, the larger web of its interrelationships is affected by the shift in the center of gravity. For example, before the Third Reich the swastika was originally a Hindu sign of goodness. The appropriation of the symbol to the Nazi agenda has radically altered the center of gravity of the symbol's meaning. This brief sketch of matrices of meanings (we will expand upon it as we proceed) provides us with a tool for understanding and analyzing the situation named above, the experience that from within a given discourse the arguments hold together, but when we look at the discourse from a different set of presuppositions or with a different set of questions the coherence is less evident. Communities of shared discourse, after all, inhabit a common space defined by a shared matrix of meanings.[14] Some aspects of their shared matrices are so deeply ingrained in their categories of thought, the questions they

[12] The nature of the interrelationship of meanings has been theorized in different ways. Derrida's system of "differences" owes much to Saussure's structuralism. Others have developed the idea of the meanings of words in terms of "binary oppositions" of terms. A common element in this approach to meanings has been to emphasize the distinction or difference between terms. I would like to suggest the need to complement this understanding by one that can find its justification in psychoanalytic analyses of the human unconscious: associations. Meanings are also constituted via the associations or linkages we make among terms, concepts, and the realities they name. This observation has important methodological implications. Especially when we are dealing with an issue of human living, it suggests that efforts to define the concept naming that issue by exclusion of difference (seeking a "pure" or "true" specification of the concept) intrinsically falsifies the concept. It extracts a clear concept by extricating it from the associations that give the issue its reality. I see this as a problem in Derrida as well as in the Anglo-American philosophical approaches. On this score I believe the psychologists are nearer to the mark when they recognize a broader range of connections. But the point is that the meaning of the reality identified by the term is not best captured by a definition that excludes whatever is not convenient.

[13] This is why I prefer the image of a matrix of meanings to the notion of a paradigm or the image of a house; it incorporates the tension between relative stability and fluctuations or changes over time more effectively.

[14] The identification of a matrix of meanings as "shared" does not indicate univocal understanding or complete uniformity in acceptance of all the constitutive meanings

ask, and the ways they approach their questions (methods of inquiry) that they remain unthematic (implicit, not articulated) "givens." They function as the basement of the building. What is erected upon them therefore presupposes the shared foundations, acts upon them, and—either explicitly or implicitly—confirms them.

Two immediate consequences flow from this mutual correlation of explicit and implicit, of presuppositions and analyses, within a given community of shared discourse. First, to those who "dwell" within the building (share the matrix of meanings) the terms of its construction make sense because the foundations are presupposed. But second, to those who do not inhabit this space, or now inhabit a house built on other foundations, the first house appears unstable. To an outsider the arguments presented presuppose premises that are not obvious, but rather must be demonstrated. In other words, from outside the shared matrix, if pressed enough, an argument can take on the appearance of circular reasoning, even of "question begging."

Thinking of the faultlines in the discussions as reflecting different matrices of meanings can help us as we move forward with our project. Initially it helps to explain the "double vision" described above. The perspective we hold with respect to a given presentation of forgiveness will be a reflection of our relationship to the shared matrix of meanings on which the position is based. If we share most of the presuppositions, the position will more or less make sense. If we do not, it will not. The image of matrices of meanings also helps us to understand why, up to this point, there has been little fruitful dialogue across the boundaries represented by the two faultlines. Those occupying significantly different matrices of meaning, even when seeking to talk about "the same" phenomenon, can be reduced to gaping at one another across the faultline in mutual incomprehension.

Beyond this, thinking of the faultlines as reflecting distinctive matrices of meanings also suggests a direction and some limitations for our own project. It will not be our task to "define" forgiveness, although in the course of our inquiry an operative definition may emerge. We are also not setting out to "prove" someone else's perspective "wrong," although we may well disagree with it on specific points. Rather, our task in part 2 will be to find a way to name forgiveness as a human enactment inde-

---

involved. It suggests, rather, a sufficiently common fund of meanings appropriated by those who share it in a sufficiently common way to enable communication.

pendently of appeals to religious presuppositions, but to do so in a way that others can recognize as having merit, as correlating with their own experience. We are not attempting to define, but to describe the dynamics of forgiveness as such. In other words, we will be attempting to sketch out a matrix of meanings in relationship to our own question while drawing on insights gained by our examination of discussions already under way.

To accomplish our task, given the conflicting approaches evident in the faultlines, we will have to do some excavation at key points on the terrain of each discussion. We will need to uncover the embedded assumptions, their interrelated values and methods, and their limitations *from the perspective of our questions.* In other words, our task is to construct the specific matrix of meanings that responds to our questions and to present it in relationship to a broader matrix of shared meanings we will elaborate as we proceed.

In the present chapter we shall direct our attention to excavating the reasons why the various positions on either side of each faultline appear to exhibit the kind of "circularity" mentioned above. These will point us to aspects of the human experience we will need to take into account in our own formulation of forgiveness. We will also make note of related issues as they impinge either on our method of proceeding or on frequently recurring disagreements besides those represented by the faultlines.

In chapter 5 we shall probe more deeply into the nature of the one for whom forgiveness is a question, the one Ricoeur called the "capable agent." This focus on the human person as the "subjective" pole of the experience of forgiveness will necessarily be balanced with an analysis of the phenomenon that gives rise to the need for forgiveness, the experience of harm.

With these elements in place, in chapter 6 we shall spell out our understanding of forgiveness as a basic human enactment. We will examine whether it meets the criteria derived from chapters 4 and 5, and we will reflect on its status with respect to some of the open questions raised by our inquiry up to that point.

### The First Faultline: Conditional or Unconditional Forgiveness?

The first of our two faultlines appears under different headings. It is the disagreement about whether forgiveness is to be unconditional or conditional. The most evident conflict along this faultline places the French-Continental discussion (unconditional) in opposition to the Anglo-American and much of the psychological (conditional). (Evidence of this opposition also appears in the language of "pure" forgiveness [Derrida] versus discussions of "true" forgiveness among the Anglo-American and psychological sources.[15]) However, drawing the contrast too strongly in terms of these camps is somewhat misleading. As we saw in chapter 1, Paul Ricoeur's analysis of forgiveness can be aligned with those who see forgiveness as conditional, and among those in the Anglo-American and psychological camps we find some who advocate what is also called "unilateral" forgiveness.[16] Unilateral forgiveness is contrasted with a forgiveness worked out interrelationally, under the condition that victim and offender are in communication with one another about the event and its status.[17]

---

[15] See, for example, Jeffrie G. Murphy, *Getting Even: Forgiveness and Its Limits* (New York: Oxford University Press, 2003), 84. Griswold contrasts ideal with non-ideal enactments of forgiveness in relationship to his proposed paradigm in his *Forgiveness: A Philosophical Exploration* (Cambridge: Cambridge University Press, 2007), 113–33. Joram Haber raises questions about the utility of the distinction between forgiveness and true forgiveness in theories that equate forgiveness with the overcoming of resentment in his *Forgiveness* (Savage, MD: Rowman & Littlefield, 1991), 21–22. However, in his pursuit of a better grounding for judgments regarding forgiveness he is positively implicated in the concern for what constitutes "true" forgiveness and how one can know it. See also Jeffrie G. Murphy, "Forgiveness in Counseling: A Philosophical Perspective," 41–53, in *Before Forgiving: Cautionary Views of Forgiveness in Psychotherapy*, ed. Sharon Lamb and Jeffrie G. Murphy (New York: Oxford University Press, 2002), at 49; Varda Konstam et al., "Forgiveness in Practice: What Mental Health Counselors Are Telling Us," 54–71, in *Before Forgiving*, at 63; Coleman, "The Process of Forgiveness in Marriage and the Family," 79. On "pseudo-forgiveness" in the psychological literature, see Denham et al., "Emotional Development and Forgiveness in Children," 129–30; Freedman, Enright, and Knutson, "A Progress Report on the Process Model of Forgiveness," 394; Sue Walrond-Skinner, "The Function and Role of Forgiveness in Working with Couples and Families: Clearing the Ground," *Journal of Family Therapy* 20 (1998): 3–19, at 11–12; James N. Sells and Terry D. Hargrave, "Forgiveness: A Review of the Theoretical and Empirical Literature," *Journal of Family Therapy* 20 (1998): 21–36, at 25, citing Ellen Bass and Laura Davis, *The Courage to Heal: A Guide for Women Survivors of Child Sexual Abuse* (New York: HarperCollins, 1994), 162 and 164.

[16] Both Griswold and Haber mention unilateral forgiveness. Haber maintains that forgiveness is unilateral. Griswold sees this as conceptually coherent only within very clearly defined restrictions. Such an expression of forgiveness would be conceivable in relationship to "forgiving the dead," but only in the "subjunctive mode." That is, forgiveness would be in the mode of a hope about what might be if the circumstances were different. See Charles L. Griswold, *Forgiveness: A Philosophical Exploration*, 120–22; and Haber, *Forgiveness*, 11. See also Freedman, Enright, and Knutson, "A Progress Report on the Process Model of Forgiveness," 400.

[17] Advocates of this approach include Griswold (*Forgiveness: A Philosophical Exploration*); Lamb ("Women, Abuse, and Forgiveness: A Special Case," 155–71, in *Before*

Unilateral forgiveness, therefore, even when discussed by Anglo-American philosophers and psychologists, resembles the unconditional forgiveness of the French-Continental philosophical discussion.

The contrast between conditional and unconditional forgiveness is not new. As indicated above, Derrida points to its presence in the Abrahamic traditions from which many contemporary Western understandings take their starting point. Where one stands in relationship to these two options determines one's position with respect to the faultline. In what follows we shall look at positions on each side of the divide, but we shall do so as outsiders. We shall identify specific points that are integral to each presentation and that from within their matrices of meanings are "self-evident" but from an outside perspective require demonstration. In other words, we shall look for and dig beneath points in the presentations that from an outsider's perspective appear to exhibit circular reasoning. We shall begin with Derrida's discussion of "pure" forgiveness as paradigmatic of unconditional forgiveness before turning to various articulations of conditional forgiveness among the Anglo-American philosophers.

### Unconditional Forgiveness: Derrida's Pursuit of Purity

Jacques Derrida's deconstructive analysis of forgiveness is of a piece with his larger ethical concerns. In *On Cosmopolitanism and Forgiveness* he makes it clear that he is troubled by overly facile political appropriation of the language of forgiveness.[18] The "universalzation" of the Abrahamic language and concept(s) of forgiveness threatens to eviscerate the very meaning of the term. Moreover, this globalization of forgiveness language and its deployment on large scales and small is often at the service of another end. This, Derrida maintains, renders both the concept and the enactment something other than pure forgiveness.

> I shall risk this proposition: each time forgiveness is at the service of a finality, be it noble and spiritual (atonement or redemption, reconciliation, salvation), each time that it aims to re-establish a normality (social, national, political, psychological) by a work of mourning, by some therapy or ecology of memory, then the "forgiveness" is not

---

*Forgiving*, at 166); Bill Puka ("Forgoing Forgiveness," 136–52, in *Before Forgiving*, 145, 149, 151); and Miroslav Volf (*The End of Memory: Remembering Rightly in a Violent World* [Grand Rapids: Eerdmans, 2006], 205).

[18] Derrida, *On Cosmopolitanism and Forgiveness*, 27–28.

pure—nor is its concept. Forgiveness is not, it *should not be*, normal, normative, normalising. It *should* remain exceptional and extraordinary, in the face of the impossible: as if it interrupted the ordinary course of historical temporality.[19]

Derrida has therefore set himself the task of understanding forgiveness in such a way that it cannot be perverted by deployment for political ends, economic exchange, or any other finality, not even to achieve reconciliation!

To support this formulation Derrida engages in a phenomenological pursuit of the "thing itself," the purity of forgiveness, its essence, and plays this "pure" forgiveness off against any conditioned expression. In part this involves a process of excluding the conceptual and pragmatic considerations that normally attend what we mean when we use the term. In this Derrida is very thorough. (We have seen this process already at work in the exposition of his treatments of hospitality and of the gift.) He calls into question any kind of intention for the deployment of forgiveness, as the statement above indicates. In a manner reminiscent of his exclusion of symbolic exchange in the giving of a gift, he also brackets from our awareness any knowledge or memory of the forgiveness.[20] If it is to be "pure," forgiveness cannot be known as such.

Derrida then employs his analysis of the concept to deconstruct it. This appeal to the aporetic structure of the concept of forgiveness serves a strategic role in relationship to the pursuit of an ethics beyond ethics: the grounding of responsible action. It destabilizes its presumed comprehensibility. This serves to eliminate any firm conceptual grasp on forgiveness that would enable it to be deployed according to one's own convenience or any ulterior motives (such as he perceives in the political use of the term). As a consequence, when faced with a harmful event one is left with a choice that cannot be resolved by appeal to ethical principles. One must make a *responsible* choice, a choice for which one is accountable.

Unfortunately, according to the logical strictures imposed by the aporiae and the requirements of purity, such an act is impossible. Our know-

---

[19] Ibid., 31–32.

[20] Ernesto Verdeja examines the problems with this aspect of Derrida's understanding of forgiveness in Ernesto Verdeja, "Derrida and the Impossibility of Forgiveness," *Contemporary Political Theory* 30, no. 1 (April 2004): 23–47. He applies Derrida's argument on the necessity of an absolute forgetting if there is to be a gift to the question of forgiveness. See Derrida, *Given Time: 1. Counterfeit Money*, trans. Peggy Kamuf (Chicago: University of Chicago Press, 1992), 16.

ing and choosing are necessary to the historical enactment of forgiveness. But through our knowing, our act falsifies what forgiveness purports to make real. And yet, without that knowing and intending, and without memory of the event to which it is extended, we would not be moved to deploy forgiveness. Hence, for Derrida, forgiveness ("if there is such a thing") is impossible, but if it were to be possible it would only be in relationship to the unforgivable, an event of such horror and offense to humanity that it places itself outside the realm of ethics. No ethical rules or norms can address it. By its nature, *this* kind of offense (the unforgivable) is such that forgiveness *might* be evoked as a responsible answer to the crime committed. Such an event calls for responsibility within the rupture of ethical norms in a context in which no economic exchange can be anticipated.

From within the terrain bounded by Derrida's deconstructive analysis this presentation possesses coherence. It hangs together. But when we approach it from the standpoint of our question regarding forgiveness as a human enactment, problems emerge. The most immediately obvious is the conflict in our starting points. We are asking about forgiveness in terms of human enactment, precisely the aspect that Derrida's analysis renders "impossible." At first glance this would seem to suggest that we must choose between Derrida and our own question. Either we stand with Derrida in the pursuit of a "pure" forgiveness that invalidates our inquiry from the start, or we ignore Derrida and "settle" for conditional forgiveness of "venial sin" (minor offenses) in which, according to Derrida, "the very idea of forgiveness would disappear."[21]

But if we examine Derrida's position more closely, as outsiders who do not share all of Derrida's presuppositions, questions surface, questions about the warrant for the claims of "purity" and the nature of the "pure" forgiveness at the heart of Derrida's argument. His use of both these terms requires closer examination, for from our outsider's perspective they are the loci of the appearance of circularity in his argument.

Derrida's use of the term "pure" in relationship to forgiveness is especially intriguing. He links this concept with the unconditional strand of the Abrahamic tradition. "Pure" forgiveness is absolutely unconditional, in his view. More precisely, the "pure" concept of forgiveness requires that there be no conditions on it.[22] But is the exclusive ascription of "purity"

---

[21] Derrida, *On Cosmopolitanism and Forgiveness*, 32.
[22] Ibid., 31–32.

to absolutely unconditional forgiveness warranted? On what basis does the claim that conditional forgiveness is not "pure" rest?

It appears that Derrida has imported into his preference for one strand of the Abrahamic tradition a value-laden concept derived from Greek philosophical thought, a concept that is quite alien to the Abrahamic tradition. The idea of "purity" Derrida has associated with an unconditional forgiveness reflects a kind of Platonic preference for the concept, abstracted from any conditions of its instantiation. The "pure" concept is unsullied by intercourse with finite reality. It *must*, therefore (*ex supposito*), stand opposed to any conditional expressions.

Whether this oppositional relationship between the two strands of the tradition is the only and therefore necessary reading is an open question. But for the present it is important to note that this reading of "pure" forgiveness carries with it an embedded value judgment, a premise about the status of conditional forgiveness. Yet this premise—that conditional forgiveness is not "pure" and that it does not even merit the name "forgiveness"—is precisely the point that needs to be demonstrated. The use of the term "pure," deployed according to an understanding that privileges the conceptual over the actual, effectively loads the dice against conditional forgiveness and imports into the discussion in a disguised manner the very conditions of impossibility that Derrida "discovers" there.

To approach the issue from a different angle, we are raising a question about the legitimacy of Derrida's understanding of forgiveness at the most basic level. Is it legitimate to sunder a concept of "pure" forgiveness from the conditions of its possible enactment, to elevate that concept to the ideal, and then to claim that what does not meet the ideal—precisely because it must be enacted according to conditions intrinsic to human functioning—is therefore not forgiveness? From the perspective of the question we are raising in this study (and of those standing on the other side of the faultline), such a position does not make sense.

The second term we need to examine is Derrida's understanding of forgiveness itself. It is intriguing to note that Derrida does not define what he means by the term. He appears to operate on the assumption that it is commonly understood. Two aspects of his treatment of forgiveness suggest what he understands to be the basic content of the concept. First, he recognizes and takes for granted that forgiveness arises as an issue in response to an experience of harm. Given his argument that only the unforgivable is the appropriate object of forgiveness, one could also surmise that the harm must be very great, that the perpetrator of the harm is morally responsible for it, and that it stands outside the bounds of the ordinary rules of morality.[23] Second, the consequence of forgiveness—or the definition of its nature?—is a restoration of relations among those alienated by the offense, relations identical to those that existed before its occurrence. This restoration is to be so complete—if it is to be pure—that neither the offense nor the forgiving of it remains in memory.[24]

According to these prescriptions, for Derrida forgiveness would seem to be a state of relatedness in which relations had been restored. But the understanding of forgiveness in terms of the "purity" Derrida advocates requires that we conceive of this restoration apart from the conditions that would be necessary for its enactment.[25] "Pure" forgiveness is conceived as a static state: a state of having been forgiven and of having forgiven, preserved in its purity by loss of memory of all conditions surrounding it. This understanding of forgiveness, consequently, defines it in terms that make it unlike anything one would ordinarily understand by the word. It removes forgiveness from the realm of human interaction by abstracting it from the normal media of human relationship. Thus the state of relatedness named by forgiveness (according to the implications of Derrida's discussion) would be amnesiac, a-historical, and a-relational. It would be impossible.

Once again, the question of circular reasoning arises. Is it legitimate to an understanding of forgiveness to conceive it as a state of (a-relational) relatedness apart from the human enactments that would bring it about? Derrida takes the legitimacy as given, even as the "meta-condition" of purity. From outside Derrida's matrix of meanings, however, it appears that he has imported into the discussion as concealed premises what his argument ought to have demonstrated, namely: that it is valid to talk about forgiveness at all in a way that so significantly revises its meaning.

These observations on Derrida's understanding of "pure" forgiveness bring to light an issue we will need to address later in part 2. When naming forgiveness, how do we resolve the tension in understanding that

---

[23] In fact, this point is underscored by Derrida's (ill-conceived) appeal to the concept of "mortal sin." See ibid., 32–33.

[24] Ernesto Verdeja explores this issue in Derrida's thought. See Verdeja, "Derrida and the Impossibility of Forgiveness," esp. 32–33. His analysis builds on the necessity of forgiving outlined by Derrida in the discussion of the Gift in Derrida, *Given Time: 1. Counterfeit Money*, 16.

[25] On this point Derrida follows the conditions for forgiveness developed by Jankélévitch. Forgiveness "happens" (if it happens) as an event: spontaneously, unplanned, unexpectedly. It possesses the characteristics of time itself. See Vladimir Jankélévitch, *Forgiveness*, trans. Andrew Kelly (Chicago: University of Chicago Press, 2005).

arises between the "pure" *concept* of forgiveness and what it purports to name? What is the relationship between concept and referent? Does the "pure" concept express the ideal meaning over against the experience? To embrace this perspective would be to adopt a kind of Platonic idealism, one that implicitly bears the judgment that finite expressions of the idea are always less perfect (and therefore less good) than the ideal. Alternatively, one could locate the truth of the term in the particular experience(s) in a way that holds the concepts to be accountable to that experience of the contingent and particular. We shall hold these questions in abeyance for now as we turn our attention to the other side of the faultline.

### Conditional Forgiveness: Anglo-American "True" Forgiveness

If Derrida has staked out the terrain of unconditionality for the discussion of forgiveness and has elided that with the concept of "purity," the Anglo-American philosophical approach has embraced conditionality as a given in the discussion, thereby placing itself on the opposite side of the faultline. It has concerned itself with the conditions necessary to arrive at "true" forgiveness. This contrast in terms is telling. "Pure" forgiveness defines itself in relationship to an ideal removed from the conditioning aspects of its enactment. "True" forgiveness measures itself, by way of contrast, with the adequacy of any enactment to meeting the conditions considered necessary to its fulfillment. This latter approach opens the door to variability in the satisfaction of the requirements of forgiveness, and therefore to varying degrees of conformity to that truth, however defined.[26] Here the "ideal" (or "paradigmatic") expression of forgiveness is identified with "true" forgiveness, but other, less complete expressions are (often) acknowledged as being within the scope of forgiveness.[27] The philosophers we examined in chapter 2 share many common concerns. Most evident is their interest in clarifying the moral conditions under which forgiveness can legitimately be enacted. This common concern leads each to identify what they perceive to be limitations in the analyses that have preceded their own interventions. They therefore set out what they see to be the practical consequences and necessary responses to the requirements of morality that, in their perspectives, have not yet been adequately satisfied. In further contrast to the discussion on the opposite side of the faultline, they also devote con-

---

[26] The question of degrees of fulfillment, and therefore of greater or lesser expressions of forgiveness so long as minimal conditions have been met receives extensive attention in Griswold, *Forgiveness: A Philosophical Exploration*, esp. 113–33.

[27] Ibid.

siderable attention to the role of affective, cognitive, rational, and relational dynamics in the process of forgiving and in assessing the morality of the enactment of forgiveness. In other words, in contrast to the unconditional side of the faultline, the Anglo-American discussion places human agency at the center of the discussion.

On the basis of the common ground just identified we can say that the philosophers we examined in chapter 2 operate on the same landscape; they make their arguments on the basis of a (largely) shared matrix of meanings. The differences between their approaches, however, while sharing many "basement-level" convictions, give evidence that other factors are at work. They do not, after all, arrive at the same conclusions. Each author approaches the topic of forgiveness from a distinctive perspective that could be called a "personal matrix of meanings."[28] This personal matrix holds many of its basic assumptions, values, and methods in common with the larger shared matrix but adapts them in light of the specific personal concerns of the individual author. Each author then analyzes the problems, formulates a question, and constructs a resolution (a *specific matrix of meanings*) in accord with the criteria internal to the personal matrix and consonant with what will be acceptable to those who participate in the shared matrix.

As with Derrida's perspective, so also with the Anglo-American authors we have examined: from within their personal matrices of meanings their arguments hold together. The specific matrices they construct to address the problems they identify possess integrity, but when one approaches them as an outsider that integrity can take on the appearance of circular reasoning. In what follows we will focus our attention on points of apparent circularity in the arguments of three of those authors, Murphy, Haber, and Griswold.[29] In so doing we will pay special attention to the way in which each specifies the conditions necessary for "true" forgiveness.[30]

---

[28] As indicated above, a "personal matrix of meanings" is the appropriation of a shared matrix by an individual, as that appropriation has been modified in the light of individual experience. It can be identified with the "sense of self" we will be exploring in the next chapter. It is distinguished from a "specific matrix of meanings" in that it constitutes the resources on which someone draws in seeking to make sense of the world or to resolve a question. The meanings brought to bear in resolving a question, and recognized as having resolved the question, constitute a "specific matrix of meanings."

[29] Hieronymi's presentation, perhaps because briefer than the others, does not exhibit a circularity distinctive to her particular project.

[30] The language of "true" forgiveness is not universally employed, but the conceptual content entailed in the phrase is consistently present as a driving concern in each author, even where not explicitly named.

## Jeffrie Murphy and "Moral Reasons" to Forgive

Jeffrie Murphy's discussion of forgiveness draws our attention to the role of our feelings, particularly resentment, as presenting occasions for forgiveness. Drawing on Bishop Butler's analysis but refining it further, he defines forgiveness (as we saw in chap. 2) as "forgoing resentment *for moral reasons.*" This emphasis is integral to Murphy's understanding of forgiveness as a moral enactment. Murphy understands forgiveness to be a virtue. If one forgives for immoral reasons, forgiveness ceases to be a virtue, a praiseworthy action.[31] It therefore ceases to be forgiveness. The definition of virtue, the understanding of forgiveness in relationship to resentment, and the requirement of moral reasons interrelate to support the definition of forgiveness.

But from the perspective of our question, this definition itself exhibits hints of circularity. Joram Haber gets at the key issues when he critiques Murphy's understanding of virtue and his inclusion of moral grounds in the definition of forgiveness itself.[32] From the perspective of forgiveness as a virtue Haber points out, contra Murphy, that a virtue is still a virtue when practiced for immoral reasons; it just does not count as one. (Courage is still courage even when practiced by a criminal in the pursuit of criminal ends. It just does not count as morally praiseworthy in those circumstances. But the nature of courage as a virtue has not changed.) Murphy's understanding of virtue as only deployable in accord with moral motivations is necessary if he is to circumscribe forgiveness within his moral theory. To guarantee that forgiveness is a moral enactment governed by moral requirements, he conceives it under the category of virtue. But he must also specify that a virtue can only be deployed according to moral requirements, else it ceases to be a virtue. By this reasoning "forgiveness" deployed not according to moral reasoning is not forgiveness. It is something else.[33]

This argument secures the topic of forgiveness for moral philosophy, but it does so in a manner that appears circular outside this matrix of meanings. Haber draws our attention to a pivotal issue in the circularity of Murphy's position when he observes: "But surely we *can* forgive in

---

[31] Haber takes issue with this argument in his *Forgiveness* (Savage, MD: Rowman & Littlefield, 1991), 17.

[32] Ibid., 5–6.

[33] See, for example, Jeffrie G. Murphy and Jean Hampton, *Forgiveness and Mercy* (Cambridge: Cambridge University Press, 1988), 20.

the absence of a moral reason; we can even forgive for no reason at all. And we can do so without conceptual confusion."[34] In point of fact, many people claim to do so. Murphy's approach would charge them with being involved in something other than forgiveness. The warrant for this charge is intrasystematic, relying on acceptance of the matrix of meanings specified by Murphy (or one sufficiently similar).

A second locus of circularity appears in Murphy's understanding of the nature of resentment in relationship to the definition of forgiveness. Murphy defines forgiveness as the forgoing of resentment for moral reasons, but only on condition that the resentment itself is first morally justified. The focus of his argument is to distinguish forgiveness from excusing and justifying.[35] However, the logic involved suggests a wider scope to the point being made. He claims that "we may forgive only what it is initially proper to resent; and, if a person has done nothing wrong or was not responsible for what he did, there is *nothing to resent*."[36] The issue we need to raise here is how to define what it is proper to resent.[37] Murphy tells us that resentment is only proper when it "is directed toward *responsible wrongdoing*; and therefore, if forgiveness and resentment are to have any arena, it must be where such wrongdoing remains intact."[38]

This definition of resentment fits well with Murphy's understanding of forgiveness as a virtue. It also supports his desire to locate the discussion of forgiveness within moral philosophy. But the argument must presuppose the assertion of the moral restriction on resentment in order to secure the understanding of forgiveness as a virtue. At the same time it must presuppose Murphy's understanding of forgiveness as a virtue

---

[34] Haber, *Forgiveness*, 6.

[35] Murphy and Hampton, *Forgiveness and Mercy*, 20.

[36] Ibid., 20 (emphasis in original).

[37] The problem of judging what is proper to resent parallels another difficulty in the argument, the judgment of what constitutes a moral reason. Murphy and Haber disagree on this issue, as we saw in chap. 2. Murphy's moral reasons allow for considering the history of relationship and other factors. Haber requires that one have explicitly repented and apologized, regardless of other relational factors. When it comes to making a moral determination about forgiveness, both criteria and locus of judgment become crucial.

[38] Murphy and Hampton, *Forgiveness and Mercy*, 20 (emphasis in original). This reasoning is likewise supported by the arguments of Haber and Griswold. See, for example, Haber, *Forgiveness*, 6, 32–40, and the discussion of resentment as a moral sentiment in Griswold, *Forgiveness: A Philosophical Exploration*, 26.

in order to impose the requirement that resentment be "proper." The reasoning is circular.[39]

Both of these points of apparent circularity in Murphy's discussion appear coherent when we stand within his frame of reference, but when we position ourselves outside the desire to circumscribe the discussion of forgiveness within moral theory and within a particular understanding of virtue—that is, when we regard these issues from the terrain of our inquiry about forgiveness as a human enactment—we can recognize that the circularity we observe serves to exclude from consideration as forgiveness many enactments that are commonly identified as such. That renders these parts of Murphy's analysis problematic from the standpoint of our project.

## Joram Graf Haber and Demonstrable Reasons to Forgive

Haber's approach to forgiveness as a moral enactment emphasizes the verifiability of the judgment that forgiveness is morally justified. It presupposes that a moral agent has committed a moral offense.[40] Verifiability means that the offending party must act in ways that distance himself or herself from the action; there can be no moral forgiveness without this step. Haber then proposes a speech-act paradigm as the standard against which other efforts at forgiveness are to be measured.

This raises an immediate question about Haber's attitude toward unilateral forgiveness. His argument does recognize this possibility but sees it as problematic. In the absence of clear evidence that the offender has repented, to forgive, according to Haber, would not be "morally respectable."[41] The unilateral forgiveness allowed by Murphy is excluded. Haber therefore requires that the offending party perform actions that give

---

[39] The deeper motivation for this definitional move appears to be the desire to justify treating forgiveness as a legitimate topic within moral philosophy. I think it is such. However, one can arrive at this result, it seems to me, by specifying that many (most?) instances of forgiveness involve the experience of harm and the perception of an injustice, or at least the feeling that one has been treated harshly. One can then limit the analysis of forgiveness for the purposes of discussion to those situations in which moral harm has been established, leaving other situations open.

[40] This places him with Murphy in rejecting from consideration non-moral harms as occasions for forgiveness. Haber is, in fact, even more insistent in his exclusion of non-moral harm. The use of the term in other contexts he terms "idiosyncratic." See Haber, *Forgiveness*, 32–33.

[41] Ibid., 98–99.

evidence of a change of attitude with respect to the offending act. This change of attitude is one in which the offender recognizes the wrongness of the act and chooses to distance himself from it. This is a precondition if forgiveness is to be a moral enactment. According to Haber's schema, forgiveness occurs through the revision of a judgment on the basis of rational consideration of behaviors displayed by the offender.

The paradigmatic moral basis for arriving at such a revision of judgment must be, according to Haber, that the offending party has distanced himself or herself from the offending act by an acknowledgment of the wrongness of the offense, an expression of repentance.[42] Shy of this expression, the offended party cannot forgive without—in Haber's perspective—undermining his or her own moral standing, for to forgive without this expression of repentance would be, in Haber's mind, condonation of the offense.[43] Further, it would be an expression of lack of self-respect.[44]

Haber's formulation, at this point, appears solid. However, an examination of his argument from the standpoint of our own questions points to three loci of circular reasoning. The first has to do with the understanding of condonation. For Haber, to forgive without a clear, prior expression of the offender's repentance and efforts to distance himself or herself from the offense equals condonation *tout court*. This claim, however, needs to be demonstrated rather than asserted. Haber's argument does not make the case. The fact that the offended party regards the matter as potentially requiring forgiveness and undertakes to respond to it by forgiving implies that the offended party in fact does not condone the behavior.

Although the discussion of condonation appears to be concerned with the attitude of the offended party to the offense, the real issue for Haber is how the offender (or a third party) views the situation. It is true that if the offended party remains silent about the forgiveness, that silence can be *construed* as condonation.[45] (It might also be construed as rejection or

---

[42] This contrasts with Murphy's presentation in which the injured party "makes the separation." From the perspective Haber is laying out, Murphy's approach would be the same as condonation.

[43] Haber, *Forgiveness*, 90.

[44] Ibid., 78.

[45] In fact, Haber appears to have made this construal. This shows up in the argument by which he judges forgiveness in the absence of repentance to be "essentially no different from condonation of wrongdoing." What his argument does not acknowledge is that, in accord with the priority he places on empirically observable evidence of repentance, he is relying on an interpretation of the observable data and making a judgment about the

condemnation!) And if the offended party were to make the forgiveness explicit to the offender without her prior expression of repentance, the offender also might *construe* that expression as condonation, and therefore as permission to continue the offensive behavior.[46] (It might also be construed as condescension!) However, such a construal would be contrary to the implications of the act of forgiveness, for to forgive without saying one has done so and to express forgiveness explicitly are both responses in which the offended party affirms that she found the action objectionable, whether this "affirmation" is made public or not, whether it is recognized and embraced by the offender or not. The potential that someone might construe any explicit action or non-action as condonation does not necessarily make it so.

But Haber's paradigm of forgiveness as a speech-act—something empirically demonstrable, performed according to the rules of a speech-act—requires that the offender have repented and expressed that repentance to the offended party. Without those conditions the speech-act paradigm does not work. However, to ensure that the paradigm is paradigmatic, Haber must construe cases that do not conform to his "solution" as non-moral forgiveness or as morally defective forgiveness. Haber must find a way to keep the offender and the offended in relationship if the speech-act paradigm is to work. He must therefore invalidate the moral worth of unilateral forgiveness. The rejection of unilateral (or unexpressed) forgiveness (apart from the speech-act paradigm) as condonation is necessary to establishing the paradigmatic status of the speech-act paradigm *as paradigmatic*. But the validity of Haber's speech-act paradigm *as paradigmatic of forgiveness* is necessary to justify the moral disapproval of unilateral forgiveness, or forgiveness in the absence of the prior expression of repentance, as condonation. Although often implicit, the reasoning remains circular.

A second element of circularity in Haber's argument appears when we consider one of his criticisms of Murphy. Haber argues that it is the

---

morality of someone else's action. He writes: "If, as I have argued, forgiveness is to be valued as a moral response, it must be tendered for a reason that is distinctively moral. It must reflect, that is, the idea that people have rights that ought to be respected. Thus, if the 'ought' of forgiveness is to be anything more than a counsel of prudence, it must be directed at repentant wrongdoers. Otherwise, forgiving behavior is essentially no different from condonation of wrongdoing. This is true regardless of the positive utilities that result." Haber, *Forgiveness*, 108.

[46] This is implicit in the arguments presented in critique of consequentialist justifications for forgiveness. See ibid., 106–7.

offending party who must effect the separation between himself or herself and the offending act.[47] Otherwise, forgiveness is not moral. His cavil with Murphy here is based on an overly narrow reading of Murphy's argument. Murphy presents the repentance of the offender as the first case in which one has grounds for recognizing a separation between the offender and the act, but he allows that one can find moral grounds in other cases as well. It is not clear that he requires that the victim "make" the separation between the agent and the act, as Haber maintains. Rather, Murphy's argument recognizes that the victim must reflexively grasp that the separation/distinction is validly operative in the situation. The issue is a matter of cognition and judgment.

This is the same cognitive process Haber requires. The conditions Haber specifies may differ from Murphy's, but the one forgiving must still make the judgment that the necessary conditions (however specified) have been fulfilled. But Haber's proposal, if it is to justify its performative utterance (speech-act) paradigm, must require that the repentance occur *and* that it be demonstrated. Otherwise, according to Haber's own criteria, the judgment that one has moral grounds for forgiving cannot be verified. But this is asserting the same claim in the conclusion (the offender must effect the separation between himself or herself and the offense) as was asserted in the premise necessary to demonstrate the conclusion. It is a circular argument.

Moreover, Haber's formulation really does not lift the burden of responsible, cognitive judgment from the victim. It simply transposes it from the context of the larger history of relationship with the person and the larger context of the consequences of the offense for the offender (as in Murphy's other cases) to a much narrower context: the willingness to believe that the speech-act has in fact fulfilled the requirements, that it does in fact demonstrate an actual change of disposition on the part of the offender. It is still the responsibility of the victim to make such a judgment.

It seems to me that Haber has missed the mark. The real issue is whether the only moral reason for revising one's judgment about the offender lies in the offender's repudiation of the specific offensive act, or whether other moral considerations can come into play. The answer to this question hinges on what one understands oneself to be doing when one is forgiving.

---

[47] See ibid., 104–5.

A third element of circular reasoning in Haber's argument is related to the second and the first. In order for forgiveness to be moral, according to Haber, it must be done for moral reasons—among them, respect for oneself. Haber's argument suggests that the only self-respectful reason for forgiving is that the offender have separated himself or herself from the act and that this repentance be verifiable in observable behavior. But this begs the question of the origin and structure of self-respect, something measured against a scale of values beyond any individual act. *Whether* one's self-respect requires holding onto resentment in the absence of repentance, it seems to me, would rest not on Haber's assertion that self-respect conform to his conditions or on any intrinsic content of the principle of self-respect, but on the constitution of the individual self and the structuring elements of one's sense of self. Haber's judgment that someone else's decision to forgive in the absence of the offender's expressed repentance constitutes a lack of self-respect is, in fact, begging the question it needs to respond to if his construct is to hold. Absent such a demonstration, his assertion is, in his own word, "idiosyncratic."[48]

Nevertheless, it is important to notice that the appearance of idiosyncrasy comes into focus only if one stands outside the matrix of meanings within which Haber's argument operates. Within that matrix the interrelationship of the components that, from our perspective, look like circular argumentation has the appearance of coherence. The pieces fit together. And yet, from the standpoint of our interest in forgiveness as a human enactment, aspects of his proposal appear to be question-begging.

## CHARLES GRISWOLD'S REVISION OF NARRATIVE AND RECONCILIATION

Like Haber, Charles Griswold argues for a paradigm of forgiveness, a model against which other claimants to the title of forgiveness must measure themselves. Like Haber he also defines the rationality of forgiveness in terms of a requirement that is empirically demonstrable—an expression of apology. Unlike Haber, Griswold edges very close to providing a definition of forgiveness that can buttress the conditions for "true" or "genuine" or "complete" forgiveness represented by his paradigm.[49] He does so, however, only obliquely, through the question he poses as the agenda for his book. Recognizing that evil is present in the world and

---

[48] Ibid., 33.

[49] See the detailed analysis of non-paradigmatic cases of forgiveness (imperfect forgiveness) in Griswold, *Forgiveness: A Philosophical Exploration*, chap. 3.

that it requires a response, Griswold wonders how one can be reconciled with evil and not simply be resigned to acceptance or avoidance of it. He observes:

> Forgiveness is a prime candidate in part because it does not reduce either to resigned acceptance or to deluded avoidance. But to say this is simply to restate the question: how can one accept fully that moral evil has been done and yet see its perpetrator in a way that counts as "reconciliation" in a sense that simultaneously forswears revenge, aspires to give up resentment, and incorporates the injury suffered into a narrative of self that allows the victim and even the offender to flourish?[50]

This is the driving question behind Griswold's engagement with the topic of forgiveness. It is a legitimate and important question. But in its formulation it not only sets the criteria for assessing the adequacy of the paradigm Griswold will propose; it also contains an implicit definition of forgiveness. The implicit definition includes the following elements: a moral offense, a responsible offender, revisioning of the offender, a repudiation of the evil, some sort of "reconciliation," forswearing revenge, and orienting oneself toward giving up resentment. In addition, Griswold specifies that, in forgiving, one must appropriate the offense into a narrative that revises its significance from its prior status as grounds for alienation from the offender. Ultimately, the end in view is the "flourishing" of all parties.

The paradigm Griswold specifies coheres in its specifics with the requirements of this implicit definition of forgiveness. His proposal adds to the discussion the idea that forgiving requires that one situate the hurtful event within a context of meanings that allows for the separation of the offender from the offense. This reappropriation involves a "rewriting" of the narrative of the events. This revision of narrative would (ideally) begin with the offender repenting and expressing repentance while the offended party reassesses the offender and the deed in light of the expressed repentance. In this context, reassessment of the deed would entail a revised judgment not of its moral status but of its meaning in relationship to the offender and the offender's revised narrative. It would also require that the offended party revise the narrative, taking this expressed repentance into account. These conditions, and the human forgivability of the offense, are

---

[50] Ibid., xxv.

the minimum conditions that must be satisfied for forgiveness to occur, according to Griswold.[51]

There is much in Griswold's account that, from the perspective of the present inquiry, is very appealing. In particular the emphasis on narrative and the narrative structure of interpersonal meaning is very important. So, too, is the related issue of the capacity to revise or restructure meaning. (We will return to these in the next chapter.) But from the standpoint of our inquiry an element of circularity appears. It surfaces in the relationship between forgiveness and reconciliation.[52] The question is whether reconciliation can legitimately be incorporated into the definition of forgiveness (or the paradigm that exhibits it) as a condition for specifying that the ideal of forgiveness *qua* forgiveness has been achieved. Yet this is exactly what Griswold has done. He has formulated his paradigm of forgiveness on the understanding that reconciliation between the estranged parties is integral to accomplishment of forgiveness as such.

Within Griswold's paradigm of forgiveness the specification of the conditions in this way works well. However, this specification blurs a distinction that, as far as my research can determine, most philosophers and psychologists take as a given: forgiveness and reconciliation are not the same, nor are they coterminous.[53] Most other writers agree that one can forgive without being reconciled and that one can be reconciled without having forgiven. This departure from common usage requires greater justification than Griswold has provided.

Why does Griswold make this move? It appears to be necessary to justify the particular paradigm he wants to promote as a solution to the problem of responding to evil in a manner that is neither acceptance nor avoidance of confrontation. Griswold presents as his paradigm that the parties to an offense (offender and victim) engage in a sharing and revising of narratives that is mutually communicated. It requires a dyadic structure. The effecting of "forgiveness" in Griswold's paradigm does not work without mutual engagement, for "the transformations that the

---

[51] Ibid., 115.

[52] I believe there is an integral relationship between forgiveness and reconciliation (to be addressed in chap. 6).

[53] Haber implicitly accepts such a distinction when he approves part of Richard Fitzgibbons's observations on the relationship of forgiveness to reconciliation in Haber, *Forgiveness*, 107. Jean Hampton recognizes the distinction and the separability of the actions in Murphy and Hampton, *Forgiveness and Mercy*, 42–43 n. 9, as does Jeffrie Murphy in Murphy, *Getting Even: Forgiveness and Its Limits*, 14–16.

offender and victim undergo are mutually dependent, in our paradigm case of dyadic forgiveness."[54]

But this is more than just a paradigm for Griswold; it is an operative definitional condition of forgiveness itself. For in the cases where establishing the dyadic exchange do not occur—specifically when the offender is deceased or when one attempts to forgive unilaterally—forgiveness, according to Griswold, is not achieved *precisely because this condition is unmet.*[55] As he states with respect to forgiveness of the unrepentant, "my claim is that whatever it is that the injured party is doing proleptically, it is not forgiving, but something else that seeks to become forgiveness but has not yet crossed the threshold as defined at the start of this chapter."[56] Were Griswold to accept such cases as forgiveness, the paradigmatic status of his dyadic, dialogical paradigm would be called into question.[57] Griswold has essentially rewritten the definition of forgiveness to make it conform to his paradigm rather than devising his paradigm to correspond to the most commonly held approaches to forgiveness.

As a description (and perhaps even a paradigm) of interpersonal *reconciliation*, Griswold's presentation has much to recommend it. But as a presentation of forgiveness it begs an important question: the relationship of forgiveness to reconciliation. Griswold's appropriation of reconciliation into the definition of forgiveness in order to support a paradigm of forgiveness that requires reconciliatory dynamics looks, from the perspective of our concerns, like circular reasoning.

## Taking Stock

At this point, where do we stand? Thus far we have identified one of the faultlines dividing the landscape of forgiveness. It marks the boundary between understandings of forgiveness that see it as unconditional (particularly in Derrida) and those that see it as a conditional and conditioned enactment (Anglo-American philosophy, psychology). On either side of the faultline we have noted distinctive presuppositions and methodological moves that, if those assumptions are granted, make sense; they

---

[54] Griswold, *Forgiveness: A Philosophical Exploration*, 47.

[55] Ibid., 120–22.

[56] Ibid., 121–22.

[57] Karen Hoffman challenges Griswold on the paradigmatic status of the paradigm he proposes in Hoffman, "Forgiveness without Apology: Defending Unconditional Forgiveness."

hold together. For those who participate in a given realm of discourse, the discussions are reflective of a shared matrix of meanings. But when questioned from beyond the limits defined by that shared matrix, aspects of the arguments can take on the appearance of circular reasoning. They appear to have presupposed elements they need to demonstrate.

We can observe this phenomenon on both sides of the faultline. But how do we explain the differences that occur among those who stand on the same side of the faultline, those who agree on the general premise of "conditional forgiveness"? Can the metaphor of a matrix of meanings provide a way of accounting for these differences? I believe so. In differentiating themselves from one another, each author (Murphy, Haber, and Griswold) argues toward his conclusions on the basis of presuppositions he takes to be given. That is, although these three authors operate in a landscape (conditional forgiveness) that is defined by a largely shared matrix of meanings (moral philosophy), they have appropriated aspects of that matrix differently. They have assimilated into their perspectives priorities, judgments, and convictions the others would reject or would evaluate differently. Though they operate to some degree within a shared matrix of meanings, the particular meanings they each hold to be relevant to specifying forgiveness as a moral enactment are not identical. The image of partially overlapping matrices of meanings can assist us in explaining this phenomenon. This becomes even clearer if we examine more closely the distinction between the shared matrix of meanings and two other levels of matrices: *personal* and *specific*.

Each author approaches the landscape of forgiveness having already appropriated much of the shared matrix that defines the terrain of moral philosophy. Each author has internalized and integrated that shared matrix into the larger horizon of shared meanings that shape his worldview. But each has also modified the matrix in the process of the appropriation, integrating it from the perspective of his own experience and questions and reshaping it according to the nuances drawn from that distinctive, personal perspective. That is, participation in the shared matrix is always also mediated by the *personal matrix of meanings* of the individual author, and it is shared only to the degree that it is integrated into that personal matrix.

*Specific matrices of meanings* arise when each author encounters a cognitive gap or lacuna in the understanding provided by his currently existing personal matrix of meanings. Failing to find a resolution to the lacuna (answer to the question it raises) in his personal matrix, he draws on his experience and on wider resources of the shared matrix to resolve the question in what he considers a satisfactory and stable manner. More simply put: a question arises. We examine the data available and interpret them in ways that, when brought together into a coherent whole, resolve the cognitive tension arising from the lacuna. This resolution, existing as a structured set of interrelated meanings for the purpose of resolving a specific cognitive lacuna or question, is a *specific matrix of meanings*.

This specific matrix of meanings proposes a resolution to a cognitive lacuna. But the proposed resolution must be verified. The elements integrated into the resolution of the lacuna must recognizably resolve the tension arising from that lacuna in a *stable* and *coherent* manner before it can be considered to be correct. But the resolution must also admit of coherent, stable integration into the personal matrix of the individual author and, if it is to gain wider acceptance, stable integration into a more broadly shared matrix of meanings. (The hope for this latter integration is what motivates the writing of books!)

Sometimes the resolution of a cognitive lacuna in a specific matrix of meanings cannot be stably integrated into an existing personal or shared matrix. This produces a kind of crisis, affecting us on cognitive, affective, and intellectual levels (and often also on political, social, and religious levels). That specific matrix is then sometimes rejected, or, if the evidence and persuasive power of the resolution is "weighty" enough, the specific matrix of meanings can realign the interrelationships of large aspects of one's personal matrix or of a commonly shared matrix. This we commonly refer to as a "conversion"—whether intellectual, moral, social, or spiritual.[58]

Thus our authors have encountered cognitive gaps (lacunae) in the explanation of forgiveness as a moral enactment on the terrain of moral philosophy. Each has therefore formulated a question or questions arising from that experience. They have then drawn on resources in the shared matrix of meanings of their engagement with moral philosophy that they

---

[58] We can see this kind of phenomenon throughout human history. It is clearly operative in religious transformations. The transition from Jewish Christianity to the acceptance of Gentiles into the Christian fold and the rupture of the Western church sparked by Martin Luther's insights into the doctrine of salvation by grace alone would be two obvious examples. The Civil Rights movement in the United States, the Women's Liberation movement, and the transition from South African apartheid to a postapartheid society also exhibit such realignments of meanings as a consequence of (and via the process of) integrating new specific matrices of meanings into their respective shared matrices.

consider relevant to address the question. The particular questions our authors believe need to be addressed, the issues they consider relevant to the question, the methodological moves they value as legitimate, and the larger context of the discussion (as they understand it) all contribute to the *specific matrix of meanings* each presents as a resolution of the question raised.[59]

Despite the differences in their specific matrices of meanings, Murphy, Haber, and Griswold are all committed to analyzing and articulating the conditions of forgiveness as a moral enactment within the landscape of moral philosophy exclusively. It is interesting to note that in each case— although by different means—the effort to secure that terrain, rendering forgiveness the exclusive provenance of moral philosophy, has relied on circular reasoning. For example, Murphy's dual insistence that one have moral reasons to forswear resentment *and* that the resentment must be morally justified serves to limit discussion of forgiveness as such to the realm and the methodological constraints of moral philosophy. However, the definition of forgiveness thus employed, as indicated above, is based on circular reasoning. Unless one already accepts that limitation of the scope of forgiveness, the restriction falls.

Haber and Griswold pursue a different strategy. They sidestep arguing on the basis of a definition of forgiveness and instead propose and argue for a paradigm (in which an implicit definition is, nonetheless, operative!) against which other claimants to the title "forgiveness" must measure themselves. These paradigms are likewise committed to restricting forgiveness to the realm of moral philosophy. Even further, they are committed to excluding from consideration as acts of forgiveness those cases in which the harm experienced is not a "moral" harm. But in both cases the paradigms presented—intended to *describe* an ideal act of forgiveness—actually operatively *redefine* forgiveness so as to conform to the conditions specified by the ideal. The ideal is then read *prescriptively* back into the definition of forgiveness to indicate what the author thinks we *ought* to understand forgiveness to mean if it is to be a moral enactment. Consequently, if our response is not to a specifically moral harm it is not forgiveness.

---

[59] A specific matrix of meanings is the constellation of meanings brought together and organized into a coherent whole for the purpose of resolving a cognitive lacuna— answering a question. The specific matrix is an adequate resolution when it is internally coherent, addresses the relevant questions regarding the lacuna, and can be confirmed in relationship to a larger horizon of meanings, a shared matrix of meanings.

Murphy, Haber, and Griswold all fall into circular reasoning in their attempts to restrict forgiveness exclusively to a response to moral harm. There are two points to be made here; both have implications for our method of proceeding. The first is that the appearance of circularity in the arguments does not invalidate the arguments as such. It illustrates, rather, that any argument—any specific matrix of meanings—will have to base its formulation on presuppositions that, within its shared matrix of meanings, will be largely accepted. Alternatively, it will need instead to present its case in ways that, although not recognizably on the terrain of a shared matrix of meanings, can make sufficient connections to the reader's own experience and self-understanding that the argument can be verified independently of the theoretical presuppositions from which the author begins.

The second point is that we are not and will not be exempt from this same fundamental reality we have observed in our interlocutors. The argument we will be pursuing will also be based on presuppositions that, from within the shared matrix of this line of inquiry, will be self-evident, or at least verifiable as a legitimate understanding by appeal to common experience. Nevertheless, critics who do not share those presuppositions can and will (quite legitimately!) question the justification of those premises. It will therefore be our task to be as transparent as possible about the pivotal moves we make in pursuing a response to our question.

### Faultline 2: Forgiveness and Moral Harm

Our examination of the arguments in the Anglo-American discussion of forgiveness has brought to light in each proposal aspects that appear to beg the questions they intend to resolve. We have also noted that, in the three cases considered, at least one facet of the circularity in question served an important role in securing the topic of forgiveness on the ground of moral philosophy by excluding as cases of forgiveness those enactments that respond to harm *other* than moral harm. This is precisely the location of the second faultline.

#### Excluding Non-Moral Harm

The main lines of the arguments for excluding non-moral harm have already been presented. We will not belabor them. However, there are two additional observations to be made before we consider the other side of this faultline. The first is that the faultline cuts primarily across the terrain occupied by psychology. Most Anglo-American philosophers and some psychologists engage forgiveness discussions from the standpoint that a moral harm is required before forgiveness becomes an issue. Many other psychologists do not. Thus the opposite side of the faultline will be occupied in large part by psychologists.

Second, this commitment to the necessity of a moral harm shows up in different ways and in varying degrees. Among philosophers, some (Murphy, Haber, Griswold) present arguments that require an absolute exclusivity. If the harm is not a moral harm, then whatever response one makes to it is *ex supposito* (or *ex definito*) not forgiveness.[60] Others will allow that forgiveness can be enacted in cases of non-moral harm, but since they are primarily concerned with the question of moral enactment they do not devote great attention to it.

Psychologists who align with the Anglo-American moral philosophical discussion on this point likewise span a range of perspectives, but for different reasons. Since as psychologists, not moral philosophers, they are not concerned specifically with parsing the conditions under which forgiving would count as a moral enactment, many appear simply to presuppose that this is the normative understanding of the term.[61] Others who do not appear on the basis of their arguments to be overly committed to the necessity that the harm be moral nonetheless employ terminology laden with moral overtones when discussing the harm.[62]

### Inclusion of Non-Moral Harm

Although some psychologists appear to take the moral nature of an offense as a condition for treating it as an occasion of forgiveness, others do not. Many, in fact, prescind from the question of the moral status of the harm. This is evident both in the language they use to describe the

[60] The same perspective is found in Bernardo Cantens, "Why Forgive? A Christian Response," *Proceedings of the American Catholic Philosophical Association* 82 (2009): 217–28, at 218.

[61] For example, Enright, Freedman, and Rique, "The Psychology of Interpersonal Forgiveness"; Macaskill, "Just-World Beliefs and Forgiveness in Men and Women."

[62] For example, the term "wrongdoer" and the related term "wrongdoing" carry the overtone of a moral breach. However, a specifically moral breach does not appear to be necessary to the argument being presented in such authors as Étienne Mullet and Michèle Girard, "Developmental and Cognitive Points of View on Forgiveness," 111–32, in *Forgiveness: Theory, Research, and Practice*; Denham et al., "Emotional Development and Forgiveness in Children," 130.

experience that evokes forgiveness as a response and in the kinds of occasions in which they recognize that the process individuals undertake to deal with a given situation is, in fact, a process of forgiveness. Both these elements bear closer examination.

First, the language many psychologists use to describe situations requiring forgiveness as a response is often neutral with respect to the moral content of a harm. For example, some psychologists approach the issue of forgiveness as a response to experiences of loss or of pain *simpliciter*.[63] As Paul Coleman has observed:

> When people have experienced a deep loss, they are forever changed. Even if they can forgive, even if they can rebuild the basic assumptions about life, love, and relationships that were shattered as a result of the injury, they are different. They must be in order to have successfully integrated what has happened to them into their scheme of things. Forgiveness offers a direction for healing that makes the "new" person less likely to become hardened and cynical, calloused by the hurts against him.[64]

This experience of loss affects the individual in question in a manner that is painful and life-changing. On the basis of Coleman's experience the facet of loss that calls forth forgiveness as a response is the pain produced. Others have employed a similar understanding in their work on experiences of trauma as the occasion for forgiveness.[65] Among these psychologists the issue that evokes forgiveness as a possible occasion for therapeutic intervention is not harm *qua* moral, but harm *qua* harm.

---

[63] See, for example, Richard Fitzgibbons, "Anger and the Healing Power of Forgiveness: A Psychiatrist's View," 63–74, in *Exploring Forgiveness*, at 64, 70–71; Frederick A. DiBlasio, "The Use of a Decision-Based Forgiveness Intervention within Intergenerational Family Therapy," *Journal of Family Therapy* 20 (1998): 77–94, at 79, 88.

[64] Coleman, "The Process of Forgiveness in Marriage and the Family," 89. Coleman's presentation can be read as overly optimistic. The concerns raised by Murphy and Lamb (*Before Forgiving*) regarding forgiveness "boosterism" might well apply here. However, if one recognizes that Coleman states that forgiveness "offers a direction for healing"— that is, can be helpful in many cases—the concerns raised by Murphy and Lamb can be mitigated.

[65] See, for example, Exline and Zell, "Does a Humble Attitude Promote Forgiveness?" 236; Noll, "Forgiveness in People Experiencing Trauma," 364, 371; Sandra Rafman, "Restoration of a Moral Universe: Children's Perspectives on Forgiveness and Justice," 215–34, in *Women's Reflections on the Complexities of Forgiveness*, at 221, 223.

To press this point further, from a psychological perspective it is not simply the experience of harm *as harm* that provides the possible occasion for forgiveness. It is the *perception* or *recognition* of a harm as a harm that triggers the affective and behavioral responses to which forgiveness is potentially a response. In other words, one must undergo a cognitive process of identifying something as harmful. Once a situation has been thus recognized or perceived, it is potentially a candidate for a forgiveness response, regardless of whether or not the harm is "moral harm."

From the perspective of the moral philosophical arguments we have examined, this would make no sense. If no real moral harm has occurred there is no occasion for forgiveness. But from the context of psychological concerns it is perfectly consistent. If one does not perceive that one has been harmed, one will not react with resentment, anger, or any of the other affective states (see below) that forgiveness addresses. On the other hand, if one perceives a harm—whether moral or non-moral, intentional or accidental—one can nevertheless react to it in a manner that calls for forgiveness as a resolution.

At issue here is what it means to forgive. From the standpoint of the psychological perspectives that allow non-moral kinds of harm, the starting point for understanding forgiveness is less a presupposed definition than a recognition of the psycho-dynamic changes an individual must go through to move from an unforgiving affective state and mode of action to a forgiving state. In other words, psychologists who are open to seeing forgiveness operative in addressing non-moral harms appear to recognize the same psycho-dynamic processes at work in those cases as they see in cases of moral harm, where forgiveness would be recognized as a legitimate issue on both sides of the faultline.

The approach to forgiveness within this broader horizon of harm (beyond, but inclusive of moral harm) is paralleled by a broader discussion of the affective states to which forgiveness is potentially a response. While recognizing and speaking of resentment as a relative constant in an examination of forgiveness, many psychologists also see forgiveness as a response to such affective states as disappointment, anger, and fear.[66]

---

[66] For discussion of forgiveness in relationship to disappointment, see, for example, Robert Karen, *The Forgiving Self: The Road from Resentment to Connection* (New York: Doubleday Anchor, 2001), 6, 9; Andrew B. Newberg, Eugene G. d'Aquili, Stephanie K. Newberg, and Verushka deMarici, "The Neuropsychological Correlates of Forgiveness," 91–110, in *Forgiveness: Theory, Research, and Practice*, at 102; and Walrond-Skinner, "The Function and Role of Forgiveness in Working with Couples and Families," 10. Anger

It is important to note that the commonality among those who allow for non-moral harm does not translate into an agreed-upon definition of forgiveness. Psychologists have been just as vexed in arriving at such a definition as have philosophers. The shared interest in the human psyche—its cognitive, affective, developmental, and behavioral dynamics—provides the boundaries for the terrain in the forgiveness landscape that they explore. However, as with the philosophers, their broader shared matrix of meanings is further divided by their specialized research interests, their schools of psychology, and the specific questions that drive their concerns. This has led McCullough and Worthington to formulate a general description of the common characteristics of forgiveness.

> Rather than attempt to offer a comprehensive definition of forgiveness—the kind of definition that philosophers highly prize—we propose that interpersonal forgiveness rests on three crucial features. First, interpersonal forgiveness occurs in the context of an individual's perception that the action or actions of another person were noxious, harmful, immoral, or unjust. Second, these perceptions typically elicit emotional responses (e.g., anger or fear), motivational responses (e.g., desires to avoid the transgressor or harm the transgressor in kind), cognitive responses (e.g., hostility toward or loss of respect or esteem for the transgressor), or behavioral responses (e.g., avoidance or aggression) that would promote the deterioration of good will toward the offender and social harmony. Third, by forgiving, these negative emotional, motivational, cognitive, or behavioral

---

as a potential affective state requiring a forgiveness response appears in Helen Chagigiorgis and Sandra Paivio, "Forgiveness as an Outcome in Emotion-Focused Trauma Therapy," 121–41, in *Women's Reflections on the Complexities of Forgiveness*, at 134; Exline and Zell, "Does a Humble Attitude Promote Forgiveness?" 236; Fitzgibbons, "Anger and the Healing Power of Forgiveness," 64, 66–67, 70–71; Aponte, "Love, Wellspring of Forgiveness," 39; Mona G. Affinito, "Forgiveness in Counseling: Caution, Definition, and Application," 88–111, in *Before Forgiving*, at 92; Patrick F. Cioni, "Forgiveness, Cognitive Restructuring and Object Transformation," *Journal of Religion and Health* 46, no. 3 (September 2007): 385–97, at 386, 388–89. For discussion of fear in relationship to forgiveness, see Jeffrey M. Brandsma, "Forgiveness: A Dynamic, Theological and Therapeutic Analysis," *Pastoral Psychology* 31, no. 1 (Fall 1982): 40–50, at 44, 47–48; and John Gartner, "The Capacity to Forgive: An Object Relations Perspective," *Journal of Religion and Health* 27, no. 4 (Winter 1988): 313–20, at 316. Brandsma draws attention to the way in which anger, when arising out of a self-protective reflex, is related to fear. Gartner, pointing to some of the deeper (sometimes unconscious) dynamics involved, devotes attention to anxiety.

responses are modulated, so that more prosocial and harmonious interpersonal relations can possibly be resumed. This is a common definition for a construct that is both common and transcendent.[67]

Within this general formulation McCullough and Worthington draw attention to the role of the individual's perception in the generation of emotional responses. Their list of different kinds of responses (emotional, cognitional, motivational, and behavioral) should not be understood as alternative options but rather as potentially mutually interrelated aspects of an integrated response. The understanding of the occasions that might require forgiveness and the aspects of the psychic life implicated in a process of forgiving are sketched much more broadly in some of the psychological discussions than they are in the moral philosophical analyses.

Thus this side of the faultline holds that there are occasions of harm that are not moral harm, but to which forgiveness is a potential response. Those making this claim (while allowing for variability of definition and emphasis) on the basis of a generally shared understanding of forgiveness as a psychodynamic process that seeks to overcome the intra-psychic and interpersonal consequences arising from the experience of harm. Examples of such non-moral harm scenarios might include a physician who "botches a surgery and disfigures a person for life"[68] or instances in which "the legitimate changes of the people we love, like a grown child's moving away or falling in love with someone else, become not just hurts to be dealt with but the beginnings of grudges."[69] In cases of divorce, when a parent moves out, a child experiences the hurt of "abandonment." Even though the parent's decision to move out might be perfectly moral and handled in a legitimate way, for the child the hurt may require a forgiveness response.[70]

---

[67] Michael E. McCullough and Everett L. Worthington, Jr., "Religion and the Forgiving Personality," *Journal of Personality* 67, no. 6 (1999): 1141–64, at 1142–43; see also McCullough et al., "Interpersonal Forgiving in Close Relationships: II. Theoretical Elaboration and Measurement," *Journal of Personality and Social Psychology* 75, no. 6 (1998): 1586–1603, esp. 1587. There the authors further underscore the importance of the perception of harm as they distinguish avoidance and revenge responses as both requiring forgiveness. They also draw attention to the fact that—in cases of avoidance responses—the affective states addressed by forgiveness include other than retributive emotions, for example, self-protective emotions.

[68] Norman S. Care, "Forgiveness and Effective Agency," 215–31, in *Before Forgiving*, at 218.

[69] Karen, *The Forgiving Self*, 53.

[70] Fitzgibbons, "Anger and the Healing Power of Forgiveness," 65, 70–71.

These examples involve experiences of harm in which a responsible agent of the harm is readily identifiable. Some psychologists also extend the possibility of forgiving responses to harm when a moral agent of the harm is ambiguously identifiable or (for a more limited number of psychologists) not identifiable at all. For example, terrible things happen to individuals in the midst of war. Often the person or persons most responsible for a given instance of harm are not identifiable except as "them." This would be a case of an ambiguously identifiable moral agent. Non-agential harm that some psychologists argue can be occasions for forgiveness would include loss of a loved one through death or the experience of a natural disaster. These instances are sometimes referred to as "situational forgiveness."[71]

These latter cases of possible forgiveness are more controversial than those in which a responsible moral agent can be identified. However, they bear mentioning for two reasons. First, they illustrate the role one's shared and personal matrices of meanings have in defining the scope of a topic. If the issue in forgiveness is the experience of harm that provokes resentment, anger, fear, and other such emotions, and that thereby places a barrier to one's future flourishing in psychic life and interpersonal relationship, then the understanding of forgiveness can be quite broad. It might even include non-agential harm. But if one limits the matrix of meanings to the context of a moral harm committed by a responsible moral agent, then ambiguously agential and/or non-agential harm would not be occasions for forgiveness. Thus the matrix of meanings from within which one operates will shape the outcome of the inquiry.

Second, drawing attention to the ambiguously agential and non-agential harms and the possibility of forgiveness as a response to them raises questions we will need to resolve as we try to name forgiveness as a human enactment. Are the dynamics at work in responding to non-agential harm sufficiently similar to those in forgiving agential harm to qualify as forgiveness?[72] If not, we can leave them out of consideration. If so,

---

[71] See the discussion in Macaskill, "Just-World Beliefs and Forgiveness in Men and Women," 39, 41. Macaskill rejects as illogical the notion of "situational forgiveness" understood as forgiveness of a situation in which no responsible moral agent is identifiable. On the other hand, Noll, "Forgiveness in People Experiencing Trauma," 364, clearly maintains that the topic, although not the focus of her research, is humanly meaningful. The recognition that both perpetrator-specific harms and natural disasters can produce PTSD renders the latter potentially subject to forgiveness responses.

[72] Macaskill ("Just-World Beliefs and Forgiveness in Men and Women," 55) has argued that they should be understood as situations of acceptance rather than of forgiveness. This

then the way we name forgiveness as a human enactment will need to provide a justification.

Psychology brings to our attention a further consideration on this side of the faultline. This is the dynamic interplay between our conscious life and the dynamics of the psychic structures that are not directly accessible to conscious thought, those lodged in the unconscious. Traumatic experiences (not necessarily moral breaches) can affect the structures and dynamics of our most basic psychic processes in ways we do not recognize. Like the basement-level presuppositions described by Taylor, they are so much a part of our self-awareness that we do not even know they exist and are affecting us until some (usually therapeutic) intervention helps us to recognize them.

Some of these traumas, as psychologists tell us, have their roots in experiences prior to our ability to formulate them in concepts and words, yet their influence on our perceptions of reality and our psychic resources for dealing with them continue to resonate in our adult lives. Others may occur later in life but be repressed for a variety of reasons. Despite that repression, their impact on our engagement with subsequent trauma (and life in general) can be profound. An experience one person might shrug off with little further thought can be experienced by another as a devastating blow. The former would not need to address the event as a matter of forgiveness. The latter might well. Theorists who define forgiveness exclusively in terms of responses to moral harm may set aside some of these latter cases as examples of forgiveness. Appealing in one manner or another to the presence of distorted perceptions of harm and therefore distorted perception of moral breach, some will dismiss the relevance of forgiveness in these cases. No moral harm has been done, therefore forgiveness is not warranted.

Apart from the presence of circular reasoning in such positions (which we have already seen), dismissing such cases in this way highlights another basis for the opposition defined by the second faultline. There are at least two reasons why those who accept non-moral harm as potentially

---

argument, however, raises a further set of questions: What is the relationship of acceptance to forgiveness? Are they in fact distinct, or are they possibly mutually implicated in each other's enactment? Might it in fact be the case that forgiveness carries acceptance as an inner constitutive movement of its own realization? This would seem to be the implication of Pamela Hieronymi's argument in "Articulating an Uncompromising Forgiveness," *Philosophy and Phenomenological Research* 62, no. 3 (May 2001): 529–55, at 551. Alternatively, might acceptance carry forgiveness as an inner constitutive movement within it?

engaging forgiveness responses do so. The first is based on the understanding that forgiving is characterized by a dynamic process of psychic factors. These same psychodynamics can be engaged by an individual in response to a moral harm or other kinds of harm. If the dynamic processes are the same, then the phenomenon can appropriately go by the same name. But second, the psychologists who accept the possibility of non-moral harm as an occasion for forgiveness also recognize that the psychic factors (conscious and unconscious) shaping one's cognition of an experience play a decisive role in whether or not one attempts to respond to that experience according to the dynamics of forgiveness.

### Findings beneath the Faultlines

Our examination of the discussions of forgiveness has led us to identify two major faultlines. The first traces its origins to the Abrahamic tradition. It is the presence of two distinct understandings of forgiveness: one unconditional, the other conditional. The second concerns the necessity (or not) of a specifically moral harm if one is to engage in forgiving. We have introduced the concept of matrices of meanings to help explain the existence of these faultlines. This concept has allowed us to see the internal coherence of individual positions while also explaining their irreconcilability. But it has not provided us with a basis for choosing between different options. Rather, it has indicated that we must recognize the limits of every perspective, including the one we will be developing in the remainder of this book. Every perspective relies on a matrix of meanings that may not be persuasive to those who do not share it.

In the course of this examination a deeper issue has surfaced. It concerns the relationship between concepts and words and what they seek to name. That is, we have encountered the problem of definition. Derrida's aporetic analysis of forgiveness has, among other things, destabilized the concept of forgiveness. It has argued for the impossibility of its realization. But in the process it has also called into question the possibility of definition itself. If a concept as commonly invoked as "forgiveness" can collapse into impossibility because of the aporiae inherent in its meaning, can we be so bold as to define anything? Although the Anglo-American discussion of forgiveness operates within a matrix of meanings that does not intersect with Derrida's concerns, the very fact that the authors we have considered disagree with each other on the fundamental conditions of forgiveness illustrates the difficulty. Defining forgiveness is a vexing endeavor.

The efforts to define forgiveness, whether directly or by means of definitions operative in paradigms, point us toward a deeper problem. At least in the cases we have considered, the definitions operative in the discussions are actually intrinsically interwoven with a kind of soft violence, both conceptual violence and existential violence. The conceptual violence shows itself most clearly in the exclusion of non-moral harm from consideration as an occasion for possible forgiveness. The authors have found it necessary to explicitly exclude such considerations. For the sake of a clearer concept and greater precision in definition, as well as for the sake of establishing the legitimacy of circumscribing the discussion of forgiveness within the bounds of moral philosophy, the authors have rejected as occasions of forgiveness instances that others commonly embrace. Conceptual clarity and intrasystematic stability are purchased at the price of a kind of conceptual imperialism. "Your experience which you recognize as forgiveness does not conform to my definition. Therefore you are wrong to call it forgiveness. It is something else." This, it seems to me, does violence to the meaning of forgiveness. It limits the understanding of this human experience, not on the basis of the human experience or to serve the human need to grapple with the reality of forgiving, but for the sake of the coherence of the philosopher's system.[73]

The conceptual violence involved in this move can also incline toward a kind of existential violence. The definition of forgiveness in terms of the moral content of the harm (and/or response to the harm) and the articulation of its conditions as a moral enactment carries the force not of a conceptual judgment but of a moral judgment against those who do not comply with its requirements. The arguments are not merely definitional; they aim to be prescriptive, telling us how one *ought* to forgive. This can provide the basis for a kind of moralizing coercion in interpersonal relations. "The offending party has fulfilled the conditions I have specified, yet you do not forgive. There is something wrong (morally) with you."[74]

---

[73] In postmodern parlance, the moral philosophers are deploying a kind of meta-narrative by virtue of the exclusion of non-moral harm. Their definition allows them to silence the voices that would otherwise interrupt the neatness of their systems of thought.

[74] I am not suggesting that the authors we have examined have made this move. Indeed, their presentations are much more nuanced than this. For example, while Haber does make the claim (*Forgiveness*, 78) that failing to feel resentment in occasions that are morally justified can be a moral defect, he also recognizes that one might have moral grounds for withholding forgiveness. But if this were to be a habitual mode of response to offenses it could well be a moral defect (ibid., 101–3.) However, setting the question

The irony is that both the conceptual violence and the existential violence arise from the desire to promote forgiveness *as a moral enactment*, yet in the process these approaches can actually provide occasions for furthering alienation, the very reality that they understand forgiving as an element in overcoming! Another aporia!

It appears to me that this latter violence reflects a further difficulty with the moral philosophical approaches we have examined. Content with an operative definition of forgiveness as a moral enactment in response to a moral harm and concerned to prescribe the conditions for the moral enactment itself, they neglect to consider *why* so many find it difficult to forgive. This, it seems to me, is a serious oversight. If we want to understand forgiveness—even if we want to define it (which I do not)—our grasp of the phenomenon will be truncated if we do not attend to the dynamics that must be engaged when trying to overcome resistance to forgiving. This resistance is precisely what makes forgiving difficult. The enactment of forgiveness must therefore be understood to include those dynamics by which the resistance is overcome. These would certainly be part of forgiving and are therefore relevant to the attempt to name forgiveness and to specifying the conditions for its fulfillment.

The problem here arises from the emphasis on prescribing how forgiveness *ought* to be (or how it *ought* to be practiced). The prescriptive approaches I have highlighted here emphasize forgiveness as a response to moral harm. But there is an alternative approach to getting at the meaning of forgiveness that does not begin from prescriptions or from the presupposition of moral harm. We catch a glimpse of it among the psychologists who allow for a broader range of occasions for forgiving. We also see it in the approach to naming forgiveness offered by McCullough and Worthington. They have focused on description of the characteristics observable when occasions for forgiveness arise and when it is attempted and achieved (or not). In other words, they operate on the basis of a kind of phenomenology of the experience of forgiveness and measure their conceptualizations against the experience of struggling with forgiving as attested by a wide range of subjects.

These findings have two implications for our manner of proceeding. First, they draw our attention to questions we will ultimately need to

---

of forgiveness within the effort to lay out moral conditions for its practice and nonpractice is done for the purpose of making moral judgments. These judgments themselves can be used coercively, although whether or not this practice itself would be moral is another question.

be able to address as we formulate our own way of naming forgiveness. We will certainly need to find a way of addressing and justifying our response to the questions posed by the two faultlines. How are we to deal with the opposition between conditional and unconditional forgiveness? Otherwise stated: is there a way to overcome the evident contradiction between the two strands of the Abrahamic traditions on forgiveness? We will also need to address the question of the relationship of morality to forgiving. In addition, we will need to find a way of naming the relationship between forgiveness and reconciliation. Finally, in our account of forgiveness we will need to ask why forgiving is often so difficult, why it meets with such resistance.

Second, these findings point us to criteria for our method of inquiry. At the very least we will need to try to avoid the conceptual and existential violence identified above. This will be particularly challenging because it will require that we try to avoid starting from an approach to naming forgiveness that might exclude from consideration experiences of forgiving that do not conform to an implicit (or explicit) theoretical understanding. As noted earlier in the chapter, definitions can, despite one's stated intentions, be operatively present in an argument. Indeed, insofar as we make use of terms to specify meaning we are going to be operatively employing definitions. To minimize the potential violence named above, we shall proceed by means of a descriptive approach. We shall describe the dynamics that appear to be operative when people understand themselves to be confronting the possibility of forgiving and attempting to enact it. Here we shall strive to be as inclusive as possible.

This approach orients itself not to the requirements of a theory of morality but to human experience. It requires that we pay careful attention to the occasions that provoke forgiveness as a possible response and that we attend to how the person confronted with that occasion experiences it. It further requires that we probe what actually happens when one undertakes to forgive. Some of what takes place, we will discover, is conscious; some is unconscious. Some is accessible to "free will"; some is resistant to our efforts to choose. These are the issues we shall explore in chapter 5.

# $C$hapter 5

# The Becoming Self
# and the Experience of Harm

## Preliminaries

$T$he process of excavating beneath the two faultlines identified in chapter 4 has left us with many questions. It has also set out criteria for our method of proceeding as we seek to name forgiveness. We are to avoid the "soft violence" entailed in previous efforts that have begun with restrictive definitions of forgiveness. Instead, we are to cast as wide a net as possible, including under the rubric of forgiveness experiences that have been excluded by some moral philosophers but that those who undergo them identify as calling for forgiveness. That is, we are to try to uncover the dynamics involved in the broad range of phenomena that, other than in moral philosophical circles, are called "forgiveness."

This shift in approach toward a more phenomenologically governed excavation of the experience of forgiveness leads us to pose a different kind of question from that found among the Anglo-American philosophers we have considered. Rather than asking "What is forgiveness?" or "Under what conditions can one deploy forgiveness morally?," the question we will be exploring is "What is one doing when she undertakes to forgive?" As we adverted to in the previous chapter, not all of this "doing" is taking place on the conscious level. We therefore need to broaden the scope of our inquiry to include unconscious dynamics. There are two foci to the question we are posing: the one harmed who engages the challenge of forgiveness and the nature of the harm when it has been recognized

145

*as* harm, that is, the nature of the harm as consciously appropriated by the one who experiences it.[1]

This second focus of our questioning requires some elaboration. The full justification for this particular way of posing the question will have to await the completion of this chapter, but by way of anticipation we can say that a harm only becomes an occasion calling for forgiveness when it has been *recognized as a harm*.[2] If it is not recognized as a harm, it will arouse neither a retributive response nor the multifaceted dynamics we call forgiving. In other words, engaging the process of forgiveness presupposes that our cognitional processes have led us to identify that we have been harmed. (More on this shortly.) This is confirmed both among the moral philosophers we have considered and in the psychological discussions.[3] Indeed, psychologists have observed that sometimes conditions we take to be normal we later recognize as harmful only in the light of the process of therapeutic intervention. Only at that point are we confronted with questions of forgiveness with respect to those conditions.[4] Cognition is integral to the experience of harm as potentially forgivable. Therefore, as we seek to uncover what is happening when we undertake to forgive, we will need to devote careful attention to the dynamics of cognition itself.

The larger question we are attempting to answer, "What is one doing when she undertakes to forgive?" can be parsed into more specific questions. What is the individual *doing* (volitionally directed activity) when undertaking forgiveness? What is happening that is not under direct

---

[1] A third focus to the question, that which unfolds within the one attempting to forgive, or, alternatively, the dynamic interaction that takes place when forgiving, will be the focus of the next chapter.

[2] "Recognized" in this context does not require that one have reflected, "I have been harmed," in an explicit way. Most commonly the recognition occurs instantaneously at the moment the meaning is perceived. The meaning could be experienced as physical pain, shame, a feeling of rejection or loss, a feeling that one is in danger or threatened. The judgment that one has, in fact, been harmed is a subsequent cognitive act that confirms the perception of meaning. It, too, can be instantaneous, but it can also be the consequence of an intentionally thematic process of reflection on the event.

[3] Some of the moral philosophers have suggested that there is something wrong with the individual who does not recognize a moral harm as a moral harm. Perhaps; but the issue here is that recognition of the harm as such must precede the decision to engage the harm as an occasion for forgiveness.

[4] For example, when a child grows up in an abusive household, behaviors taken as normal will only be recognized for their harmfulness when one's criteria for evaluating "normal" have shifted through the process of becoming healthy.

volitional control but is nonetheless integral to the enactment of for-giveness? Is anything taking place within the individual that underlies and sustains the intentional movement toward forgiving? To prepare the way to answering these questions, in this chapter we shall dig more deeply into the underpinnings of the two foci mentioned above. We shall examine the nature of harm such that we experience it as harmful and we shall consider what it is about us that makes us susceptible to such an experience. This will give us a clearer basis on which to name what is taking place when one undertakes to forgive.

Before proceeding we must take note of a distinctive feature of the question we have posed. Although we can specify two foci to the question, the way in which the question is formulated compels us to examine the individual who experiences the harm, the harm itself, and the cognition of the harm in their *intrinsic interrelationship* within the dynamics of forgiveness. As we delve into the deeper analysis of each of these foci of our question we must bear in mind that the other focus is intrinsically implicated. The understanding of each focus presupposes to some degree what we will find in our examination of the other. To put this in terms we identified in chapter 4, the excavation we are undertaking at this point is directed toward articulating a matrix of meanings from within which we can name what is occurring when we undertake to forgive. The mutual interrelationship of the elements is an intrinsic characteristic of constructing that specific matrix. To those who do not stand within this matrix it will look like circular reasoning. From within our shared matrix it will look like coherence.

As already noted in chapter 4, this binocular disjunction in assessment is not entirely avoidable; it is a consequence of the fact that we inhabit distinctive matrices of meaning. But even assuming that you (the reader) and I have sufficient common ground not to perceive what follows as a circular argument, we are still faced with a conundrum: where do we begin? We cannot talk about the experience of harm without clarifying what we mean by the "self" who is harmed. But the experience of harm and the nature of that experience constitute the occasion that raises the question of forgiveness. As such, our understanding of harm conditions the understanding of the "self" we need to clarify. We are left with a "chicken and egg" dilemma.

In order to get past this dilemma I shall simply jump into the question. I shall first explore the nature of harm, taking as a given that it is an assault on the self and examining the implications of this conviction for an understanding of harm. The justification for assuming this starting point will unfold later, in the discussion of personal becoming and the sense of self in relationship to matrices of meaning. These two sections will, in a sense, be converging on the same terrain, but from different starting points. Proceeding in this way will set the stage for a discussion of the relationship between the recognition of harm and the becoming of the self, before we conclude with the implications of these explorations for naming forgiveness.

## Probing the Experience of Harm

It can seem like a statement of the obvious to claim that harm, when it is recognized as such, is experienced as an assault on the self. In the philosophical and psychological literature we have examined up to this point, this conviction appears to be taken for granted. Put in its baldest terms, "For damage to an individual to occur, there must be a sense of the self. After all, there must first exist a self that can be injured before it can actually be injured."[5] A sense of self is necessary in order for an experience of harm to occur. Obvious indeed. But what is it about harm that makes it harmful specifically to the self, or, as Andrew Newberg and associates named it, the "sense of self"? What does harm do?

Much of what we have examined in previous chapters can help us to answer that question. As a starting point we can say that the experience of harm destabilizes us. It creates a disruption.[6] Different authors have

---

[5] Andrew B. Newberg, Eugene G. d'Aquili, Stephanie K. Newberg, and Verushka deMarici, "The Neuropsychological Correlates of Forgiveness," 91–110, in *Forgiveness: Theory, Research, and Practice*, ed. Michael E. McCullough, Kenneth I. Pargament, and Carl E. Thoresen (New York: Guilford Press, 2000), at 102.

[6] Julia Kristeva gets at the sense I am intending here in her discussion of "abjection" in the early differentiation of the object from the "I" in Julia Kristeva, "Hatred and Forgiveness; or, From Abjection to Paranoia," 183–94, in eadem, *Hatred and Forgiveness*, trans. Jeanine Herman (New York: Columbia University Press, 2010). She describes (p. 184) the abject in terms that will resonate with our discussion of cognition below as "an intertwining of affect and meaning" and elaborates: "The abject has only one quality of the object—that of opposing the I. But while the *ob-jeu* or the transitional object, by opposing me, gives me equilibrium in the fragile web of desire for meaning, the abject excludes me and pulls me to where meaning collapses. 'Something' I do not recognize as a thing. A weight of nonsense that has nothing significant about it and yet crushes me." It is worth noting the language of equilibrium, web, and meaning. This seems to me to provide oblique support for the understanding of the sense of self and matrices of meaning I will be elaborating shortly.

named this in different ways: detracting from our sense of self-worth or our personal dignity,[7] causing trauma,[8] creating an experience of loss.[9] Again, this seems obvious. But how does harm do this? Why does it have such an effect?

To anticipate an explanation that will appear in the next section, let me assert for the moment that harm has this effect because (1) it is an event of meaning and (2) we experience that meaning as an attacking or disrupting of how we make sense of ourselves and of our world to ourselves. The experience of harm destabilizes how we experience ourselves. Both the psychological and the philosophical literature point toward this destabilization and suggest that it occurs on two interrelated levels. On the first level the destabilization to the sense of self can be experienced as an assault on the self as such, a repudiation of one's worth or dignity. This first level is attested in both the psychological literature[10] and in

---

[7] This is often discussed in terms of the moral necessity of acting out of respect for oneself as well as respect for the human dignity of the offender when undertaking forgiveness as a moral enactment. See, for example, Charles L. Griswold, *Forgiveness: A Philosophical Exploration* (Cambridge: Cambridge University Press, 2007), 43–47; Joram Graf Haber, *Forgiveness* (Savage, MD: Rowman & Littlefield, 1991), 36, 38, 72–73; Jeffrie G. Murphy and Jean Hampton, *Forgiveness and Mercy* (Cambridge: Cambridge University Press, 1988), 16–19; Margaret R. Holmgren, "Forgiveness and Self-Forgiveness in Psychotherapy," 112–35, in *Before Forgiving: Cautionary Views of Forgiveness in Psychotherapy*, ed. Sharon Lamb and Jeffrie G. Murphy (New York: Oxford University Press, 2002), at 118ff.

[8] See, especially, Jennie G. Noll, "Forgiveness in People Experiencing Trauma," 363–75, in *Handbook of Forgiveness*, ed. Everett L. Worthington, Jr. (New York: Routledge, 2005); Beverly Flanigan, "Forgivers and the Unforgivable," 95–105, in *Exploring Forgiveness*, ed. Robert D. Enright and Joanna North (Madison: University of Wisconsin Press, 1998), at 97–99; Helen Chagigiorgis and Sandra Paivio, "Forgiveness as an Outcome in Emotion-Focused Trauma Therapy," 121–41, in *Women's Reflections on the Complexities of Forgiveness*, ed. Wanda Malcolm, Nancy DeCourville, and Kathryn Belicki (New York: Routledge, 2008); Sandra Rafman, "Restoration of a Moral Universe: Children's Perspectives on Forgiveness and Justice," 215–34, in *Women's Reflections on the Complexities of Forgiveness*, at 222–23, 229.

[9] Robert Karen, *The Forgiving Self: The Road from Resentment to Connection* (New York: Doubleday Anchor Books, 2001), 47, 122; Jeffrey M. Brandsma, "Forgiveness: A Dynamic, Theological and Therapeutic Analysis," *Pastoral Psychology* 31, no. 1 (Fall 1982): 40–50, at 41. The experience of loss is also at issue in Pamela Hieronymi's discussion of the need on the part of the forgiver to absorb a cost. See her "Articulating an Uncompromising Forgiveness," *Philosophy and Phenomenological Research* 62, no. 3 (May 2001): 529–55, at 551.

[10] See, for example, Brandsma, "Forgiveness: A Dynamic, Theological and Therapeutic Analysis," 41; Newberg, d'Aquili, Newberg, and deMarici, "The Neuropsychological

philosophical discussions.[11] The experience of harm is a personal experience of disruption because it is *my* experience and it assaults my sense of myself at the core of my sense of worth.

But on the second level the experience of harm disrupts my sense of self *as inhabiting a world*. "World," in this context, is not a physical place but a complex of meanings in relationship to which and from within which we understand ourselves and position ourselves with respect to what is "other."[12] The experience of harm shakes not only my feelings of personal worth but also my security vis-à-vis the larger context in which I am situated and from within which I appropriate my sense of self.[13]

The psychological discussions we have examined signal this point in different ways. Some psychologists write of the loss of a sense of "self-world congruence."[14] This phrasing states the point directly, but elsewhere in the literature the same idea is implicit in the varied ways of naming the process of recovery from harm. This process involves reconstituting or reshaping the understanding of the larger context of one's relationships, particularly with the offender. Jennie Noll, in reflecting on the process for recovery from deep trauma, indicates the need in recovery to "make sense of trauma by understanding how the trauma fits with one's view of the world and reorganizing beliefs."[15] Paul Coleman hints at this damage

---

Correlates of Forgiveness," 91–92; Suzanne Freedman, Robert D. Enright, and Jeannette Knutson, "A Progress Report on the Process Model of Forgiveness," 393–406, in *Handbook of Forgiveness*, at 400; and Noll, "Forgiveness in People Experiencing Trauma," 369.

[11] The connection is often more implicit in the philosophical discussions than in the psychological. The general idea, as seen in chaps. 1 and 2, is that moral harm is an undeserved assault on one's dignity or worth. See the discussions of self-respect, personal dignity, and self-worth in Griswold, *Forgiveness: A Philosophical Exploration, passim*; Murphy and Hampton, *Forgiveness and Mercy, passim*; and Haber, *Forgiveness, passim*.

[12] See, for example, Ann Macaskill, "Just-World Beliefs and Forgiveness in Men and Women," 39–59, in *Women's Reflections on the Complexities of Forgiveness*; Rafman, "Restoration of a Moral Universe: Children's Perspectives on Forgiveness and Justice." See also Bernard Lonergan, "A Definition of Metaphysics," in *Understanding and Being: The Halifax Lectures on Insight*, ed. Elizabeth A. Morelli and Mark D. Morelli, *The Collected Works of Bernard Lonergan* (Toronto: University of Toronto Press, 1990), 181–99, at 182–83, where Lonergan discusses the idea of a "world."

[13] The notion that one appropriates one's sense of self from within a "world" will be justified in the next section.

[14] Newberg, d'Aquili, Newberg, and deMarici, "The Neuropsychological Correlates of Forgiveness," 102.

[15] Noll, "Forgiveness in People Experiencing Trauma," 370; see also 369–71.

to one's world in his allusion to "reframing" the harm that has occurred in a relationship.[16] Ann Macaskill makes a similar point in her article exploring the damage done to one's "Just-World beliefs."[17]

The same kind of indirect support for this conviction appears in the philosophical discussions of the Anglo-American philosophers we have examined. They emphasize that the experience of harm is of a *message communicated*. It is an experience of meaning that not only repudiates the recipient's worth but also, by that very fact, posits a world in which it is legitimate to denigrate the worth of the victim.[18] Pamela Hieronymi draws attention to precisely this aspect of harm when she highlights the meaning of harm as a future threat, for, as she observes, "not only the guilt of the offender but also the meaning of the misdeed, i.e., the threatening claim, persists in social space."[19]

This meaning of the harm, as a message disrupting the sense of self and of the self's world, is the dimension that elicits a response. The response called for seeks to address precisely the meaning communicated by the offense; it must be a meaningful response. It must be meaningful to the person who recognizes that she has been offended. It must respond to the meaning of the event as recognized by her.[20] (In this response the offender may or may not be directly or explicitly included.) And it must be a response that restores a sense of stability or integrity to the sense of self of the injured party, both in herself and in her self/world relations.[21]

---

[16] Paul W. Coleman, "The Process of Forgiveness in Marriage and the Family," 75–94, in *Exploring Forgiveness*, at 88, 91. Coleman's discussion of reframing is echoed in much of the philosophical literature as well. Griswold's emphasis on reconstituting the narrative of the event overlaps substantially with this idea. See Griswold, *Forgiveness: A Philosophical Exploration*, 53–58.

[17] Macaskill, "Just-World Beliefs and Forgiveness in Men and Women," 42.

[18] See, for example, Murphy and Hampton, *Forgiveness and Mercy*, 17, 24; Murphy, *Getting Even: Forgiveness and Its Limits* (New York: Oxford University Press, 2003), 35, 43; Haber, *Forgiveness*, 38 (citing Murphy); Griswold, *Forgiveness: A Philosophical Exploration*, 45–46.

[19] Hieronymi, "Articulating an Uncompromising Forgiveness," 550.

[20] For example, the response may be directed toward restoring a sense of power as an expedient for reaffirming one's own worth and one's place in the world. See Julie Juola Exline and Anne L. Zell, "Does a Humble Attitude Promote Forgiveness? Challenges, Caveats, and Sex Differences," 235–51, in *Women's Reflections on the Complexities of Forgiveness*, at 236.

[21] See, for example, Noll, "Forgiveness in People Experiencing Trauma," 369. See also the description of post-divorce adjustment in Anthony Giddens, *Modernity and*

How one responds to any given experience of harm can vary according to the individual personality,[22] but we can conceive of non-forgiving
responses as generally falling into one of three main categories.[23] The first
is retributive. It demands some sort of compensation from the offender;
it wants "payback," to "get even."[24] This is the direction of the impulse
beneath resentment and the pursuit of vengeance. The second kind of
response is withdrawal. One simply cuts off relationship. The third kind
of response continues the relationship, whether by choice or necessity,
but does so in a manner in which the lingering effect (but also affect)
of the offense imposes a kind of barrier to future depth of relationship.
One lives with a functional reconciliation but stops short of interpersonal
reconciliation.[25]

---

*Self-Identity: Self and Society in the Late Modern Age* (Stanford, CA: Stanford University
Press, 1991), 10–12. Giddens draws here on Judith Wallerstein and Sandra Blakeslee,
*Second Chances* (London: Bantam, 1989).

[22] See, for example, Norman S. Care, "Forgiveness and Effective Agency," 215–31,
in *Before Forgiving*, 223; Varda Konstam et al., "Forgiveness in Practice: What Mental
Health Counselors Are Telling Us," 54–71, in *Before Forgiving*, at 57.

[23] These categorizations are for heuristic purposes. In actual practice it is possible for
there to be blending of categories. It is also possible that a given person might shift back
and forth from one mode of response to another. These categories have been formulated
with a view to responses to harm in which there is an identifiable agent. Similar responses
might also be possible in situations of nonagential harm but, lacking an offender to
blame, they might express themselves indiscriminately—against others who have not
offended—or in a generalized orientation toward life. This latter point is affirmed in the
psychological discussions below.

[24] See, for example, Exline and Zell, "Does a Humble Attitude Promote Forgiveness?"
236.

[25] Many people are forced to live with functional reconciliation—children in the homes
of abusive parents, employees under the heel of abusive bosses, the disabled who must
rely on the care of resentful caregivers. In such situations, conditions require coexistence
and cooperation for survival. In such circumstances one may be able to cooperate with an
offender, but internal barriers are maintained for the sake of self-protection. Interpersonal
reconciliation is of a different sort. It is not merely functional. In the deeper reconciliation
that forgiveness appears to intend (see next chapter) it is not necessary to maintain the
inner protective walls. The level of trust is restored, or at least in the process of restoration.
See, for example, Freedman, Enright, and Knutson, "A Progress Report on the Process
Model of Forgiveness," 400; Harry J. Aponte, "Love, the Wellspring of Forgiveness: An
Example of Spirituality in Therapy," *Association for Family Therapy and Systemic Practice*
20 (1998): 37–58, at 41; Noll, "Forgiveness in People Experiencing Trauma," 372; Janice
Haaken, "The Good, the Bad, and the Ugly: Psychoanalytic and Cultural Perspectives

Each of these kinds of responses seeks to restabilize the sense of self disrupted by the offense and to restabilize the self's sense of its relationship to the world. But these three approaches fall short of their intended purpose. They do not reverse or repudiate the meaning of the event effectively or in a manner that produces or restores the kind of stability that has been ruptured.

Retribution gives the appearance of repudiation or reversal of the offensive meaning, assuming that the retribution is understood as a response to the offense. However, as numerous philosophical discussions have pointed out, this approach is futile. It seeks to eradicate the message as though it had never been communicated. It wants to turn back the clock, but cannot.[26] Beyond this, in another way, seeking retribution can undermine the very message it is trying to send. It implicitly affirms that one's worth and one's place in the world are contingent on their being recognized by those who have called them into question with their actions. That is, it reconfirms in a non-thematic way that one's worth is contingent on its recognition by others, including the offender(s).

Moreover, to the extent that retribution is achieved by means of power, suppressing the one who produced the offending message, it is a vindication of violence as a means of self-affirmation. This too, paradoxically, can serve to undermine the legitimacy of one's own protest. At best, retribution may win the particular battle, but it loses the war for a stable sense of self. It continues the dynamic by which one's sense of worth is dependent on someone else and on the world functioning as one would like, and it vindicates in principle the use of violence—possibly even the use of violence like what was experienced as harm.

Withdrawal from relationship (as an alternative to forgiving) would appear to avoid the pitfalls of retribution in reestablishing stability to the sense of self and of one's world. Withdrawal is a self-protective strategy.[27]

---

on Forgiveness," 172–91, in *Before Forgiving*, at 182; Jerome Neu, "To Understand All Is to Forgive All—Or Is It?" 17–38, in *Before Forgiving*, at 25.

[26] Several authors draw on Hannah Arendt's articulation of the problem in *The Human Condition* (Chicago: University of Chicago Press, 1958). She writes of the "predicament of irreversibility." What has been done cannot be undone. See the reference in Griswold, *Forgiveness: A Philosophical Exploration*, xv, 100; Haber, *Forgiveness, passim*.

[27] Self-protective strategies do not necessarily always look "protective"; sometimes the self-protective aspect is concealed beneath the anger that gives power to the response. See, for example, Brandsma, "Forgiveness: A Dynamic, Theological and Therapeutic Analysis," 41. Self-protection is a natural reaction and has a good purpose. But in the dynamics

One may repudiate the meaning of the offense in one's own mind or among a narrowed cadre of like-minded associates. However, if one does nothing more than withdraw from the context of the harm, the very fact of having withdrawn to protect oneself entails that the meaning of the message has become structured into one's pattern of relating. It continues to exercise power. The message of the offense can influence one's future relationship to others, to self, and to world. In such a scenario the anger at the individual who provoked the harm can become generalized and directed toward others not related to the offending event.[28] Far from equalizing the relationship with the offender, this strategy can give the offender and the message of the offense power over one's future.

A similar dynamic operates in strategies of truncated reconciliation. One retains a self-protective posture, fueled by the painful memory and resentment of the offense,[29] but the meaning of the offense is not overcome and the experience of the hurt continues to exercise its influence on the future course of one's relationships—with the offender and with others.[30]

In "real life" these categories are not always clearly distinct. In a given situation an offended party might, at different times, employ different combinations of these strategies (in their varied forms of expression) to vitiate the meaning of the harm. Moreover, these characterizations are only generalized statements in the abstract about the directions in which the three options can tend. Individual circumstances and responses always involve multiple extenuating conditions. Nevertheless, the point remains: the movement (trajectory) described in each of these non-forgiving responses is ultimately self-defeating. When enacted, these strategies actually embed the meaning of the harm in the individual's future orientation to self and to world. The meaning of the harm shapes the person's future becoming in a manner that retains its power for harm in the life of the person.

---

of relationships it can hinder relational flourishing. See Michael E. McCullough et al., "Interpersonal Forgiving in Close Relationships: II. Theoretical Elaboration and Measurement," *Journal of Personality and Social Psychology* 75, no. 6 (1998): 1586–1603, at 1587.

[28] See Brandsma, "Forgiveness: A Dynamic, Theological and Therapeutic Analysis," 41.

[29] See Exline and Zell, "Does a Humble Attitude Promote Forgiveness?" 236.

[30] Brandsma underscores the manner in which unresolved angry feelings can become channeled into passive aggression or generalized in one's response to the world generally. Brandsma, "Forgiveness: A Dynamic, Theological and Therapeutic Analysis," 41–42.

Forgiveness presents itself as an alternative mode of response. It is a different strategy for restabilizing the self and the self/world relationship in the wake of a recognized harm.[31] To appreciate why this is so, we now need to shift our attention.

## Personal Becoming, the Sense of Self, and Matrices of Meaning

Now we need to examine the question of harm from the perspective of the self. We will ask a different kind of question: What is it about the self such that it could experience harm as an assault on the self? Alternatively, why is it that an act of meaning can be experienced as harm?

Our explorations up to this point suggest two locations where we may look for an answer. First, as is clear from the possibility of experiencing harm itself, but also from our foray into psychological literature, we are creatures who undergo change. More to the point, we are persons who are constantly *in the process of becoming our selves*. We emerge from a past and move toward a future and, in the process, we become "other" even as we remain "ourselves."[32] To make this concrete: in one sense the person who graduates from medical school is "the same" as the person who began it. But over the course of studies that person has also become "other" than she was before beginning. Thus one of the places we should explore more deeply is the landscape of "personal becoming." We will need to uncover the dynamics of personal becoming.

---

[31] The term "strategy" is used here with some hesitation. I do not intend to suggest that forgiveness is deployed with the conscious intent of accomplishing something other than itself, like some sort of gambit in chess. Rather, the point is that it involves a response to the experience of harm different from those entailed either in retribution or in the other nonforgiving responses that retain and solidify the experience of harm as an obstacle to future interpersonal reconciliation.

[32] The topic of "selfhood" has generated a great deal of literature in both philosophy and psychology. Questions of the nature of the self, its relationship to "identity" or "continuity" over time, whether it is static or constructed are among the many topics under discussion. More recently the postmodern emphasis on "decentering" the self has risen to prominence. It is not my purpose to engage or adjudicate among the competing theories currently under discussion. My approach will be to describe characteristics of the experience of the self in a way that would be recognizable to anyone engaged in reflection on her or his own experience of self as a self. In doing so I will be drawing from the writings of philosophers and psychologists who are committed to different theoretical orientations but who, no matter the orientation, would, I hope, find the formulation of the particular points as such unobjectionable.

Second, this process of becoming occurs intrinsically via the mediation of our cognitive processes. Our ability to engage cognitively with the world around us, to recognize its meaning(s) and respond to it meaningfully, is essential to the process of becoming the unique persons we are and will be. We will therefore need to dig more deeply into the question of the relationship among cognition, meaning, and the sense of self. In doing so we will also need to draw out why the self/world relation is so important for the coming-to-be of the sense of self and what role it plays in the harm that can evoke forgiveness as a meaningful response.

### The Dynamics of Personal Becoming

In contrast to what has been termed the "modern subject," an understanding of the person as essentially a complete, self-possessed, rational mentality that must somehow cross a great divide between its inner world and the world outside itself,[33] contemporary philosophy and psychology have emphasized the *in*completeness of the human person, that we are constantly in the process of *becoming*.[34] Who we are grows into itself over the course of our personal history. Moreover, this growth does not "spin itself out of its own resources."[35] Rather, there is a twofold dynamism at work in the process of personal becoming.

---

[33] Commonly this shift in understanding is characterized in terms of the move in recent thinking away from the understanding of the self reflected in the writings of René Descartes, Immanuel Kant, and modern philosophy, to what is now termed "postmodern." See Dan Zahavi, "Is the Self a Social Construct?" *Inquiry* 52, no. 6 (December 2009): 551–73, at 562; and Edward E. Sampson, "Deconstructing Psychology's Subject," *Journal of Mind and Behavior* 4, no. 2 (Spring 1983): 135–64, at 142.

[34] This idea is reflected in Bernard Lonergan's thought. See Lonergan, "The Mediation of Christ in Prayer," 160–82, in *Philosophical and Theological Papers 1958–1964*, ed. Robert C. Croken, Frederick E. Crowe, and Robert M. Doran, *Collected Works of Bernard Lonergan* (Toronto: University of Toronto Press, 1996), at 171; Bernard Lonergan, "Common Sense," 84–108, in *Understanding and Being*, at 98–103; and idem, "A Definition of Metaphysics," 181–99, in *Understanding and Being*, at 188.

[35] My phrase. In psychoanalytic discussions there is some controversy on this point. One reading of Freud holds to mental structures of the infant working themselves out via the instinctual drives inherent in the infant. This contrasts with some strands of Object Relations theory, which requires the engagement with the other to provide both content and the occasion to activate/actualize the inherent dynamic possibilities in the infant. It is beyond the scope of the present work to adjudicate this dispute. It is also not necessary for what follows. Both ends of the theoretical spectrum recognize the existence of internal, dynamic structures operating in infant relationships at initial stages of development. Both

In one moment of this dynamism we are mediated to ourselves by the encounter with what is other than ourselves. There is a sense in which we come to ourselves "passively" by being affected by what is other than ourselves.[36] But in another moment of the dynamism we are active participants, directing our participation in the process and intentionally (and also unintentionally) affecting others, even as our choices shape who we are becoming.[37]

Through the interplay of these passive and active engagements with the "other" over the course of a lifetime we come to "self-possession." But the current state of our self-possession is always playing itself out in tension with our encounters with the world that is other and with those aspects of ourselves that are not directly under our conscious, intentional control.[38] Thus my sense of self at this moment will undergo change as my social relationships change or the political climate in my city changes or when a close friend dies unexpectedly. My becoming will be shaped by those "external" aspects of my world that are beyond my control. But, as psychological research reminds us, the same is also true with respect to "internal" forces, unconscious feelings or memories that shape my response to the experiences of my conscious life.[39] They, too, have a part to play in my becoming.

---

also recognize that these initial relational dynamics have enduring effects on one's later psychic and relational life: one's sense of self, the self/world relation, one's relationships with other persons. Both also affirm that these early structural elements remain operative at an unconscious level and impact conscious life. These three points, although theorized differently by different psychoanalytic schools, are held in common. They are the points most relevant to the present discussion.

[36] Zahavi, "Is the Self a Social Construct?" 565ff., makes this point, drawing on the writings of Edmund Husserl. Part of Zahavi's project is to indicate that one can hold for a "transcendental I" and still give full weight to the social mediation of the content (I will speak of "meanings") to the "I" via engagement with the other.

[37] This is the basis for the conviction that we do have responsibility for whom we become/the characteristics of our future selves that emerge from our present intentional actions. See Lonergan, "Mediation of Christ in Prayer," 172–74; idem, "Ethics and God," 225–51, in *Understanding and Being*, at 229–33.

[38] Julia Kristeva alludes to this psychological dynamism in her discussion of passion operating in the unconscious realm in Kristeva, "The Passion According to Motherhood," 79–94, in *Hatred and Forgiveness*, esp. 80–82.

[39] See, for example, the discussion of complexes, their formation, and their impact from the realm of the unconscious on later conscious life in Gustav Bovensiepen, "Attachment-Dissociation Network: Some Thoughts about Modern Complex Theory," *Journal of Analytic Psychology* 51 (2006): 451–66, esp. 452–54. Joseph Sandler discusses the

Both philosophical and psychological research have provided resources for explaining *why* our personal becoming operates in this way. Philosophical reflection, partly drawing on research in psychology, has elaborated an understanding of cognitional dynamics in our coming to know.[40] Making use of Bernard Lonergan's cognitional theory, we can summarize these dynamics as follows. First, through the medium of our senses we encounter what is "other." (Lonergan speaks of "data," "objects," and "subjects.") Our sensory engagement with what is "other" awakens the desire to understand. It stimulates "wonder" or "questioning," the desire to know.[41] We assemble aspects of previous acts of understanding in the process of coming to insight into the present experience. That is, we have an act of understanding. But sometimes our initial insights are wrong.[42] Further observation or additional information leads us to revise what we thought we knew. So we also subject our understanding to verification against a wider horizon of confirmed understandings, insights we have come to judge to be "true."[43] This verification in judgment characterizes

---

interconnection of unconscious and conscious via the language of self-representation (or object representation) and fantasy in Sandler, "Fantasy, Defense, and the Representational World," *Infant Mental Health Journal* 15, no. 1 (Spring 1994): 26–35, at 27–28. For the role of affects, both conscious and unconscious, in our behavior, see ibid., 29.

[40] As with the notion of the "self," so also with cognitional theories. There are many articulations and numerous points in dispute. For what follows I will be relying on the terminology of Bernard Lonergan's cognitional theory as sketched out in his "Cognitional Structure," 205–21, in *Collection*, ed. Frederick E. Crowe and Robert M. Doran, *Collected Works of Bernard Lonergan* (Toronto: University of Toronto Press, 1988), and elaborated in greater detail in Bernard Lonergan, *Insight: A Study of Human Understanding* (New York: Philosophical Library, 1970). The basic philosophical understanding of cognition I will be articulating is not particularly controversial. In any case, the claims I will be making are open to verification (or falsification) by the reader's reflection on her or his own processes of cognition.

[41] We might not actually formulate a question when this activation of wonder occurs. But when we reflect on the experience of wonder, the dynamism of inquiry is unmistakable.

[42] See, for example, Bernard Lonergan, "Judgment," 109–32, in *Understanding and Being*, at 122, on the revisability of insights.

[43] See Lonergan, "Judgment," 115, where he observes: "You make a judgment because you grasp the sufficiency of the evidence. But your grasping the sufficiency of the evidence can depend upon past judgments; as soon as someone disputes the judgment, you begin invoking those past judgments to justify your present judgment. Again, you invoke them to limit, qualify, clarify, and explain just what you mean when you make this judgment. A judgment occurs within a context of other judgments, within a context of some determi-

the transition from simply "having an idea about something" to being able to claim that we "know" something.[44] What we have understood and then confirmed by means of judgment as "known" can then serve as the basis for determining a course of responsible action.

This brief sketch of cognitional process and its movement from experience of the other to the attainment of knowledge has several implications. First, it tells us that knowing is what Lonergan terms a "formally dynamic structure."[45] It is a structure composed of parts that are themselves dynamic: moving toward something. The interrelationships of the parts in their operations means that knowing cannot be reduced to any of its parts (e.g., seeing, hearing, getting an idea, forming a judgment) but only occurs when the parts fulfill their operations within the dynamic movement toward knowing. Its formally dynamic structure means that knowing is a self-assembling (and self-correcting) process. Second, it implies that our cognitional processes are directed toward a grasp of what Lonergan terms "the real."[46] But third, that grasp is always of the real as understood—that

---

nate development of intelligence, and this contextual aspect of judgment is fundamental. We know our worlds not by one judgment but by an accumulation of judgments, as the fruit of a long series of judgments, and the meaning of any judgment is dependent upon a retinue of other connected judgments that explain it, give it its presuppositions, exhibit its consequences, exhibit all the other complementary things that, in some extremely delicate fashion, qualify and elucidate the particular judgment we are making."

[44] See Lonergan, "Judgment," and idem, "Philosophical Positions with Regard to Knowing," 214–43, in idem, *Philosophical and Theological Papers 1958–1964*, ed. Robert C. Croken, Frederick E. Crowe, and Robert M. Doran, *Collected Works of Bernard Lonergan* (Toronto: University of Toronto Press, 1996), at 224–25.

[45] Lonergan, "Cognitional Structure," 206–8; idem, *Method in Theology* (New York: Seabury, 1979), 12–13.

[46] See Lonergan, "Cognitional Structure," 211–14. Although he does not use the phrase "the real" in this context, the point is the same. See also Lonergan, "Judgment," 110–11, where he observes: "The act of judgment is the act that adds assent to a proposition, that changes a proposition from the expression of an object of thought, the expression of some bright idea that comes into your mind, into an object of affirmation." This affirmation is of "the real," that it is thus. See also Bernard Lonergan, "Method in Catholic Theology," 29–53, in *Philosophical and Theological Papers 1958–1964*, at 40–41; idem, "Common Sense," 106–7, and the discussion in idem, "Knowing and Being," 133–55, in *Understanding and Being*, esp. 148–49. In *Insight*, 252, Lonergan comments: "Our own position, as contained in the canon of parsimony, was that the real is the verified; it is what is to be known by the knowing constituted by experience and inquiry, insight and hypothesis, reflection and verification."

is, as *interpreted*—from within a horizon of acts of understanding that have already been attained and confirmed in judgment.[47]

In other words, understanding—and therefore knowing—is always based on a hermeneutic act; it presupposes an act of interpretation of the data of experience.[48] Fourth, our knowing is always affectively charged. It is motivated by desire at its basis. But, as will be clarified below, it is also colored by affective associations related to prior experiences of understanding, both those that are consciously accessible and those that operate unconsciously until such time as we draw them into reflexive awareness. These associations shape our disposition even in the initial moments of encounter before we have moved from experience of the other to an act of understanding.[49] Thus the "real" is always mediated to us by *affectively charged* meaning.[50]

[47] This horizon of prior meanings I have termed a "personal matrix of meanings." We will be drawing the explicit connection and distinctions between these two conceptual-izations shortly. Lonergan gets at this point indirectly in "The Form of Inference," 3–16, in *Collection*, at 7, when he states: "Similarly, the implication of the conclusion in the data is not any general principle or rule. It arises from the intuition of the moment; its ground is the objective configuration of the moment as interpreted through the accu-mulated insights of experienced judgment; its value is just the value of that judgment; its only court of appeal is the event, and when the event has come, then, except on a theory of identical historical cycles, its day of usefulness is over forever. To attempt to apply symbolism to such inferences would be to misunderstand symbolism. The data can hardly be stated, much less abbreviated. The implication is not a general correlation to be employed repeatedly but the unique coincidence of a complex objective configuration and a complex subjective interpretation and judgment." See also the quotation in n. 46 above.

[48] To say that all knowing is mediated by interpretation is not to claim that it is a matter of "anything goes," capricious fancy, or absolute relativism. It is to recognize the limits imposed on our knowing by the processes of knowing themselves. But knowing is always oriented toward the real and, in principle, admits of correction. Correction occurs when our understanding is challenged. It is measured against the horizon of our prior attainments of verified judgments and the horizon of knowledge enshrined in the shared matrix of meanings we inhabit. But it is also subject to revision in light of new encounters with the real that may call prior attainments into question. See Lonergan, "Judgment," 115; and n. 46 above.

[49] For example, my prior experience may have led me to conclude that a particular professor is a boring lecturer. When I enter into a new lecture situation my prior history can color my affective receptivity to what is about to unfold, even before the professor has spoken a word.

[50] See Lonergan, *Method in Theology*, 30–31, where he writes: "The feeling relates us, not just to a cause or an end, but to an object. Such feeling gives intentional consciousness its mass, momentum, drive, power. Without these feelings our knowing and deciding would

This brief sketch of cognition has implications for our experience of personal becoming. Our personal becoming arises from our engagement with the world around us. It is cognitively mediated as we seek the real. But our grasp of the real is always intrinsically interpretive, colored by our prior acts of understanding and by the affective nuances that precondition our present engagement and give energy to our intentional orientation to the world around us.[51]

Psychological research leads to similar conclusions regarding our cognitional processes, but it also focuses attention on other aspects of the dynamics of becoming as it seeks to understand our psychic operations. One of the aspects of psychological research that will be of particular importance for our discussion of personal becoming has already been hinted at: relationality.[52] Our personal becoming is intrinsically relational. This confirms what philosophy observes, that we are awakened to awareness of ourselves

---

be paper thin. Because of our feelings, our desires and our fears, our hope or despair, our joys and sorrows, our enthusiasm and indignation, our esteem and contempt, our trust and distrust, our love and hatred, our tenderness and wrath, our admiration, veneration, reverence, our dread, horror, terror, we are oriented massively and dynamically in a world mediated by meaning." See also Lonergan, "Time and Meaning," 94–121, in *Philosophical and Theological Papers 1958–1964*, at 98–100; idem, "The Analogy of Meaning," 183–213, in *Philosophical and Theological Papers 1958–1964*, at 189–91.

[51] There are other aspects of meaning operative as well. These will be discussed below.

[52] This idea has become broadly accepted in philosophy as well as in psychology. We have already seen traces of it in philosophy in the references to Husserl in Zahavi, "Is the Self a Social Construct?" 563–65. We also find it in Sampson, "Deconstructing Psychology's Subject," 136; Ruth Abbey, "Charles Taylor, *Sources of the Self: The Making of the Modern Identity*," 268–90, in *Central Works of Philosophy, Vol. 5: Quine and After*, ed. John Shand (Durham: Acumen, 2006); and in Charles Taylor, *Sources of the Self: The Making of the Modern Identity* (Cambridge, MA: Harvard University Press, 1989), 35–39. The psychological literature, likewise, takes this as a given. Present discussions focus on the pros and cons of various theoretical frameworks for articulating the dynamics involved in infancy and in later development. For a brief sampling, see Bovensiepen, "Attachment-Dissociation Network: Some Thoughts about Modern Complex Theory"; Sandler, "Fantasy, Defense, and the Representational World"; Lynne Murray, "Intersubjectivity, Object Relations Theory, and Empirical Evidence from Mother-Infant Interactions," *Infant Mental Health Journal* 12, no. 3 (Fall 1991): 219–32. For a critical appraisal of the empirical research that supports some of the theoretical constructs regarding infant relational development, see Katrine Zeuthen, Signe Holm Pedersen, and Judy Gammelgaard, "Attachment and the Driving Force of Development: A Critical Discussion of Empirical Infant Research," *International Forum of Psychoanalysis* 19 (2010): 230–39.

by encounter with the other.[53] Paradigmatically, we can understand this in the differentiation of the infant from her mother, which occurs before the development of language.[54] In this initial phase the recognition of an other who does not conform immediately to the inarticulate desires of the infant instills the sense of otherness that underlies later differentiation.[55] This experience of "otherness" is the ground from which the sense of self as different from the other emerges. The self is self-in-relation, or, to place the stress on the self-constituting aspect of relation to the other, one could say that the self initially experiences itself as other-than-the-other.[56] Our sense of self emerges from this primordial experience of relationality.

The manner in which one negotiates this early emergence to "self-awareness" has an enduring importance in the later life of the person. The differentiation itself is "meaning laden"; it bears meanings that *shape how we interpret the world* and how we enter into future relationship. The meanings emerging in that early self-differentiation can color

---

[53] Lonergan discusses this as the "first period of human life," one characterized by engagement with objects. This engagement "makes one what one is." See Lonergan, "The Mediation of Christ in Prayer," 171.

[54] Julia Kristeva makes oblique reference to this in "The Passion According to Motherhood," 82, and eadem, "The Triple Uprooting of Israel," 213–21, in *Hatred and Forgiveness*, at 215, where she observes: "The microcosm of psychoanalytic investigation uses the same logic: from Freud to his modern disciples, the analytic experience discovers that the child becomes a subject of speech, thought, and meaning when he is able, under certain biological and familiar conditions, to lose his mother as well as her narcissistic and phallic omnipotence, and from this foundational 'exile'—'separation,' according to Freud, 'depressive position,' according to Melanie Klein, 'lack,' according to Lacan—to find the object and the other again in psychic representation and language, by means of the imaginary and the symbolic, in what might—under these conditions alone—become the precarious freedom of the human condition. Moreover, our acts of creativity, which are the rebirths of our subjectivity throughout life, demand the capacity not to renounce the self but to stay away from the old Self or 'object,' so as to give it a different meaning in new ties, new transferences, a continuous 'transitional space' (D. Winnicott), which is the private side of civilization, and culture."

[55] Attachment theory explores the implications of this phase of development and its later repetitions in other relationships. It argues that poorly negotiated separations and distinctions can embed harmful relational dynamics into one's later relational patterns. See Bovensiepen, "Attachment-Dissociation Network: Some Thoughts about Modern Complex Theory," 453–54, 456–57.

[56] Kristeva writes: "[Reflexive consciousness] is a matter of the capacity for an encounter (or sharing) of the same with the other and, simultaneously, of the same with oneself as another" (Kristeva, "The Passion According to Motherhood," 80).

one's fundamental disposition with respect to the world one only later comes to understand through the symbolic mediation of language. For example, an infant who negotiates the transition into "otherness" (selfhood) surrounded by nurturing and the reinforcement of affirmation will presumably (barring other traumatic interventions) approach the world with greater openness, optimism, and trust than one who has not experienced such a secure early life.[57] The meanings associated with the transition to a sense of self, even though occurring in a pre-linguistic phase of development, remain dynamically effective in later life, but at an unconscious or subconscious level.[58]

Similarly, as linguistic skills develop the child appropriates meanings that are largely predetermined by the socio-linguistic context. Although relatively stable for the child who is just learning, language itself, and the meanings it conveys, are constantly in flux. The language we have inherited, after all, has had a history of development of its own. Terms have taken on shades of meaning and reversals of meaning in the course of their use as a medium of relationship. Our mastery of language is part of the process of our coming to a sense of self and is, to a significant extent, constitutive of our sense of self. It provides us with the tools we need to interpret ourselves (and our world) to ourselves (and to one another). But our engagement with the meaning borne by language is not passive. Part of our development into selfhood is the acquisition of sufficient mastery of language and of the socio-culturally embedded meanings within it that we can begin to differentiate ourselves from the meanings that have been given—choosing to identify with some and embrace them, and choosing to distance ourselves from others. We become agents in shaping language and in shaping the shared matrix of meanings we inhabit as social beings.[59]

[57] See the discussion in Murray, "Intersubjectivity, Object Relations Theory, and Empirical Evidence from Mother-Infant Interactions."

[58] Drawing on the work of Mario Jacoby, Verena Kast and Daniel Stern, Bovensiepen discusses "Representations of Interactions that have been Generalized" (RIGs). "RIGs are the infant's early interaction patterns with his mother, saved in the implicit memory which depicts a behaviour expectation and a pre-verbal representation. According to the affective colouring of these RIGs, they then enter into dynamic complexes" (Bovensiepen, "Attachment-Dissociation Network: Some Thoughts about Modern Complex Theory," 453). The author then goes on to note that such patterns "proved to be very stable in later life."

[59] See Sampson, "Deconstructing Psychology's Subject," 145, where he cites the work of Anthony Giddens on the reciprocality of influence. On the importance of language and our role in shaping it, see Alexander Kremer, "Richard Rorty's Interpretation of

*Personal Becoming and Personal Matrices of Meaning*

We can recast what has been said up to this point about personal becoming and the mediation of meaning in terms of matrices of meaning.
The personal becoming we experience, our process of becoming selves, is
the process of constructing a personal matrix of meanings. This process is
a function partly of what occurs to us and partly of how we interact with
what occurs as we grow in our capacity to determine our own choices.

At an initial stage we can say that the world is mediated to us by
meanings.[60] These meanings predate our arrival on the scene. They inhabit
a shared matrix (that they constitute and by which they are constituted)
by which larger social units (family, community, nation, religion) name
themselves and their relationships to the larger world. Some of these
meanings are directly accessible to reflection as we grow in our ability to
use the linguistic symbols we have inherited, but some of them are also
deeply embedded in the foundations beneath those meanings accessible
to direct reflection. They only come to conscious awareness through much
struggle.[61] For example, gender role distinctions in family and public life
were broadly accepted and not reflected on as an object of criticism until
the women's suffrage movement gained currency. As individual women
began to assert themselves publicly, their actions shaped what other
women and men could begin to imagine about their relationships.[62]

These "given" meanings, however, to be effective in the emerging self of
the individual, have to be appropriated, and appropriation always includes
*interpretation*.[63] Although a process of communication and critique of

---

Selfhood," 191–99, in *Self and Society: Central European Pragmatist Forum*, vol. 4, ed.
Alexander Kremer and John Ryder (New York: Rodopi, 2009), at 195–96. For an interpretation of the role of narrative in our self-constitution, see ibid., 197–99. Without
committing myself to the whole of Rorty's philosophy I simply note the convergence of
aspects of his thought with the argument I am making. It is important in this connection
to attend to his use of the phrase "web of relations" at p. 198, which coheres with the
conceptualization of matrices of meanings, regardless of whether one accepts Rorty's
particular understanding of language.

[60] Lonergan, *Method in Theology*, 28, 76–77, 238.

[61] This is the principle behind psychoanalysis as a therapeutic model.

[62] Charles Taylor's image of the basement level of meanings applies here.

[63] This is evident in the elaboration of "interpretation" as a functional specialty in
Lonergan, *Method in Theology*, 127. See also his discussion of the problem of interpretation, which draws the connection between interpretation as a functional specialty and
the interpretive dynamic intrinsic to coming to understand, in ibid., 154. One can see
the connection as well in the analogy Lonergan draws between the doing of history

understanding can keep interpretation of important values within a range of possibilities, a certain amount of "drift" in understanding can occur because each of us understands against the horizon of our own personal prior appropriations of meaning. Most of these prior appropriations will come from the shared matrix (matrices) we inhabit, but in their particulars they, too, will have undergone some "drift" because they, too, will have been interpreted in the process of appropriation. That is, the world mediated to us by meaning is always a world *interpreted* by the one who encounters it. Thus the relatively stable center of gravity in the meaning can, in the process of appropriation, undergo change even without our adverting to it.

Apart from the unnoticed and unintended changes in the meanings we appropriate from the matrix we share with others, in the process of our growth in self-direction we develop the capacity to choose to embrace some meanings and reject others. Our own intentional acts have an impact on the shared matrix. On the one hand, the meanings we choose to embrace and on which we choose to act take on for us the status of meanings affirmed. We value them.[64] In doing so we communicate in the public space an affirmation of the value as it preexists in the shared matrix. On the other hand, meanings we choose to reject, despite their positive valence in the shared matrix, take on a different status for us individually and for those in our circle of associates.[65] They are now colored for those around us by our having rejected them.

If the world is, in fact, mediated to us by meanings, then we can also make the more striking claim that we are mediated to ourselves

---

and the individual's idea of himself or herself; both are interpretive. See Lonergan, "The Philosophy of History," 54–79, in *Philosophical and Theological Papers 1958–1964*, at 73.

[64] It is not entirely clear whether, in the course of choosing to affirm a particular meaning, we ascribe a positive value to it first and then choose it or we choose it and then appraise its value in a way that justifies it to ourselves. The process could be either or both. Certainly, in the early stages of the formation of a sense of self many meanings are "given" and therefore accepted as normal and good, prior to any independent capacity for making judgments about normality and goodness.

[65] It is not that our associates will necessarily share our assessment of the meaning. The point is, rather, that they will recognize that our assessment of the meaning is negative. They may therefore evaluate it as a matter to be avoided in conversation or as a basis for distancing themselves from the relationship. This impulse of avoidance would be an indication that an additional meaning had been attached to the initial meaning, apart from any denotation of its content.

by meanings.[66] Our self is mediated to itself by meanings. The earlier discussion of philosophical and psychological contributions to the notion that we are in a process of becoming, mediated by our cognitional engagement with the surrounding world, bears this out. The fact that we are mediated to ourselves by meanings shows in the process by which we come to self-awareness, differentiating ourselves from the "other," the process of appropriating language and symbolic reflective activity, emerging into the capacity to apply symbolic bearers of meaning to reflection upon our selves.

These are stages in the process by which we come to a sense of self. It is important to note that this sense of self is self-assembling.[67] The dynamism of cognition, awakened to itself through encounter with the other, is not static. It engages with the world. This dynamism of engagement is an ongoing correlate of conscious life. It is the dynamic foundation of the possibility of a personal history of interaction with a larger world, the engagement by which we appropriate (and adapt) the meanings with which and by means of which we understand the world and, more importantly for the present moment, by which we identify ourselves to ourselves.

This self-assembling constructs our personal matrices of meanings. Our interpretation of the world and of ourselves contributes to a more-or-less stable, integrated understanding of "the real." The different meanings, in their interrelationships, sustain that stability. Most of the meanings in this

---

[66] This point is implied in Lonergan, "The Philosophy of History," 73. The point is further underscored by his discussion of self-presence and its distinction from reflective self-awareness in which we objectify a concept of ourselves (I would say "objectify our sense of self") in order to reflect on ourselves. In both cases the mode of access to ourselves is mediated by meaning—the meaning(s) of the objects we are regarding in self-presence and the meaning(s) of the objectified self in reflective self-awareness. See Bernard Lonergan, "Self-Appropriation and Insight," 3–32, in *Understanding and Being*, at 15–17; idem, "Elements of Understanding," 33–58, in *Understanding and Being*, at 33–35; idem, "Knowing and Being," 139–41; idem, "Metaphysical Analysis and Metaphysical Integration," 200–224, in *Understanding and Being*, at 219–24; and idem, "Philosophical Positions with Regard to Knowing," 221–26.

[67] This is a consequence of the fact that our sense of self is always cognitively mediated. As our knowing is a self-assembling process, in its appropriation of verified meanings it provides data from which we assemble a sense of self. This assembly occurs obliquely in the form of self-presence as we attend to what is other and it occurs reflexively as we attend to ourselves as the ones doing the attending. See the discussions of self-presence and self-appropriation referenced in the previous note.

matrix we experience as directly accessible to conscious reflection; others are buried more deeply; yet all of them exercise a potentially powerful impact on our sense of self and our integration of new experiences and understandings into our sense of self.

The point I want to make here is that our sense of self *is* a personal matrix of meanings. Our access to our personal selves is mediated through the meanings we have assembled into our sense of self and of the world *through* our engagement with what is other by means of the dynamics of cognitional processes. Within this sense of self we can affirm the presence of both consciously accessible "meanings" and others that are dynamically operative below the level of conscious reflection. Both levels are operative in the sense of self because both are at work in the processes of appropriation, interpretation, and construction of meaning. This personal matrix of meanings is the only way we have reflective access to ourselves. It *is* our sense of self.

Nevertheless, the sense of self we possess (the personal matrix of meanings through which we possess ourselves) is not static. It is in a constant state of tension because it is in a constant process of becoming. Our dynamic processes of integrating meaning into our sense of self and of the world are constantly operative. Prior achievements of meaning provide the basis for integrating new meanings and for their interpretation. But those prior attainments, when they are challenged, can also be revised, disrupted, undone by encounters with other meanings. Thus the continuity of our sense of self depends to a certain extent on the stability over time of the matrix we have achieved—the stability of our core complexes of meanings and values. We actually participate in this process of stabilization and reformation. Our intentional responses to the tension between stability and change in our personal matrix of meanings is the locus of our responsibility for our own future becoming.

This presentation of matrices of meaning and the becoming of the sense of self can help to make sense of the claim that the experience of harm disrupts the stability of the sense of self. The dynamic character of our sense of self—that it is constantly in the process of becoming—is also the basis of its vulnerability to disruption. Because we are mediated to ourselves by meaning and because our sense of self is structured by the appropriation and integration of new meanings into itself, the encounter with meanings that challenge our sense of self can unsettle its structural integrity.

This destabilization touches both the sense of self and the self/world relation. Some assaults on the sense of self are experienced primarily as personal attacks. For example, a spouse violates trust by engaging in an extramarital affair. This personal experience of harm can destabilize the sense of self but can also unsettle the harmed party's sense of her or his place in a larger world. Alternatively, a child's experience of her or his parents' divorce will destabilize the child's world but will also, consequently, destabilize the child's sense of self. Sense of self and sense of self/world relation are integrally related because both are constituted by the appropriation of meaning into the meaning structures (matrices of meanings) of the individual through which we come to a sense of self, of world, and of our place in the world.

### Structures of Meaning in the Sense of Self

The descriptive account of the self as a personal matrix of meanings provides a useful framework for conceiving what is taking place in the experience of harm and will prove valuable for naming forgiveness. But up to this point the presentation has been rather abstract, particularly with respect to the meanings that both constitute the self and are disrupted in the experience of harm. These meanings, I have proposed, do not exist within the matrix in isolation, as discrete entities. Rather, they are dynamically interrelated. The very concept of a matrix indicates a flexibly structured set of relations from which new structures can arise. Before we return our attention to the phenomenon of harm, it will be helpful to say something about the structures of meanings within the sense of self, their distinctions and their interrelationships.

### PROMINENT KINDS OF MEANINGS IN THE SENSE OF SELF

The first point to note is that there are different kinds of meanings at work in the sense of self. As meanings they are dynamic; they possess energy that can manifest itself in a kind of directed "movement" with respect to another or to oneself. As meanings within a matrix they mutually condition one another. Consequently, some of the meanings are implied in the specifications of other meanings. Although we distinguish different meanings with the terms we use, the distinctions are somewhat malleable. The boundaries between one "meaning" and another can in some circumstances be fluid. Nevertheless, it will be helpful to identify some of the kinds of meanings that have already been implicated in the discussion. Here it will be important to remember that "meanings" are not reducible to "concepts," but we must use concepts to identify them.

These concepts point toward the "center of gravity" in the dynamism of each kind of meaning.

The first kind of meaning we can call "affective." It includes the whole range of feelings from attraction through indifference to repugnance.[68] As indicated above, affective energy is the driving force behind our engagement with the world and, by extension, behind our coming to our sense of self. It is integrally related to the second kind of meaning, "perspectival" (alternatively: "standpoint"). This includes the range of data we have experienced (already affectively charged) and our interpretations of it in relationship to *our* questioning (seeking to understand) precisely because it is ours. It is therefore also the coloration we bring to any experience by virtue of the standpoint from which we engage the world. It is the nuance of meaning that occurs because this world of meanings is "mine." A third kind of meaning, "judgment," refers to our capacity for assessment and evaluation.[69] We noted above that judgment is an integral part of the process of verifying acts of understanding and thereby effecting the transition from insight to "knowledge." But judgment's evaluative capacity has broader application. It is brought to bear in assessing practical matters, determining what is a rational line of thought, and deciding what would be a moral way of proceeding.

Affective, perspectival, and judgmental kinds of meanings mutually condition one another in the process of cognition itself. They are clearly implicated in the appropriation and construction of meaning. But as we noted earlier, relationality, a fourth kind of meaning, is likewise integrally involved. It is the encounter with the other that awakens the self to itself. But "others" are not just "others." Some are friends, some are unknown, some are enemies. Our capacity for relating and the meanings we attach to relationships will be shaped by affectivity, cognition, and judgment, but also by a fifth kind of meaning, historicality, the givenness of our location in time, place, culture, and social status, as well as the fact that we accumulate a history (itself a construct of meanings) and contribute to the histories of others. In addition, relationality and historicality are shaped by a sixth kind of meaning, temporality, the awareness that we are

[68] See, for example, the discussion of passions and desires in Kristeva, "The Passion According to Motherhood," 80–81. See also Lonergan, "The Mediation of Christ in Prayer," 168–70.

[69] In this context "judgment" does include Lonergan's notion of the function of rationality in the verification of insight, but it also includes the broader evaluative dynamism involved in weighing alternatives and critiquing the merits of different states of affairs.

situated in time. Our time is limited. Our access to the past is mediated by memory. We apprehend ourselves in the present, but we also project ourselves into the future; we anticipate and aspire. We envision a world in continuity with the world we currently inhabit, but changing within an anticipated range of possibilities. Our awareness of ourselves as moving through time therefore co-conditions our experience of ourselves as in relationship and as historically situated. It contributes to our sense of self and of our self/world relation.

The meaning of temporality, especially in and through our aspirations, draws into focus a seventh, related kind of meaning, intentionality. In this context intentionality refers to the significance of the fact that we direct our attention and efforts toward an objective, whether something to be known or a goal to be accomplished.[70] The energy in our intending is the guiding force in cognitional processes, in our relationality, our judgments, and our exercises of freedom, but in its turn it is shaped by affectivity, perspective, judgment, freedom, and valuation. Freedom is the eighth kind of meaning. It is more than the capacity to choose; it is fundamentally the capacity to make responsible choices about the direction of the course of our becoming. It is presupposed by intentionality. It is the locus of the sense of ourselves as responsible for our actions. Freedom is presupposed by our intentionality, but it is not absolute.[71]

Historicality, temporality, relationality, and perspective play decisive roles in shaping the context within which we exercise our freedom, imposing the concrete limitations that make intentional action possible.[72]

Finally, valuation is that range of meanings by which we prioritize among competing interests. Often experienced in alignment with affectivity, valuation also overlaps with judgment in shaping the exercise of freedom.

These nine kinds of meanings do not exhaust the possibilities. One could identify others. One might also find it more useful to collapse some into others. As indicated above, the boundaries between them are somewhat fluid. But naming these kinds of meanings in this way serves

---

[70] Intentionality is the operation within consciousness that orients our consciousness toward some object or other. See Lonergan, *Method in Theology*, 12, 34, 73. For an application of intentionality analysis to the project of method in theology, see ibid., 340–43. See ibid., 106–7 for a discussion of the relationship of intentionality to action. See also Lonergan, "The Mediation of Christ in Prayer," 168–70.

[71] See Lonergan, *Method in Theology*, 240.

[72] See the distinction between essential freedom and effective freedom in Lonergan, "Ethics and God," 230–32.

a twofold heuristic purpose. First, it provides a common vocabulary that will allow us to parse more carefully the inner workings of the experience of harm, and therefore to understand in more detail what is at stake in forgiving. Second, it can help us to conceive of the sense of self more clearly as structured in a matrix of meanings.

## Constellations of Meaning

This second point, that the sense of self is structured in a matrix of meanings, requires some elaboration. Each of the nine kinds of meanings mentioned above admits of a range of possibilities. If we think of them as dynamic forces, each of these kinds of meanings can be conceived as moving in different possible directions with respect to a given event, person, or possibility. Or, to turn this around, when we are confronted with any given event, person, or possibility our response will be negotiated among the different possible alignments of the energies represented by each of these kinds of meanings.

Taken individually, each kind of meaning represents an axis of possible impulses. We can therefore talk about these kinds of meanings individually as "axes" of meanings. The names we have used for these different kinds of meanings distinguish these axes in terms of their salient characteristics. However, the axes do not operate within our sense of self— our personal matrix of meanings—as isolated energies. They mutually influence each other. They converge and intersect in different ways with respect to different events, persons, and possibilities—past, present, and anticipated in the future—within our sense of self.

These convergences and intersections are not always stable. At times meanings align very comfortably with respect to a given object or experience. Our feelings, judgments, histories, anticipations of the future with respect to our family of origin, for example, might be quite harmonious. The meanings mutually sustain one another in their interrelationship. At other times they might not hold together as stably. The values of loyalty to family and maintaining peace in relationships, for example, might run afoul of a sense of responsibility, anxiety, and uncertainty about the future if one confronts abusive behavior by one of the family's members. Thus within the sense of self, in addition to axes of meanings we can also conceive of "constellations of meaning," loci where the convergences of meaning and the alignments of axes are such as to give greater structural stability to that constellation. The structural stability of the constellations can then shape the ways in which other, less complex meanings are integrated. Constellations, therefore, can possess a kind of "gravity" in the sense of self, providing stability to other meanings and complexes of meanings.

Conversely, these constellations can also collide with other constellations or meanings in ways that produce instability. Some constellations of meanings we have inherited from the world around us. They pre-existed our arrival on the scene. We appropriate them in the process of coming to ourselves, taking them as "givens." We can think of them as foundational complexes of meanings that contribute to the stability of the shared matrix of meanings from which we draw in the construction of our sense of self. Among these complexes are our cultural heritage, our religious belief systems, family traditions, our attitudes with respect to groups other than our own, and so on. We appropriate these (and other) complexes into our sense of self. Depending on circumstances, they can be so deeply internalized as to structure the "basement level" of meanings through which we interpret the rest of our subsequent experiences. These constellations of meaning provide centers of gravity or anchors or (relatively) stable foundations in relationship to which other meanings can be arranged as we appropriate them in the ongoing process of our personal becoming.

In addition to the constellations of meanings we inherit (the givens), there are also constellations we construct via our own engagement with the world around us. We fashion them in a kind of dialogical tension with the complexes of meanings we have inherited. Among these would be our personal friendships, the interests we pursue, our course of studies, the choice of a career, and the choice of a life-partner, as well as our responses to experiences of illness, personal tragedy, deaths of those we love, and so on. As with the constellations of meanings we inherit, those we construct as our personal complexes of meanings over the course of our becoming possess (acquire) a kind of gravity in our sense of self. They are integral to who we experience ourselves as being and becoming.

## STABILITY AND CHANGE IN CONSTELLATIONS OF MEANING

These constellations of meaning provide stability to our sense of self. Significant complexes of meaning become the lenses through which we interpret ourselves, our relationships, and our present experience of becoming. I will illustrate with a personal example. In my pre-adolescent years my parents underwent a turbulent divorce. This became for me a prominent lens through which I viewed and interpreted myself to others throughout my adolescence and into adulthood. The constellation of meanings in relationship to that experience formed a powerful center of gravity for my sense of self.[73] However, over time that constellation of meanings has diminished in importance in my sense of self. It has been replaced by an adult history of relationships, commitments, accomplishments, and interests. The "weight" of these meanings has, over time, replaced the significance of the earlier constellation in my sense of self over the course of my personal becoming.

This brings to light two aspects of these constellations of meanings. The first is that, once they have assumed a relatively stable structure, they exhibit a kind of inertia. They resist change. In a manner analogous to the resistance to scientific revolutions examined by Thomas Kuhn, the constellations of meanings by which we interpret ourselves to ourselves and by which we organize our relationship to the wider world exert energy to maintain their structural integrity.[74] This makes sense. In the scientific realm new, unexpected data are first interpreted from within the prevailing framework of understanding. This integration is undertaken with as little disruption to the prevailing framework as possible. So also in the case of the individual person. We attempt to integrate new meanings by appropriating them to our existing constellations with as little disruption as possible. Constellations of meaning operate conservatively within our sense of self. They are like centers of gravity, organizing less "weighty" meanings in relation to themselves.

---

[73] Recent philosophical discussions have focused on the "narrative" self. What I am getting at here intersects with the concerns in those discussions. In general terms I would agree that our interpretations of ourselves to one another and to ourselves are fashioned into narrative form. However, I have chosen to focus on the deeper constituent components of narrative, meanings and their constellations. This approach will allow us to discuss in greater detail the experience of harm and what is at stake in undertaking forgiveness. For further information on the "narrative" self, see Kremer, "Richard Rorty's Interpretation of Selfhood"; Kenneth Baynes, "Self, Narrative, and Self-Constitution: Revisiting Taylor's 'Self-Interpreting Animals,'" *Philosophical Forum* 41, no. 4 (2010): 441–57; John Christman, "Narrative Unity as a Condition of Personhood," *Metaphilosophy* 35, no. 5 (October 2004): 695–713; Roger Frie, "Identity, Narrative, and Lived Experience after Postmodernity: Between Multiplicity and Continuity," *Journal of Phenomenological Psychology* 42 (2011): 46–60; Anthony Rudd, "In Defence of Narrative," *European Journal of Philosophy* 17, no. 1 (2007): 60–75; Fred Vollmer, "The Narrative Self," *Journal for the Theory of Social Behavior* 35, no. 2 (2005): 189–205, for different approaches to the contemporary discussion of narrative and selfhood.

[74] Thomas S. Kuhn, *The Structure of Scientific Revolutions* (Chicago: University of Chicago Press, 1962).

But this is only part of the story. Constellations do in fact undergo structural change, realignment, and in some cases are largely disassembled before their constituent elements can be realigned into a new stable constellation within a larger matrix of meanings (personal matrix of meanings). There are many reasons such a realignment may occur. However, for the purposes of this inquiry into forgiveness we limit our focus to the experiences of meaning that disrupt our sense of self, that is, experiences of harm. This occurs when one is confronted with a new meaning that defies integration into the existing complex. We experience such meanings as "disruptive." We have to respond to them.

Shy of a major realignment of the structure of one's matrix of meanings, when we are confronted with disruptive meanings there are three potential kinds of responses. One is a rejection or refutation of the meaning. This is commonly expressed in a rejection of its claims or its warrants and takes the form of (an) argument(s) about why the meaning is wrong. (The condemnation of Pelagius's understanding of grace and the mutual condemnations on several fronts by emerging ecclesial groups during the Protestant Reformation would be good examples of this kind of response.) A second potential response is an unreconciled coexistence of conflicting meanings. A kind of chasm of nonengagement with the meaning (or complex of meanings) keeps the two apart. (For example, the practical acceptance of scientific paradigms of knowing and its consequences—use of electricity, air travel, computers—side by side with scriptural literalism illustrates the disjunction.) Or third, one can engage in denial, refusing to acknowledge that the other meaning exists. (The virtual absence of dialogue between the Derridian and Anglo-American approaches to forgiveness would be a case in point.) These three kinds of responses may in actual practice be interwoven with one another in the effort to distance oneself from the claims of the disruptive meaning.

It is important to note that these three kinds of response directly parallel the responses one can make to the experience of harm. This is not accidental. If, as I am contending, our response to harm is a response to the meaning of the event, then the options available in such cases will resemble the options available to us in responding to any kind of meaning we would rather not embrace or integrate into our experience. But if this parallel holds, it also suggests that we will find a mode of response to disruptive meanings that parallels the response of forgiveness. This is, in fact, the case.

If we encounter a meaning that is disruptive of our personal matrix of meanings, and if we do not resist its advances, the alternative to the three kinds of responses identified above is to realign the constellations of meaning to which the new meaning is relevant. On a large scale this can involve the effort to integrate into a stable matrix whole constellations of meanings that, at an earlier time, we took to be opposed. On the level of shared matrices of meanings, the ongoing discussions about the relationship of science to religion exemplify this process. On a more individual and personal level, in the life of a child whose parents are divorcing, this realignment might express itself in the effort to reconcile the hurtful behavior of parents toward one another and toward their children with the trust children place in the goodness of their parents. In addition to the large-scale realignments of multiple complexes of meanings in the examples just mentioned (whether in a shared or personal matrix of meanings), one can think of the reconfiguration of an individual constellation of meanings in the light of incontrovertible new information. (For example, when a child learns in adolescence that she has been adopted, this can significantly reconfigure her sense of self as a member of a family.)

New meanings we appropriate into our personal matrix of meanings always involve some sort of adjustment. In a non-disruptive mode there is a mutual correlation between those meanings already operative in the matrix and what is experienced as new. (For example, the discovery that one does not like the taste of anchovies, or the experience of meeting a new person for the first time, can both be integrated into an existing personal matrix of meanings without disruption.) The new is integrated *as* understood by and *as* confirmation of the existing matrix. But disruptive meanings require more. They call for a restructuring of the existing constellation of meanings to which they are addressed. This restructuring can have reverberations throughout the entire matrix because the disruptive meanings destabilize the prior alignments of meanings in the matrix and call for a new configuration.

This restructuring in response to disruptive meanings has the character of a "conversion."[75] The term "conversion" here does not indicate a

---

[75] Lonergan describes conversion in terms of a "change of direction" that, potentially, impacts the whole of one's life. He observes: "Conversion, as lived, affects all of man's conscious and intentional operations. It directs his gaze, pervades his imagination, releases the symbols that penetrate to the depths of his psyche. It enriches his understanding, guides his judgments, reinforces his decisions." *Method in Theology*, 131; see also, 52, 130–31, 267–69. On the different kinds of conversion, see Lonergan, "Method in Catholic Theology," 37. On the interrelationship of intellectual, moral, and religious conversion,

religious change (although the parallels in dynamics are obvious). We can see this kind of conversion in what Kuhn has termed "paradigm change." It is a realignment of meanings and their structured interrelationships, potentially along each of the axes of meaning whose intersections form the fundamental constellations of meanings in our sense of self.[76]

Two examples will illustrate what I am getting at here. First, the recognition that differences of gender and race must not be used to justify discrimination in society reflects the appropriation of complexes of meanings that have had reverberations throughout our civic life. The embrace of these complexes of meanings has called for (and continues to call for) a conversion at all levels and in all areas of interpersonal relationship. It reshapes the meanings we identify in those relationships and, consequently, recasts the meanings we recognize in matters that intersect with them. Second, in a similar way, falling in love has the effect of a conversion. In the light of that experience one's priorities shift. The way we perceive ordinary objects changes; they become imbued with new meaning ("*She* left this note for *me!*" "This is the park where we first met.") because of the reordering called for by the complex of meanings associated with falling in love.

At this point it is worth pausing to note a distinction between these two examples of conversion. In the first the conversions involved emerged through much struggle. They encountered resistance—often violent resistance—before they gained sufficient force to dislodge the complexes of meanings opposed to them. Moreover, as many women and members of racial and ethnic minorities will attest, the conversions called for are not complete. The reverberations of the new complexes of meanings have not completed the realignment of the meanings structuring our civic life. By contrast, in the second example, falling in love, the conversion is (normally) readily embraced, at least at the start. It is experienced as an occasion of hope, joy, liberation, and a source of vitality for life. But even here, once the initial flush of excitement has passed, the process of realigning deeply embedded meanings to correspond with and support this new constellation may take a great deal of time.

---

see Lonergan, "Natural Knowledge of God," 117–34, in *A Second Collection*, ed. William J. F. Ryan and Bernard J. Tyrrell (Toronto: University of Toronto Press, 1974), at 127–30.

[76] Lonergan gets at this point when he maintains: "As history, so also interpretation does not promise univocal results. The interpreter may understand the thing, the words, the author, and himself. But if he undergoes conversion, he will have a different self to understand, and the new understanding of himself can modify his understanding of the thing, the words, and the author" (*Method in Theology*, 246).

In other words, conversions can result either from long struggle or spontaneous realignments of fundamental meanings in one's sense of self or of world (or both). But in either case integrating the new complex of meanings into the sense of self (whether on the social or the individual level) will be an ongoing process. The conversion sets a trajectory for future becoming but, once undertaken, that trajectory must be ratified in subsequent decisions over time. We do not convert "into" something different; we convert "toward becoming" in a different way—different from what our prior trajectory would have produced.[77]

## Recognition of Harm, Responding to Harm, and the Becoming Self

The preceding account of personal becoming, cognitional processes, the self, and matrices of meaning helps us to understand why harm affects us as it does—that, in fact, it disrupts our sense of self. It also helps us to see that the way we respond to the experience of harm will shape our future becoming.

To summarize, harm must be recognized as harm if it is to be a potential object of forgiveness. If it is not recognized as harm, it may well affect our personal becoming, but only if it is recognized as harm—as disruptive of the meanings by which our sense of self is constituted—will it potentially evoke a forgiveness response.

This recognition of a harm *as* a harm is a matter of interpretation. That is, we can only recognize it as harm when we appropriate its meaning through the horizon of prior acts of understanding and knowing that are themselves the result of interpretation of the meaning of other experiences. Some of these prior appropriations of meaning will be directly accessible to conscious reflection; others will not. But both conscious and unconscious meanings can shape our interpretation of present experience.

When harm *is* recognized as harm it is experienced as an assault on the self. (One could state this from the reverse angle: when one experiences something as an assault on the self it is recognized as a harm.) As an experience of meaning, the harm disrupts the matrix of meanings that constitutes our sense of self. The self then seeks to restabilize its personal matrix of meanings (sense of self) in response to the harm. This restabilization occurs in and through the interaction of the engagement

---

[77] Lonergan gets at this point in his discussion of religious conversion in *Method in Theology*, 283–84.

between the meaning of the harm and the meanings that constitute the personal matrix of meanings (sense of self).

To this summary I will add a further point. The intensity or degree of disruption caused by the meaning of the harm is directly correlated to the difficulty that will be encountered in overcoming its meaning. An insulting comment from someone about whom one does not really care will have less of an impact when it is expressed in private than if the individual broadcasts it—without objection by one's friends—in the public square. Integrating the disruption to one's sense of self into one's matrix of meanings will probably be less difficult in the former case than in the latter; the latter would call into question the larger complex of meanings centered on the personal relationships involved.

This summary points us toward the importance of the question of forgiveness. How we respond to an experience of harm will shape the person we are in the process of becoming. It will certainly have an impact on our sense of self in relationship to the particular harmful event and the one who occasioned it (if such a one can even be identified). But as the psychological literature indicates, especially in cases of trauma that lodges itself deep within our unconscious life the manner in which we engage the harm we experience can also affect our relations with others who have no relationship to the original event. The meaning of the harm can have a wide reach in the life of the one harmed. Consequently, the decision to forgive or not to forgive potentially has profound implications beyond the parties most intimately involved in the harm.

At the same time, despite the implications for our personal becoming, choosing to forgive can be very difficult. Two aspects of this difficulty come immediately to mind. First, in the face of a significant harm we can often feel great reluctance to even consider the possibility of forgiving. We simply do not *want* to forgive. We *want* to retaliate. Even if we recognize in a dispassionate moment that we *should* forgive, that does not automatically move us to desire to forgive. This is the experiential side of the paradox that we cannot "will" ourselves to will differently than we do. We can experience ourselves as "stuck" in an unforgiving frame of mind and heart. We sometimes speak of being internally divided.

Second, even if we *do* move to the point of desiring to forgive and embrace forgiving as our desired response to the event (and the perpetrator), we are not entirely at the disposal of our own volition. Some of the energy that underlies our hostility to the meaning of the event (and to the perpetrator) lives at the unconscious level. Although for the moment our conscious life may be oriented by the intention to forgive, at some later time the impulse to seek retribution may percolate to the surface from the deep recesses of the unconscious. It may impel us, despite our earlier resolve, to use the history of the event against the offender. Worse still, these energies might also impel us to act in retributive ways toward people uninvolved in the original offense but who, on some unconscious level, remind us of the parties who were involved.

We can understand these difficulties on the basis of what has been said so far. The impetus to desire or not desire anything is negotiated among a variety of meanings that in their interrelationships constitute our sense of self. We cannot rise above that reality to realign the dynamic orientation of any particular meaning or any complex of meanings "at will." Instead, the realignment, if it occurs, does so partly through our choosing and partly in a manner beyond our control. Consequently, coming to the point of embracing forgiveness toward an offender is often experienced as a "conversion." *As* a conversion, entering into forgiveness defines a trajectory for our future becoming with respect to the offense, the offender, and a broad range of other possible relationships.

We will need to bear these factors in mind as we turn to the project of naming forgiveness itself.

# $C$hapter 6

# Forgiveness
# as a Human Enactment

## Preliminaries

*I*n part 1 of this exploration we surveyed the landscape of the contemporary discussions of forgiveness. That survey drew our attention
to questions that, although commonly recognized as important for
understanding forgiveness, continue to evade resolution. In part 2 we have
been engaged in a task of excavation, digging beneath the complexities
that make some of these questions so intractable. Initially this led us
to probe the sources of major faultlines in the discussion (chap. 4). The
tensions revealed by our efforts directed our attention to consideration
of the person for whom forgiveness can be a question, the one who has
experienced a harm (chap. 5). In the process we have at last come to the
point at which we can name forgiveness as a human enactment.

The task of the present chapter is twofold. First, drawing on the insights of chapter 5, I shall present an account of forgiveness as a human
enactment. This will be in the mode not of definition, but of description.
That is, making use of the analyses of harm, meaning, and personal becoming presented in chapter 5, I shall describe from the perspective of the
human experience of forgiveness what is happening when one undertakes
to forgive. Once the dynamics operative in forgiving have been described,
the second task of this chapter will be to return to some of the important
unresolved questions raised thus far. To put this task in the form of a
question, we shall ask: "How might this descriptive account of forgiveness
affect the way we address those unresolved questions?" Initially we will
apply this question to tensions and disagreements that surfaced in part
1, the survey of the landscape. Then we will turn our attention to the
faultlines from chapter 4. The completion of these two tasks will bring to

a conclusion the discussion of forgiveness as a basic human enactment, but it will also set the stage for part 3, where we return to the question of specifically "Christian forgiveness."

## Naming Forgiveness as a Human Enactment

The approaches to forgiveness we have explored thus far have devoted a great deal of attention—quite legitimately—to retributive emotions. Particularly among the Anglo-American moral philosophers, but also within many of the psychological discussions, the emphasis has been on addressing and resolving (overcoming, forswearing, etc.) retributive emotions, particularly resentment. This concern has shown itself in the various attempts, whether philosophical or psychological, to define forgiveness in relation to those feelings.

These various efforts have merit. However, from within the matrix of meanings that has been taking shape in these pages the emphasis on the modification of or response to resentment and other retributive emotions in defining forgiveness seems misplaced. It appears to be based on a misidentification of the significance of resentment (and the other retributive emotions). Those retributive feelings and impulses are not the problem forgiveness addresses. They are much more like the canary in the coal mine. Their presence signals that something much deeper is amiss. They are symptoms of a more profound reality, the destabilization of the sense of self and of the self/world relationship.

The claim I have just made finds its justification in the line of inquiry that shifts attention away from definitions and surface-level feeling states to the deeper dynamics involved in responding to harm. If, instead of asking "what are the moral conditions under which one can morally forgive an offense?" or "how can we help clients to forgive?" we pose the question "what is taking place in the person who attempts to enact forgiveness?" it becomes readily apparent that there is much more involved in forgiving than management of feelings or behaviors. The process of forgiving is much more deeply interwoven with our psychic life and in our processes of becoming than is commonly recognized. We therefore need another way of naming forgiveness than has been provided up to this point.

Drawing on the results of the previous chapters, I would suggest that we can provide a descriptive account of what is happening when one undertakes to forgive in terms of three main headings: the nature of the harm, the trajectory of the forgiving response, and the characteristics of the response for the one who forgives.

*The Nature of the Harm*

In chapter 5, drawing on indications that had already surfaced with some consistency in other discussions of forgiveness, we probed the nature of the harm for which forgiveness is potentially a response. As all the authors we have considered affirm, whether explicitly or implicitly, the harm that evokes a potential response is recognized as meaningful. The meaning we recognize is one we experience as diminishing our worth, dignity, or person in some way. It is experienced as an assault. Sometimes we can experience it as a direct attack on ourselves. At other times we experience an assault on our "world" that impinges on the stability of our self/world relationship. Sometimes the harm disrupts both simultaneously; at other times the harm to one will also disrupt the other. In any case, the harm is experienced as damaging to one's *self*, to *me*. It is personal.

As we noted, for this harm to evoke a forgiving (or retributive) response, it must be *recognized* as a harm. Sometimes this recognition is thematic; it is explicitly named as harm. These are the cases most commonly addressed in the literature. Among the Anglo-American philosophers we have examined, this is the exclusive kind of recognition taken into consideration. But as our brief examination of psychic processes suggests, recognition might also occur on an unthematic—we could say "unconscious" or implicit— level. The meanings inscribed in the structures of the unconscious can, at times, identify something unconsciously as a personal affront. On the conscious level we might not acknowledge the harm, but unconscious, affective energies can shape our conscious life in ways that are, in fact, retributively driven. Our visceral responses, at times mysterious to our own conscious processes, can reveal that harm has been "recognized unconsciously."[1]

The experience of harm, as an experience of meaning, can call into question any (or many) of the kinds of meanings by which my sense of self

---

[1] It should be obvious that in this instance the use of the term "recognize" is only analogous to its use in relation to conscious recognition. It implies that on some level not directly accessible to conscious reflection we have made an association or connection between a currently presenting event and a prior event to which we do not, at the moment, consciously advert. Such connections are affectively charged. The feelings associated with a prior event attach themselves to the present event. In such cases the present event appears to mediate by means of what it symbolizes to us out of our past (and often forgotten) experiences an access to affective energy still retained from the past event. That energy discharges itself on the present event, often surprising those who witness its expression. The specific point of contact with prior history may only come to conscious awareness after much probing.

is constituted in my personal matrix of meanings. Affective, perspectival, judgmental, relational, historical, temporal, and any other kind of meaning: all are potentially disrupted by the experience of harm. Because these kinds of meanings are interrelated within the structure of one's personal matrix it is quite likely that the one who undergoes the disruption will experience it in relation to multiple axes of meanings simultaneously. It is that disruption we experience as harm, as an assault on our personal dignity. These meanings are all implicated not only in the constitution of our sense of self but also in our self/world relation, and by extension they are implicated in our relationship to the one who occasioned the experience of harm.

Indeed, the meaning we attribute to the person responsible becomes part of the meaning of the harm itself. For example, if a total stranger cuts me off in traffic and almost causes me to have an accident, the anonymity of that stranger is part of the meaning of the event. I cannot find the individual again to redress the harm, but the retributive feelings can percolate within my psyche and, despite my best intentions, be directed at other drivers on the road with me. The meaning of the event incorporates the anonymity of the offender into the interpretation of the event and its consequences and it shapes my relationship to the larger world. Alternatively, when someone I have taken to be a good friend maligns me to another person, the intensity of the harm and the affectively charged meaning associated with it are colored by the prior history of the relationship and the trust I had placed in that friend. Such an experience can cause me to question myself and my understanding of "my world" in addition to any questions it may raise about my relationship with my friend.

The disruption caused by the experience of harm calls for a response, not just a reaction. A reaction occurs spontaneously. A response requires some sort of conscious and considered decision. It is an act of responsible freedom. Whereas a reaction might express spontaneously the state of the injured self as it has come to be up to and including the moment of harm, a response is a *respons*ible choice about *how I want to become* in relationship to the harm. A reaction arises without consideration, out of the accumulated history of my becoming. A response seeks to direct my future becoming.

### The Movement and Intention of the Forgiving Response

Another way of stating the distinction between reaction and response is that a response sets a trajectory for future becoming. It is guided by a responsibly embraced intention in its movement forward in time. The primary objective governing the movement of a forgiving response, viewed phenomenologically, is to overcome the destabilization produced by the experience of harm.[2] This will require that the axes of meaning and the constellations of meaning within the personal matrix of meanings realign themselves to appropriate the history of the harm and the meaning it has communicated.

The movement toward restabilizing the sense of self and of the self/ world relationship possesses certain distinguishing characteristics. These have already been hinted at in chapter 5. The first characteristic of this movement is precisely that it does seek to integrate the history of the event and its meaning into the sense of self. It tries to realign the disrupted meanings with as little disturbance of unaffected axes and constellations of meanings as possible.

In part this will involve recasting the meaning initially recognized in the event. The emphasis on reframing the event, presented in both the philosophical and the psychological discussions, gets at this need to recast the meaning.[3] But we should note that refashioning a narrative may not be sufficient. Not just any narrative will do. In order for the narrative to

---

[2] The phrase "viewed phenomenologically" is important here. I am describing the objective (we could also think of this as an "intention" or "trajectory") embedded within the movement toward forgiveness as one undertakes to forgive. On a conscious level one might identify the response differently, in terms of consciously appropriated values. But the dynamics of the process of forgiving, viewed through the lens of psychology, indicate that there is a significance beneath the conscious processes. One way of naming that significance is in terms of what the dynamism is designed to accomplish. This is what I am identifying.

[3] See, for example, the presentation on "seeing the offender in a new light" in Charles L. Griswold, *Forgiveness: A Philosophical Exploration* (Cambridge: Cambridge University Press, 2007), 53–59; Varda Konstam, et al., "Forgiveness in Practice: What Mental Health Counselors Are Telling Us," 54–71, in *Before Forgiving: Cautionary Views of Forgiveness in Psychotherapy*, ed. Sharon Lamb and Jeffrie G. Murphy (New York: Oxford University Press, 2002), at 63; Suzanne Freedman, Robert D. Enright, and Jeanette Knutson, "A Progress Report on the Process Model of Forgiveness," 393–406, in *Handbook of Forgiveness*, ed. Everett L. Worthington, Jr. (New York: Routledge, 2005), esp. 395, 397, 401 n. 6, where the authors respond to criticism raised by Joanna North; Paul W. Coleman, "The Process of Forgiveness in Marriage and the Family," 75–94, in *Exploring Forgiveness*, ed. Robert D. Enright and Joanna North (Madison: University of Wisconsin Press, 1998), 91; Ann Macaskill, "Just-World Beliefs and Forgiveness in Men and Women," 39–59, in *Women's Reflections on the Complexities of Forgiveness*, ed. Wanda Malcolm, Nancy DeCourville, and Kathryn Belicki (New York: Routledge, 2008), 42.

be effective in the integrative movement, it must *arise from the realignment of the meanings* used to constitute the narrative.[4] Affective, perspectival, judgmental, valuational, historical, and other kinds of meanings, before they can be integrated into a story that satisfies the requirements of the restabilizing intentionality, must be reoriented within the personal matrix of the one attempting to enact forgiveness. If enough of these axes of meaning are oriented in a manner opposed to forgiving, the narrative constructed will lack the energy and stability needed to effect a trajectory toward forgiveness. Thus the axes of meanings implicated in the harm and in the attempt to revise a narrative of the event must align with the forgiving intention.

One of the consequences of this realignment may touch directly on the location of the sense of self. The extent and nature of one's invest-ment in the meanings disrupted by the harmful event might result in a fundamental realignment of the sense of self. This realignment could relocate the center of gravity of the sense of self into values or complexes of meanings other than those disrupted. If, for example, one's sense of self is heavily invested in success in a particular career and one is humiliated and fired for one's performance in that field, it is possible (likely?) that the process of restabilization following such an event will also include a relocation of the center of gravity of that sense of self into a (or many) different complex(es) of meanings (for example, family relations, religious commitments, etc.).

A second characteristic of the movement toward forgiving an offense is its opposition to non-forgiving responses to the meaning of the harm. Forgiving excludes from the outset any capitulation to the meaning initially recognized in the harm. It excludes using the history of the harm to definitively close off the possibility of future relationship. It also excludes using the history of the harm as a justification for retributive action. Such non-forgiving responses either close off the possibility of future relationship or place it under a reversal of the direction of oppres-sion and violence: now my violent (retributive) response will define our

---

[4] This is an important point. The discussions of narrative identity and narrative mean-ing implicitly presuppose the presence of meanings available for the construction of the narrative. I am suggesting a dual relationship between narratives and meanings: narratives shape meanings, but meanings also shape narratives. My concern with "meanings" does not exclude narrativity or narratability of meanings, but gives greater emphasis to meanings as logically and psychologically prior to the construction of narratives, even though our access to those meanings in reflexive awareness will be embedded in narrative.

relationship. By contrast, the movement of the forgiving response engages the struggle to (re)open a relational space within which a future, positive (nonviolent) relationship to the offender is possible.[5]

It is important to note at this point that the space for possible future relationship opened by the movement of forgiveness is not the same thing as reconciliation. It is the precondition for it. This is a point to which we will return below.

In addition to the characteristics just named, the movement toward forgiveness, the trajectory set out by the intention of forgiving, produces effects within the one forgiving as the movement progresses. The first effect concerns the recast meaning of the experience of harm. In the process of forgiving, the experience of the harm takes on a new meaning for *me* as the one forgiving. Its meaning is no longer merely the meaning first recognized as harm, the violence done to my sense of self. It has taken on the meaning of a harm *I have engaged in a forgiving manner*. The decision to forgive becomes for the forgiver part of the meaning (of the harmful event) that results from the realignment of the disrupted axes and complexes of meaning.

This new meaning *might* be facilitated by the prior expression of re-pentance on the part of the offender (as is paradigmatic for Haber and Griswold),[6] but it might not; prior repentance is not necessary. The new meaning given to the offensive events by my entering into forgiveness of them might also *provide* a new meaning to the offender (if any), making it available to her interpretation of the event, or to those allied with the meaning of the offense, opening the space for a possible reconciliation. But even if the offender (if any) does not recognize or embrace this new meaning of the event—the meaning of the harm *as one toward which the victim chooses to enact forgiveness*—it has still taken on this new signifi-cance for the victim.

A second effect of the effort to engage forgiveness in response to the harm concerns the power of the harm. When one undertakes a forgiving response to a harmful experience, the power of the harm to continue to exercise disruptive energy on one's sense of self and one's self/world

---

[5] As I will argue below, in cases where there is no identifiable offender this relational space opened by forgiving is made available to all those against whom the individual might otherwise have enacted retributive or hostile responses, regardless of their inno-cence of the original harm.

[6] See, for example, Griswold, *Forgiveness: A Philosophical Exploration*, 49–52; Joram Graf Haber, *Forgiveness* (Savage, MD: Rowman & Littlefield, 1991), 90–95.

relation is diminished. The process of realignment of meanings involved in a forgiving response goes hand in glove with a diminishment of the affective charge in the offense. As I reconstitute or restabilize my sense of self—my personal matrix of meanings—following an experience of hurt, and as I do so in the direction of forgiveness, the pain of the offense, as disruptive, diminishes along with the affective impulse toward retribution.[7] In other words, the restabilization of the personal matrix of meanings in the process of forgiving carries with it a *revaluation* of the experience of harm, one that diminishes its power to extend its disruptive influence into my future becoming.

### Characteristics of the Realignment of Meaning

Just as the trajectory of forgiving has distinctive characteristics, so too does the realignment that occurs during the process of forgiving. These characteristics are also part of naming forgiveness; they tell us something essential to answering the question about what is happening when we engage the process of forgiving.

### An Exercise of Freedom in Becoming

The first characteristic of the realignment of meaning is that it is an exercise of freedom in becoming. When we seek to forgive, we engage our capacity for responsible action. The specific way we engage that capacity is future oriented. It impinges on our future actions. Moreover, we engage it not simply for the present moment but as an intended trajectory of becoming into the future, an intended mode of choosing for our future. Forgiving, therefore, has the character of a *commitment*.

Nevertheless, commitment, despite our resoluteness at the time we make it, is marked by uncertainty. The very possibility of commitment being a meaningful enactment is due to the fact that our future personal becoming is open-ended. At some time in the future we can reverse our commitments. Part of what makes a commitment to be a commitment is a willingness to face and respond to the future—with *all* of its uncertainties—from the

---

[7] It is important to note that I am describing what appears to be happening when one forgives. I am not indicating how we can make forgiveness happen. Some of what happens, as will be discussed below, is volitional; we choose it. Some is beyond our direct volitional control. The way of effecting this transformation is largely individual, a matter of one's own personal becoming.

terrain of the commitment itself. But that willingness—the alignment of meanings within our personal matrix that gives energy to making the commitment—can shift. We can, at a future time, question the value and meaning of the commitment or, over the course of time, the incremental decisions that could affirm the commitment do not and the commitment itself—in a state of things often unrecognized until too late—erodes into nothingness. Thus our commitments are marked by uncertainty in a way intrinsic to the dynamics of personal becoming. The trajectory of our personal becoming can change.

In addition, our commitments are marked by uncertainty by virtue of the conditioning elements of the very human freedom we engage when we make a commitment. We are not fully under our own volitional control. Two aspects of this limitation of freedom are illustrative. First, in any free decision we make we are negotiating that decision among the centers of gravity of sometimes competing complexes of meaning that are integrated into and constitutive of our sense of self. The unfolding course of personal history can realign and reshape the relationships among those complexes of meaning in ways that can undermine any commitment we have made. The intensity of feeling about a commitment at one moment may cool and fade at a later time.

Consider, for example, a young couple, too young to marry. They are intensely "in love" but also have dreams about their future careers. They want to celebrate their love sexually. They believe they are committed to each other and that their love will endure. Once a child has been conceived and some of the costs of committed love take center stage in their awareness, the complexes of meanings related to other aspects of their hoped-for future life will collide with the practical reality of the commitment they expressed earlier and the consequences of their actions. Competing values come into play and the commitment will be challenged.

Something similar can occur with freedom to forgive. At a given moment we might embrace forgiveness toward someone who has hurt us. Feelings of graciousness, generosity, nobility, and even genuine affection can lead us to value forgiving the offender to such a degree that, at that moment, it seems easy to undertake forgiving. But at a later time the feelings that sustained the "commitment" may lack the motive force to override other values that still remain destabilized by the offense. These latter values could so realign our affective energies that the freedom to remain consistently aligned with the trajectory of the commitment is called into question.

This brings us to the second way in which our freedom is not fully under our control. As we noted in chapter 5, the meanings shaping the direction and exercise of our freedom operate on both the conscious and the unconscious levels of our psyches. Consciously accessible meanings might realign toward forgiving while unconscious meanings resist that trajectory (or vice versa). The tension caused by the different trajectories operating on the conscious and unconscious levels, it seems to me, accounts—at least in part—for the experience of the resurgence of resentment and other retributive emotions after one has engaged forgiveness. It also provides a plausible explanation for the expression of retributive behaviors via passive-aggressive patterns of relationship after one has consciously decided to forgive.

These elements of uncertainty in our commitments to forgive tell us something about our freedom and about commitment itself. Our freedom is not absolute, but it is also not a static capacity. We can grow and develop in freedom. The range of responsible self-direction of one's own personal becoming grows (we hope) as we mature from childhood into adulthood. It does so by being exercised in ever larger and more diverse circumstances. The complexes of meaning arrayed against any particular commitment to forgive become the test of our freedom. Although there might be momentary setbacks in the face of the upsurge of those forces, our freedom grows by engaging with and resisting their erosion of the commitment to forgive. I might at one moment give in to a retributive impulse despite the commitment to forgive. This does not falsify the commitment;[8] it discloses the limits of my freedom. For the measure of the commitment is not the momentary setback. The measure of the commitment is the consistency with which I reaffirm the trajectory of personal becoming intended by the commitment as each new setback comes to light.

## An Experience of Conversion

The second characteristic of the realignment of meanings that takes place in forgiving shows itself precisely in those moments when we encounter the limitations of our freedom and the uncertainty of our commitment to forgive. The realignment that takes place, insofar as it cannot be completely effectuated by an act of will, possesses the character of a *conversion*.

---

[8] The Anglo-American philosophical discussion is marked by claims that the resurgence of retributive feelings and/or actions is an indication that one has not forgiven. The claim calls into question two aspects of the discussion: the reality of the enactment and its completeness. The lack of completeness appears to be read as invalidating the enactment. I argue that the completeness envisioned by the philosophical discussion as necessary for saying "I have forgiven" is inhuman. It ignores the dimensions of personal becoming, the limitations of human freedom, and the nature of any commitment undertaken by such persons.

As was just discussed above, in addition to any impulses to forgive we also often have internal resistance, conscious and unconscious, to forgiving. The pain of the disruption to our sense of self and our self/world relation gives power to the retributive impulses. Even though other complexes of meanings may incline us to desire to forgive (or at least to desire to desire to forgive), the inaccessibility of some meanings within our unconscious processes and the intractability of some complexes of meanings more directly accessible to our consciousness can resist the realignment required for forgiveness. We experience our will as divided.

This presents a real conundrum to the effort to engage forgiveness. The impetus to forgive derives its energy from the alignment of meanings according to a specific trajectory. Without that alignment there is no such impetus. What then can move us to align in the direction of forgiveness if there is no motive energy? We can experience ourselves as helpless to orient ourselves toward forgiving. But when we are partially inclined to forgive and partially disinclined, or when we are just coming to the point of even raising the question of forgiveness, the case is different. What can move the will—our volitional capacity—toward forgiving when the valences of the meanings beneath our volition have themselves been oriented totally or substantially toward retribution?

The answer to that question is unclear. It is important to note the question, however, because it points to a common experience relevant to the claim about conversion. When confronted with an experience of harm we can often experience our own orientation toward the prospect of forgiveness as ambivalent, simultaneously pro and con. Often the resistance seems insurmountable, and yet, people do undertake to forgive.

The transition from inability to ability to forgive is often experienced as surprising. Vladimir Jankélévitch seems to have had this experience in mind when he wrote of the "event" quality of forgiveness.[9] Something has changed in a manner I did not control. It has come as a gift or a grace (to use his language).[10] In this experience one feels that she has been liberated, and on many levels. She experiences a liberation from the power of the harm, from the tension generated by self-protective impulses occasioned by the harm, from the power of a past event to shape the course of her future becoming. But the liberation also has a forward direction. It sets one free to direct her future becoming, unhampered by the meaning of the

[9] See the discussion in Vladimir Jankélévitch, *Forgiveness*, trans. Andrew Kelly (Chicago: University of Chicago Press, 2005), 34–38.

[10] Ibid., *passim*. See esp. 30–31.

pain and free for the possibility of new or renewed relationship. Hence the liberation is experienced as energizing a willingness to forgive and to orient oneself toward a distinctive future not constrained by retributive impulses.

These qualities—the event character, the liberation, and the energy to commit oneself to forgiving—indicate that a realignment of meanings has occurred. Insofar as this realignment is experienced as beyond one's volitional control (an event), it has the character of a conversion. As liberating, this conversion makes commitment to forgiving possible. As energizing, the conversion reflects an affective shift that moves in the direction of a decline in retributive emotions.

It should be noted, however, that a conversion to forgiving, despite its "event" character, is not a one-shot deal. A conversion is experienced as an "event" in the moments of one's first awareness that a significant realignment of one's personal matrix has occurred. However, as the explanation of personal matrices has indicated, there are numerous complexes of meaning constituting our sense of self. A significant realignment of meanings in an event of conversion must still work its way through the many complexes of meanings and centers of gravity in our sense of self. That takes time. It also involves struggling with meanings resistant to the implied realignment. Hence conversion is an ongoing process.

Indeed, the process of conversion may never be complete. As persons in the process of becoming we are constantly faced with choices that possess multiple layers of significance. Recognizing their relevance to our enactment of forgiveness and choosing accordingly are not easy, and even if all of our conscious meanings have been successfully and resolutely aligned with forgiving, we still must reckon with the meanings operative in our unconscious. Thus, once forgiveness has been undertaken, it remains a dimension of our exercise of freedom—whether affirmed or refused—over the course of the rest of our process of becoming. That process is not completed until our death.

## An Eschatological Orientation

The uncertainty and incompleteness intrinsic to both the commitment to forgive and the conversion toward forgiving bestow on forgiveness an eschatological quality.[11] The commitment and the conversion both aim

---

[11] This has already been noted in relationship to Derrida's discussion of the "impossibility" of forgiving. There is a kind of deferral of possibility/judgment about actuality into an unspecified future. See also the introductory remarks contextualizing the epilogue in

at a completeness, an irrevocability. But as long as we are in the process of becoming and as long as aspects of our personal matrices of meanings are beyond volitional control, we can never be certain that the desired completeness—forgiveness in the perfect tense—has been achieved.[12] That judgment can only be reached when our becoming itself is at an end: at the end of life, looking backward in time.

This implies that forgiving is intrinsically bound up with a distant future even as it is lived out in the present moment. It places the one who undertakes to forgive in a temporally ambiguous space. We stand between the "already" of the commitment undertaken and the "not yet" of the commitment completed. Insofar as my personal becoming confirms the orientation of the commitment to forgiving, the eschatological fullness is actualized at this moment, although its irrevocable completeness has not yet come to pass. If my personal becoming at some point fails to confirm that orientation, the question remains open whether this lapse constitutes a new trajectory against forgiving the particular event or whether it will become the occasion for a renewal of the basic trajectory toward forgiving via an intensification of the forgiving realignment of meanings and the ongoing process of conversion.

### Forgiving and Remembering

Forgiving is oriented toward the future according to a specific movement. It aims at a possible reconciliation, even if that reconciliation must, for now, be deferred to an unspecified time. As such, forgiving possesses the character of *hope*. It is *aspirational*. It reflects a desire that emerges in our conscious life, directing our exercises of freedom in becoming. But this directed impulse, if it is to be effective in the future, implies something about remembering. Forgiving requires that we remember.

As we have already seen, this claim is a matter of dispute. Jacques Derrida argues against this view in two ways. Both are related to his understanding of "pure" forgiveness. One argument is that any finality

---

Paul Ricoeur, *Memory, History, Forgetting*, trans. Kathleen Blamey and David Pellauer (Chicago: University of Chicago Press, 2004), 457.

[12] The point here is that the claim that forgiveness of the deceased or third party forgiveness that Griswold places, with some merit, in the "subjunctive mode" actually applies to all enactments of forgiveness insofar as they are deployed under the conditions of what it means to be human. See Griswold, *Forgiveness: A Philosophical Exploration*, 120–41.

other than forgiveness itself distorts the purity of forgiveness.[13] To render this critique in the terms of the present exposition, any other finality shifts the meaning of forgiveness from forgiveness itself to the desired end. Memory is a medium for accomplishing the end; therefore it serves something other than forgiveness. The second aspect of his argument against the place of remembering in forgiving is an extension of his argument about the gift. To remember is, for Derrida, *ipso facto* to render the forgiveness part of an economy of exchange. As he argues, for forgiveness (if it is possible) to be pure, it must be forgotten at a level even beyond the conscious. The forgetting must extend to an eradication of any traces of its presence in the unconscious.[14]

By contrast, Jankélévitch maintains that "the discontinuity of forgiveness is rendered possible by the fullness of memories. Nothing could be more evident: in order to forgive, it is necessary to remember."[15] The implications of Paul Ricoeur's presentation, although supportive of Derrida's concern about reducing forgiving to an economy of exchange, appear to align more directly with Jankélévitch. Ricoeur translates the pursuit of equalization through a horizontal mediation of offense and response into an utterly gratuitous vertical crossing of the abyss between the offender and the offended. This crossing requires that the one forgiving remember the offense, at least until the moment when forgiveness has been achieved.

The Anglo-American philosophers, like Jankélévitch and Ricoeur, presuppose the necessity of memory for forgiving. The effort to forge a separation in the mind of the injured party between the offender and the offense is a cognitive (as well as affective) process. It requires that one be able to direct one's attention toward the responsible party and her involvement in provoking the experience of harm. This is especially clear in Griswold's description of the process of revising the narrative of the event.[16] The psychological discussion of "reframing" echoes this sensibility and likewise presupposes an active memory of the event.[17]

---

[13] Jacques Derrida, *On Cosmopolitanism and Forgiveness* (London: Routledge, 2001), 31–32.

[14] Jacques Derrida, *Given Time: 1. Counterfeit Money*, trans. Peggy Camuf (Chicago: University of Chicago Press, 1992), 16.

[15] Jankélévitch, *Forgiveness*, 56.

[16] Griswold, *Forgiveness: A Philosophical Exploration*, 47–59.

[17] See Coleman, "The Process of Forgiveness in Marriage and the Family," 91; Macaskill, "Just-World Beliefs and Forgiveness in Men and Women," 42; Keith E. Yandell, "The Metaphysics and Morality of Forgiveness," 35–45, in *Exploring Forgiveness*, 39, 44.

Although there are differences in the presentation of the role of memory among these distinctive approaches opposed to Derrida, it is worth noting a common presupposition beneath each of their arguments. Each takes as a given that forgiving is a human enactment and that people do, in fact, attempt to realize it. This places these approaches, at least in some respects, on common ground with the descriptive account of forgiving being presented. Indeed, once we step onto the terrain of the human enactment of forgiveness and take into account the intrinsic cognitive dimension of any such enactment, remembering is inescapable.

The understanding of forgiving being described here involves an intentional choice of a trajectory of personal becoming with respect to the offense and the offender. Although not totally resolvable on the level of a moment of decision, forgiving is enacted by freedom in the form of a commitment not to use the meaning of the harm as a basis for retribution or closing off all possibility of future relationship. This commitment stands in tension with meanings that have not yet been aligned according to the commitment's intended trajectory. To be faithful to the commitment requires memory of the event and of the commitment itself. Without this memory the energy arising from meanings not yet aligned toward forgiving has greater potential to turn the commitment itself into a passing whim. Memory provides the freedom of personal becoming with an orientation point in light of the commitment to forgive the offender for the offense. Insofar as forgiving entails a struggle against energies within oneself that are not directly under one's volitional control, forgiving requires a conversion. Memory serves to maintain awareness of the tension between contrary alignments of personal complexes of meaning so that freedom can exercise itself to cooperate with the movement of the conversion that originally opened up the possibility of forgiving.

From this perspective memory is essential to forgiving. But what kind of memory? In the descriptive account of forgiving spelled out here, memory is of the event (and the offender, if there is one) as the object, recipient, or occasion of my commitment. My commitment, as indicated above, changes the meaning of the event and the offender *for me*. In the realignment of meanings disrupted by the offense I give new meaning to the harm, to the agent of the harm, and even to my own self and my self/world relationship. The harm becomes a harm I have committed myself to forgiving. In view of that commitment I have bound myself not to invoke it as a pretext for reciprocal harm. The agent has become the one whom I have forgiven. I have affirmed that, in the future, I shall restrain the retributive impulses from asserting themselves in our relationship. I no longer invest the history of that harm with the power to damage my sense of worth or my security in the world. Instead, the larger matrix of meanings that mediates to me my sense of self (my personal matrix of meanings), in the process of its realignment following the harm, draws upon a broader range of values, relationships, personal history, and so on, to confirm my sense of worth and my security in relationship to the larger world. The memory of the forgiveness I have undertaken becomes part of my sense of self.

Yet, even if memory is integral to the understanding of forgiving being described here, it does not exclude all forms of forgetting. In a weak sense we can say that forgetting is a normal part of human experience. To the extent that, after making a commitment to forgive an offense, and as the most basic complexes of meaning disrupted by the offense come into alignment with the intention to forgive, the intense, initial preoccupation with the harm will often fade. It will no longer occupy my attention as consistently as it did in the first blush of the offense. As I go about my life, I forget the offense—not in the sense that I *cannot* recall it, but in the sense that it *does not come to mind*. In this sense, when a further event evokes a meaning I associate with the offense, or when the history of the harm comes back to mind for some reason, I remember that harm, but *as forgiven*—as something I have committed myself to forgiving.

The stronger sense of forgetting—that identified by Derrida as necessary to preserve the purity of forgiveness—is not necessary in the understanding of forgiveness I have been describing. Indeed, I question whether, barring physical trauma to the brain or pharmacological intervention, it is even possible. (This seems to me to have been part of Derrida's point regarding the impossibility of forgiveness; it is not possible to completely forget, therefore it is not possible to forgive.) But beyond the impossibility of forgetting, in light of the description of forgiving presented here, I would argue that such forgetting is not even desirable. If I am to be responsible for my own future in personal becoming (acknowledging the limitations involved), I need the capacity to remember, especially the capacity to remember my commitment to particular enactments of forgiveness.

## Rethinking Tensions in the Discussion of Forgiveness

The approach to understanding forgiving just presented represents a significant shift in the landscape of forgiveness. It relocates the discussion from the pinnacle of pure concept and draws it out of the box canyon defined by the question of the conditions for the moral enactment of forgiveness. Instead, drawing on aspects of both of those discussions and on the resources of psychological research, it locates the question in the broad plain of human enactment and personal becoming. By naming the different dynamics (processes, movements) involved when one seeks to undertake forgiving as a response to harm, and by describing the characteristics of this complex phenomenon in comparison to other human experiences, this descriptive account provides us with a different way of reading and responding to some of the unresolved issues that have surfaced in the different discussions up to this point.

In what follows we shall return to some of the places of tension that have emerged thus far and view them from the perspective of this newly articulated matrix of meanings. (It will not be possible to address all the tensions we have observed in the various discussions. However, the approach taken to responding to some of the main tensions we have encountered should provide a sufficient basis on which others can take up those unresolved questions.) The points of tension we will address can be grouped loosely under two headings: the relationship of forgiving to reconciling, and the implications of unilateral forgiveness.

### The Relationship of Forgiving to Reconciling

The course we have traced across the landscape of forgiveness has brought to light differences of perspective on the relationship of forgiveness to reconciliation. Derrida's analysis appears to conflate the two; the integral place of absolute forgetting in his understanding of forgiving points toward an ideal in which relationships proceed unaffected by the experience of harm. In the realm of conditional forgiveness sketched out by Griswold both the definition from which he starts and the paradigmatic status of enactments based on "speech act theory" subsume reconciliation into the meaning of forgiveness itself; forgiveness without reconciliation is not complete forgiveness.

Other authors see a distinction between forgiving and reconciling. Both Jeffrie G. Murphy and Joram Graf Haber allow that forgiveness might possibly lead to reconciliation, but they see them as distinct phenomena.[18] As Murphy points out, "there can be forgiveness without

---

[18] Haber appears to allow for this possible relationship in his cautious comments on Richard Fitzgibbons's work. Haber's point, however, is to raise caution about any uncritical advocacy for forgiveness on psychological grounds. See Haber, *Forgiveness*, 107. Murphy's

reconciliation and reconciliation without forgiveness."[19] This perspective appears to be the one most commonly accepted in the psychological literature as well.[20] From a therapeutic standpoint one might find it valuable to forgive an offender, but dangerous to reestablish relationship.

The account of forgiveness presented above aligns with those who make a clear distinction between forgiving and reconciling. However, there is more to this question than at first meets the eye. Derrida's ideal of forgiveness, despite my hesitations, does point to a kind of eschatological vision compatible with that identified in the descriptive account of forgiveness presented above, and Griswold's definition of forgiveness in a manner inclusive of reconciliation, although I maintain that this is an expression of circular reasoning, does draw attention to an important point. Even though there is a distinction between forgiving and reconciling, forgiving does have an intrinsic orientation toward reconciliation.

As the descriptive presentation of forgiveness indicates, forgiving is an activity directed toward overcoming the consequences of a harm. It is enacted by the one harmed. One of these consequences is the damage done to relationship. Even if reconciliation is not actively pursued (or even desired at the time forgiveness is undertaken), an integral dimension of forgiving is that it (re)opens the *possibility* of reconciliation.[21]

---

discussion takes up the question more directly in Murphy, *Getting Even: Forgiveness and Its Limits* (New York: Oxford University Press, 2003), 14–16.

[19] Ibid., 14.

[20] See, for example, Michael E. McCullough, Kenneth I. Pargament, and Carl E. Thoresen, "The Psychology of Forgiveness: History, Conceptual Issues, and Overview," 1–14, in *Forgiveness: Theory, Research, and Practice*, ed. Michael E. McCullough, Kenneth I. Pargament, and Carl E. Thoresen (New York: Guilford Press, 2000), at 7–8; Walter J. Dickey, "Forgiveness and Crime: The Possibilities of Restorative Justice," 106–20, in *Exploring Forgiveness*, at 108; Yandell, "The Metaphysics and Morality of Forgiveness," 45; and Everett L. Worthington, Jr., "Initial Questions about the Art and Science of Forgiving," 1–13, in *Handbook of Forgiveness*, at 9.

[21] Jankélévitch gets at this idea when he writes of forgiveness as having no "because" and as restoring the guilty to innocence. He observes: "This is all the more reason why forgiveness is in no way anticipated by the causality of value, of merit, or innocence—and we say 'all the more reason' because such a causality is evidently the most normal. Not only is it not because the accused is innocent that forgiveness forgives him (innocence, on the contrary, rendering forgiveness superfluous), rather it is much more because forgiveness forgives that the guilty person becomes innocent. On the condition of being innocent itself, of claiming nothing, forgiveness converts the sinners whom it pardons to innocence" (Jankélévitch, *Forgiveness*, 145).

Interpersonal reconciliation can be understood as the fulfillment of the trajectory of forgiving, but it is also a distinct kind of enactment. It is the enactment of the coming together of parties who were alienated, of actually restoring a relationship. But it is a coming together in which the harm of the past is no longer a threat because the offender and the offended have come to a shared understanding of the harmful action as something not to be repeated (in the case of moral harm).

Yet even in the absence of the enactment of reconciliation, even if reconciliation must remain an eschatological possibility never achieved, one can still undertake and enact forgiveness. Thus, while forgiving is a necessary precondition for interpersonal reconciliation, even if reconciliation does not occur, so long as we engage the enactment described above, we are forgiving. Forgiveness of an offender can be enacted unilaterally. Reconciliation with an offender cannot.

There is a caveat to this presentation of reconciliation. When dealing with a moral harm, as Griswold and others have argued, it is necessary that the offender repent.[22] (Griswold, Haber, and others make the repentance of the offender a requirement for the morality of forgiving. In the absence of repentance, forgiveness could be construed as condonation. More on this shortly.) The necessity for repentance as an absolute requirement for the moral enactment of forgiveness, as presented in these arguments, presupposes the restriction of questions of forgiveness to moral harm. If non-moral harm is also potentially an occasion for forgiveness, then the requirement of repentance becomes incoherent.

Some of the psychological discussions presented in chapter 3 accepted the possibility of forgiving a non-moral harm. The understanding of forgiveness as a human enactment I have outlined does not require moral harm as a condition for its enactment. If we recognize that the same dynamics are operative in responding to experiences of harm whether we see them as moral affronts or merely as harmful, the basis for restricting the forgiveness to moral harm appears arbitrary. Indeed, when we look at forgiving as a human enactment and do not presuppose a moral harm as necessary it becomes clear that the claims for the necessity of moral harm in order to call forth the response of forgiveness need to be justified. The moral content of the harm is not integral to the enactment of forgiveness as such.

[22] See, for example, Haber, *Forgiveness*, 90ff.; Griswold, *Forgiveness: A Philosophical Exploration*, 47–59.

If this is so, then the question of repentance must be reexamined. In the case of a moral harm, the reason why an offender must repent before reconciliation can occur is obvious. If the offender does not repudiate the meaning of the offense, the one harmed is making herself available for further abuse. Although she might forgive the offender for the harm— and thereby open the possibility of future reconciliation—to seek to effect reconciliation when the offender clings to the message of the harm would be to open oneself to further harm.

However, in the case of a non-moral harm repentance does not necessarily work that way. If someone were to intervene, for example, to stop a friend from drug or alcohol abuse, the intervenor is not necessarily acting immorally. Certainly the evident intention is moral. However, the addict's personal matrix of meanings will be seriously disrupted by this intervention. That disruption might well (as it often does) elicit retributive responses from the addict and a rupture of relationship. For there to be a future in relationship, the addict's personal matrix of meanings must be realigned. This will involve appropriation and integration of the disruption into the personal matrix of meanings via a realignment of the various kinds and complexes of meanings that constitute the addict's sense of self. In light of the realignment the addict will then have to commit himself not to use the history of the disruption as a basis for retribution or for closing off future relationships. He will need to exercise his freedom in an ongoing process of realigning those meanings that resist that commitment. He will need to orient them in a direction supportive of it. He will experience that process as a struggle with unfreedom. This will be experienced as both an expression of choice and as ongoing conversion, embraced on the basis of the remembered harm and the commitment not to consent to the movement of retributive impulses. In short, the addict will need to enact the same dynamics as one does when forgiving a moral harm.

The same could be argued *mutatis mutandis* with respect to other non-moral harms. For example, when one party to a romantic relationship, without committing any moral harm, decides that this is not the relationship she wants to pursue, the decision can be perfectly legitimate, but the pain it initiates in the lover who is being set aside must still be dealt with. It may well require the kind of process described here as enacting forgiveness.[23] Similarly, in the case of an economic downturn

---

[23] Whether or not the case actually does require forgiveness will depend on many factors. It will be a matter of decision based on what the rejected lover recognizes as the meaning of the event in relationship to his personal matrix of meanings. This, in turn, will

when one is let go from a job, the disruption caused can be much more than financial. The processes the newly unemployed person may need to engage with respect to those who made the decision might well be those of enacting forgiveness.

In cases such as these, for reconciliation to occur it is not necessarily the one who occasioned the experience of harm who needs to repent. Nothing immoral has been done. However, it *might* in some cases be necessary for the one who experiences the harm (disruption) to undergo change in a way that is more or less analogous to repentance. This is evident in the case of the addict. He will need to repent of his self-destructive behavior, and perhaps also of his hostility toward the intervenor. In the case of the jilted lover or the fired employee one could, perhaps, say that they will need to repent of any hostile behaviors provoked by the retributive emotions following the experience of harm before reconciliation can occur. But in none of these cases would the one who provoked the experience of harm (disruption) need to repent of his or her disruptive actions.

One further point in relationship to reconciliation bears mentioning. It is a parallel between the dynamism of forgiving and that involved in reconciliation. Forgiving aims toward reconciliation as the fulfillment of the trajectory to which one has committed oneself in response to a harm. This trajectory becomes etched into the most fundamental movement of one's personal becoming into the future. Interpersonal reconciliation, likewise, aims toward a future beyond itself. Reconciliation is initiated at a moment when two or more estranged individuals reestablish positive relationship. But relationship, and therefore reconciliation, is not a static state. It is constantly changing in the light of new experience we appropriate as meaningful. Relationship moves toward the future, just as forgiving and commitment do. As long as the relationship continues, the reconciling—the mutual welcoming following upon the commitment of forgiving and the revision of meaning of the event of harm—continues to develop and unfold as a part of that relationship. Thus reconciling has a trajectory toward an ever-deeper interpersonal communion. Without appealing to religious language, one could describe the fulfillment of reconciliation in terms of what Derrida was wrestling with in his writings on hospitality and the gift. Reconciliation aims at a welcome and a self-giving without restriction. This, too, is an eschatological hope.

---

be a reflection of the manner in which the rejected lover has integrated the relationship into his sense of self along such axes of meaning as relationality, orientation to the future, affectivity, the scale of values according to which he prioritizes different values, and so on.

## Unilateral Forgiveness

The idea that unilateral forgiveness is a possibility is fairly widespread in philosophical and psychological discussions.[24] The implications of Derrida's aporetic analysis of forgiveness, especially his insistence on an absolute forgetfulness of the offense, would seem to *require* that the enactment be unilateral. Psychological discussions may differ on whether unilateral forgiving is preferable or advisable for a given client but they recognize that it is a possible option.[25] The understanding of forgiveness presented above clearly sees unilateral forgiveness as a possibility. Indeed, one might even make the claim that focusing the investigation of forgiveness in terms of what one is doing when forgiving (or what is happening within one when undertaking to forgive) makes unilateral enactment the most basic—one could even say "paradigmatic"—manifestation of forgiveness. On such a view other exercises of forgiveness would then measure themselves in relation to this unilateral exercise.

Such a claim would, of course, be anathema to some among the moral philosophers, for while some recognize the *possibility* of a unilateral enactment, many raise the objection that unilateral enactment of forgiveness could (some would say "does") run afoul of moral requirements. Three particular areas of concern have surfaced thus far in our investigation: the question of condonation of the offense, the requirements of self-respect, and the separation of the offender from the offense. All three are

---

[24] Among philosophers, Haber clearly affirms that forgiveness is a unilateral enactment, although the moral conditions for enacting forgiveness require the repentance of the offender (Haber, *Forgiveness*, 11). Griswold's formulation, by contrast, envisions forgiveness as paradigmatically dyadic in structure. He therefore only sees unilateral forgiveness as a "subjunctive mode" experience and as invocable only in limited cases. See Griswold, *Forgiveness: A Philosophical Exploration*, 116, 120–22. Among psychologists addressing the topic, Suzanne Freedman sees unilateral forgiveness as a legitimate possibility (Freedman, Enright, and Knutson, "A Progress Report on the Process Model of Forgiveness," 400), while those associated with the work of Sharon Lamb express reservations and critique unilateral forgiveness for potentially undermining moral requirements. See Lamb, "Women, Abuse, and Forgiveness: A Special Case," 155–71, in *Before Forgiving*, at 158, 166; and Bill Puka, "Forgoing Forgiveness," 136–52, in *Before Forgiving*, at 145, 149, 151.

[25] See, for example, Freedman, Enright, and Knutson, "A Progress Report on the Process Model of Forgiveness," 400; and Margaret Holmgren, "Forgiveness and the Intrinsic Value of Persons," *American Philosophical Quarterly* 30, no. 4 (October 1993): 341–52, at 345 for positive appreciation of unilateral forgiveness. For a more critical perspective, one that is heavily influenced by moral philosophical principles, see Lamb, "Women, Abuse, and Forgiveness: A Special Case," 158, 166.

understood in the Anglo-American philosophical discussions and in some psychological discussions to bear on the moral status of the enactment of forgiveness.

## THE QUESTION OF CONDONATION

The language of condonation shows up in both the moral philosophical and the psychological discussions of forgiveness.[26] How that language is understood varies from author to author within each discipline. Minimally, both discussions and the authors involved understand condonation as different from forgiveness. What distinguishes condonation is that it gives tacit consent or approval to an offensive act.[27] This becomes an issue in unilateral forgiveness when the forgiveness enacted by the one harmed is not expressed to the offender. The offender can take the silence as consent or approval. Alternatively, the offender could see forgiveness as condonation if the forgiveness is expressed but the act is not clearly condemned.[28]

---

[26] Among psychological discussions, see Marjorie E. Baker, "Self-Forgiveness: An Empowering and Therapeutic Tool for Working with Women in Recovery," 61–74, in *Women's Reflections on the Complexities of Forgiveness*, at 65; Nancy DeCourville, Kathryn Belicki, and Michelle M. Green, "Subjective Experiences of Forgiveness in a Community Sample: Implications for Understanding Forgiveness and Its Consequences," 1–20, in ibid., at 2; Julie Juola Exline and Roy F. Baumeister, "Expressing Forgiveness and Repentance: Benefits and Barriers," 72–87, in *Forgiveness: Theory, Research, and Practice*, at 145; McCullough, Pargament, and Thoresen, "The Psychology of Forgiveness: History, Conceptual Issues, and Overview," 7–8; and Jennie G. Noll, "Forgiveness in People Experiencing Trauma," 363–75, in *Handbook of Forgiveness*, at 367. In the Anglo-American philosophical discussions, concern about condonation is a pervasive theme. See, for example, Norvin Richards, "Forgiveness as Therapy," 72–87, in *Before Forgiving*; Griswold, *Forgiveness: A Philosophical Exploration, passim*, esp. 54–55, 121–22; Haber, *Forgiveness, passim*, esp. 59–60; Murphy and Hampton, *Forgiveness and Mercy, passim*.

[27] Griswold, drawing on the work of Paul M. Hughes, provides a useful distinction between two kinds of "condonation." "One may condone in the sense of accepting while not disapproving (by not holding the wrongdoing against its author), or in the sense of tolerating while disapproving (a sort of 'look the other way' or 'putting up with it' strategy)" (Griswold, *Forgiveness: A Philosophical Exploration*, 46 n. 7).

[28] I introduce this as a limited condition in cases in which the harm being forgiven is, in fact, morally objectionable. Since I do allow that one can forgive for reasons other than moral harm, condemnation of the event experienced as harm is not necessarily presupposed. The necessary condition for forgiving is that one experience something as disruptive, even if it is a morally praiseworthy action.

The question that arises in such cases is whether the forgiveness undertaken by the one harmed, if it is not made explicit or if the harm is not explicitly condemned, *ipso facto* constitutes condonation. This is the point of disagreement. The pronounced tendency among moral philosophers is to argue that, in the absence of repentance by the offender, forgiveness runs the risk of constituting condonation. However, even on this point the perspectives cover a range, some (like Haber) arguing for an *ipso facto* collapse of forgiving into condonation,[29] others (like Jean Hampton) recognizing the *possibility* that unilateral forgiveness without explicit condemnation of the offense could constitute or be construed as condonation.[30] Among psychologists the tendency is to recognize the distinction between forgiveness and condonation and to repudiate condonation but reject the notion that unilateral forgiveness and the absence of explicit condemnation of the offense automatically collapse forgiveness into condonation.

It is important to note that both philosophers and psychologists are sensitive to the moral problems associated with condonation. However, the differences in the larger frameworks of inquiry between philosophers and psychologists lead to differences in the assessment of the problem. The Anglo-American philosophical discussion, focused as it is on the conditions for the moral enactment of forgiveness, analyzes the question of condonation in relationship to the forgiver's responsibility to the "moral community."[31] We are obligated to uphold the moral values that sustain the life of our moral community. Related to this concern is the moral obligation to uphold and defend one's own worth and dignity in the face of an offense. The intrinsic worth of the individual must be preserved and defended, as must the larger social fabric of moral values

---

[29] Haber, *Forgiveness*, 110. Griswold sees the same danger in *Forgiveness: A Philosophical Exploration*, 54–55, 57, 64, 121–22.

[30] This is implicit in her argument against the position of Aurel Kolnai. See Murphy and Hampton, *Forgiveness and Mercy*, 84; see also 39–43.

[31] The phrase "moral community" as a point of reference for the obligation to act morally runs throughout Griswold's analysis. See, for example, *Forgiveness: A Philosophical Exploration*, 29, 49, 52–53, 69, 90. Although less prominent in Haber's analysis, the concept is explicitly mentioned in a similar vein (Haber, *Forgiveness*, 82, 99, 103). It appears with less prominence in some of the psychological literature. See, for example, Sandra Rafman, "Restoration of a Moral Universe: Children's Perspectives on Forgiveness and Justice," 215–34, in *Women's Reflections on the Complexities of Forgiveness*, 222. Mona G. Affinito emphasizes the relationship of the victim to the larger community context in her "Forgiveness in Counseling: Caution, Definition, and Application," 88–111, in *Before Forgiving*, 95, 105, 107, 109.

(shared matrix of moral meanings).[32] Hence the range of perspectives in this philosophical context spans a spectrum from cautious allowance of unilateral forgiveness to vigorous opposition to it on moral grounds.

The moral dimension is present but generally less emphasized in the psychological discussions. For some authors the moral aspect of condonation does occupy a significant place in their analysis.[33] However, more commonly the concern behind the discussion of condonation is whether the failure to condemn an act as harmful will increase the likelihood that the one harmed will be harmed again. The distinction between this approach and that of the moral philosophers is the attention the psychologists give to the repetition of the harm as a *psychologically damaging* event rather than (but not to the exclusion of) its status as a moral rupture. The range of perspectives in this discussion spans the terrain from cautious approval of unilateral forgiveness to vigorous support of it on psychological grounds.

[32] It is an open question for me how these two foundational values—defending self-worth and upholding the standards of the moral community—are related in the different articulations of this argument. Is the necessity to eliminate any confusion about the condemnation of the offense (avoiding any possibility that silence could be construed as condonation) argued primarily on the basis of the value of the person, or does it hinge on the inviolability of the norms of the moral community? As I will argue below, one's sense of self-worth is not necessarily bound up with the explicit condemnation of a harmful action. There are other meanings involved. Also, the appeal to the norms of the moral community appears to me to be overly abstract. There are diverse moral communities who may assess these questions differently. Those who make the argument about condonation to exclude the legitimacy of unilateral forgiveness as described here appear to be universalizing their own imagined but unspecified moral community to make absolute claims about the demands of moral reasoning. This deontological kind of reasoning ignores the particularity of diverse cultures and systems of values in making prudential moral judgments. It likewise fails to recognize the dependence of its own judgments on matrices of meanings that owe their truth claims to interpretations of reality.

[33] Lamb and Murphy, in the introduction to *Before Forgiving*, their collection of cautionary essays about forgiveness in therapeutic contexts, express concern about efforts at forgiveness actually being expressions of condonation when they observe: "no matter how frequently advocates of forgiveness say that forgiving does not mean condoning, it is hard for most of us to accept that view." She raises an interesting question: Even when the individual forgiver is helped through forgiveness, is the moral community well served in this process? See Lamb, "Introduction: Reasons to Be Cautious About the Use of Forgiveness in Psychotherapy," 3–14, in *Before Forgiving*, at 12. In that same volume the philosopher Margaret Holmgren, reflecting on moral difficulties when promoting forgiveness in therapeutic contexts, touches on the same concern. See Holmgren, "Forgiveness and Self-Forgiveness in Psychotherapy," 112–35, in *Before Forgiving*, at 122–28.

The approach to understanding forgiveness developed in this present work clearly affirms that unilateral forgiving is a possibility, but it has sidestepped the question of the morality of forgiving in general, and of unilateral forgiving in the present case. Posing our question in terms of what is happening within the forgiver when one undertakes to forgive—at least as I have presented it here—makes the moral evaluation of the enactment a second level consideration. It is subsequent to establishing a description of the dynamics of forgiveness. The operating assumption, which we will examine in more detail in the discussion of the fault-lines below, is that the moral aspect of forgiving is one of many possible valuational concerns one *might* bring to bear in deciding to undertake forgiving, but it is not an essential consideration. One can, as Haber pointed out, undertake to forgive for a variety of reasons, or no reason at all. The factors shaping the decision need not be moral considerations.

The point at issue for the moment is not the larger question of the moral enactment of forgiveness in general but rather the status of unilateral forgiveness with respect to condonation, especially when no explicit condemnation of the harm has been expressed. Is such unilateral forgiveness equivalent to condonation? Is unilateral forgiveness, on that basis (the equivalency of unilateral forgiveness and condonation), immoral? Are we, therefore, morally proscribed from forgiving unilaterally?

To address these questions from the perspective of the understanding of forgiveness described above, it will be helpful to recall some of our earlier findings. The force of the moral philosophical argument is dependent on appeal to the moral philosophical matrix of meanings and its approach to the question of forgiveness. Forgiveness is taken to be an issue for moral philosophical analysis. To secure that placement, forgiveness is defined in terms of moral harm. The moral frame (frames!) of reference circumscribe(s) the landscape in a manner that excludes enactments of forgiveness that do not conform to the delimited understanding of what qualifies as forgiveness. (If we are dealing with non-moral harm, so it is claimed, the response cannot be forgiveness.) The presupposition that forgiveness must always be in response to a matter of moral harm, and the fundamental importance of satisfying moral criteria in the moral philosophical matrix of meanings, make the moral imperative of explicit repudiation of the harm inevitable. This move is further leveraged, in some arguments, by the equation of silence with condonation.

In chapter 4, I contended that Haber's reduction of unilateral forgiveness to condonation was a circular argument. That contention applies here, too. The necessity of an explicit statement against the offensive act does not arise from the nature of forgiveness, but from the nature of the conditions for *moral* forgiveness that Haber wants to define as paradigmatic. He presents a speech-act paradigm of moral forgiveness for which relationship and communication about the offense between the two parties is a necessary condition. The charge of condonation is the lynchpin to sustaining the paradigm; without it—that is, if unilateral, unexpressed forgiveness were morally acceptable—Haber's proposal would not retain its paradigmatic status. A similar argument can be made with respect to Griswold's paradigm. The "dyadic structure" of the "forgiveness" paradigm he proposes excludes unilateral forgiveness in almost all cases. Griswold does allow for unilateral forgiveness "in the subjunctive mode" when the offending party is deceased.[34] However, he maintains that forgiveness in such cases is not really achieved because the dyadic structure has not been observed.[35]

Common to both these approaches is the way in which reconciling is embedded as an operative condition within the understanding of forgiving itself. The distinction between the two enactments is not observed. If this distinction were recognized and integrated into Haber's and Griswold's projects, the problem would be resolved, although the shape of their paradigms might well need to be seriously revised. If reconciling is indeed integral to forgiving in the manner posited by both Haber and Griswold, then unilateral forgiveness might be subject to the charge of condonation, for then to forgive without naming what is offensive in a morally objectionable act and coming to agreement in the repudiation of it *might* (ordinarily) be to condone the act (allowing it to go unchallenged, even if it is not approved of). But if forgiveness is an enactment distinct from, but related to, reconciliation—as I have argued above—the charge does not necessarily hold. Condonation becomes an issue between the parties directly involved only at the point when reconciliation—the (re) establishment of interpersonal relations—is at issue. That is the point at which the approval or condemnation of a given disruptive act must be sorted out, because coming to agreement on the understanding of the act, as Griswold rightly argues, is essential for the reestablishment of

---

[34] Griswold, *Forgiveness: A Philosophical Exploration*, 120–22.

[35] This conclusion flows from the existential situation of trying to forgive someone who is already dead and Griswold's minimal conditions for enacting forgiveness, which, as his paradigm makes clear, require a dyadic engagement. See Griswold, *Forgiveness: A Philosophical Exploration*, 113–17, for a description of the minimal conditions for imperfect forgiveness.

relationship (reconciliation), but it is not essential for the enactment of forgiveness.

Beyond the objections raised thus far to the arguments regarding the danger of condonation, there is a further concern. It seems to me that there is a form of concealed violence against the victim in some strands of the argument about condonation. Hints of that violence creep through in several places: in the appeal to the moral community, in the use of the argument about the self-worth of the victim, and, more evidently, in the concern about how third parties will view the non-retributive posture of the victim if she forgives unilaterally and does not publicly condemn the offensive action.[36] When appeals to these ideas are made to urge upon the one harmed the obligation to publicly repudiate the offense so as to avoid (*even the appearance of*) condonation, they impose a burden on the one who has been harmed. Such arguments obligate the victim to take responsibility for and to manage how others interpret her response to the harm. They then use this postulated obligation to justify a particular prescription about how forgiveness must be enacted if it is to be moral.

Such approaches serve to revictimize the victim. They reinforce the harm. The offender's actions have already disrupted the sense of self and of the self/world relation of the one harmed. According to such arguments the offender's actions have also imposed on the victim an obligation to control how the victim's responses are interpreted by others, including the offender. The compulsion behind this obligation—couched in terms of not condoning or appearing to condone the offensive action—is the threat of moral condemnation. The threat of this condemnation becomes a force binding the victim to the meaning of the event at the time of the offense. Particularly in arguments that appeal to concern about how others might read the act of forgiveness, it binds the victim to some third party's *potential interpretation* of the meaning of the act and of its forgiveness.

There *might*, indeed, be circumstances in which a person—say, a public figure—has a moral obligation to publicly communicate repudiation of an offensive act done to her. But it is by no means clear that this is a universal moral obligation regardless of circumstances, or that it can be imposed as a condition for the moral practice of forgiveness. To put the point more strongly, the implications of the concern about condonation

---

[36] See, for example, Griswold, *Forgiveness: A Philosophical Exploration*, 121. As Jennie G. Noll points out, this is most commonly a problem when forgiveness is equated with reconciliation. Noll, "Forgiveness in People Experiencing Trauma," 367.

as they appear in some of the arguments constitute a further abuse of the one harmed. This renders the moral philosophical arguments about condonation in relation to unilateral forgiveness incoherent, for to purchase the assurance that condonation (or its appearance) is avoided at the price of further violence to the victim would itself be immoral.

One possible way to avoid this predicament has already been signaled. Distinguishing forgiving from reconciling, and recognizing that condonation or its appearance is most properly an issue when undertaking reconciliation, would bypass the incoherence. In most cases the clear communication of disapproval of the offensive harm becomes important in the (re)establishment of interpersonal relations between the one harmed and the one who occasioned the harm. Here the issue is not managing how third parties will potentially interpret the event and the forgiveness extended, but whether, in the (re)establishment of relations, the offending behavior is excluded from or allowed in the future development of the relationship. If one were to take unilateral forgiveness as the paradigm case, having carefully distinguished forgiving from reconciling, and to locate the question of condonation on the terrain of reconciliation—that is, in the realm of (re)establishment of interpersonal relations between the parties directly involved—a good deal of the difficulty would disappear. This suggests that much of this problem is less a matter of the morality of unilateral forgiveness than it is a function of failure to distinguish forgiving from reconciling and the desire to justify a particular paradigm of forgiveness that does not recognize the distinction.

## UNILATERAL FORGIVENESS, REPENTANCE, AND SELF-RESPECT

The question of self-respect has surfaced in many ways in the moral philosophical and psychological discussions. Both discussions affirm that the harm that provokes a retributive emotional response is experienced as an affront to one's dignity. The offense calls into question one's self-worth. Forgiving, therefore, must be done in a manner that shows respect for one's self.

This conviction, shared by both philosophers and psychologists, has been used by moral philosophers as a basis for their argument that an offender must repent before forgiveness can be morally extended. The degree of commitment to this principle varies, depending on the philosopher. Murphy, as we have seen, allows for reasons other than repentance for forgiving someone, while Griswold limits the possibility to the "subjunctive mode" and considers the enactment of forgiveness in such cases incomplete, and Haber rejects the morality of forgiveness in the absence of explicit repentance as condonation.

Haber is the most forceful of these authors in identifying the unilateral forgiveness of an offender in the absence of explicit repentance as a sign of lack of self-respect. Griswold evinces a similar perspective.[37] Murphy, by contrast—and of necessity, given his acceptance of other reasons for forgiving than repentance—does not bind the self-respect question to the repentance of the offender. Neither, for that matter, do the psychologists. Their attention is more directly focused on the fact that one's sense of self-worth has been damaged and that forgiving will be implicated in healing the effects of experiences of harm. They thus express concern that, in forgiving, one not act in a manner counter to self-respect, but they do so primarily from the perspective of psychological rather than moral harm. The problematic issue, therefore, is the moral philosophical conviction that unilateral forgiveness in the absence of evident repentance indicates a lack of self-respect.

The approach to understanding forgiveness presented here—focusing attention on what is taking place within the one forgiving in undertaking to forgive—suggests that the connection between unilateral forgiveness and lack of self-respect is not as certain as is claimed by Haber and Griswold. We can see this by examining the question from three different standpoints already elaborated in our descriptive account of forgiveness.

The first standpoint concerns the dynamics involved in our response to the experience of harm. It is true that the harm that can occasion the question of forgiveness is experienced as an assault on the sense of self. The meaning of the harm challenges our self-worth. In the initial impact of the disruption and the period following, the pain evoked by the experience draws our attention with relentless insistence to the recognized meaning in the offense. When we find ourselves in the immediate aftermath of the event and its recognition as harm, it can seem as though our self-worth hinges on the reversal of the meaning of the event and the forceful repudiation of its message. But *does* our self-worth or our self-respect *really* depend on extracting repentance from the offender?

The account of meaning and personal becoming presented in the analysis of the experience of harm in chapter 5 gives us good reason to conclude that it does not. The dynamic process involved in forgiving suggests that part of that process—and this is especially clear in cases of

---

[37] Griswold, *Forgiveness: A Philosophical Exploration*, 43–47, 65.

unilateral forgiveness—is the relocation of the center of our sense of our own worth. It involves a reclaiming of self-respect that *might* be assisted by the offender's expression of repentance but does not, from a psychodynamic standpoint, depend upon it. Our sense of self and our self-respect are lodged in multiple complexes of meanings. A given individual *might* need to witness evidence of repentance in order to reestablish the stability of the sense of self, but another individual might not. Her sense of self and awareness of her self-worth might be more securely grounded, or might be grounded in complexes of meaning not heavily disrupted by the specific offense.

In a curious way, the arguments advanced by Haber and Griswold actually undermine their stated advocacy for the dignity of one's self-respect. They suggest that self-respect is dependent on withholding forgiveness until repentance is expressed by the offender. In the event that one does not perceive or recognize that one's self-respect is dependent on this condition, the direction of their arguments implies that they think one *should* experience it this way. The impression is that those who do not find their self-respect in retaining their resentment until evidence of repentance is forthcoming are somehow defective. Beyond the fact that this argument is another example of circular reasoning, it also makes one's self-worth dependent not on the constitutive meanings from which the sense of self emerges but on Haber's and Griswold's judgment about what *ought* to constitute the sense of self and the locus of self-worth.

This is a further example of the conceptual and potentially existential violence embedded in Haber's and Griswold's constructs. The conviction that repentance is necessary before one may morally forgive may be a necessary presupposition of their respective theories but it has little to do with self-respect as constructed out of multiple meanings and complexes of meanings. Indeed, their conviction (that failure to withhold forgiveness in the absence of the offender's repentance constitutes a lack of self-worth) is contradicted by the psychic processes by which the sense of self and of self-respect come into being and develop over time. Moreover, the very possibility of forgiving at all—of realigning the meanings in our personal matrices that have been disrupted by a harmful event and reestablishing their stability without retribution, and so on—shows that our sense of self-worth cannot be properly assessed on the basis of our response to someone's offensive act.

The second standpoint that challenges Haber's and Griswold's perspectives on self-respect in unilateral forgiveness derives from the presentation on matrices of meanings. We constitute our sense of self and our self-respect via the meanings we integrate into our personal matrix—including, but not limited to, the scale of value we attach to any given meaning. What Haber's and Griswold's positions on self-respect do not take into account on the question of unilateral forgiveness or forgiveness in the absence of repentance is that, for some, the sense of self-worth might be more readily affirmed *by* unilateral forgiveness in the absence of repentance than by holding onto resentment until repentance has been expressed. This is a judgment that, I maintain, each individual must make on the basis of prudential consideration of the competing values he or she recognizes to be implicated in the harmful event.

A third critical perspective on this issue emerges from the discussion of developmental processes in personal becoming. Just as the sense of self is something that is constantly in a process of development, so, too, is the sense of self-worth or self-respect derived from it. This ongoing development is, in fact, a condition for the possibility of being hurt in such a way that forgiveness could be a viable response to the harm done. Without the human possibility of change in one's sense of self-worth or self-respect, what we have been calling the experience of harm would have no personal impact. For a child, the judgment(s) of others form a critical piece of information about social values and norms that are appropriated into the sense of self, but part of the process of maturation is coming to increasing self-possession in relationship to external influences. Psychological research on stages of moral development provides a variety of schemas for understanding that movement in the processes of moral decision-making. Higher levels of moral maturation culminate in the capacity to make moral judgments on the basis of values embraced and affirmed in action independently of public approbation of them.[38]

According to this developmental perspective one could make the argument that the capacity for and enactment of unilateral forgiveness might be *preferable*—even *paradigmatic*—as expressions of self-respect. This perspective locates self-respect independently of the actions of the other. It might therefore be an expression of a more mature or more

[38] See, for example, the developmental schema of moral decision-making in Lawrence Kohlberg, *The Psychology of Moral Development: The Nature and Validity of Moral Stages*, Essays on Moral Development, vol. 2 (San Francisco: Harper & Row, 1984); Lawrence Kohlberg, Charles Levine, and Alexandra Hewer, *Moral Stages: A Current Formulation and a Response to Critics*, Contributions to Human Development 10 (Basel and New York: Karger, 1983). For a concise presentation, see Ronald Duska and Mariellen Whelan, *Moral Development: A Guide to Piaget and Kohlberg* (New York: Paulist Press, 1975).

highly developed sense of self and valuing of self, and of a more advanced appropriation of one's own personal freedom, than that dependent on the expressed repentance of the offender. As such it might even reflect, from a developmental perspective, a higher order of moral judgment than that proposed by Haber and Griswold.

## Unilateral Forgiveness and Separating the Offender from the Offense

Throughout the moral philosophical discussion of forgiveness we have encountered the importance of establishing a separation between the offender and the offense if forgiving is to be enacted morally. If the offender still identifies with the offensive action, to forgive—so the argument goes—would be immoral (condonation). Unilateral forgiveness is therefore excluded as a moral option. Some of the implications of this argument have already been addressed above. However, there are two additional aspects of this issue that bear examination.

The first is a conceptual conundrum raised by Derrida that has implications for the Anglo-American moral philosophical discussion. Much of the Anglo-American treatment of the separation of the offender from the offense hinges on the repentance of the offender. (Murphy is an exception to this rule. He allows for other moral reasons for forgiving besides repentance.) But Derrida poses a challenge to this reasoning. If the person has repented, she is no longer the same person.[39] She has changed. There is no longer any need to forgive, only to forget and move on.

The approach to understanding forgiveness described above provides a basis for critiquing Derrida's provocation on this point. First, as has already been presented, forgiving is distinct from reconciling. As I have argued, the repentance of the offender pertains most properly to the topic of reconciliation, not to forgiveness. Part of the power of Derrida's argument rests on the conflation of these two distinct realities. When the distinction is kept in mind, Derrida's objection does not apply.

A second critical observation concerns the claim of "difference" between the one who offended and the one who has repented. In one sense the anthropological reflections on personal becoming intrinsic to the description of forgiveness as a human enactment would seem to affirm Derrida's claim. We become "other" over the course of time. The repentance of the one who offended indicates a kind of commitment similar

[39] Derrida, *On Cosmopolitanism and Forgiveness*, 35.

to that of the one who forgives: to a change in direction with respect to one's future becoming. However, the difference does not constitute as absolute a disjuncture as Derrida's argument wants to maintain. The one who has repented is still the subject of the history of the harm. If forgiving is really, as has been argued, a personal enactment in the form of a commitment not to use a history of harm as a justification for retributive action and a commitment to the possibility of relationship in the future—a commitment arising from a restabilization of the sense of self following the harm—then the repentance of the offender is irrelevant to the enactment of forgiving. While the offender can rupture a relationship unilaterally, she cannot restore it unilaterally. The step prior to the restoration is forgiveness. That enactment lies with the one injured by the event. From the standpoint of the one injured by the event, the meaning of someone's repentance *might* be a factor in the realignment of his sense of self and his self/world relation, but it is not a necessary condition for that realignment to occur.

Third, Derrida's objection entails attributing to the repentant one a degree of "purity" in act that he does not allow to the one forgiving. To repent one must undertake an intentional act of committing oneself to identify with the values counter to those communicated by the harm. This is the mirror image of what one undertakes to do in forgiving. However, Derrida requires that the forgiver make the commitment with an absoluteness beyond human capacity if it is to achieve its purity.[40] This makes the enactment of forgiveness impossible. Yet no such requirement appears to be asked of the one repenting. A purity of enactment on the part of the repentant one appears to be presumed. To be consistent, Derrida would need to apply the same restrictions to both the repentant one and the one forgiving. Repenting would require an absoluteness equal to that of forgiving. It, too, would be humanly impossible. Therefore the assertion that the offender pre- and post-repentance are "different" people does not hold. But in the world in which harms really do occur, people do undertake to forgive, and—sometimes—people do repent of their actions. The account of forgiving that understands it to be a commitment to a trajectory of becoming in the mode of eschatological hope provides a parallel way of understanding repentance and forgiveness. Our repentance

---

[40] See Derrida, *Given Time: 1. Counterfeit Money*, 16. See also the critical engagement with this line of reasoning in Ernesto Verdeja, "Derrida and the Impossibility of Forgiveness," *Contemporary Political Theory* 30, no. 1 (April 2004): 23–47.

is likewise a commitment to a trajectory of becoming, one that looks toward a future fulfillment but is lived out day by day in the present.

There is a deeper methodological problem underlying Derrida's challenge on this point. His claim regarding a "different person" after repentance wants to hold for a kind of *ontological* distinction in what is fundamentally a matter of (moral) meaning. The kind of separation called for by the moral philosophers we have examined is on the level of relationship, meaning, and orientation toward the future. It involves a recognition of the difference between the meaning of the offender before repentance and the meaning of the offender following the repentance with respect to the initially recognized meaning of the harm. Once the meaning of the harm has been repudiated by the offender, the meaning of the offender has changed—*for those who recognize it.*

For the meaning of the offender to change for the one harmed, however, does not depend on such an act by the offender. The one harmed can forgive regardless of repentance, thereby affirming the recognition of a new meaning for the offender. Nor does the change of the meaning of the offender by his repentance necessarily entail that the meaning of the offender for the one harmed undergo change. That only occurs when the one harmed *recognizes* the change in meaning. And that recognition is a matter of necessity, not for enacting forgiveness but for enacting reconciliation.

To state this more directly in terms of the understanding of forgiving advanced in this chapter, the separation of the offender from the offense occurs via recognition of meaning. From the standpoint of forgiveness (in contrast to reconciliation) the one forgiving recognizes a change in her affective, perspectival, evaluative, historical, relational, and other kinds of meanings with respect to the offender and the initially perceived meaning of the harm insofar as these impinge on the stability of the sense of self. That realignment arises from and effects a restabilization of the sense of self in which the—now revised—meaning of the offender is understood to be not simply reducible to the meaning of the event (whether the offender has repented or not). This recognition, which might be experienced either as the consequence of an intentional effort to revise meaning or recognized after its occurrence in the mode of a conversion, or both, enables one to (re)open the space of possible reconciled relationship. It does so as an expression of an eschatological hope: initially, the hope that one remain true to the commitment of forgiving. Secondarily, in the event of actual movement toward reconciliation, it (re)opens the relational space in the hope that the offender remains faithful to the trajectory of becoming that is entailed in repentance.

A further issue related to the question of the separation of the offender from the offense surfaced in chapter 2. Haber critiqued Murphy on the grounds that his formulation requires of the victim that she effect the separation.[41] He saw this as imposing an unjust burden. Earlier I made the argument that Murphy's position is not as clear-cut as Haber believes; the separation need not be "made" by the victim. It is only necessary that such a separation be *recognized* by the victim. We are in the realm of recognized meaning. This is the same realm required by Haber's solution to the unjust burden: that the offender express repentance for the offense. The meaning of the expression of repentance must still be recognized by the victim. It is the same cognitive act in both cases. Consequently, since Haber's appeal to the injustice of requiring the victim to effect the separation does not hold, the use of that argument against the legitimacy of unilateral forgiveness carries no weight.

Nevertheless, the descriptive account of forgiveness presented above does provide some insight into how to understand who effects the separation. While Haber approached the question in terms of a disjunctive—either the victim or the offender—the understanding of forgiveness presented here suggests that the answer is more complicated. When we are dealing with forgiveness, the one forgiving does need to recognize the distinction between the meaning of the offender as the one who occasioned the harm and the offender as having meaning not reducible to the meaning of the harm. This recognition *might* be something one intentionally labors to attain. In this case there is a sense in which the victim does "make" the separation. But the recognition might also occur as a realization that simply "dawns" in the awareness of the victim. It might occur as a kind of conversion of perspective for which the victim has not made any effort, at least on the conscious level. This applies whether one is dealing with moral harm or non-moral harm. In the case of unilateral forgiveness this recognition of separation occurs within the victim; it is independent of the later actions of the offender.

The situation is different when one is dealing with reconciliation. In this case, as Griswold's argument indicates, there would need to be a mutual effort and agreement on revising the narrative of the meaning of the event. In this revision the offender would need to establish that he has distanced himself from that meaning. This is an almost absolute precondition for interpersonal reconciliation following the forgiveness of a moral

---

[41] Haber, *Forgiveness*, 104–5.

harm.[42] To engage in interpersonal reconciliation when the offender still identifies with the meaning of the moral harm would (ordinarily) be to condone that meaning (and behavior) within the relationship. Yet, even assuming that the offender *has* repudiated the meaning of the harm, it is still necessary that the victim recognize and embrace the revised meaning of the event in a manner that also recognizes the distinction between the offender and the offense. In the case of reconciliation, revision of meaning is a mutual effort.[43]

## The Question of Forgiving Non-Agential Harm

The presentation on unilateral forgiveness thus far has argued for its legitimacy. If forgiveness is characterized by the restabilization of one's sense of self and self/world relation following an experience of (recognized) harm, and if its enactment is in the mode of a commitment not to use the history of the harm as a justification for retributive action, but rather to open up a space for the possible (re)establishment of relationship, then it would seem at first glance that non-agential harm would not be an appropriate occasion for undertaking to forgive. After all, if there is no agent who caused the harm there is no one to resent, and therefore no one to forgive.[44]

This line of reasoning has already been alluded to in three objections raised to the idea of forgiving in response to harms not caused by a responsible agent. One hinges on the connection between moral harm and forgivability: if the harm is not a moral harm, the response cannot be forgiveness. In the absence of an agent there is no moral harm, therefore forgiveness does not apply. The second argument is based on rationality: if there is no agent involved, there is no rational object of resentment; therefore forgiveness is not involved.[45] The third argument is more di-

---

[42] Within the context of a basic human enactment understood independently of appeals to religious convictions it is hard to conceive of an exception to this rule. In the case of religiously motivated efforts at reconciliation it is possible that exceptions occur. This will be addressed in part 3.

[43] Griswold's account of this in his dyadic structure seems to me to be on target.

[44] See, for example, the conditions for forgiveness to arise at all in Haber, *Forgiveness*, 40. Murphy points in a similar direction when he argues that "we may forgive only what it is initially proper to resent," in Murphy and Hampton, *Forgiveness and Mercy*, 19. Nonagential harms would not, in his understanding, qualify as deserving of resentment because they do not arise from the intentional actions of moral agents.

[45] See Macaskill, "Just-World Beliefs and Forgiveness in Men and Women," 55.

rectly definitional: expanding the understanding of forgiveness to include non-agential harm would be unacceptable "definitional drift."[46]

However, a closer examination of these objections and of the understanding of forgiveness presented here calls the arguments into question. We have already critiqued the notion that forgiveness only applies in cases of moral harm. The realization that what provokes a potential forgiving response is the recognition of harm *as* harm holds independently of the moral content one might judge to be involved in the action. The ascription of moral content to the harm might serve to justify the intensity of the retributive emotions one feels, but the feelings can be evoked whether a moral harm is recognized or not.

The claim that one's resentment would be irrational in the absence of an agent certainly is plausible. But the rationality of one's retributive emotions is only a factor in determining the validity of one's judgment regarding the moral content of the harm. It does not affect the retributive emotions as such, only the judgment regarding their rationality. They still need to be dealt with. If the harm need not be a moral harm to be an object of forgiveness, then the appeal to the irrationality of resentment misses the point. The dynamic process of forgiveness described here can still be engaged, and may need to be engaged, if one is to come to a point of restabilizing one's sense of self and self/world relationship in the face of the harm, regardless of whether or not one judges the retributive feelings to be rational.

The objection regarding "definitional drift" also falls apart on closer inspection. It begs the question it is designed to settle, namely, the legitimacy of the definition of forgiveness to which the authors appeal.[47] If the definition they employ appropriately represents the dynamics we engage when we undertake to forgive, then the question arises whether the dynamics are different than those involved in responding to non-agential harm. If we are in fact engaged in two different dynamics, this needs to be demonstrated, not asserted. Conversely, if the definition appealed to (by those who fear definitional drift) does not represent the actual dynamic process involved in forgiving, the definition needs revision. In

[46] Robert D. Enright, Suzanne Freedman, and Julio Rique, "The Psychology of Interpersonal Forgiveness," 46–62, in *Exploring Forgiveness*, at 50–51.

[47] The concern about definitional drift has received some pushback from other psychologists who see the value in broadening the understanding of forgiveness on the basis of what people actually experience. See DeCourville, Belicki, and Green, "Subjective Experiences of Forgiveness in a Community Sample: Implications for Understanding Forgiveness and Its Consequences," 17.

other words, if in the light of more penetrating investigation the definition the authors take for granted is not adequate to the phenomenon it names, then we are not dealing with "definitional drift" but with the need for *definitional correction*.

Of course, these responses to the objections only point out the inadequacy of their reasoning in support of the claims they wish to make. Moreover, they do so according to the specific matrix of meanings we have been developing thus far with respect to forgiveness as a human enactment. But invalidating the objections does not necessarily imply that the counter-claim is true: that one can legitimately forgive in the absence of an agent of the harm. That requires a further argument. However, if the description of the dynamics of forgiving presented here hold, then the case for the possibility of forgiving non-agential harm can be made.

As philosophers and psychologists have agreed, unforgiven harm (disruption of the sense of self and of the self/world relation) binds us to an event in the past in a manner that affects our trajectory of future becoming. Psychological insight has also drawn attention to the fact that the retributive affective states occasioned by harm can become generalized and directed outward, toward those uninvolved in the harm and even toward ourselves. Forgiveness is the process by which we become free from the power contained in the meaning of the harm via the restabilization of the sense of self and the self/world relation. This process carries with it the diminishment of the power of retributive impulses.

Just as, in the case of agential harm, feelings of resentment (and other retributive feelings) can become generalized to shape our relationship to the surrounding world, so also can feelings arising from experiences of harm that have no agent involved. A woman's child dies at birth. Her sense of self has been deeply disrupted. Her experience of loss can generate anger and resentment that affect the rest of her relationships. There is no responsible agent toward whom to direct the feelings, but they are real. They have an impact on her relationship to the world and to other persons. They can even engender resentment toward those whose children are alive and well. The process of freeing herself from the power of that harm might well have to follow the dynamics of forgiveness. Although the feelings of resentment would have no responsible agent as their proper object (and might therefore be called "irrational" by some), they do have an impact on the individual's personal becoming and her relational capacities. The forgiveness, therefore, would come to expression in her relationships with those who enter within the sphere of her resentment-based behavior and attitudes.

## Forgiveness and the Faultlines

The responses presented to some of the many points of conflict in the discussions of forgiveness have already indicated how the present descriptive account of forgiveness would address the two larger faultlines identified in chapter 4. Before we conclude this chapter it will be helpful to return to each of the faultlines to make this response more explicit and to draw out further implications of the approach presented here.

### *Unconditional versus Conditional Forgiveness*

The main issue characterizing the first faultline as presented in chapter 2 is the difference between the Derridean "pure" forgiveness and the Anglo-American moral philosophical "true" forgiveness. This difference underlies the disagreement over whether forgiveness is properly unconditional or an enactment that takes place within certain conditions. Related to this disagreement is the question whether forgiveness is "impossible" or possible. From the very outset the present approach—asking about what one is doing when one undertakes to forgive—has assumed that forgiveness *is* possible and that it *is* undertaken according to certain conditions. Chapter 4 also presented a critique of Derrida's concept of "pure" forgiveness on the grounds that from the perspective of the present matrix of meanings it has the appearance of a circular argument.

However, the understanding of forgiveness presented here is not as hostile to Derrida's concerns and approach as this critique might suggest. This becomes clear if we examine a linguistic distinction that has made its way throughout the presentation, that between "forgiveness" and "forgiving." The term "forgiveness" possesses a kind of ambiguity. It is a noun derived from a verb. In its noun form it suggests a state in which an enactment has been completed, a "perfect-tense" state. This is the implication of the phrase, "I have forgiven you." The act is complete. It is done.

The descriptive approach to forgiveness articulated above calls this understanding of the phrase into question. Given the kind of beings we are—always in the process of becoming, participating in that process by our responsible decisions, always influenced by our conscious understanding *and* by unconscious factors not directly accessible to our intentional control—we can never be certain that the forgiveness we pronounce in such statements *is in fact* complete and irreversible. It would be truer to our human condition to understand the statement "I have forgiven you" to mean "I have committed myself to be forgiving toward you—not to use the history of the event of harm as an occasion for retribution or to foreclose the possibility of future relationship." Then the statement would not be about a completed state of being but about a commitment to an ongoing trajectory in (inter)personal becoming.

This understanding of the pronouncement of forgiveness in interpersonal relations as a statement about a commitment to the future, and therefore a statement about a hope, actually brings us very close to Derrida. Most directly, it means that, despite identification with the possibility and the conditionality of forgiveness, this understanding also incorporates a kind of impossibility into the understanding of forgiveness. But it transfers that impossibility from the aporia of the concept to the existential/phenomenal realm at the intersection of human becoming, the inaccessibility of parts of our own motivations, the limits of lives, and the open-endedness of a future we do not control. As indicated above, the moment at which it would be possible to pronounce truthfully in the perfect tense that "I have forgiven you" is the exact moment at which I can pronounce nothing at all because my personal becoming has ended. Thus, for the individual, it is impossible to know with certitude that one has indeed forgiven.

On the other hand, it is possible to know that one has forgiven in the sense that she has at this moment (or up to this moment) made (and held to) the commitment entailed in enacting forgiveness. She can claim "I forgive you" in the sense of "I am forgiving you"—an ongoing enactment. And this she can know to be true even in the midst of the conditions specified above. This possible forgiveness will always be played out in the conditions of one's own concrete experience, mediated by the meanings of one's own shared and personal matrices of meanings. Even an upsurge of retributive impulses need not falsify it, for they are taken into account in the unconditionality of the commitment, both at the moment of the commitment itself and in every moment at which the commitment is reaffirmed. In a sense such upsurges serve as the test that can verify (or falsify) the truth of the commitment, not by the fact of their having arisen but by the response made to them. The character of the commitment, therefore, introduces the element of a kind of intentional unconditionality back into the conditional expression of forgiveness. But the unconditionality is, in this case, aspirational—a hope—and it is circumscribed by the meaning of the specific harm.

In other words, the understanding of forgiveness presented here recognizes the presence of both conditional and unconditional aspects, possible and impossible dimensions to its enactment. What emerges as a faultline separating the Continental-French from the Anglo-American discussions is, in the present reading, simply an index of the many facets and complexities of the dynamics involved in enacting forgiveness.

## *Moral Harm versus Non-Moral Harm*

The second faultline lies between those who maintain that forgiveness only applies in cases of moral harm and those who allow the possibility that forgiveness can be a legitimate response to non-moral harms. In chapter 4 we saw how the exclusion of moral harm, at least in some forms of the argument, rests on what from our standpoint is circular reasoning. In the analysis of the experience of harm and personal becoming (chapter 5), we also argued that the fundamental issue in forgiving is not the moral content of the harm but the recognition of the harm *as* harm; this is what occasions the possibility of forgiveness as a meaningful response. The same multifaceted dynamism involved in restabilizing the sense of self and of the self/world relation following a moral harm (which we call forgiving) is operative in responding to non-moral harms. It is therefore no surprise that the present descriptive account of forgiveness as a human enactment recognizes the application of forgiveness to non-moral harms.

Nevertheless, there is more that needs to be said on this subject, in two respects. First, our examination of the cognitive dimension of meaning and its role in recognition of harm raises further problems with the exclusion of non-moral harm from consideration. These touch on the issue of moral judgment. But second, even though the present proposal accepts that non-moral harm is legitimately a potential occasion for forgiveness, forgiving is always engaged with questions of moral value. These two points need to be spelled out before this discussion comes to a conclusion.

## COGNITIONAL PROBLEMS WITH EXCLUDING NON-MORAL HARM

As we have already seen, the arguments presented by Murphy, Haber,[48] and Griswold[49] exclude non-moral harms as occasions for forgiveness. Murphy makes the point when he claims that one can only forgive what it is initially proper to resent.[50] The arguments presented by these authors all hinge on the ability of the one harmed to recognize the moral harm,

---

[48] Haber, *Forgiveness*, 40.

[49] Griswold, *Forgiveness: A Philosophical Exploration*, 40, 42.

[50] See Murphy and Hampton, *Forgiveness and Mercy*, 20, as well as the discussion in chap. 2, pp. 46–47.

that is, to recognize the harm and to arrive at a judgment that the harm arises from a moral breach. Were there no specifically moral breach, according to their arguments, there would be nothing to forgive.

This understanding of forgiveness, if we embrace it, leads to a serious conundrum—one that calls into question the possibility of ever knowing whether forgiveness has been enacted. The problem lies in the establishment of the (im)morality of the offense. The recognition of the immoral status of the offense depends on the interpretation of the offense in relation to a horizon of previously confirmed meanings: those judged to be true in relation to the matrix of meanings against which they were measured. As Griswold points out, however, there are many conceivable circumstances in which one might fail to recognize the moral content.[51] There are also conditions in which one might ascribe moral offense where no moral breach has in fact occurred. According to the premise of the argument, for forgiveness to be invoked we must have a *bona fide* instance of a moral harm. If we cannot know whether such a harm has occurred, we do not know whether we are enacting forgiveness.

This problem becomes further complicated if we ask about the point at which the judgment of the moral content occurs. It might be that the judgment of moral content occurs coterminously with the recognition of the harm. One's matrix of meanings might include the judgment that all cases of "X" constitute a moral breach. If I recognize that "X" has occurred, then the moral character of the instance is presupposed and is recognized simultaneously with the recognition of the event as such. But there is no unassailable standard against which to measure or evaluate the validity of this judgment, either in the particular case or as a general rule. The standards themselves are already embedded within and dependent on the matrix of meanings of the one making the judgment.

Alternatively, one could make the judgment that a moral breach has occurred subsequently to the recognition of the harm as harm. In either case the judgment that the breach is a moral breach is reached by the individual on the basis of an interpretation of the event experienced as harm. But what is the function of this judgment in the dynamics of forgiveness? According to the moral philosophers we have considered, it is a necessary condition if we are to invoke forgiveness as a response and if we are to justify the specific conditions for the enactment of forgiveness that each author wants to promote. That is a plausible argument.

---

[51] Griswold, *Forgiveness: A Philosophical Exploration*, 40.

However, it fails to take into account an alternative. The judgment of the harm as a moral breach might also be a psychological strategy (however unconscious) to justify to the one injured the feelings of resentment provoked by the offense.

We are left with the problem of distinguishing "real" moral harm from "unreal." If we cannot make that distinction with certitude, according to the premises of these moral philosophers, it becomes impossible to know whether forgiveness has *ever* been enacted. We arrive at a point very close to Derrida's impossible forgiveness. We are then left with the necessity of finding an "objective" judge of the morality of the event in question or a universally-agreed-upon standard of assessment, the application of which avoids any ambiguity.

This problem depends on the claim that forgiveness only applies to moral harms. The consequences of that claim, if followed through, are not supportable. However, if forgiveness is not bound so exclusively to moral harm but is in fact a potential response to the experience of the recognition of harm as harm, then invoking forgiveness and knowing that we are doing so is considerably less problematic. We can enact forgiveness when we recognize that we have experienced a harm. Moral harms are simply a subset of the range of possible experiences to which forgiveness can be extended.

## The Issue of Moral Value

The preceding arguments raise critical questions regarding the definition of forgiveness in terms of moral harm. Making the understanding of forgiveness contingent on the judgment of moral harm leads to serious conceptual difficulties. However, the descriptive account of forgiveness presented in this chapter does not exclude moral value from the discussion of forgiveness. Indeed, one could argue that moral value is always implicated in forgiving, even as it is implicated in any human or relational act.

The question naturally arises: How then is one to incorporate moral judgments into the enactment of forgiveness? It is not the purpose of the present inquiry to provide a moral philosophical response to that question. However, if the critiques of the moral philosophical approaches we have considered do have merit, then any approach will need to avoid the pitfalls we have identified. They will need to begin from a clearer understanding of the phenomenon of the enactment of forgiveness prior to the imposition of theories of virtue, speech-acts, or deontological ethical principles, and certainly prior to the formulation of "solutions" to the question of the "moral" enactment of forgiveness. To put this in other terms, theories about moral enactment will need, at least in the case of forgiveness, to begin from the phenomenon of the experience of harm and the capacity to recognize moral values as relevant to experiences of harm. The descriptive account of forgiveness presented in this chapter may serve as a first step in that direction.

# Part Three

# The Landscape of Christian Forgiveness

*U*p to this point our exploration of the landscape of forgiveness has been restricted to realms in which no explicit appeal is made to religious sensibilities. This has provided us with a benchmark of forgiveness as a basic human enactment. To accomplish this we surveyed three prominent lines of inquiry—French-Continental philosophical discussions, Anglo-American moral philosophical discussions, and psychological discussions of forgiveness—in part 1. In part 2 we dug beneath these three discussions, excavating resources that assisted us in describing forgiveness as a basic human enactment. Our approach has been to uncover what is going on within us and in our orientation toward others when we undertake to forgive.

The results of these explorations led to the conviction that current accounts of forgiveness are not adequate to the question we have been posing. If one accepts the foundational presuppositions of any of these approaches and embraces the intention(s) driving their inquiries, the discourses possess coherence. However, as we have seen, if one steps outside the matrices of meanings from within which those different discussions take place (for example, by posing our question about human enactment), many common assumptions on which those discussions are based do not hold up. Consequently, chapter 6 presented an alternative description of forgiveness and applied it to several problematic issues that had emerged in other discussions.

With this descriptive account of forgiveness established, we are now in a position to venture into the landscape of Christian forgiveness and to return to the question that motivates this entire work: is there a distinctively Christian forgiveness? As we take our first steps into this new realm it will become apparent that the landmarks by which we will need to orient our exploration differ from many of those we have encountered thus far, for in the land of Christian forgiveness the shared matrix of meanings through which we interpret and evaluate enactments of forgiveness is shaped by the Christian narrative. Rather than drawing our attention to "impossible forgiveness" (Derrida) or to the moral conditions under which one may or may not forgive (Anglo-American moral philosophers) or to the psychodynamics of forgiveness (psychologists), the Christian narrative orients us in relationship to God's action: God's saving, redeeming work in Christ as God's forgiveness of us. Christians are to make sense of their own call to forgive and of their own individual enactments of forgiveness from within this narrative. The reference to this narrative is what makes the diversity of Christian approaches identifiably Christian.

Yet even before we take our first steps onto this terrain we must make note of a significant challenge. It has its parallels in the three discourses we examined in part 1. Just as, in each of those discussions, we met a range of voices, each reflecting its own appropriation of a larger shared matrix of meanings, so, too, Christian contributions to contemporary reflection on forgiveness are many and diverse. Like their counterparts from the secular discussions, Christian authors pose distinctive questions, employ various methods of inquiry, and make their own judgments about which data to consider and how to interpret them in addressing their particular questions. What unites these authors is that each engages the question of forgiveness *because* of a personal commitment to Christian faith and a conviction that the promotion of forgiveness is a requirement of that faith commitment.

The challenge arises because, despite the common motivation and the appeal to a (more or less) common narrative, there are also significant differences among the many voices claiming to present the Christian account of forgiveness. It will not be possible to name and explore all the variations available. But on what basis is a selection to be made? Any selection runs the risk of being labeled "arbitrary" or "stilted" by those whose preferred accounts do not receive the attention they believe their favored versions merit.

Although this will not satisfy all readers, the criterion of selection employed in what follows will be methodological in two senses. In one sense it will meet a methodological objective. The authors selected will provide benchmarks on a spectrum of perspectives. This will allow the exploration to span a breadth of approaches in a manageable way, but it will also allow readers who favor other authors to assess where they stand in relation to the spectrum presented. In a second sense the criterion is methodological because it will focus on an aspect of the methodology used by each author. The criterion has been adapted from the christological language of the latter half of the twentieth century, which distinguished "Christology from below" from "Christology from above." Some approaches to Christology emphasize the humanity of Jesus and seek to "ascend" to the creedal affirmations regarding his divinity (Christology from below). Others emphasize the pre-existence of the Divine Logos and the "descent" to the world (Christology from above). Whatever the limitations of these modes of conceptualizing christological discussions, they do provide an analogy to different trajectories in Christian expositions of forgiveness.

The three Christian authors selected for discussion in what follows represent an approach to forgiveness "from below" (Louis Smedes), an approach "from above" (Miroslav Volf), and an approach located between the two, one that emphasizes theological arguments "from above" but attempts to draw connections to practices that promote the embodiment of forgiveness "from below" (L. Gregory Jones). These three authors with their different approaches will help us to clarify the boundaries and to identify many of the landmarks on the terrain called "Christian forgiveness." They will provide a starting point for engaging the question whether Christian forgiveness really *is* distinctive, and if so, why.

This selection of authors requires further comment. The three authors selected theologize from within different Protestant matrices of meaning: Reformed, Lutheran, and Methodist. My own background is Roman Catholic, interpreted from within my experience as a Jesuit priest. This raises two questions. First, why are no Catholic sources among those chosen? Second, is what follows going to be setting up for a Catholic polemic? This latter question is especially pointed because Volf bases his theological analysis of Christian forgiveness explicitly on his appropriation of Martin Luther's theology. Both of these questions require response.

To the first question: we will be focusing on these three authors because each of them occupies an important place in present-day discussions. Their works are discussed by others who wrestle with the question of Christian forgiveness. Apart from some contributions in the self-help vein and some devotional literature, there is precious little from a distinctly Catholic perspective on the questions we will be exploring. Nevertheless, the kinds of issues we will address and the critical perspectives that will be proposed are not exclusively Protestant issues; they are a challenge to perspectives commonly held by Catholics as well.

This provides a partial response to the second question. Many of the critical issues that will be raised apply to Catholic approaches to forgiveness, but my hope is that the critical engagement with these authors will provide a basis for identifying whether there is a distinctive Christian forgiveness as well as a justification for attempting to rethink it. The "rethinking" will, of course, be from within a Catholic shared matrix of meanings, but it will be pursued in the landscape of *Christian* forgiveness. That is, it will be pursued in a manner that I hope will be recognizably in accord with the intentions of the authors under consideration. Thus, my hope is to make a Catholic contribution in an ecumenical spirit to furthering reflection on a matter of importance to all Christians.

It should already be apparent from what has been said that no one of the authors under consideration presents "the" Christian understanding of forgiveness; there are many. So also, the rethinking of Christian forgiveness toward which we will be moving will not be "the" Catholic understanding. This is a project in constructive theology; the very notion of "rethinking Christian forgiveness" already indicates as much. The exploration that follows will therefore be proposing a new way of drawing together the resources of the Christian theological heritage in order to name a truth of Christian faith in a new way: one, it is hoped, that can address itself effectively to the circumstances of the present day and to a broad range of Christian perspectives.

The approach of part 3 will parallel on the terrain of Christian forgiveness the course followed in parts 1 and 2 in the realm of secular discussions of forgiveness. Chapter 7 will survey the landscape, focusing on the three authors named above. The agenda will be primarily expository (paralleling part 1), but will situate the different positions on the spectrum "from below"/"from above." This will provide us with a preliminary account of distinctively Christian forgiveness.

The task of chapters 8 and 9 will parallel that of chapter 4: to excavate deeper issues within the discussion. The purpose will be twofold. First, it will be to expose "instabilities" or "shaky ground" in these Christian accounts. Some of these will be related to their diagnoses of the context challenging Christian forgiveness. Others will be more specifically theological. Both kinds of instability will point to the need to rethink Christian forgiveness. Second, they will also provide us with some of the criteria a rethought Christian forgiveness must satisfy.

In chapter 10 we shall begin the task of "rethinking." We will reorient ourselves on the Christian landscape by rethinking the Christian narrative so as to address the challenges raised in chapters 8 and 9. Chapter 11 will articulate a revised understanding of Christian forgiveness, thereby paralleling chapter 6. It will bring this revised understanding into dialogue with the three Christian approaches presented in chapter 7, but also with the secular approaches examined in parts 1 and 2.

# Chapter 7

# Surveying the Landscape of Christian Forgiveness

### Getting Oriented in the Christian Landscape

*T*he introduction to this exploration of Christian forgiveness observed that there are many different expressions of what it means to be Christian. Initially one could say that these differences have their roots in historical disputes about the fundamental meaning of discipleship: what it means to profess Jesus as "Lord" and what it means to "follow him" in one's life. This is certainly true, as far as it goes. But as our examination of personal becoming suggests (chap. 5), there is more to the story than that. Each of us appropriates the shared matrix of meanings called "Christianity" from our own individual standpoint. We integrate the Christian message (or not) into our personal matrices of meanings in a way unique to each of us, but sufficiently (we hope) in common with the shared matrix from which we draw to remain identifiably within the fold.

When we relate the Christian story to others we draw on our own appropriation of it, but we also shape the story in accord with the circumstances that move us to write or speak. Our interpretation of the need (lacuna) that prompts us to write, in creative interaction with the story as we understand it, and with our own trajectory of personal becoming, impresses itself on both the form and the content of our retelling of the story.

This situation, this tension between the specificity of a shared matrix of meanings and the inevitable variation that takes place during one's personal appropriation and re-presentation of it, imposes certain limitations on any effort to name Christian forgiveness, but it also highlights the reason why Christian writers find it so important to tackle the question. The situation imposes limitations because any general description of Christian

230

forgiveness will differ to some degree from the actual appropriation of Christian self-understanding lived out by any particular individual. It will also differ from other Christian accounts because each rendering is based on the denominational histories, theological presuppositions, and specific questions moving each individual author.

Naming the characteristics of Christian forgiveness and its relationship to a shared matrix of meanings identified with a normative Christian self-understanding is of vital concern to Christians who fear the loss of what it means to be Christian—or alternatively, who take seriously the Christian mission to advance the Kingdom of God. The potential for "identity drift" inherent in the difference between the normative standards of a given shared Christian matrix of meanings and the way those standards are appropriated carries with it the danger of "identity confusion" or worse, the loss of what is essential to being Christian.

Thus, on the one hand, our task is to identify a distinctively Christian forgiveness (if there is such a thing). Given the many different shared matrices of meanings that identify themselves as "Christian," it is probable that some self-identified Christians will take exception to aspects (or all) of what we might identify as distinctively Christian forgiveness. This cannot be avoided. Therefore it will be necessary to remember that the best we can hope for is *an* articulation of Christian forgiveness; it will be one among many possibilities. Moreover, this articulation will be shaped not only by the way my own personal matrix of meanings has appropriated the Christian narrative but also by the specific questions I am seeking to address. On the other hand it will be essential that this account, as an articulation of *Christian* forgiveness, be truly rooted in those aspects of the shared Christian matrix of meanings under which distinctive Christian approaches are arrayed. It will need to account for the place of forgiveness in Christian self-understanding in a manner that, despite possible novel formulations, is recognizably grounded in the foundational story of Christianity broadly defined.

As we first step into the landscape of Christian forgiveness it will be helpful to survey the terrain. Yet, as the immediately preceding comments indicate, and as the presentation of matrices of meanings in chapter 5 helps to explain, there are as many approaches to Christian forgiveness as there are Christians who undertake to explain it. The literature on Christian forgiveness is expansive, covering genres from purely devotional to self-help to scholarly. It is not possible within the limits of this study to do justice to all the distinctive nuances evident in the literature. We shall therefore need to approach our survey of the landscape in a way that allows us to sketch the breadth of the distinctively Christian terrain while at the same time providing access to important details in the discussions.

To do so we shall examine the works of three Christian writers who have made significant contributions to contemporary reflection on forgiveness: Lewis Smedes, Miroslav Volf, and L. Gregory Jones. Their approaches are diverse, as are the concerns that move them to write. But each is aware that forgiving is challenging, that it is central to Christian self-understanding, and that there are many obstacles to engaging in forgiveness. The distinctive manner in which each grapples with these issues will serve our inquiry in two ways. First, each of these authors will raise issues that a presentation of Christian forgiveness will need to address. They will introduce us to the breadth and details of the landscape of Christian forgiveness. But second, viewed in relationship to each other these three authors will present a spectrum of possible approaches to the question of Christian forgiveness. Other Christian approaches can then be assessed in relation to that spectrum.

## Lewis B. Smedes and the Healing Power of Forgiveness

Contemporary Christian reflection on forgiveness has flourished since the rise of self-help literature in the 1980s. Lewis B. Smedes (1921–2002), a theologian in the Reformed tradition who taught for twenty-five years at Fuller Theological Seminary, is among the best-known Christian contributors to the genre. His *Forgive and Forget: Healing the Hurts We Don't Deserve* (1984) has secured a prominent place of respect in the popular Christian literature on forgiveness.

Late in his life, reflecting on the success of *Forgive and Forget*, Smedes observed: "The trade journal *Publisher's Weekly* described it [*Forgive and Forget*] as a 'crossover' book. A 'crossover' book is a bridge book that connects the academic and the ordinary reader just as it bridges the gap between Christian and secular readers."[1] This brief recollection aptly identifies several points of importance for understanding his contribution to naming Christian forgiveness. First, Smedes understands his work as an act of communication with a wider audience than his academic peers and his co-religionists. Although it arises from his Christian theological commitments, it is intended to speak to the experience of readers who

---

[1] The quotation is excerpted from Smedes's memoir, *God and I at the Writing Desk*, in Lewis B. Smedes, *Forgive and Forget: Healing the Hurts We Don't Deserve* (New York: HarperCollins, 1984), 165.

might not be inclined to plumb the depths of complex theological arguments but who can reflect critically on their own human experience. Second, the book is written so as to appeal to non-Christians as well as Christians. It does so by staying grounded in descriptions of readily identifiable human experiences that are common to human persons independently of their religious commitments. It is meant, therefore, to be as inclusive as possible. As a consequence, although Smedes's own motivations are rooted in his Christian commitments, his mode of expression is broadly humanistic. References to God are few; references to Christ are fewer.[2] Where they do occur they are mainly illustrative from a Christian perspective of points that could be adduced from reflection on human experience. Thus in his presentation Smedes does not identify anything as distinctively Christian with respect to forgiveness.

The nature of this work, intended for a broad readership, affects Smedes's mode of presentation. It is an analysis of forgiveness "from below." Because his work does not presume that his readers share his Christian faith, Smedes must couch his analysis and promotion of forgiveness as a practice in terms with which his readers can identify. He must start with human experience. One of the most prominent metaphors he employs to achieve this is "healing." The experience of harm is painful. The pain indicates that something is wrong. Holding onto resentment and retributive feelings does not resolve the pain. Forgiving has the potential to do so. Thus one aspect of his advocacy of forgiveness is its benefit to the one who forgives. This is, in fact, primary in his exposition.

But Smedes appeals to other reasons as well, and these are related to personal integrity in a world harmed by human choices. In response to the question "why forgive?" Smedes offers four reasons, each comprising a chapter in his work. First, he argues that forgiving "makes life fairer."[3] It is fair to the wrongdoer because it requires that we recognize the reality of the harm and hold the offenders responsible for what they have done. "You will forgive only when you dare look at people eyeball to eyeball and tell them that they are responsible for what they did. Forgiving is fair to wrongdoers because it holds them to the incriminating touchstone of their own free humanity."[4] Forgiving does not undo the history of the

---

[2] Smedes refers to God 117 times but only refers to either Jesus or Christ sixteen times during the course of the book.

[3] Smedes, *Forgive and Forget*, 125–33.

[4] Ibid., 130. By way of anticipation it is worth noting that the concern to hold offenders responsible has its parallel in Miroslav Volf's interest in "remembering rightly." See

relationship or excuse the offense. It carries within it the clear recognition that "I have experienced harm because of what you have done."

The alternative to forgiving would be to "freeze yourself in the unfairness of a cruel moment in the past." This would be unfair to the well-being of the victim of the harm. As Smedes elaborates: "Forgiveness is not the alternative to revenge because it is soft and gentle; *it is a viable alternative because it is the only creative route to less unfairness.*"[5] When we seek revenge instead of forgiving we are seeking to equalize the experience of harm, yet we can never do so. What we consider commensurate punishment or retribution is experienced by the recipient as excessive, thereby promoting a further retributive response. So the cycle of vengeance perpetuates unfairness. Forgiving offers a way out of the unfairness.[6]

A second reason Smedes names for forgiving is that it is "a better risk."[7] It is better than forgetting what has been done.[8] To forget would be to risk repetition of the harm, but to remember can be harmful, too. Memory *can* be an inducement to perpetual alienation and hostility. It can fuel a predisposition to future violence. Again, forgiveness offers an alternative. "There is a *redemptive remembering.* There is a healing way to remember the wrongs of our irreversible past, a way that can bring hope for the future along with our sorrow for the past. Redemptive remembering keeps a clear picture of the past, but it adds a new setting and shifts its focus."[9] Redemptive remembering sees the harmful event in a new light.[10] This is one of the few places in the book where Smedes draws explicitly on the Christian narrative to exemplify his point. He explains:

> The Christian community, too, was told from the beginning not to forget the sufferings of its founder. Remember the terrible death

Miroslav Volf, *The End of Memory: Remembering Rightly in a Violent World* (Grand Rapids: Eerdmans, 2006); idem, *Exclusion and Embrace: A Theological Exploration of Identity, Otherness, and Reconciliation* (Nashville: Abingdon Press, 1996), 131–32.

[5] Smedes, *Forgive and Forget*, 131 (italics in original).

[6] Ibid., 130–31.

[7] Ibid., 134–37.

[8] Ibid., 135.

[9] Ibid., 136. The language Smedes uses here is clearly drawn from a Christian matrix of meanings.

[10] Smedes does not make this explicit, but part of that new light would seem to be precisely that we now remember the event *as forgiven.* There is a close relationship between what Smedes is getting at here and the description of forgiveness as a basic human phenomenon presented in chap. 6.

of Jesus until he comes again at the end of time—so early believers were commanded to do. But this remembrance is not meant to stoke the fire of resentment against the unfairness of his dying; just the opposite. The point of remembering is to be renewed again and again by the life that rises from the aftershocks of his unfair death. Redemptive memory is focused on love emerging from ashes, light that sheds darkness, hope that survives remembered evil.[11]

It is possible that the harm done to the founder of Christianity could be revisited upon the Christian community. But the remembering to which they are called is that in which God has taken the risk of forgiving and shown that forgiving is the way to redemption and to new life. Hence it is a better risk to forgive in favor of the possibility of new life than to cling to anger, hatred, and resentment.

Third, Smedes argues that forgiving is a stronger response than holding onto hatred. As he elaborates, it is "realism" because it requires us to deal with the reality of what has happened. It includes confrontation with the offender (in Smedes's formulation). It is an expression of personal freedom. And forgiving finds its roots in the power of love, a power that makes it possible for us to live with the vulnerability that comes with forgiving. Consequently, forgiving is an expression of strength.[12]

Finally, Smedes makes the point that forgiving is appropriate for "faulty people." As he explains, we are all enmeshed in a context of relationships in which we both participate in harm toward others and also contribute to the harm we experience as done to ourselves. Thus, on the one hand, "we are never as pure as we feel."[13] Our own motives for the actions we take are themselves mixed with both good and evil. Yet, on the other hand, when we have been harmed "we are seldom *merely* sinned against. We often contribute to our own vulnerability. Sometimes we invite pain, not because we love somebody too much, but because we are stupid."[14]

---

[11] Smedes, *Forgive and Forget*, 137.

[12] Ibid., 138–46.

[13] Ibid., 147. Volf develops this theme in *Exclusion and Embrace*, 84; and in *The End of Memory*, 124–25.

[14] Smedes, *Forgive and Forget*, 147. There is a valid point here. Not all who claim to be victims are purely so. However, this moves close to "blaming the victim" for the offense and using this co-responsibility as a moral compulsion to enact forgiveness. In my terms there is a risk here of "soft violence" against the victim.

Recognizing these truths about ourselves brings us into contact with the ambiguity of our own moral standing. This ambiguity does not vitiate the validity of our umbrage at the offense, but it does chasten us to attenuate our impulse to vengeance. Consequently, when we examine our experience of having been harmed honestly we also unmask the illusion of our moral superiority with respect to those who have harmed us. The moral distance between us is not as great as our impulse to blame might suggest. Smedes therefore summarizes:

> Forgiving fits faulty folk. And we are all faulty. The best of us belong to that catholic club where nobody dares throw the first stone. For us to forgive others, then, has a certain congruity about it, a kind of fittingness, for the mixed bag of vice and virtue that we all are. All this explains why Jesus was so tough on sinners who refused to forgive other sinners. He saw the laughable incongruity of people who need to be forgiven a lot turning their backs on people who need a little forgiving from them.[15]

These four points, added to his arguments about personal healing, form the core of Smedes's effort to persuade his readers that engaging the task of forgiving the harms we have experienced is worth the effort. But what *is* forgiveness? What are its characteristics? And how does Smedes's articulation of forgiveness stand with respect to the question of a distinctively Christian enactment?

Smedes identifies the characteristics of forgiveness both negatively and positively. Negatively, he distinguishes forgiving from forgetting, excusing, suppressing conflict, accepting others, and tolerating offensive behaviors.[16] Forgetting simply does not engage with the challenge posed by the experience of harm. Excusing removes responsibility from the perpetrator. Suppressing conflict prevents forgiving from taking place by controlling interactions. Acceptance of others does not entail approval of what they do; forgiveness includes disapproval of offensive actions. Toleration implies going along with what one knows to be offensive. This also is not forgiveness.

Positively, Smedes holds that forgiving requires that one know and be prepared to identify what is offensive and why. It involves letting go of

---

[15] Smedes, *Forgive and Forget*, 149–50.
[16] Ibid., 39–45.

the "right" to seek retribution,[17] and it includes a revision of our affective orientation toward the offender, or at least a desire to make such a revision.[18] This can take place when we "rediscover the humanity of the person who hurt us,"[19] thereby making it possible for us to "desire the good" for the offender.[20] Ideally this will issue in "complete forgiveness," a situation in which relationship is restored.[21] But whether or not it does so, the process of coming to the point of forgiving the offender will still bring with it healing for the one harmed.

At this point two observations are in order. First, although his own Christian faith may be a motive force behind his writing on the subject of forgiveness, the arguments Smedes develops to motivate others to undertake forgiveness are not explicitly Christian. They are, first, personal well-being (healing) and second, restoration of the social fabric of relationships damaged by the harm. Certainly Christianity would support these motivations as positive values, but they are so because they are common to human well-being, not because they are distinctly Christian. Second, and by extension, Smedes presents nothing to suggest that there is anything distinctive about "Christian forgiveness." It appears that for Smedes this phrase would merely refer to common human forgiveness as practiced by Christians. Smedes's presentation will therefore come under fire from other Christian writers.[22]

---

[17] In *The Art of Forgiving: When You Need to Forgive and Don't Know How* (New York: Ballantine Books, 1996), 110, Smedes writes of "surrender[ing] your malice" as a characteristic of forgiving. In the same work, pp. 5–10, he discusses "surrender[ing] our right to get even."

[18] Ibid., 10.

[19] Ibid., 6–7. This "rediscovery" intersects with what is discussed among the philosophers and psychologists under the heading "separating the offender from the offense." It also appears to be implicated in "reframing" an event.

[20] Ibid., 73–74.

[21] See chap. 4 of Smedes, *Forgive and Forget*, 31–37, "We Come Together." Smedes is well aware that there are conditions under which such a reunion is neither possible nor advisable. When an abuser, for example, has not forsworn the abusive behavior, to return to relationship would be dangerous. In such conditions, the character of the forgiveness achieved has, in his mind, a kind of incompleteness.

[22] Most notably, Smedes is criticized by L. Gregory Jones for his "therapeutic forgiveness." L. Gregory Jones, *Embodying Forgiveness: A Theological Analysis* (Grand Rapids: Eerdmans, 1995), 39–53, esp. 48–53. The criticism is echoed by Chris Brauns, *Unpacking Forgiveness: Biblical Answers for Complex Questions and Deep Wounds* (Wheaton, IL: Crossway, 2008), 64–72. Smedes contests that his emphasis on the therapeutic value of

## Miroslav Volf and the Generosity of God

Among contemporary Christian theologians writing on forgiveness, Miroslav Volf is perhaps the most prolific, examining the issues involved from a variety of angles. A central theme in his writings is effecting the kind of reconciliation between enemies that Christian faith holds out as the eschatological sign of the Kingdom of God. Such reconciliation requires in the first place that we speak truth about the reality of what has ruptured relationships. This theme he takes up with respect to ethnic violence in Yugoslavia in *Exclusion and Embrace*.[23] Further, reconciliation also requires that we remember rightly, a theme Volf examines at length in *The End of Memory*.[24] But his most extensive exploration of forgiveness occurs in *Free of Charge: Giving and Forgiving in a Culture Stripped of Grace*.[25]

In *Free of Charge*, Volf examines two interrelated ways of being and acting that, he argues, *should be* characteristic of the life of the Christian: generosity and forgiveness. His treatment of the Christian obligation to generosity in the first part of the book lays out the foundations for his argument about the obligation to forgive in the second part. "Generosity," in his terms, is more than a willingness to give "things" to others; it is fundamentally about giving of oneself. This giving, he believes, is essential to healthy human relationships yet, he maintains, our culture has become "graceless"; it does not reflect the generosity and the forgiving spirit that ought to be there. As he explains:

> Maybe my experience on the streets of southern California was an exception. But it fits into a larger pattern of what we may call the gracelessness that is slowly spreading like a disease throughout

---

forgiving corresponds to the substance of Jones's charge—particularly that it is "cheap grace." The fact that Smedes argues that one must recognize the harm for what it is (in truth) and confront the offender with the harm for reconciliation to occur would seem to cast some doubt on the aptness of Jones's critique. However, there is another aspect to Jones's argument that Smedes does not address, namely, the question of motivation. Jones appears to hold that self-interest, as such, disqualifies forgiveness as Christian. We shall return to this issue in later chapters. A further plausible element of Jones's criticism of Smedes is methodological. It arises because of the contrast between approaching forgiveness "from below" rather than "from above."

[23] Volf, *Exclusion and Embrace: A Theological Exploration of Identity, Otherness, and Reconciliation.*

[24] Volf, *The End of Memory.*

[25] Miroslav Volf, *Free of Charge: Giving and Forgiving in a Culture Stripped of Grace* (Grand Rapids: Zondervan, 2005).

many of our cultures. Some may suggest that we are no worse off today than we were fifty years or even two centuries ago. My sense is that we are. But my main point is not to note a decline; rather, to name a problem. We live in a culture in which, yes, extraordinary generosity does happen. But at the same time, that culture is largely stripped of grace.[26]

Some of this gracelessness he traces to the commodification of life. He argues that there is a tendency in modern culture to live from a mentality in which all things are to be treated as resources to be bought or sold. Consequently, the thought of giving without expectation of repayment becomes culturally unsustainable. But beyond that, because of this commodification, and the drive to gain a profit (however measured), there is also a pressure to cut corners, to cheat, to deal unfairly with one another. As a result our relationships become distorted. Volf argues that these cultural influences undermine Christian faith and practice. They are not the only influences, but they are significant.[27]

In order to overcome this gracelessness and its corrosive impact, not only on culture generally but even more on Christian discipleship, Volf argues for the retrieval of generosity as an expression of "true self-interest."[28] This would be a self-interest formed in relationship to the understanding of human fulfillment revealed by God in Christ. By drawing attention to this self-interest he hopes to correct false or inadequate understandings of human responsibility in the light of Christian faith claims and to clarify the meaning of the Christian faith itself.

---

[26] Ibid., 14. Volf's reference is to an encounter with a hostile and threatening police officer when, overwhelmed with excitement at being about to meet his soon-to-be-adopted son, he mistakenly turned the wrong way on a one-way street.

[27] Volf makes it clear that he is identifying tendencies, not absolutely operative modes of behavior. However, he believes that the behaviors he observes are indicative of a powerful orientation or trajectory of development in modern culture. This trajectory he sees as contrary to fundamental Christian values. See *Free of Charge*, 14–15.

[28] Ibid., 20–21. The idea of "true self-interest" parallels the preference for forgiving rather than holding onto resentment that was developed in chap. 5. Not holding on to resentment allows for a different trajectory of personal becoming than holding on to it. That trajectory seeks to exclude the experience of past harms from influencing the progress of all of one's relationships, not just those directly implicated in the harm. The difference in these two formulations is that Volf ties the content of "true self-interest" directly to principles drawn from the Christian narrative, whereas the understanding of self-interest in chap. 5 lacks such a coordinating narrative.

He presents his case starting with a Christian reading of the generosity of God toward us. That generosity shows itself in the fact that God created us (and continues sustaining us in being) and has redeemed us (and continues to labor for our redemption).[29] God made us with the freedom to respond to God's generosity, a freedom sustained by grace. Through faith we can come to recognize God's hand at work, blessing us with so many gifts.[30] This recognition ought to stir within us a sense of gratitude that in turn should lead to generosity. For the gifts God bestows, although certainly for our own benefit, are given primarily for the fulfillment of God's plan to draw all into communion.[31] Thus, moved by gratitude for what we have received, we are to be generous to those we meet. By cooperating with the intention of God's plan we make ourselves available as instruments in the service of God.[32] This, as Volf explains, is part of our own communion with God. We participate in God's life at work within us.

> A toddler may participate as his mom sweeps the garage by taking his own small broom and copying her. They are working together. The son does what he sees his mother do. He participates in his mom's work by imitating it. It's different in our relationship to God. We do imitate God, but not just by observing at a distance. God is not only above us. Jesus Christ is not just a figure from the past. God is in us. Christ lives through us. We imitate God as instruments of God: God gives and forgives, and we make God's giving and God's forgiving our own.[33]

The point Volf is making here applies to both his analysis of giving and his understanding of forgiving. Indeed, in the presentation of forgiving in *Free of Charge*, Volf builds on ideas presented in the discussion of generosity. But whereas the argument with respect to generosity emphasizes God's *creative* work (while also noting the generosity of the redemption), in the discussion of forgiveness Volf focuses primarily on God's (generous) *redemptive* action in Christ.

Volf's treatment of forgiveness, beginning with God's forgiveness of us and then moving to the forgiveness we (Christians) ought to extend

---

[29] Volf, *Free of Charge*, 34–35.
[30] Ibid., 45.
[31] Ibid., 85, 100, 161–62; Volf, *Exclusion and Embrace*, 23, 100.
[32] Volf, *Free of Charge*, 48, 165.
[33] Ibid., 165.

to those who offend us, is heavily influenced by his reading of Martin Luther.[34] God's forgiveness of humankind is worked out in the dramatic tension between God's justice and God's mercy when confronted with human sin. God's justice evokes God's wrath at sin, which God justly condemns.[35] This places God in a bind.

> You can sum up where we've landed in four simple sentences. The world in sinful. That's why God doesn't affirm it indiscriminately. God loves the world. That's why God doesn't punish it in justice. What does God do with this double bind? God forgives.[36]

Drawing on Luther's theology of substitutionary atonement, Volf articulates the dynamics of God's forgiveness in terms of "'satisfaction': God doesn't forgive until the demands of justice have been satisfied."[37] Christ bears the punishment humanity has earned. He substitutes himself for us.[38] Because Christ has "paid what we owed"[39] we are freed from the obligation to pay the debt. How does this satisfy justice? How can God punish the innocent Jesus in our place and still call it justice? Volf's response follows the classical lines of the substitutionary atonement theory, particularly as articulated by Martin Luther:

> What happened when God "made him [Christ] to be sin who knew no sin, so that in him we might become the righteousness of God" (2 Corinthians 5:21)? The answer is simple: God placed human sin upon God! One God placed human sin upon another God? No, there are not two Gods. The God who is One beyond numbering and yet mysteriously Three reconciled us by shouldering our sin in the person of Christ who is one of the Three. That's the mystery of human redemption made possible by the mystery of God's Trinity: The One who was offended bears the burden of the offense.[40]

But how does this action of Christ come to touch the individual believer? As Volf explains, the offenses (sins) must "be removed from

---

[34] Volf acknowledges this fact, already made obvious by his explicit engagement with Luther's theological corpus in the formulation of the argument, in *Free of Charge*, 171.

[35] Ibid., 139–40.

[36] Ibid., 140.

[37] Ibid., 144.

[38] See ibid., 144; and Volf, *The End of Memory*, 120.

[39] Volf, *Free of Charge*, 144.

[40] Ibid., 145.

the sinners, blotted out, dispersed." Because Christ is one with us in our humanity, his death "enacts" our death as payment for sin. His death, as payment of sin, is an inclusive substitution—embracing our death as payment as well.[41]

The effects of this substitution reach to humankind via two forms of union with Christ. We are united to Christ in one way because he is united to us in his humanity. But this generic union is not sufficient. For the effects of this redemptive substitution to touch us individually we must each personally become united to Christ by faith. The grace that bestows this faith, an act of generosity on God's part, moves us to place our trust in the merits of Christ, not in our own works, and thereby frees us from the power of sin. Then Christ comes to live within us. When we live by this faith, although we remain sinners, the righteousness of Christ is imputed to us.[42] Both the personal union with Christ through faith and the imputation of Christ's righteousness to us are at work in the transformation of the sinner.

> God doesn't count our sins to us but instead counts to us Christ's righteousness. Why is this second effect needed if Christ lives in us and through us? How is it that we still sin when we are transformed by Christ's presence? A person's transformation will be complete only in the life to come. During this life, sin besets us in two ways. We fail to live trusting in God, which is our root sin, and on account of that failure, we also fall into many and varied sins. When we are united with Christ, both the great sin of unbelief and the individual sins that grow out of it "are covered." God "does not want to hold us accountable for them." Instead, God counts to us Christ's righteousness. This is the second effect of the union with Christ.[43]

In view of God's generous forgiveness of us, and to the extent that we are united with Christ and undergoing transformation into his life, Volf argues, our own lives should exhibit the same kind of forgiveness toward those who offend us as we have received from God. We have a duty to be generous in forgiving, but this generosity is more fundamentally the

---

[41] Ibid., 146–47.

[42] Ibid., 149–50.

[43] Ibid., 150. It is worth noting that in this formulation it is not so much that we are changed but that God's attitude toward us is changed. Exactly what Volf means by "transformation" will become a question in the next chapter.

expression of the love to which Christians are called—even a love of one's enemies.[44]

The characteristics of this forgiveness reflect the characteristics of God's forgiveness of us. God's forgiveness involves releasing the offender from the burden of debt arising from the offense.[45] This entails releasing the offender from guilt[46] and actively seeking the offender's good.[47] The good in view is, ultimately, full participation in the life of communion to which all are called and for which we are made. Thus, by implication, this Christian forgiveness foregoes the imposition of punishment on the offender.[48] Rather, Christian forgiveness is unconditional, at least in its offer, and it must be so.

> Why should we forgive unconditionally and indiscriminately? We don't do it simply because a law demands we do so. We forgive because God has already forgiven. For us to hold any offender captive to sin by refusing to forgive is to reject the reality of God's forgiving grace. Because Christ died for all, we are called to forgive everyone who offends us, without distinctions and without conditions.[49]

For Volf, to refuse to forgive in this way is to stand outside the ambit of God's generosity toward us. To make his point he draws on the parable of the unforgiving slave from Matthew 18:23-35. In that story a servant owing a vast amount of money to the king, his master, is in danger of being sold, along with his wife and children, to pay off the debt. In response to his pleas for mercy and time to repay the debt (impossible, given the amount owed), the king forgives the entire debt. He absorbs the loss as his own.[50] Shortly thereafter the slave encounters a fellow slave who owes him only a small fraction of what he himself owed. The first slave treats the second mercilessly and has him thrown into prison. When the king learns of this he calls the first servant back, condemns him for his lack of mercy toward his fellow servant, and throws him into prison.

---

[44] Volf, *Free of Charge*, 189.

[45] Ibid., 130.

[46] Ibid., 172.

[47] Ibid., 130.

[48] Ibid., 171.

[49] Ibid., 180.

[50] This parallels the point made by Hieronymi that the one who forgives agrees to absorb the cost of the offense. Pamela Hieronymi, "Articulating an Uncompromising Forgiveness," *Philosophy and Phenomenological Research* 62, no. 3 (May 2001): 529–55.

In his commentary on this parable Volf avoids a common reading that sees the king's reimposition of the burden of debt as a punishment for the servant's lack of generosity. Instead, he suggests,

> The point of the story may be simply that God's forgiveness and our forgiveness go hand in hand as do God's unforgiveness and our unforgiveness. Jesus may not have been suggesting that our unforgiveness causes God's unforgiveness. Rather than triggering a loss of God's forgiveness, our unforgiveness may just make manifest that in fact we haven't allowed ourselves to receive God's pardon.[51]

Those who have received God's pardon would, supposedly, be moved to extend the same, generously, toward those who have offended them. If we do not extend that forgiveness, the responsibility lies with us for rejecting the forgiveness extended to us by God.

Moreover, as Volf maintains, forgiving others as God has forgiven us is a Christian duty.[52] The point here is that, as with other gifts we receive from God, forgiveness is given to us for our benefit, but not *only* for *our* benefit. It is bestowed as part of God's active labor for the transformation of the world. Hence it is a gift given in order to be shared. It fits into a "larger and active strategy of conquering evil 'with good.'"[53] This introduces a missionary element into the discussion. The Christian narrative of God's salvation includes being called into a relation of discipleship with Jesus. Discipleship is oriented toward mission, being sent into the world to carry on the work of the master.

Human forgiveness, if it is to imitate the forgiveness God has extended to us, requires that, with respect to what offends us, we assume a stance analogous to God's posture with respect to sin. We are to condemn offenses as such, but we are to suspend the punishment they deserve.[54] We are to offer forgiveness without condition. But, according to Volf, for forgiveness to reach completion it must issue in reconciliation.[55] That

---

[51] Volf, *Free of Charge*, 156. I share Volf's sensibilities on this issue. However, I believe a stronger case can be made for this argument. The discussion of grace and sacramentality in chap. 9 will sketch the foundations for such a case.

[52] Volf, *Free of Charge*, 160.

[53] Ibid., 161.

[54] Ibid., 176.

[55] The description of "complete" forgiveness makes this apparent. "Still, in rare situations, forgiveness may reach completeness. Imagine that a close friend has wronged you, a friend who is deeply sorry and to whom friendship with you matters a great deal.

is, it must be received by the offender who recognizes her offense and repents of it.[56] Thus Volf ties the completion of the act of forgiveness to its having been recognized and embraced by the offender, together with its condemnation of the offense.

When the offer of forgiveness has been received we can enter into the final phase of forgiveness, according to Volf. We can begin to forget the offense. Drawing on references from the Scriptures, Volf argues that God "forgets" our sins.

> It's not just that God doesn't reckon them to us, forgoing both pun-ishment and imputation of guilt, or that God removes sin from us like a heavy burden, dispersing it like morning mist. Scripture explicitly states that God doesn't even remember our sins. They don't come to God's mind (Jeremiah 31:34; Hebrews 8:12; 10:17). So it's not just that we're innocent at the moment we are forgiven. In God's memory, we've been made innocent across the entire span of our lives. God looks at us and doesn't superimpose on us our former transgressions. Our transgressions don't exist anywhere anymore. They don't stick to us as guilt, and they don't stick to God's memory of us. We were sin-ners, but we are no longer sinners—in a sense, not even sinners past![57]

If Christians can remember what God does in forgiving us and live from gratitude, then, according to Volf's argument, that memory ought to engender in our hearts a generosity that can counter something of the gracelessness in our contemporary culture. In imitation of God's "forget-fulness" of offenses we can let the sins against us slip into oblivion. Indeed, he argues, this "not remembering offenses rightly crowns forgiving."[58]

---

Imagine also that you can be certain she will never wrong you that way again. You've forgiven her. As you did, you both remembered the wrongdoing, you both condemned it; you released her from punishment and guilt, and she's repented of it and thanked you for the gift" (ibid., 176). He makes a similar point when writing of "full-fledged forgiveness." His argument is that it is not achieved until the forgiveness has been re-ceived, essentially until there is reconciliation. See ibid., 182. This same line of thought is evident in *Exclusion and Embrace* (pp. 125–26), where the image of "embrace" functions as a metaphor for reconciliation. Forgiveness, in that context, is the boundary between offense and reconciliation.

[56] Volf, *Free of Charge*, 181–86.

[57] Ibid., 173–74.

[58] Ibid., 175. I will take issue with this appraisal of remembering in the final chapter. At this point it is worth noting that Volf's appraisal does not take into account how forgiving changes the meaning of the offense for the one offended.

Although Volf's account contrasts strongly with Smedes's in its explicit grounding in the Christian narrative, there are many similarities in their perspectives. Both recognize the importance of naming the truth of the harm, but neither requires that the offender repent before forgiveness can be enacted; forgiveness is unconditional. However, Volf does go beyond Smedes on this point in making the claim that the offender can only benefit from forgiveness and the release from guilt it entails if she first repents of the offense and receives the forgiveness as mercy in the context of the condemnation.[59] Both Smedes and Volf maintain that forgetting the offense can occur once the reconciliation has taken place, and both talk about transformation of the one harmed. Smedes emphasizes the transformation as a result of human effort; Volf emphasizes the transformation that God works in the sinner by grace.

It is at this point—the emphasis on God's work—that the differences between the two authors come into sharpest focus. Volf clearly approaches forgiveness "from above." The content of the Christian narrative of God's forgiveness of us provides the foundation for the motivation to forgive others. In this presentation Volf, unlike Smedes, devotes little attention to the internal workings of the human struggle to enact forgiveness. He focuses instead on the interplay of sin and grace in God's transformation of the sinner. Volf also introduces a missionary element into the discussion. Christians are sent to bring God's forgiveness in Christ into the world. This might be inchoately present in Smedes's presentation but, lacking an explicit narrative of relationship with God, it is not developed. And Volf identifies a specific culprit in the erosion of Christian forgiveness: generally, "sin" in the world, but sin as mediated by a culture stripped of grace.[60]

In summary, we can find in Volf's presentation characteristics that distinguish Christian forgiveness. It is a response to God's action. It is motivated by gratitude and expressed in generosity. It is unconditional. But the emphasis on what God has done (from above) and what we should do (and why) does not tell us much about what Christians *are doing* when forgiving, at least in the sense in which the present work is posing the question, nor does it tell us much about whether or how that enactment might be different from other enactments of forgiveness. The

[59] This additional element is consistent with Volf's long-standing concern with reconciliation.

[60] Volf discusses obstacles to forgiving in *Free of Charge*, 193, 214; and *The End of Memory*, 86.

major distinguishing factor appears to be the role of the narrative matrix in grounding the motivation to forgive.

## L. Gregory Jones, Forgiveness, and the Dynamics of Trinitarian Life

Many of the themes and concerns raised by Miroslav Volf echo those found in the work of L. Gregory Jones, but Jones's diagnosis of the problems associated with forgiveness in the Christian community and his proposed solution are set within a different framework. He elaborates his assessment of the state of Christian forgiveness in his masterful work, *Embodying Forgiveness: A Theological Analysis.*[61] Expressing his conviction that the practice of forgiving is a central dynamism distinguishing Christian individual and ecclesial existence, Jones writes:

> Forgiveness is at once an expression of a commitment to a way of life, the cruciform life of holiness in which people cast off their "old" selves and learn to live in communion with God and with one another, and a means of seeking reconciliation in the midst of particular sins, specific instances of brokenness. In its broadest context, forgiveness is the way in which God's love moves to reconciliation in the face of sin. This priority of forgiveness is a sign of the peace of God's original Creation as well as the promised eschatological consummation of that Creation in the Kingdom, and also a sign of the costliness by which such forgiveness is achieved. In this sense, then, forgiveness indicates the ongoing priority of the Church's task to offer the endlessly creative and gratuitous gift of new life in the face of sin and brokenness.[62]

This densely packed statement exhibits at the outset many similarities with Volf's perspective. Jones emphasizes God's action in effecting forgiveness. This is to lead toward reconciliation in the Kingdom of God. God's forgiveness of us also grounds a mission to share forgiveness with others. That forgiveness, given by God and further shared by the church, is to be transformative—for the individual who receives it and for the world in which it is received. But beyond Volf, Jones argues that the church must embrace practices that cultivate the "embodiment" of forgiveness in the Christian and in the church. This additional move, beyond the

---

[61] L. Gregory Jones, *Embodying Forgiveness: A Theological Analysis* (Grand Rapids: Eerdmans, 1995).

[62] Ibid., 5.

approach presented by Volf, places Jones between Smedes's discussion of forgiveness "from below" and Volf's approach "from above," but with a stronger emphasis on the "from above" as what shapes his (Jones's) discussion of the "from below" elements.

Why is the cultivation of ecclesial practices for promoting the embodiment of forgiveness necessary? Jones maintains that, despite the centrality of forgiveness to the Christian narrative, the Christian practice of forgiveness has been and is being eroded. It is in danger of being undermined by forces both internal and external to the church itself. External to the church, the rise of what Jones terms "therapeutic" forgiveness in the broader cultures of the West has begun to supplant commitment to the "costly" forgiveness on which Christianity is based. Drawing inspiration from the writings of Dietrich Bonhoeffer, Jones identifies the primary characteristic of this "therapeutic" forgiveness as allowing us to "'feel' or 'think' better" about ourselves "without having to engage in struggles to change or transform the patterns of their [our] relationships."[63] "Making myself feel good" becomes the objective, not overcoming alienation and restoring relationship. Something of the social orientation of forgiving has been lost.[64]

This danger stands in relationship to another: "the tendency for forgiveness to become eclipsed by sin and evil, and more specifically by violence."[65] The prevalence of violence in our world—one could also add, the glorification of violence in our entertainment—teaches us to respond to violence with violence. We can despair of the power of forgiveness to overcome evil and violence. These external influences find their way into the life of the Christian community. Christians can lose hope that forgiving can transform a world mired in violence. As a consequence, both a distorted understanding and practice of forgiveness and the overwhelming effects of violence in the world at large can undermine the Christian disciple's commitment to embody the forgiveness that should be a distinguishing characteristic of Christian life.

---

[63] Ibid., 6–9.

[64] Jones explicitly cites Smedes's work. I do not believe that the charge is entirely fair to Smedes. However, as a way of getting at a trajectory of thinking and feeling broadly disseminated in our culture—that is, away from responsibility in relationship toward a kind of narcissism—it does identify a real danger. The degree to which it is operative, and to which it applies to Smedes, is open to dispute.

[65] Jones, *Embodying Forgiveness*, 32.

In addition to these external influences—and perhaps as a result of them—Jones also identifies with Dietrich Bonhoeffer in critiquing the Christian desire for "cheap grace."[66] Cheap grace is characterized by the pursuit of a word of forgiveness or absolution in a privatized context without having to do the serious work of confronting my offense or its implications for the people against whom I have sinned. Quoting Bonhoeffer, Jones elaborates:

> "The preaching of forgiveness without requiring repentance, baptism without church discipline, Communion without confession, absolution without personal confession." Within such an approach to Christian life, the forgiveness of sins is proclaimed as a general truth, and "my only duty as a Christian is to leave the world for an hour or so on a Sunday morning and go to church to be assured that my sins are all forgiven."[67]

This erosion of attitudes and the decline in the valuation of forgiveness and the place it ought to occupy in Christian life are not simply a matter of the influence of the modern world in which we find ourselves. They also reflect a long history of changes in ecclesial practices of forgiveness and the interplay of those changed practices with our ways of conceptualizing forgiveness.[68]

In order to address this deterioration in the understanding and practice of forgiveness, Jones sets out to name Christian forgiveness in its distinctiveness. This will involve clarifying what Christian forgiveness entails, why Christians should forgive, and the integral relationship of Christian forgiveness to Christian discipleship. The aspect of Christian faith Jones finds most essential for drawing these elements together is the distinctively Christian understanding of God as Trinity.[69] According to Jones, by understanding ourselves and the call to forgive from within

---

[66] Ibid., 8.

[67] Ibid., 13, quoting Dietrich Bonhoeffer, *The Cost of Discipleship*, trans. R. H. Fuller (New York: Macmillan, 1963), 47, 45, 54.

[68] Bonhoeffer, *The Cost of Discipleship*, 37–38.

[69] Jones is expressing a common concern in Christian theological circles that the doctrine of the Trinity has lost its place in the heart of Christian life. He reflects an emerging theological consensus that this doctrine, if properly understood and integrated into Christian self-understanding, would have a transformative impact on Christian life and practice. This concern runs throughout two masterful works on the doctrine of the Trinity: Walter Kasper, *The God of Jesus Christ* (New York: Crossroad, 1986), and

the revelation of God as triune we can arrive at a deeper (correct) grasp of Christian forgiveness and its essential place in Christian life. This revived perspective will then help us to recognize the importance of developing those practices that help the Christian community to embody forgiveness in a distinctively Christian manner, reflective of the dynamics of God's own life as revealed in Christ.

Jones develops his trinitarian exposition of Christian forgiveness in three chapters. He first examines the dynamics of trinitarian life as revealed in the Scriptures (chap. 4).[70] This involves attending to the activities of each of the persons of the Trinity in their interrelationships as revealed in the Scriptures. He then brings those to bear on the question of forgiveness: God's forgiveness of human sin and the forgiveness Christians are called to exercise toward one another (chap. 5).[71] He devotes particular attention to the importance of the "judgment of grace" and the need for repentance. On this his position is very close to Volf's. He then rounds out this exposition of distinctively Christian forgiveness by examining the way in which the Christian community historically expresses itself as the embodiment of the forgiveness it proclaims (chap. 6).[72] In this context Jones explores the central practices of the Christian community and their relationship to forgiveness: Baptism, Eucharist, Reconciling Forgiveness, Prayer, and Healing.[73]

The trinitarian framework of Jones's presentation allows him to situate a distinctively Christian forgiveness within the full range of the Christian story of salvation. God, who is a Trinity of self-giving love in communion, desired to share communion with created beings. We have therefore been constituted in such a way that communion with God is a real possibility (though always a matter of God's freely bestowed grace). But the capacity for meaningful communion carries with it the capacity for rejecting that communion: the capacity for sin.[74] Sin entered human history through the misuse of our capacity to choose. Over time, the history of sinful choices has embedded itself in patterns of social relations (social structures) and histories of exercises of freedom such that they

---

Catherine Mowry LaCugna, *God for Us: The Trinity and Christian Life* (San Francisco: HarperSanFrancisco, 1991).

[70] Jones, *Embodying Forgiveness*, 101–34.

[71] Ibid., 135–62.

[72] Ibid., 163–205.

[73] These are the subdivisions of chap. 6, "Practicing Forgiveness."

[74] Jones, *Embodying Forgiveness*, 113–15.

contribute to the promotion of further sinful choices.[75] The world is thus marred in its capacity for sharing divine life by the milieu of prior sin in which we live, the pressures toward further sin arising from that milieu, and the individual sinful choices we make that contribute to perpetuating that sinfulness. Our capacity for communion with God is suppressed by the power of the sin that lives within us. We therefore stand in need of forgiveness. As Jones explains:

> Christians claim that this fundamental condition of Sin manifests itself in particular and specific sins, sins that are often difficult to learn to identify and name in one's own life and in the lives of others. Forgiveness is necessary for such sins, as Israel well knew. And repentance is necessary for such sins to be forgiven. This is so whether the offense is against God or is the inevitable damage that we human beings inflict on one another, on ourselves, and on the whole Creation.[76]

This sinful condition is a predicament that afflicts all people individually and society as a whole. As Jones elaborates: "The crisis of the human condition is not simply my individual guilt, but rather the evil, suffering, and brokenness—the 'universal situation of disaster'—that undermines not only my communion with God but *our* communion with God and with one another."[77]

In light of this predicament—that God has made us for communion with God and with one another and that we are mired in the alienating consequences of sin—God took action on our behalf. God initiated a "new breakthrough" to restore us individually and collectively to the possibility of the communion for which we were (are) created.[78]

This new breakthrough is the inauguration of the Kingdom of God with the advent of Jesus Christ. Through the incarnation, Jones argues, God initiates a "shift in understanding the purpose and scope of God's forgiveness."[79] God, in Jesus of Nazareth, enters into the wholeness of the human condition to transform it. In the process Christ discloses that repentance is no longer the price that must be paid prior to forgiveness; it becomes the mode of response by which we receive the forgiveness

[75] Ibid., 117.
[76] Ibid.
[77] Ibid.
[78] Ibid., 117–18.
[79] Ibid., 119.

offered.[80] But Jones also emphasizes that there is an element of continuity in the newness. "What is at stake in the doctrine of the incarnation is the affirmation that the self-giving love of God manifested in Jesus is neither different from God's creative and forgiving love nor unrelated to the communion of God's own life."[81] Jones thus points to an integral relationship among the Christian doctrines of incarnation, creation, redemption, forgiveness, and communion. God is proactive in seeking out the "lost."[82] By his self-emptying (*kenosis*) to take on the human condition in Jesus, the Second Person of the Trinity demonstrated something of God's own way of loving. God goes forth into created reality in order to call back to communion those who are alienated by sin.

The ministry of Jesus proclaims the Kingdom of God, in which reconciliation with God in communion of love is a real possibility. He therefore expresses God's forgiveness to those he encounters. But, as Jones argues, Jesus also brings judgment. He brings God's forgiveness to the sinner but he pronounces judgment on those who refuse to forgive.[83] On this point Jesus stands in opposition to the sensibilities of his day (and ours!). Whereas his contemporaries demanded clear signs of repentance before considering forgiveness, Jesus offers forgiveness before repentance. But this does not make repentance irrelevant. Rather, repentance becomes the personal transformation necessary if we are to receive the benefits of forgiveness, the reentry into communion in relationship that forgiveness makes possible. Forgiveness is the necessary but not sufficient condition for the reconciliation that leads to communion. "For Jesus, forgiveness cannot be earned, whether through repentance or by any other means. But our repentance is the only adequate response to God's forgiveness."[84]

Unfortunately, the people of his day do not universally embrace the offer of God's Kingdom that Jesus inaugurates and embodies in his own person. Much the reverse: "Rather than bringing us to repentance, Jesus'

---

[80] "This shifts the emphasis from Judaism's assumption that repentance precedes human forgiveness to an assumption that repentance will become an indispensable component of the habit of forgiveness." Ibid., 121.

[81] Ibid., 119.

[82] The parables of the lost sheep, the Prodigal Son, and the lost coin, as well as Jesus' own practice of spending time with those considered outside the Law, reflect this proactive, missionary posture.

[83] Jones, *Embodying Forgiveness*, 120.

[84] Ibid., 121. The line of argument developed here parallels Volf's. Repentance is necessary if one is to benefit from the effects of the forgiveness being offered.

ministry only heightens our desire to be the judges. So we judge him." In Jesus, "God then submits to our judgment, to our freedom to reject God. In this sense, Jesus is sent to the cross as the One judged *by* humanity, the One rejected by humanity, the One killed by humanity."[85] Drawing on insights from Karl Barth, Jones argues that God allows humankind to pass judgment on Jesus in order to reveal both the corruption of our own judgment and the righteousness of God's, a judgment of grace that continues to bestow forgiveness and call to repentance. By accepting his fate on the cross Jesus took upon himself our sins, expressed in the form of our judgment (rejection) of him and of the kingdom he brought. God's judgment shows itself as grace both by revealing at the cross our sinfulness and need for repentance and by revealing in the resurrection, by which God vindicates Jesus, that our hope for forgiveness and reconciliation has not ended with our folly.[86] "The crucified and risen Christ thus fulfills the work of his ministry and definitively reveals the gracious character of the God who forgives to reestablish communion."[87]

We can come to participate in that communion, but the price for doing so is our transformation. We must accept the grace of God's judgment by recognizing our participation in sin and repenting of it. We then enter into a lifelong process of transformation so as to—increasingly—"appropriate and embody Christ's forgiveness."[88]

There are two driving forces in this transformation. The first is the Holy Spirit. We must experience ourselves as called to repentance and transformation by the power of the Holy Spirit. It is the Spirit who unites us with Christ, enabling us to share in his life. By this Holy Spirit we are then empowered to enter into the ongoing work of Christ. At this point the second force comes into play, namely, human freedom. But this is always preceded and sustained by the Holy Spirit's liberating and transforming action. Thus "the Spirit enables those who have been forgiven by Christ also to become those who forgive, seeking to restore communion with others in analogous fashion to the ways it has been restored to them."[89]

Jones draws on two resurrection accounts from the Gospel of John to illustrate the twofold role of the Holy Spirit. The Spirit is both the communicator of a grace offered to all and the one who mediates that

---

[85] Jones, *Embodying Forgiveness*, 123.
[86] Ibid., 123–25.
[87] Ibid., 125.
[88] Ibid., 281.
[89] Ibid., 129.

common grace to our personal, distinctive experience. The first illustration from John's Gospel is in the encounter of the Risen Lord with Mary Magdalene at the tomb (John 20:11-18); the second is in his exchange with Peter at the Sea of Tiberias (John 21:1-17). The contrast between these two encounters illustrates the common transformative dynamism even in the midst of significantly different personal histories. Jones explains that Mary, as one who knew herself to have been forgiven by Jesus before the crucifixion, feels lost with the disappearance of his body from the tomb. In her encounter with the Risen Lord, as she comes to recognize him, she receives a new identity in a new relationship. This bestows on her a "new life that, presumably, would entail a willingness to proclaim and embody Christ's forgiveness in relations with others."[90]

Peter, by contrast, had sinned against the Lord in his threefold denial of him. He did not have the opportunity to experience Christ's forgiveness of that offense before the crucifixion, but at the Sea of Tiberias, in his encounter with the Risen Lord, Peter is confronted with the truth of his sin (judgment of grace) by means of the threefold question about his love for Jesus. "Yet even as he recalls Peter's sin, he [Jesus] communicates his forgiveness and reconciliation by giving Peter a renewed mission."[91] The transformative encounter with the Risen Lord sets Peter free for a future in service to the church and the Gospel.

The similarity in diversity of these two encounters illustrates the work of the Holy Spirit in the community of Christ's disciples.

> The Spirit not only makes particular the universal significance of Christ's forgiveness; the Spirit also takes the particular identity of Christ and makes it universal through the practices and friendships of the Body of Christ, the Church. Jesus authorizes and obligates his disciples to forgive and be forgiven in God's name; more precisely, the disciples are called and enabled to do so by the power of the Holy Spirit, the Spirit of Truth.[92]

Thus it is the Spirit's work in the life of the individual that awakens the recognition that the judgment on *my* sin is a judgment of *grace* and that the grace offered to all is really and particularly offered to *me* in my distinctiveness: to me *personally*.[93]

---

[90] Ibid., 130.
[91] Ibid., 131.
[92] Ibid.
[93] See ibid., 157.

By the second force in this transformation—personal effort under the impulse and guidance of the Holy Spirit—we internalize God's way of forgiving as revealed in Christ. Jones argues that the sacramental practices of the church, prayer, the confession of one's sinfulness, and so on are means by which the Body of Christ can help foster the awareness and embodiment of forgiveness in the lives of the members so that they, too, in the power of the Spirit, can "embody them forth" to bring Christ's transforming forgiveness to the larger world. By this means the communion of the Kingdom of God can itself become more widely embodied in the world as the work of the Holy Spirit draws us toward the eschatological fulfillment of that Kingdom.[94] Through its emphasis on the encouragement of practices that can promote the embodiment of forgiveness, Jones's presentation draws together a theological articulation of forgiveness "from above" with a practical approach to forgiveness "from below."

The dynamics of Christian forgiveness, as Jones presents them, include, first, the judgment of grace. This judgment confronts us with the reality of our own responsible, sinful acts and participation in the patterns of sin in the world, but it confronts us also with the simultaneous offer of forgiveness. Repentance is the acceptance of that judgment (the condemnation of our sin) and turning away from it so as to reestablish relationship with God in Christ. That is, repentance makes it possible for us to receive and accept forgiveness and thereby to reconcile with God and neighbor. Further, Jones shares Volf's perspective that as those who have been forgiven and have accepted forgiveness in recognition of our own sinfulness we ought to be stirred by gratitude for this gift. This gratitude, in turn, should move us to generosity toward those who sin against us.[95]

But the forgiveness we offer is to reflect the dynamics of God's forgiving. It is to be offered in the face of a clear recognition of the truth of what is being forgiven. As Jones puts it:

> So Christians ought to insist more than anyone else on the importance of accountability and culpability—but they should do so within a context in which the judgment *of grace* is the determinatively prior aim and where eschatological holiness is the ultimate goal. It ought to make us acutely aware of and sensitive to the haunting effects of being sinned against, and not only of Sin *per se*.

[94] Ibid., 133.
[95] Ibid., 160–62.

It ought also to inspire a passionate concern for the cultivation of
communities where human destructiveness can be transformed into
new life, where despair can be transformed into hope.[96]

This summary statement draws together the elements of responsibility,
judgment of grace, and transformation toward eschatological holiness
in a way that highlights a further aspect of Jones's analysis. Christian
forgiveness is not *just* for the sake of the individual. In his description
of "therapeutic" forgiveness Jones criticized the tendency to privatize
and cheapen the reality of forgiveness. With this summary statement he
makes clear that forgiveness in the Christian context has a social scope,
indeed, a social-transformational mission. The trinitarian relations of
self-giving love and the form of the revelation of the Triune God in the
life, death, and resurrection of Jesus are the inspiration and the icon of
the forgiveness to which Christians are called and for which they are sent
into the world in the power of the Holy Spirit.

### Contrasting Landscapes

The three Christian authors whose views of forgiveness we have just
surveyed do not by any means cover all the diverse approaches Christians
have taken to articulating forgiveness. There are as many variations on
the theme of forgiveness among Christian authors as one can find among
philosophers writing on the subject. However, this initial foray into the
approaches of three specific Christian theologians does give us a starting
point for probing the question of a distinctive Christian forgiveness more
deeply. It has drawn our attention to some of the issues that surface most
frequently in Christian reflections on forgiveness. It has given us a basis
on which to identify some of the similarities and differences between the
various approaches to forgiveness we have seen thus far, and it has presented the distinctive perspectives as representatives of three positions on
a spectrum of approaches ("from above"/ "from below"), a spectrum that
can be used as a starting point in approaching other Christian authors.

These first steps on the terrain of Christian forgiveness have made clear
that there are differences between approaches that espouse (or merely
presuppose) a distinctive Christian forgiveness and those presented in the
philosophical and psychological discussions. Articulations of a distinctive
Christian forgiveness also differ from the phenomenological description

---

[96] Ibid., 156.

of forgiveness as a basic human enactment presented in chapter 6 and from the presentation offered by Lewis Smedes. It will be helpful to identify some of these similarities and differences before subjecting the proposals for a distinctive Christian forgiveness to a more critical analysis.

### Similar Contours

Among the similarities, three stand out. First, as in most of the philosophical discussions, these Christian writers understand forgiveness as an issue exclusively in relationship to a moral breach, "sin." Their reasons for doing so differ from those of the Anglo-American moral philosophers. In the Christian context the question of sin is evaluated in relation to the eschatological hope for divine/human communion with God in love. Positive proscriptions ("Thou shalt not . . .") and prescriptions ("Love your enemies") draw their force from the revelation of God's desire for communion with humankind in love as the graced fulfillment of human destiny. Personal relationship with God and ultimate hope for salvation, understood in terms of the Christian narrative, underwrite the moral judgments associated with the proscriptions and prescriptions. Conversely, those prescriptions and proscriptions are directed toward fostering that saving relationship with God. By contrast, moral philosophical approaches make their appeal to moral principles accessible to human reason without appeal to the divine. Nevertheless, the emphasis in both the Christian and the moral philosophical accounts is on a harm that stands under some sort of moral condemnation.

Second, like the moral philosophers the Christian writers maintain that there is an integral connection between forgiveness and reconciliation. At times they write as though there is a difference between the two.[97] On those occasions the distinction appears to reflect the approach of the phenomenological description (chap. 6), emphasizing the differences in the enactments of forgiveness and reconciliation. In other places, however, the distinction almost disappears. This occurs when the Christian writers

---

[97] See, for example, Jones, *Embodying Forgiveness*, 154–55. Volf also writes at times as though there is a clear distinction between forgiving and reconciling. One cannot reconcile with another unless the other repents, but one can forgive even if the offender does not repent. See Volf, *Free of Charge*, 183. On the other hand, Volf at times appears to conflate forgiving and reconciling as when he argues in terms of a less than "full-fledged forgiveness." Complete forgiveness, in this formulation, requires reconciliation. See Volf, *Free of Charge*, 182.

view both forgiveness and reconciliation from the perspective of a final end toward which both forgiveness and reconciliation are oriented: God's desire to draw all into communion. Understood in terms of a divinely mandated *telos* (end goal, ultimate purpose), the term "forgiveness" is sometimes taken to refer to the entire process of the movement from estrangement to (eschatological) communion.[98]

This ambiguity comes to expression in a third point of similarity with the moral philosophers and some psychologists: the language of *degrees of forgiveness*. In the absence of a reconciliation between the estranged parties forgiveness is understood to be incomplete or imperfect. In Volf and Jones this incompleteness is correlated to the non-acceptance of forgiveness by the offender that, in turn, hinges on the refusal of the offender to repent.[99]

### Distinguishing Features

Despite these similarities, there are differences between the explicitly Christian accounts and those found in the mainstream of philosophy and psychology. These differences are important in grounding the claims to a distinctive Christian forgiveness. They are thus especially evident in the case of those authors who emphasize the distinctiveness. The most important differences for the purposes of the present inquiry can be grouped under three interrelated headings: the Christian narrative, the motivational impulse, and the idea of "transformation."

### THE CHRISTIAN NARRATIVE

The most obvious point of difference between the approaches to a distinctively Christian forgiveness, as represented in Volf and Jones, and the philosophical and psychological accounts (as well as the descriptive account in chap. 6) is the prominent place of the Christian narrative in shaping the presentations of Christian forgiveness. Unlike the secular accounts of forgiveness, the Christian account draws its significance from a shared matrix of meanings that carries with it a clearly articulated cosmology (overarching vision of reality) and *telos* (ultimate purpose). While

---

[98] This would be an example of "synecdoche," naming one part of a larger reality as a stand-in for the whole.

[99] See, for example, the extended discussion in chaps. 6 and 8 in Jones, *Embodying Forgiveness*, esp. 168, 180, 192, 194 n. 41. See also Volf, *Free of Charge*, 176.

the *telos* identifies a trajectory of preferred development in relationships, the overarching vision of reality—the Christian narrative—provides the basis for rules according to which that development is to operate.

One of the striking elements of this narrative is that it takes the individual up into a matrix of meanings that goes beyond the individual experience of those offenses in which forgiveness arises as an issue. Responding to individual experiences of sin with forgiveness still retains the significance of a specific enactment, but this individual enactment is grasped in its relationship to a larger, integrative horizon of meaning. It is not just that I forgive, but that my forgiving is somehow part of God's larger project/hope for the world. For the Christian this relationship of individual enactment of forgiveness to the larger context of meaning can lend the individual enactment greater significance in the sense of self of the individual Christian than would ordinarily be the case in the enactment of forgiveness in a secular context.

The common sensibility in both Volf and Jones is that no act of forgiveness is purely one's own, nor is it merely between the victim and the offender. As Volf puts it:

> If forgiveness involved only two parties, the one who forgives (the wronged person) and the one who receives forgiveness (the wrong-doer), it would not be easy to defend it against the objections contained in such probing questions. But it doesn't. For Christians, forgiving, like giving in general, always takes place in a triangle, involving the wrongdoer, the wronged person, and God. Take God away, and the foundations of forgiveness become unsteady and may even crumble.[100]

The meaning of forgiving within a Christian context, therefore, is always co-determined by the understanding of God and of one's relationship to God. Perhaps better said, the Christian matrix of meanings proffers relationship with God and God's ongoing action in the world as the foundational meaning that, in Christian enactments of forgiveness, as such, co-determines the meaning of the enactment for the one forgiving.

---

[100] Volf, *Free of Charge*, 131. I would extend the argument to say that it includes the broader range of personal relationships of both the offender and the offended, since the decision whether to forgive or not will shape the personal becoming of both and is reached only through the matrix of meanings in which those others are already implicated as co-constituting the sense of self of those directly involved in the harm.

By forgiving because of my Christian sense of self I reaffirm and intensify the trajectory of my personal becoming *as Christian*.

## THE MOTIVATION TO FORGIVE

This relationship to God and God's involvement in the act of forgiving also points us toward the second significant difference between these accounts of Christian forgiveness and the secular approaches we have considered. The difference has to do with motivation to forgive. In the three Christian authors we have examined, and in the shared Christian matrix of meanings as a whole, the issue of the motivation to forgive is paramount. The explicit motivations identified by Smedes do not appeal to the Christian narrative. They are directed toward the legitimate self-interest of the individual (personal healing) and then extended to a broader range of interrelational motivations.[101] But those motivations presented by Volf and Jones are profoundly and explicitly rooted in the soil of the defining Christian story. Fundamentally, the motivation to forgive should be gratitude arising from the belief that we have first received forgiveness from God in Christ and that this has been extended to us by the power of the Holy Spirit.

The analyses presented in the latter two accounts appeal both to the fact of our having been forgiven and to the sacrifice offered by Christ in dying on the cross. The believer, knowing herself to be a sinner yet forgiven, should be moved by reflecting on God's beneficence to gratitude for God's mercy.[102] That gratitude should, in turn, issue in generosity toward those who sin against her; it is a gratitude that finds its expression in generously extending toward those who offend her the same kind of forgiveness God has already bestowed on her. This is, fundamentally, an act of love.[103]

## PERSONAL TRANSFORMATION

A third distinguishing feature of Christian forgiveness that both Volf and Jones emphasize is transformation. By grace the sinner comes to

---

[101] This is the reason why Jones criticizes Smedes for offering a merely "therapeutic" forgiveness. See Jones, *Embodying Forgiveness*, 50, 53, 57.

[102] See Jones, *Embodying Forgiveness*, 184. The point is dispersed throughout Volf's argument in *Free of Charge*, but for some of the highlights see pp. 45, 203, 209, 217 in that book, and esp. 149–50.

[103] See, for example, Jones, *Embodying Forgiveness*, 293; Volf, *Free of Charge*, 20–21, 189.

recognize the judgment of God, to experience it *as* grace, and to repent of the offense (sin). God's action in the life of the repentant sinner initiates and sustains a multifaceted transformation. The relationship of the sinner with God is transformed. The sinner changes in her relationship to her sin, repenting of it and, implicitly or explicitly, repudiating it. Grateful for God's grace of forgiveness, the sinner experiences gratitude and is disposed to act with generosity toward the sin of others, forgiving what would otherwise have been retained as an occasion for retribution.

The first part of this transformation occurs each time the sinner recognizes herself as sinner before God. Jones is very explicit that this transformation marked by repentance must be an ongoing part of the life of the Christian; we must be constantly renewed in repentance.[104] The practices of the ecclesial community are to promote this ongoing transformation through repentance. Volf is less explicit on this point. The latter part of the transformation is a matter of continuous, ongoing change in orientation toward those who sin against us. We are to grow into Christ's way of being toward the sinner.[105]

The idea of ongoing transformation suggests a point of possible contact with the phenomenological account in chapter 6 of forgiving as a human enactment: personal becoming. This is a valid comparison. However, the transformation Volf and Jones are talking about specifies a content and direction to the personal becoming, one given by the Christian narrative itself. It has many different names within that narrative: holiness, the life of Christ within us, *theosis*, deification. All of these names point to a greater participation in the divine life. They indicate that one is already living, in increasing degree, the life of the Kingdom of God as one is transformed into the way of holiness that extends forgiveness to others.

### Initial Features of a Distinctive Christian Forgiveness

This initial survey of three Christian authors on forgiveness leaves us with some preliminary indications of what might distinguish Christian forgiveness as a practice or enactment from other expressions of forgiveness. Three aspects stand out: the Christian narrative, the motivation for forgiving, and the transformation that Christian forgiveness is supposed to engender in the Christian. All three draw our attention to the question of meaning: the meaning of the narrative, the meaning of the motivation,

---

[104] See, for example, Jones, *Embodying Forgiveness*, 168, 171, 179.
[105] See Jones, *Embodying Forgiveness*, 160; Volf, *Free of Charge*, 63, 165.

and the meaning of the transformation. These three elements mutually inform each other, forming a shared matrix of meanings out of which the Christian interprets the world.

Within this matrix Christian forgiveness is understood to be an expression of the same benevolent, merciful generosity to others that the sinner has experienced from God. The forgiveness Christians extend to others is a duty commanded by God, but it is also part of a mission that belongs to Christian discipleship. That mission is unconditional, as is the forgiveness that embodies it.

However, there is a further point to be made about the relationship between Christian forgiveness and the narrative that grounds it. The narrative is not closed. As the narrative takes increasing hold in my personal matrix of meanings I become increasingly implicated in the narrative itself. My story becomes part of the living present of the Christian narrative. Reciprocally, the Christian narrative is expanded and developed as it increasingly becomes my story. Thus, ultimately, Christian forgiveness cannot be understood exclusively in terms of isolated (punctual) enactments. The meaning of individual enactments comes from the whole of the story—my story and its relationship to the Christian story—that is still unfolding. Nor can it be driven by extrinsic motivations. The extent to which one enacts distinctively Christian forgiveness is the index of the degree to which the Christian narrative has become one's own, and conversely of the degree to which one's own narrative has become Christian.

Thus the meaning of the Christian narrative is not simply its story about the past. It is a story about the present, too, and about the future. It is a story in which those who proclaim it and those who receive it are implicated. They are implicated in terms of the meaning of their own personal becoming, both with respect to the motivations that drive that becoming and in terms of the transformation that opens them up (or not) to the motivations embedded in the values of the narrative itself. Narrative, motivation, and transformation are to mutually condition each other in the personal becoming of the Christian and are to come to expression in the embodiment of Christian forgiveness.

## Conclusion

The three approaches to forgiveness presented by Lewis Smedes, Miroslav Volf, and L. Gregory Jones have sketched out a range of possible Christian approaches: from Smedes's Christian-motivated but humanistically formulated account of forgiveness "from below" to Volf's "from above" articulation, emphasizing God's work throughout, to Jones's effort to engage the middle ground, drawing together a trinitarian narrative of redemption with practical pedagogical interests. Volf and Jones have drawn our attention to the crucial connection between the narrative of God's forgiveness of us in Christ and the motivation that should impel Christians to forgive others. Both presentations, even in their differences, stand within the larger shared matrix of meanings called "Christianity."

These explicitly Christian presentations of forgiveness reflect the depths of the distinctive heritages from which they spring. They deserve the respect they have garnered from their readers. Nevertheless, they are not the last word. What I read in them does not address the questions I am posing about Christian forgiveness, or at least they do not do so in a way that fully satisfies me, given my Christian theological matrix of meanings. There are aspects of these presentations of Christian forgiveness I find problematic and that, therefore, lead me to believe that Christian forgiveness as it is traditionally articulated needs to be rethought. My reservations touch on each of the three distinguishing features of Christian forgiveness mentioned above. Each is more problematic in ways not apparent in Volf's and Jones's presentations. Making that argument is the task of the next two chapters.

# Chapter 8

# Testing the Ground
# of Christian Forgiveness

## Preliminaries

The questions that have guided this project up to this point have been: Is there such a thing as Christian forgiveness? Is it distinct from forgiveness understood as a basic human enactment (independently of faith claims)? If there is a distinctive Christian forgiveness, might we need to rethink our understanding of it? The authors considered in the previous chapter have, each in his own way, provided valuable resources for approaching these questions in their Christian specificity. The work of Lewis Smedes, although not clearly affirming a distinctive Christian forgiveness, has served two purposes. It has drawn attention to the importance of the human side of forgiveness for a Christian thinker and, by the reaction it has evoked from some Christian writers, it has cast into relief key dimensions of some explicitly Christian articulations of forgiveness. In particular, Smedes has drawn attention to a tendency to undervalue the theological significance of human internal processes as they relate to forgiveness.

Both Volf and Jones, by contrast, have underscored their specifically Christian interest in forgiveness. Each appears to hold that Christian forgiveness is distinctive. Each in his own way has emphasized the role of the Christian narrative in that distinctiveness. Indeed, as both authors implicitly argue, the relationship between narrative and practice is crucial. To use our own terms, the Christian narrative provides the matrix of meanings that makes the practice of forgiveness intelligible as an expression of Christian life. It provides guidelines for the enactment of forgiveness and for Christian assessment of enactments of forgiveness as a mode of action in the larger world. The narrative is, therefore, integral to Christian motivations for forgiving.[1]

As a formal proposition I agree with the implicit conviction shared by Volf and Jones (and others) that Christian forgiveness must be understood in relation to the narrative that gives it its meaning. I also agree that this narrative provides the basis for identifying what might be distinctive about Christian forgiveness. But not all Christians tell the story in the same way. Indeed, even Volf and Jones present different emphases, at least in part because of the distinctive concerns that move them to write. It is therefore important, and the task of this chapter, to pose the critical question: How adequate are their presentations of Christian forgiveness?

Here the question of adequacy is, in the first place, about the ability of Volf's and Jones's presentations to satisfy the questions guiding this inquiry. But we can be even more specific. As presentations of Christian forgiveness: (1) are they adequate to the contemporary context of meanings in which Volf and Jones want to promote the practice of Christian forgiveness? (2) do they provide a basis for distinguishing Christian forgiveness from other approaches to forgiveness? and (3) are they theologically coherent? We shall explore the first two of these questions of adequacy in the present chapter; the third will occupy our attention in chapter 9.

These questions are interrelated. For example, theological coherence is not just a matter of logical consistency, it is also a matter of correlation with a larger horizon of meanings within which the theology is being articulated. The context of meanings in which we seek to promote forgiveness is therefore implicated in the assessment of coherence. Similarly, the distinctiveness of Christian forgiveness must be articulated on the basis of a theology that possesses such coherence if it is to make a compelling appeal to enactment among those who inhabit the contemporary context of meanings.

The present chapter will take up the question of adequacy in relation to the contemporary cultural context of meanings. Volf and Jones attempt

---

[1] For the purposes of the questions underlying this present work the Christian narrative is also crucial for identifying the distinctiveness of Christian forgiveness. It does not just exhort to performing forgiveness by doing the same things anyone else would. Instead, it exhorts to forgiving even in circumstances and under conditions that others find problematic. The Christian narrative provides a matrix of meanings that not only impels toward distinctive modes of enactment but also supports, within that matrix, the conviction that this distinctiveness is a superior mode of forgiving. We shall return to these points later.

to address themselves to this culture as they seek to promote the practice of Christian forgiveness. We will be exploring whether their presentations adequately address the obstacles to forgiving represented by this contemporary cultural context. If they do not, we will have preliminary grounds for taking up the task of rethinking Christian forgiveness.

## The Traditional Narrative

Mirsolav Volf and L. Gregory Jones present two distinct articulations of an approach to Christian forgiveness that, in its basic outline, is widely accepted in the mainstream of Western Christianity, in both its Protestant and Catholic expressions. It is based on the theory of substitutionary atonement classically articulated by Anselm. In Western Christianity this account of the saving work of Christ has achieved quasi-canonical status. For the sake of convenience we can call this the "traditional account." Broadly considered, most Western Christians are likely to recognize this narrative and affirm the gist of it as naming the meaning of Christian forgiveness. This is the narrative whose adequacy to our questions we need to evaluate.

Taken at face value, the differences of approach we have just explored in chapter 7 already suggest that some rethinking, or at least clarification, is in order. If we consider the approach taken by Lewis Smedes, Christian forgiveness would seem to be no different from that offered by anyone else. What distinguishes it as Christian forgiveness would be the fact that this common enactment happens to be undertaken by a Christian. But does that mean that every enactment of forgiveness undertaken by a Christian is, *de facto*, Christian forgiveness? If so, then the expression "Christian forgiveness" would be empty except as a means of identifying the one forgiving as Christian. Volf and Jones would, I believe, reject this way of understanding Christian forgiveness, but the question remains. Does the distinctive Christian matrix of meanings—the traditional narrative of Christian forgiveness as represented by Volf and Jones—provide sufficiently stable ground for us to lay claim to a distinctive Christian forgiveness?[2]

---

[2] The language of "stable ground" bears some explanation. In what follows I will argue that the traditional narrative has become unstable—structurally unsound—as a way of promoting the practice of forgiveness in the present, postmodern context. Part of this instability is a function of shifts in the shared matrix of meanings in contemporary culture. Part of it is inherent in the traditional narrative itself. Beyond this, the traditional narrative does not adequately support the claims to a distinctive Christian forgiveness.

When we direct our attention to Christian forgiveness as a human *enactment* we are drawn to probe more deeply. The traditional account lays emphasis on the way the Christian narrative is supposed to shape motivation. Does lodging the distinctiveness of Christian forgiveness in the motivations derived from the Christian narrative really distinguish Christian forgiveness from forgiveness as a basic human enactment? The implicit claim is that it does. But this point is assumed, not demonstrated. If this assumption is justified, however, then we are faced with the further question of the relationship between this distinctive motivation and how forgiveness is enacted in a distinctively Christian forgiveness. This draws us to engage with the issues raised in parts 1 and 2 about forgiveness as a phenomenon enacted by human beings: persons in the process of becoming.

If we contrast the Christian accounts of forgiveness with the secular presentations examined in parts 1 and 2 the responses to these questions are inconclusive. Certainly the conditions for enacting forgiveness as presented by the Christian authors differ from the mainstream of the Anglo-American moral philosophical accounts in that Christian authors do not (usually) require the repentance of the offender in order to undertake forgiveness. However, to that extent the terrain these Christian writers wish to encompass in their understanding of forgiveness overlaps with that embraced by both the mainstream of psychological approaches and the descriptive account of forgiveness presented in chapter 6.

Nevertheless, the Christian accounts differ from all these others insofar as the authorization to forgive does not rely on arguments based exclusively on philosophical reason (moral philosophical approach), nor does it rely on promotion of personal healing (although, as I will later argue *contra* the protests against "therapeutic forgiveness"—explicit in Jones and implied in Volf—personal healing might be a legitimate motivation for a Christian to undertake forgiveness). Rather, traditional accounts appeal to the authority of a revelation received by the Christian community as its normative, self-identifying story. Moreover, as exemplified in Volf and Jones, these accounts rely on the individual member of the community recognizing this story as her own truth in such a way that it actually does motivate her to undertake forgiving.[3] The revelation can, therefore,

---

Thus the traditional narrative is not a stable basis on which to build either the claims to distinctiveness or the promotion of forgiveness.

[3] This is the moment of grace identified by Volf by which the person comes to faith, but I am describing it "from below"—from the perspective of human experience—as a moment of recognition.

ground a distinctive motivation to forgive, but this does not lead to the conclusion that the Christian story, at least as it has been told in the common accounts, can ground claims to a distinctive Christian enactment.

Indeed, when we examine the characteristics of the enactment of forgiveness as contained in the Christian accounts the close resemblance between these accounts and what we have already encountered in other discussions renders questionable the claims to a distinctive practice. Forgiveness becomes an issue in the face of an experience of having been harmed (sin).[4] That experience has damaged or destroyed a pre-existing relationship. Most commonly it is understood as including a breach of the moral order. The one harmed recognizes the harm and is provoked to a retributive disposition toward the one who caused the harm. By undertaking forgiveness the one harmed commits herself not to use the harm as a pretext for retribution. She opens up the possibility of reconciliation by appropriating the meaning of the harm, as forgiven, into her sense of self.

### Christian Narrative, Motivation, and Distinctiveness

At this point, claims that there is a distinctive Christian forgiveness appear to rest on shaky ground. As is clear from the presentation in chapter 7, Smedes does not make a case for a *distinctive* Christian forgiveness. Jones argues that Smedes's position, in fact, distorts Christian forgiveness.[5] The reasons for Jones's judgment are twofold. First, Smedes emphasizes the importance of self-healing as a dimension of and a motivation for undertaking to forgive. This is counter to the un-self-interested generosity that, according to Jones and Volf, should be the motivating force for Christian forgiveness.[6] They underscore this obligation to forgive with the language of "duty." Jones apparently sees the appeal to self-

---

[4] The relationship of what philosophers discuss as "harm" to what Christian writers and theologians identify as "sin" is complex. I shall not attempt to parse it here. For the purposes of this investigation both harm and sin are appropriately understood as occasions for forgiveness.

[5] Jones, *Embodying Forgiveness*, 48–53. Indeed, he argues that Smedes's approach "trivializes and undermines central Christian practices and understandings of forgiveness" (ibid., 52). I am sympathetic to Jones's critique of Smedes. However, I believe that Smedes's approach picks up on sensitivities that, if properly integrated, would improve Jones's articulation of a distinctively Christian forgiveness. This will become apparent later.

[6] Volf is less explicit on this point than Jones. However, his theological anthropology and his articulation of the motivations that should move one to forgive, as well as the moralistic tone of the language he uses to account for resistance to forgiving, all incline

interest as arising from and contributing to a mentality that undermines the distinctively Christian character of the commitment to generosity in forgiving.[7] Forgiving can become a self-focused enactment that bypasses the Christian call to promote reconciliation. Second, Smedes does not ground his examination and exposition of forgiveness explicitly in his Christian commitment. He gives too little attention to the Christian narrative.

Jones and Volf, by contrast, make their case for a distinctive Christian forgiveness by tying their explanations of forgiveness to the narrative of God's forgiveness of humankind in the person of Jesus. They have thus grounded the distinctiveness of Christian forgiveness, at least in part, in the motivation to forgive. The properly Christian motivation to forgive, according to both Volf and Jones, is the gratitude that should flourish in the hearts of those who *recognize* that they have been forgiven by God. This gratitude should then issue in generosity toward others, a generosity expressed in forgiveness. Forgiving becomes thereby an act of love.[8] As an act of love, it is socially situated. It intends to promote the overcoming of relational ruptures.

Nevertheless, the question of the relationship of Smedes's account of forgiveness to a distinctively Christian forgiveness remains open, despite the objections raised by Jones. In his *The Art of Forgiving*[9] Smedes himself replied to the accusation that he had sold out to a "therapeutic forgiveness." He does not revise his explanation of forgiving to make it more explicitly Christian. Instead, he appeals to the dynamics of interpersonal relationship to argue that the reciprocal relations involved in forgiving entail an integral relationship between self-healing and the benefit that comes to offenders when we forgive.[10] Smedes's point appears to be that

---

his argument in the same direction as Jones's on this point. For his thoughts on obstacles to forgiving, see Volf, *Free of Charge*, 193, 214ff.

[7] In this regard they draw close to the perspective Derrida espoused. If the absolute ideal is not achieved, then the minimal conditions for Christian forgiveness—among them lack of self-interest, apparently—render the enactment something other than Christian forgiveness. I am indebted to my Jesuit brother, Bryce Deline, for this observation.

[8] Volf explicitly names love as the Christian motivation. However, within the context of his larger argument it is clear that love arises from gratitude for the generosity of God and expresses itself in generosity, by means of love in the form of forgiveness, toward others who have offended. See Volf, *Free of Charge*, 189.

[9] Smedes, *The Art of Forgiving*, 71.

[10] It is intriguing that Volf makes a similar point when writing about healing ruptured relationships in *The End of Memory*, 82, yet when he turns explicitly to the question of

insofar as anyone undertaking to forgive has experienced harm he or she is going to want to overcome the pain of that harm as that pain lives on in the state of unforgiveness. The desire to overcome that internal pain will, therefore, be mixed with the desire to restore right relations and with any other altruistic motives. In Smedes's account therapeutic self-interest does not, *ipso facto*, exclude Christian motivation. In other words, for Smedes, Christian forgiveness does not require that our motivations be un-self-interested. Christians can forgive out of a desire for healing. Alternatively, a desire for healing can coexist with what Jones sees as Christian motivations.

If Jones is correct in arguing that Smedes has neglected the side of the process initiated by God as articulated in the Christian narrative, Smedes's response suggests that Jones does not pay adequate attention to the human dimensions of the process of forgiving—to what takes place interiorly within the forgiver as forgiveness unfolds and how feelings are implicated in the motivation to forgive. We can understand the disagreement on this point in terms of the schema identified in chapter 7. Smedes is approaching the question of forgiveness "from below." Volf has taken the "from above" perspective. Jones has placed himself between the two, but in a manner that privileges "from above." That is, he starts from what God has done for us and the obligation (duty) that imposes on the grateful recipient of God's forgiveness. Because of that obligation, and because Christians are not as obviously practiced at forgiving as the narrative calls us to be, Jones argues for the need to draw a closer connection between the telling of the story and the promotion of disciplinary practices in such a way that forgiving will be more fully embodied in Christian life.

The contrast between the approach of Smedes ("from below") and that taken by Volf and Jones (favoring "from above" and explicit reliance on the Christian narrative as foundational to the understanding and practice of forgiveness) gets us to a place of instability in the Christian landscape of forgiveness. It raises the question: to what extent is the human experience of pain and the desire for healing of that pain theologically relevant to the articulation of Christian forgiveness? The charge leveled by Jones against Smedes's presentation can give the impression that Christian forgiveness has no room for such motivations; they are theologically

---

Christian forgiveness in *Free of Charge* he does not develop the dimension of multiple motivations.

irrelevant or, if they are theologically relevant, it is because they express our "selfishness" rather than Christian love.[11] They are traceable to the power of sin in our lives.

This is another way of getting at the distinction between "from above" and "from below" approaches to Christian forgiveness: the theological relevance of human experience—the experience of pain, the experience of desire for healing, and also the experience of resistance to the call to forgive. We can see the instability this contrast brings into articulations of Christian forgiveness when we examine in greater depth how Volf and Jones discuss our experience of the obstacles to forgiving.

### Stumbling Blocks to Christian Forgiving

It is a commonplace in contemporary literature on forgiveness (secular and Christian) to start from the premise that the virtue of forgiveness is observed more in the breach than in practice. But as both Miroslav Volf and L. Gregory Jones recognize, the practice of forgiving is integral to Christian self-understanding. As they point out, there are influences at work in our relationships and in our culture that move in a trajectory counter to the forgiveness to which Christians are called. Volf gets at this state of affairs by what the subtitle of his work refers to as "a culture stripped of grace." With this designation he points to the absence of generosity and the distortion of relationships that occurs when generosity is lacking. This lack of generosity, he argues, places us in oppositional, competitive relations to one another and foments violence. For Christians, he claims, the cultural loss of grace goes hand in hand with the insinuation of distortions into our images of God.[12] Volf hopes that correcting these misunderstandings will help relocate forgiveness (properly understood) in the center of Christian life.

Jones's analysis identifies two distinct but interrelated kinds of problems underlying both the distorted understanding of Christian forgiveness and failure to enact it. The first kind is external to the Christian community but affects its self-understanding and practice. The second is internal to the community but shapes its engagement with the surrounding world. The first kind, external, has to do with the distorting impact of therapeutic intentions (making oneself feel good) on the understanding

---

[11] Volf, *Free of Charge*, 193, 214ff.

[12] He takes up the issue of distorted images of God with respect to giving in chap. 1 and with respect to forgiving in chap. 4 of *Free of Charge*; see pp. 21–31, 131–43.

of Christian forgiveness. The importation of a therapeutic paradigm into Christian approaches to forgiveness, he argues, undermines the social aspect of forgiveness and its relationship to overcoming the divisions within community.[13] Jones maintains that "therapeutic forgiveness" substitutes a "cheap grace" for the hard work of forgiving and reconciling.[14] I could "settle" for a forgiveness that just makes me feel better without attempting to confront or resolve the problem or work toward reconciliation. A further, external factor is the prevalence of violence in the world and the manner in which that violence can overwhelm the believer. It can make forgiving seem like a hopeless venture.

The second kind of problem, that internal to the life of the church, is the loss of practices promoting the embodiment of forgiveness. Like Volf, Jones sees the decline in distinctly Christian forgiveness as partly related to a misunderstanding of the revelation of God. This needs to be corrected. But in contrast to Volf, Jones directs attention to the dynamics of the communion of persons in the Trinity as these have been revealed in

---

[13] I have already alluded to Smedes's response to this charge. It is worth noting that on this point Jones is replicating a tendency we have also seen in the secular discussions—understanding forgiveness as inclusive of reconciliation as a constitutive and completing moment of forgiveness itself. I see the two enactments as related, but distinct.

[14] Jones draws the language of "cheap grace" from his reading of Dietrich Bonhoeffer. It is a common trope in Christian literature, particularly within Evangelical Christian perspectives. However, it has been picked up in multiple discussions of forgiveness, either with direct reference to Bonhoeffer or in referring to Jones. See, for example, Chris Brauns, *Unpacking Forgiveness: Biblical Answers for Complex Questions and Deep Wounds* (Wheaton, IL: Crossway, 2008), 63, 69; Fraser Watts, "Christian Theology," 50–68, in *Forgiveness in Context: Theology and Psychology in Creative Dialogue*, ed. Fraser Watts and Liz Gulliford (London and New York: T & T Clark, 2004), at 52; Craig L. Blomberg, "On Building and Breaking Barriers: Forgiveness, Salvation and Christian Counseling with Special Reference to Matthew 18:15–35," *Journal of Psychology and Christianity* 25, no. 2 (2006): 137–54, at 143; Ilsup Ahn, "The Genealogy of Debt and the Phenomenology of Forgiveness: Nietzsche, Marion, and Derrida on the Meaning of the Peculiar Phenomenon," *The Heythrop Journal* 51 (2010): 454–70, at 466. The language of "therapeutic forgiveness" has also made its way more broadly into Christian writings as a negatively charged designation. Brauns makes extensive use of Jones's critique of therapeutic forgiveness in *Unpacking Forgiveness*. Blomberg also expresses concern about reducing forgiveness to a therapeutic technique in "Building and Breaking Barriers," a matter likewise explored by Nathan R. Frise and Mark R. McMinn, "Forgiveness and Reconciliation: The Differing Perspectives of Psychologists and Christian Theologians," *Journal of Psychology and Theology* 38, no. 2 (2010): 83–90.

salvation history.[15] The life of the Triune God, as revealed in the person of Jesus and mediated by the Holy Spirit, is the basis on which he clarifies what Christian forgiveness is and how it is to be cultivated. That is, Jones believes that articulating the implications of the revelation of the Trinity for Christian life will set forgiveness in its proper theological context.[16] Communal practices designed to promote the trinitarian dynamics of forgiveness in the lives of believers, he hopes, will school Christians in how to embody forgiveness as Christians. This, in turn, will affect their engagement with the relational ruptures and violence they encounter in the larger world.

## Beneath the Stumbling Blocks

Volf and Jones both make valuable contributions to Christian reflection on forgiveness. They identify some of the important obstacles to the promotion of forgiveness within the Christian community. The kinds of issues they raise are commonly echoed by other Christian writers on forgiveness: the identification of obstacles to Christian forgiveness in the surrounding culture; the desire to promote the practice of Christian forgiveness; the appeal to the Christian narrative to persuade readers that forgiveness is essential to Christian life; the effort to clarify what forgiveness does and does not entail for the Christian.[17]

Volf and Jones have thus put their fingers on a throbbing nerve in contemporary Christian consciousness. However, their diagnoses of the

---

[15] This issue runs throughout Jones's presentation, but part 2 is devoted to explicit engagement with the trinitarian dynamics of Christian forgiveness. See especially *Embodying Forgiveness*, chap. 4, 101–34.

[16] Jones is not alone in his conviction that retrieving the doctrine of the Trinity is of practical importance for Christian living. See, for example, Walter Kasper, *The God of Jesus Christ* (New York: Crossroad, 1986), and Catherine M. LaCugna, *God for Us: The Trinity and Christian Life* (San Francisco: HarperSanFrancisco, 1991).

[17] Some of the popular Christian presentations taking up these issues include Brian Zahnd, *Unconditional?* (Lake Mary, FL: Charisma House, 2010); Emmanuel Katongole and Chris Rice, *Reconciling All Things: A Christian Vision for Justice, Peace and Healing* (Downers Grove, IL: InterVarsity Press, 2008); L. Gregory Jones and Célestin Musekura, *Forgiving as We've Been Forgiven: Community Practices for Making Peace* (Downers Grove, IL: InterVarsity Press, 2010); John Loren Sandford, Paula Sandford, and Lee Bowman, *Choosing Forgiveness: Turning from Guilt, Bitterness and Resentment towards a Life of Wholeness and Peace* (Lake Mary, FL: Charisma House, 2007); Philip Yancey, *What's So Amazing about Grace?* (Grand Rapids: Zondervan, 1997).

problems focus attention only on the most visible, surface-level obstacles. At least in part because of their preference for articulating distinctively Christian forgiveness "from above," from the perspective of God's action to which we respond, they neglect to probe more deeply into the human dynamics involved in forgiving and the role of those dynamics in obstructing the distinctive Christian forgiveness they wish to promote.[18] There is much more at stake than they have identified. As a result, both their analyses of the problems and their prescriptions for addressing the obstacles to what Jones calls the "embodying" of forgiveness leave important issues unaddressed.[19]

Why should one accept the assertion that Volf and Jones have overlooked relevant considerations in their examination of Christian forgiveness? The analysis that follows will provide a more complete justification.

---

[18] In the case of Volf there may also be a basement-level orientation that diminishes the importance of even asking about the human side of the question. His use of Martin Luther's framework for discussion of forgiveness carries with it some of the residue of Luther's anti-Pelagian polemics against the regnant scholastic theology of his day (as he read it) and the consequent Pelagian sensibilities among common believers. The sensibilities on which Tetzel was able to capitalize in his promotion of indulgences—ultimately provoking Luther's ninety-five theses—were broadly enough disseminated in the religious culture that Pelagian distortions were a real issue. The idea that one's own actions, apart from grace, could effect the acquisition of grace (and salvation) by means of merit (understood as obligating God to us) were enough in the air to call into question the gratuity of grace itself. Luther's response to this situation emphasized the utter depravity of the human condition after the Fall. Without grace we can do nothing good. Luther therefore emphasized our absolute need for grace. Volf's presentation, relying on Luther's account of God's saving action, continues this one-sided emphasis. Jones devotes more attention to the human side of the issue when he discusses the importance of practices that inculcate Christian virtue, the embodiment of forgiveness toward others.

[19] In making this claim I am not suggesting that simply identifying these deeper forces will automatically produce more consistent and faithful practice of forgiveness; that would be naïve. Rather, the claim being made here is that a deeper, more nuanced understanding of the forces arrayed against the embodiment of Christian forgiveness can lead to more precise development of pastoral strategies to help overcome those forces. It is not the purpose of this inquiry to prescribe those strategies. However, if there is a distinctive Christian forgiveness, and if efforts to name it thus far are found to be wanting, then some rethinking is in order. If this rethinking provides us with a theological account that also addresses aspects of the human experience that have heretofore been overlooked or not adequately integrated into our theologizing, then this rethought account of a distinctive Christian forgiveness should also illuminate how we can better address some of the problems facing the promotion of Christian forgiveness as a practice.

However, two immediate observations lend initial weight to the claim. First, the problem with forgiving is not new. Forgiving those who have offended us has been challenging to Christians from the beginning. Although present circumstances provide new matter that our impulses to resist forgiving can employ, the resistant impulse has been evident throughout Christian history. It is woven into the fabric of human processes of becoming, as the analysis of human becoming and its relationship to experiences of harm in chapter 5 attests. Consequently, directing our attention to a culture stripped of grace or to the influences of modernity in eroding our Christian identification with and practice of forgiveness—although valid up to a point—distracts from the deeper human dynamics that make it possible for such current realities to have a negative impact.

Second, the diagnoses presented by Volf and Jones fail to take adequately into account that the boundaries between Christians, the culture, and the ecclesial community as a collective are permeable.[20] Were they not, there would be no basis for the critiques of culture and modernity raised by Volf and Jones. This permeability is presupposed by both authors, yet its theological significance is unexamined. It is true that culture influences the Christian and the church, but the influence can also go in the other direction. Indeed, without the resources of culture the church would not exist in the concrete, for the church is subject to the requirements of incarnation. It must draw its substance from the world in which it lives, even as it transforms that substance into the Body of Christ: so, too, the individual Christian. To put it in other terms, the church is always situated within a culture that is the culture of its members, or, conversely, the personal matrices of meanings of those who constitute the Body of Christ are always composed of meanings drawn from the shared matrix of the ecclesial community *and* the shared matrices of the surrounding culture, simultaneously.

This is an ambivalent situation with respect to the church and Christian identity. On the one hand, as Volf and Jones argue, the influence of culture can distort Christian self-understanding. That is undeniable. On

---

[20] In *Exclusion and Embrace*, where the issue is reconciliation, Volf is most eloquent on this interpenetration of influences. But when he turns to forgiveness his emphasis on God's action appears to render this fact irrelevant to the discussion. This seems to be a consequence of both his "from above" approach to the question of Christian forgiveness and his reliance on the late-medieval theological anthropology embedded in the narrative of substitutionary atonement he has appropriated from Martin Luther.

the other hand, Christian self-understanding has always been worked out on both the corporate and individual levels via the negotiation of identity among available, competing frameworks of meaning in dialogue with the Christian narrative of salvation. Moreover, Christian identity is bound up with a mission to the world. Christians on mission to a world not identified with a Christian matrix of meanings, or only nominally so, must make use of the resources of the local culture if they are to present the Gospel in credible or recognizable ways to their audience. Mission requires creative, discerning appropriation, transformation, and employment of available cultural resources.

The diagnoses offered by Volf and Jones incline toward an understanding of Christian forgiveness that aspires to a kind of Christian integrity conceived as standing over against the contemporary culture, understood as a distorting influence. On the one hand this inclination is natural and serves an important function; it helps us clarify for ourselves who we are as a distinct group by keeping us oriented to our founding inspiration. On the other hand, it can fall victim to a kind of sectarian temptation.[21]

This is most clearly evident in the reductionistic characterization of "therapeutic forgiveness." To be sure, some psychological accounts of forgiveness may fit the characterization presented by Jones. There are credible grounds for applying the charge to Smedes, although I am not totally convinced by the evidence presented. However, the rise to reflective awareness of psychological processes is a resource that has theological significance. It can provide to theology a better understanding of the human person than anthropologies fashioned by ancient Greek philosophers and refashioned by medieval and Reformation-era theologians. A theological anthropology that refuses to grapple seriously with the dynamics of the human psyche when they are implicated in the subject under investigation is susceptible to the charge of dogmatism at best and intellectual dishonesty at worst. Such a refusal is the seedbed of sectarian thinking.

To succumb to this sectarian temptation can undermine or distort the place of the Christian mission to the world within the Christian sense of self. Both Volf and Jones would oppose the extremes to which a sectarian impulse can lead, but their critiques of cultural influence and the underdeveloped attention they give to the individual personal dynamics involved in undertaking forgiveness as a meaningful response

---

[21] Volf is keenly aware of the dangers posed by this temptation and analyzes them at length in *Exclusion and Embrace*. It is therefore surprising that he does not engage this issue in his discussion of forgiveness.

to an experience of harm can contribute to an oppositional reading of the relationship between the Christian (or the church) and the world.

To adapt a phrase, there is an element of a "Christianity against culture" mentality in both their diagnoses of the problems and the solutions they propose.[22] Although both authors are aware of the other side of the story, the positive, missiological aspects of engagement with culture are underdeveloped in their theological analyses. Both Volf and Jones affirm that Christians are called and sent to bear witness to or embody forgiveness in the world. They both give nominal affirmation to the idea that the world and its insights might enhance Christian understanding and practice of forgiveness, but this remains unexplored as a real possibility.[23] Functionally, in their presentations they relate to "the world" as "other" and as opposed to the Christian community. At the very least it is to be regarded with suspicion lest it alloy the distinctive characteristics of Christian life.[24] An understanding of Christian forgiveness that respects

---

[22] The phrase is adapted from the "Christ against culture" typology presented in the classic work of H. Richard Niebuhr, *Christ and Culture* (New York: Harper & Row, 1951), 45–82.

[23] Volf, for example, takes seriously some of the concerns about "psychological reasons" against forgetting offenses, even appealing to Sigmund Freud, when setting up the conditions for a proper "forgetting" of offenses such as he believes is integral to a Christian understanding of forgiveness (*Free of Charge*, 174). Yet the move he ultimately makes in this argument, appealing to a limited number of scriptural texts about "God forgetting" our offenses as a basis for insisting that we do the same, points to a theological approach that does not take the fruits of psychological research and insight seriously as a positive theological datum. Jones's much more articulate position on the use of resources from nontheological disciplines will be examined in more detail below.

[24] As will be discussed below, Jones does provide criteria for a positive engagement with non-Christian sources—philosophy, sociology, psychology, and so on. However, the criteria he names (in very general descriptive terms) for employing them reflect a self-protective, suspicious stance. He writes: "Even so, in order for these investigations to be integral to the craft of Christian forgiveness, Christians need to recognize and critically assess the ways in which nontheological inquiries are already embedded in traditions that may or may not cohere or overlap with a theological context shaped by and focused on the Triune God. The problem with too many modern discussions, as I suggested in the first section, is that they have increasingly diverged from such a theological context. But that divergence is a critique of their practices, not of the importance of the enterprise itself" (Jones, *Embodying Forgiveness*, 225). The call for critical assessment is valid. The question is whether there is any room in Jones's perspective for the fruits of secularly grounded disciplines to critique Christian self-understanding, including the understanding of the relationship of trinitarian dynamics to the life of the church itself.

the Christian mission to the world—and the place of forgiveness as a human enactment in that mission—requires a more nuanced account of the relationship between Christianity and culture, one that provides for the dynamics of discernment about how to engage particular cultural constructs. But this more nuanced account will require a properly Christian, theological grounding, one Volf does not provide and for which Jones only sketches the possibility.[25]

These two points (that forgiving is a perennial challenge to Christians and that we always stand in an ambiguous and ambivalent relationship to surrounding cultures) draw attention to the fact that the obstacles facing Christian forgiveness operate on a deeper level than the analyses of Volf and Jones have addressed. To put this in terms of the image drawn from Charles Taylor, the identified problem (inadequate Christian understanding and practice of forgiveness) exists on the first floor.[26] To address it, both Volf and Jones construct arguments (second floor) based on foundations (basement) presumed to be shared with their interlocutors (residents of the first floor). Although the residents will grasp some meaning in the words used to name those foundations and perhaps give assent to them, those words are apparently unable to motivate the first-floor residents to forgive—at least consistently. The problem is that the deeper foundations have shifted. The residents of the first floor may only have a notional assent to the terms presented in the argument. Their actual basement-level presuppositions and commitments might differ substantially from those of Volf's and Jones's theologizing. This difference at the basement level is, I believe, a better explanation for why Christian forgiveness is misunderstood and is so often not put into practice.[27]

To recast this in terms of matrices of meanings, the presumed shared matrix of meanings is, in fact, not held in common. Even if there is

---

[25] Jones is close to such a grounding with his emphasis on trinitarian dynamics. It may even be that his personal theological perspective would agree with the point being made here but the scope of his project did not entail addressing this question.

[26] See the use of the image of a house in Charles Taylor, *A Secular Age* (Cambridge, MA: Belknap Press of Harvard University Press, 2007), 433. See also the exposition and application of this image in chap. 4 above.

[27] Volf's concerns about the "gracelessness that is slowly spreading like a disease throughout many of our cultures" (*Free of Charge*, 14), the cultural distortions in our understanding of God in *Free of Charge*, 20–21, and the understanding of the autonomous self in *Free of Charge*, 65–66 all point to a dislocation of meanings at the basement level. So too do Jones's concerns regarding "therapeutic forgiveness." This is especially evident in his second chapter in *Embodying Forgiveness*, 35–70.

some common ground, the constellation of meanings that Volf and Jones believe *should* have sufficient gravity in the Christian's sense of self to motivate the Christian to forgive does not. It does not possess sufficient weight in the sense of self of the individual Christian (or of the Christian community) to counter the force and gravity of the retributive feelings that arise in the face of harm, nor is it sufficient to counterbalance the other cultural (and ecclesial!) meanings that co-constitute the personal matrices of the forgiveness-resistant Christian.

Volf attempts to address this imbalance by retelling the narrative, elaborating it from within the framework of Luther's theology. Jones follows a similar course (retelling the narrative), but also prescribes the retrieval of practices to inculcate the appropriate habits of behavior. By focusing their attention so heavily on what the Christian narrative tells us God has done in forgiving us, they make an argument about what *should* be the disposition and behavior of the Christian with respect to offenses (sins). But they neglect to analyze why it is so difficult for anyone, Christians included, to forgive in the first place and how retelling the story will effect the desired change in Christian practice. Instead, they retell the narrative that believers may already affirm. They prescribe what the community *should* understand about the narrative and how that *should* be reflected in behaviors supportive of forgiveness.

Jones does go further than Volf in elaborating practical suggestions for the promotion of forgiveness in the ecclesial community. For example, he prescribes that Christians seek out role models and mentors in the craft of forgiving. He also draws attention to the potential value of Christian sacramental practices for fostering a deeper embodiment of forgiving-ness.[28] But even this does not engage the deeper dislocation of *meaning* that lies beneath the lack of motivation to forgive. "Meaning" in this context must be understood not in terms of definition or concept but in accord with the broader understanding outlined in chapter 4 and applied in chapter 5. It includes personal histories, valuational priorities, aspirations, and so on. The problem is that the narrative that should motivate forgiving practices and that underlies the doctrinal explanations of the sacramental practices does not possess sufficient weight in the personal matrix of meanings of the believer (or the shared matrix of the community) to produce the forgiving behaviors and attitudes appropriate

---

[28] See Jones, *Embodying Forgiveness*, 228; idem, "Crafting Communities of Forgiveness," *Interpretation* (April 2000): 121–34, at 134.

to the Christian narrative's implications. Other meanings have greater influence in shaping the sense of self (or of communal identity), and therefore in shaping our actions.

### Naming the Dislocated Meanings

The fact of dislocated meanings permeates the Christian literature on forgiveness; it is implicit in efforts to name the problem of Christians not practicing forgiveness. It is certainly evident in Volf's and Jones's arguments. As indicated above, this dislocation occurs most profoundly at the basement level of meanings. It reshapes the often-unexamined presuppositions by which we interact with, evaluate, and make decisions about those meanings that confront us on the first-floor level. Many of the ways of naming these dislocations fall under the rubric of the transition from the modern to the postmodern mindset.[29] Admittedly, the term "postmodern" is problematic in its own right. There is no uniform agreement on what it designates. However, as a term encompassing several interrelated tendencies that have arisen as alternatives to the values and assumptions shaping modernity the term can serve to point us toward characteristics relevant to the present discussion. These characteristics touch directly on the dislocation of meanings at issue in the impediments to embodying Christian forgiveness.

Among the most commonly cited and observed dislocations of the postmodern ethos has been a growing mistrust of meta-narratives, the big stories that, on the one hand, provide a frame of reference or a horizon from within which to make sense of new experiences but, on the other hand, can suppress uncomfortable questions that might disrupt that frame of reference or horizon.[30] A growing recognition that such narratives have oppressed vast numbers of people and even led to the suppression

---

[29] This dislocation of meaning corresponds to the kind of "basement-level" shift in meanings discussed above and explored in Taylor, *A Secular Age.* For an example of such a shift in the understanding of sin, see Taylor's analysis in *A Secular Age,* 493–513.

[30] See the discussion of metanarrative and the reasons for the mistrust with which they are currently regarded in Jean-François Lyotard, *The Postmodern Condition: A Report on Knowledge,* trans. Geoff Bennington and Brian Massumi (Minneapolis: University of Minnesota Press, 1988), 31–36; idem, *The Differend: Phrases in Dispute,* trans. Georges Van Den Abbeele (Minneapolis: University of Minnesota Press, 1988), nos. 160, 200, and esp. no. 227. For critical discussion of the theological implications of critique of metanarrative, see Lieven Boeve, "Bearing Witness to the Differend: A Model for Theologizing in the Postmodern Context," *Louvain Studies* 20, no. 4 (Winter 1995): 362–79,

of indigenous cultures has produced a kind of suspicion with respect to narratives that present themselves as definitive and comprehensive accounts of reality (totalizing narratives).

The counterpart to this mistrust has been a growing acceptance of an unresolved pluralism of complexes of meaning.[31] Postmodern sensibilities are much more explicitly comfortable than modern sensibilities in living with the unresolvable tensions between complexes of meanings standing side by side within a personal matrix, a kind of bricolage sense of self.[32] The kind of conceptual coherence and rational integration so highly prized by modernity and so reflective of its optimistic meta-narrative regarding the capacities of human reason have given way to an edgy accommodation to only partial coherence, unresolved pluralism, and relativized truth claims.[33] A decisive element in this transition has been the replacement of the authority of the meta-narrative with the authority of the individual, skeptical judgment.[34] Claims of truth or value must be

---

and idem, "Critical Consciousness in the Postmodern Condition: New Opportunities for Theology?" *Philosophy and Theology* 10, no. 2 (1997): 449–68.

[31] Stanley Grenz traces this state of affairs to an epistemological shift—away from the Enlightenment idea of universal reason and knowledge to the conviction that all knowing is contextualized and that therefore all truth claims are contextualized. See Stanley J. Grenz, *A Primer on Postmodernism* (Grand Rapids, MI: Eerdmans, 1996), 14, 15, 20–22.

[32] See Grenz, *A Primer on Postmodernism*, 15; Paul Lakeland, *Postmodernity: Christian Identity in a Fragmented Age* (Minneapolis: Fortress Press, 1997), 88. See also Taylor, *A Secular Age*, 513. In the 1970s, Karl Rahner identified another basis for fragmentation, although in a different context: the sheer explosion in information and specialization in research and disciplines defies integration of knowledge to such an extent that we are more keenly aware that we cannot master any discipline. In some areas we will be experts, in others mere amateurs. This recognition provided an *apologia* for his anthropological approach to theological questions. See Karl Rahner, *Foundations of Christian Faith: An Introduction to the Idea of Christianity* (New York: Seabury, 1978), 1–8. The "bricolage" sense of self might not be a specifically postmodern phenomenon. The epistemological underpinnings of our presentation of matrices of meanings suggest that such a sense of self may, in fact, be a perennial reality. But postmodernity has brought with it basement-level shifts in meaning that now make it possible to theorize about this state of affairs as "normal," not as a defect to be overcome.

[33] See, for example, Taylor's discussion of shifts in cultural sensibilities in the period since the 1960s in *A Secular Age*, 519ff.

[34] I use the phrase "skeptical judgment" to distinguish what I am naming here from "critical judgment." The latter I take to be methodologically aware of its own processes as well as those operative around it. It can therefore subject its own functioning to critique. Immanuel Kant and Bernard Lonergan would be excellent examples of this. Skeptical

recognized *by me* if they are to lay any claim on me.[35] They cannot be leveraged on the basis of the authority of the meta-narrative.

This postmodern condition challenges the proclamation of the Christian Gospel. For those who do not reject the Gospel utterly as another oppressive meta-narrative, their identification with its message may well function as just one complex of meanings alongside many others. It might not (and for many does not) possess sufficient gravity in their personal matrices of meanings to function as a foundation or an orienting reference point for engaging the other complexes of meanings within the sense of self.[36] It might also only be appropriated piecemeal—what in some Catholic circles is disparaged as "cafeteria Catholicism." The integrity of a Christian shared matrix is itself called into question.

Within this context many of the constitutive elements of the Christian narrative are subject to being regarded with postmodern skepticism. At the very least they can undergo a shift in importance. For some people they may no longer carry any practical significance in their lives. Although the very pluralism characterizing the postmodern condition precludes making universal claims about such shifts, it is possible to identify specific themes within Christian narratives that are vulnerable to postmodern skepticism. Four of these themes relevant to the question of Christian forgiveness bear naming.

The first is an anthropological element. Broadly, it is the notion that the understanding of the normatively human is to be derived from the revelation of God.[37] To be sure, some anthropological insights found in Judeo-Christian scriptures do receive wide acceptance in the postmodern ethos. The affirmation of the intrinsic dignity of the human person would be high on the list. But these would be arrived at by other means than appeal to revelation and would be interpreted in relationship to

---

judgment, by contrast, operates on the basis of a suspicion of truth claims generally but does not subject its own skepticism to examination.

[35] Grenz, *A Primer on Postmodernism*, 15.

[36] See, for example, Taylor's description of the distanced stance with respect to religion in *A Secular Age*, 521.

[37] As John Webster points out, in the postmodern context this is no longer an unquestioned premise. He writes that Christian claims about "the nature and destiny of humankind" based on appeals to Christian revelation and belief in the triune God "are culturally marginal." John Webster, "The Human Person," 219–34, in *The Cambridge Companion to Postmodern Theology*, ed. Kevin J. Vanhoozer (Cambridge: Cambridge University Press, 2003), at 219.

a different matrix of meanings. One aspect of Christian anthropology that would be particularly problematic in a postmodern mindset touches directly on the complex of theological issues surrounding forgiveness. It consists in the claim, explicit in some branches of Christianity, that we all merit the wrath of God.[38]

Many Christians will hold such a notion in the abstract, as a statement of belief, but the depths to which it affects their sense of self or their relations with others is under challenge by postmodern matrices of meanings. Particularly as our world becomes more globally connected and Christians interact with good people from other religious or even atheistic perspectives, one can expect that explanations of Christianity that make this a central element in their narratives will have a weaker hold on the sense of self even of those who affirm the concept that all deserve God's wrath. Both the skeptical mindset mentioned above and suspicion regarding absolutes leveraged on the basis of appeals to revealed content, when confronted with concrete experience of goodness in others who do not share one's religious tradition can contribute to a displacement of this particular expression of Christian theological anthropology.

A second element, related to the first, is that the language of "sin" has lost its power. The questioning of traditional Christian narratives regarding right and wrong, shifting evaluations of behaviors previously proscribed as sinful, skepticism about absolute moral standards in general, and critical recognition of the complicity of religious leaders in behaviors that, by their own standards, are deserving of condemnation have all contributed to a marginalization of the language of sin. These conditions find further support in the emergence of psychological paradigms for assessing moral behavior. As Ann Swidler has observed: "Guilt is going out of style. While such changes are hard to document with simple questions about doctrine or practice, I would argue that there has been a general shift in religious imagery away from sin, punishment, and damnation, toward a God who is, above all, the source of something like Abraham Maslow's 'unconditional positive regard.'"[39]

---

[38] See the discussion of God's wrath in Volf, *Free of Charge*, 138–40. Jones also makes use of the theme of God's wrath, yet he inclines toward seeing it in relationship to the "judgment of grace," prodding us toward repentance and reconciliation. See Jones, *Embodying Forgiveness*, 56–57, 244, 255.

[39] Ann Swidler, "Saving the Self: Endowment Versus Depletion in American Institutions," 41–55, in *Meaning and Modernity: Religion, Polity and Self* (Berkeley: University of California Press, 2002), at 41.

The vocabulary of sin lives on in religious contexts, but the affective repugnance it once evoked appears to have declined. We can read critical comments about "therapeutic forgiveness" as a religious response to the replacement of the language of sin with the language of mental health professions.

Third, and following on the dislocation of the first two meanings, the idea of salvation has also been transformed and shifted to the margins.[40] Particularly for those in affluent (Western and largely northern-hemisphere) cultures, the "need" for salvation does not possess the existential imminence it once did. The cultural perspective that privileges autonomy and independence (modernity), combined with one that encourages skepticism (postmodernity), can lead to a deferral of concern about ultimate destiny (the afterlife, final judgment, etc.). Attention is focused on the here and now and on the intra-mundane modes of "salvation" one can grasp on one's own.[41] Moreover, with the displacement of "sin" to the margins of consciousness, the experiences of need for salvation that might come to reflective awareness occur in other dimensions of life—health, relationship crises, depression or mental health issues, and so on.[42]

Finally and most fundamentally, belief in God has been attenuated as a significant factor in the complex of meanings that shape people's actions. Most obviously, the emergence of the so-called "new atheism" represented by such figures as Richard Dawkins,[43] Daniel Dennett,[44]

[40] Ibid., 42.

[41] Hans Urs von Balthasar identified this as a malaise of modernity and its search for intramundane sources of ultimacy in his doctoral dissertation, *Geschichte des eschatologischen Problems in der modernen deutschen Literatur* (Einsiedeln, Freiburg: Johannes Verlag, 1998; originally self-published in Zürich in 1930).

[42] Swidler identifies other concerns that occupy a larger place in contemporary consciousness than guilt and sin in "Saving the Self," 42–44. Walter Lowe raises a methodological problem when Christology is approached from the standpoint of need or lack. It makes the credibility of the subsequent narrative dependent on the identification with that lack. (This imbues the narrative with its own negativity, as in the critiques of substitutionary atonement, for example.) Walter Lowe, "Christ and Salvation," 235–51, in *The Cambridge Companion to Postmodern Theology*, ed. Kevin J. Vanhoozer (Cambridge: Cambridge University Press, 2003), at 236.

[43] Richard Dawkins, *The Blind Watchmaker: Why the Evidence of Evolution Reveals a Universe without Design* (New York: Norton, 1996); idem, *A Devil's Chaplain: Reflections on Hope, Lies, Science, and Love* (Boston: Houghton Mifflin, 2003); idem, *The God Delusion* (Boston: Houghton Mifflin, 2008).

[44] Daniel C. Dennett, *Breaking the Spell: Religion as a Natural Phenomenon* (New York: Viking, 2006); idem, *Darwin's Dangerous Idea: Evolution and the Meanings of Life* (New

and Christopher Hitchens[45] directly attacks religion and religious beliefs on all levels. But even among those who do profess belief in God, the relevance of that belief to decisions in daily life is not always recognized or, when recognized, applied in practice. It must compete with other priorities and values. This is certainly the case when one is confronted with the possibility of engaging forgiveness. Indeed, this conviction underlies Volf's and Jones's efforts to correct what they regard as inadequate understandings of God and our relationship to God.

These dislocations of meaning create problems for the traditional Christian narrative of forgiveness, at least as a motivator to practice forgiveness toward others. They open a gap between the shared Christian matrix of meanings and the contexts of meaning taken as "givens" in the rest of one's life. These latter contexts of meaning, verified in daily experience, take on the status of "the real," while the Christian shared matrix is correspondingly reduced to the operative status of a myth—a comforting story unrelated to "the real world." Believers are thus faced with the challenge of correlating their religious affirmations with the contexts of meaning operative in the rest of their lives.

### Dislocations of Meaning as Call to Conversion

These fundamental shifts in the place of Christian beliefs within the sense of self of individuals (and even of ecclesial groups) have created a situation that neither Volf nor Jones has adequately addressed. The problem behind the lack of motivation to forgive is not reducible to lack of familiarity with the doctrines calling for Christians to practice forgiveness, nor can it be reduced to the influences of cultural shifts reshaping the concept of forgiveness (i.e., therapeutic forgiveness). There is also more at stake here than a decline in ecclesial practices intended to promote forgiveness. If it were merely these, the primary concern *would* be education; theological clarifications like Volf's and Jones's combined with some ecclesial disciplines (as advocated by Jones) might be sufficient. But given the kinds of displacements of meaning evident in contemporary

---

York: Simon & Schuster, 1995); idem and Alvin Plantinga, *Science and Religion: Are They Compatible?* Point/Counterpoint Series (New York: Oxford University Press, 2011).

[45] *The Portable Atheist: Essential Readings for the Nonbeliever,* selected and introduced by Christopher Hitchens (Philadelphia: Da Capo, 2007); Christopher Hitchens, *God Is not Great: How Religion Poisons Everything* (New York: Twelve, 2007); idem and Douglas Wilson, *Is Christianity Good for the World?* (Moscow, ID: Canon Press, 2009).

culture, and bearing in mind the spontaneous resistance to forgiving so prevalent in human experience in any case, the real challenge is not catechesis (religious education) or theological clarity, but *conversion*.

The kind of conversion called for is precisely that identified in chapter 5. It is a realignment of individual meanings (a limit concept) and of complexes of meanings within the structure of the matrix of meanings constituting the sense of self. This requires more than intentionally correlating different concepts, although that will play a part. It requires a realignment of the fundamental affective coloration of concepts and their location in the valuational priorities that govern our actions. This realignment must not only transform our conscious life; it must also reach even into the realms of the personal matrix (sense of self) that are not directly accessible to reflective awareness or volitional control. It must include a realignment of the dominant intentional trajectories of personal becoming that emerge from our unconscious and that come to expression in our individual choices.

Although much of the realignment called for must occur in those areas not directly accessible to reflective awareness, this deeper kind of conversion does have reverberations on the conscious level, for although it reaches into our psychic depths it must be confirmed in our conscious life by acts of freedom. These acts, for their part, will need to be understood as meaningful within the range of possible meanings available to each person's personal matrix. Indeed, the change effected by such a conversion is often experienced (as discussed in chapter 5) as a liberation. One is now free (or at least freer and more empowered) to choose and to commit oneself to what one previously experienced only as struggle or even as impossibility. As a result, the conversion emerges into consciousness as a liberating gift, as grace.[46]

The Christian narrative names this experience of conversion in terms of encounter with the God who sets us free. (Volf and Jones, theorizing about forgiveness "from above," identify it in terms of the experience of the "judgment of grace."[47]) This conversion does more than establish us in a newfound freedom. It also reveals and confirms (or establishes) personal relationship with God.[48] The two aspects go together: freedom

---

[46] Volf writes eloquently about this kind of phenomenon in terms that resonate very well with my account of conversion in matrices of meanings in *The End of Memory*, 79.

[47] See, for example, Jones, *Embodying Forgiveness*, 57, 131, 135–63; Volf, *The End of Memory*, 103, 180–82.

[48] Volf and Jones implicitly make this point in their treatment of repentance. I must recognize the sin *as sin* in order to receive the forgiveness *as forgiveness* of me. The rec-

and relationship. Moreover, although the grace is experienced as coming to us as gift from God, we do not experience it as alien when it comes. In the moment of conversion we recognize the realignment as somehow truer to our own selves than the configuration of our matrix of meanings prior to the conversion.[49] The truth we receive is our own deeper truth, despite (or perhaps *because* of) being experienced as a liberating gift. We embrace it in an act of freedom as we affirm the truth of our own self, a truth worthy of shaping our future becoming.

### Dislocated Meanings and the Need to Rethink Christian Forgiveness

At this point a clarification is in order. The argument being made here does not reject the importance of telling the Christian story or exercising ourselves in practices that help us to embody Christian forgiveness. Proclamation of the Christian narrative is an essential part of calling people to conversion and to embracing Christian forgiveness, not just in general but also in response to the particular harms we encounter personally in life. So, too, learning to embody forgiveness by means of ecclesially promoted disciplines can play a vital role. Both proclamation and ecclesial discipline can contribute to the construction of a matrix of meanings in which Christian forgiveness occupies a central place both in my interpretation of myself in relation to the narrative and in my motivation to enact forgiveness. They contribute to a context of meanings. To that extent Volf and Jones (in line with the whole history of Christian proclamation!) are on the right track.

Rather, the point at issue here is that the emergence of the postmodern ethos has unsettled what used to be considered stable ground. The obstacles on the landscape of Christian forgiveness have shifted. With the shifts in the "weight" accorded some of the most basic elements of the Christian story as these stand within the shared cultural matrices of

---

ognition of sin is a recognition of my stance before the God who offers the forgiveness. The repentance is the acceptance of the forgiveness being offered to me personally by the God who forgives.

[49] Volf and Jones get at what I am describing here when they examine the experience of repentance. Repentance comes as response to the experience of the "judgment of grace," to use Jones's terms. The awareness of oneself as sinner and as forgiven in relationship to the God who judges and forgives can occur simultaneously. We recognize the truth of our sinfulness in recognizing the forgiveness of God as personally *for us*, as the truth of who we are before God.

meanings we inhabit, *and* as we internalize these shifts into our own personal matrices of meanings, key elements in the story no longer exercise the prominent role they once might have had in shaping the personal becoming of believers. The displacements of meaning that have taken place challenge us to retell the narrative in a manner that people today will find compelling. We need to rethink Christian forgiveness.

How can we tell the Christian story in such a way that contemporary Christians and others can see themselves in it and can find in it the deeper truth of their own experience? In relation to the promotion of Christian forgiveness, how can we tell the story in such a way that people will be moved to confront their internal resistance to forgiving and will see this as a meaningful expression of their own truest selves? We need to find a way to connect the Christian narrative with what people can recognize and confirm as responding to the larger horizon from within which they interpret their own experience.

One possible approach to making that connection between the Christian message and my own truest self has been set aside under the label "therapeutic forgiveness." Neither Jones nor Volf expends much positive energy on the idea that the personal interest in finding healing for the pain one has experienced because of an offense might be a legitimate Christian motivation to forgive, but in the present, postmodern ethos the desire for healing such pain might provide a more existentially vital contact with the language and experience of salvation (and therefore with the motivation to forgive)—at least as a starting-point—than simply retelling the narrative in traditional terms. In this regard Smedes's emphasis on personal experience of the desire for healing and liberation from the pain of the offense might be of greater value in the promotion of Christian forgiveness than his critics have allowed.

Why do Volf and Jones bypass the possibility that the desire to ease one's own pain could be a theologically important—and positive—motivating factor in Christian forgiveness? A full answer to this question would take us far afield, but some preliminary indications have already surfaced. They are lodged in the personal matrices of meanings of these authors as they are shaped by a specific reading of the Christian narrative, the ways in which their matrices of meanings shape their diagnoses of the challenges to forgiving, and the specific questions they are attempting to address (specific matrices of meanings).

First, they want to locate the distinctive element of Christian forgiveness in the motivation to forgive. They see it as a response of generosity to the experience of having been forgiven by God. To allow for the desire to ease one's own pain as legitimate within a Christian understanding of forgiveness would be to open the door to "therapeutic" forgiveness and other less-than-ideal motivations. Second, and underlying this first concern, there are often elements of a "Christ against culture" mentality. Adapting one's understanding of Christian forgiveness in accord with contemporary understanding of psychic processes and the experience of the need for overcoming psychic pain, it is feared, might diminish the clarity of the distinctively Christian. It could render Christian forgiveness subject to the dictates of a merely human science. Third, by locating the distinctiveness of Christian forgiveness one-sidedly in the recognition and acceptance of the gracious action of God in forgiving us (forgiveness from above), these approaches demonstrate an implicit theological anthropology, one that views human understanding apart from revelation with suspicion. This is related to a theological tendency to view the human primarily (exclusively?) under the rubric of sin. One's own pain at having been sinned against (or harmed) can be of no significance—except, perhaps, as the cross to be borne in forgiving others.

### Missteps on the Christian Terrain

This brings us to one of the most pervasive and troubling lacunae in the traditional understanding of Christian forgiveness as represented by Volf and Jones. It is an issue deeply embedded in their theological matrices of meanings. Both authors (and many others) make an assumption about the relationship between our actual sinfulness and our consciousness of the character of our relationship to God. They assume that our reflective awareness of encounter with God will necessarily include reflective awareness of our sinfulness. Further, they argue that this awareness of ourselves as forgiven sinners is *the* basis for the gratitude that motivates the Christian to forgive others. Indeed, in their presentations, awareness of ourselves as forgiven sinners is the operative criterion for the authenticity of the experience of God. By implication, without understanding ourselves in these terms—and therefore being motivated to forgive for these reasons—the "Christian-ness" of our forgiveness is questionable. This thinking lies behind the criticisms leveled against Smedes.[50]

The conviction that this awareness of self as forgiven sinner is necessary to Christian forgiveness is a lynchpin of this kind of argument. It is

---

[50] See Brauns, *Unpacking Forgiveness*, 64–65. Brauns echoes the arguments raised by Jones.

essential to the theological coherence of the presentation. Nevertheless, it remains an unsubstantiated hypothesis.

*That* we are all entangled in the Sin of the world—the web of relations and dynamics shaped by prior sinful choices and pressuring us to continue them—cannot be denied by any Christian. *That* we contribute to the power of that Sin by our individual sinful choices is likewise undeniable. *That* the life, death, and resurrection of Christ reveal and effect the overcoming of the power of sin and our resurrection with God, I affirm wholeheartedly. But that does *not* mean that all experiences of encounter with God will be reflexively grasped in terms of our forgiven sinfulness, *nor* does it mean that awareness of our own forgiven-ness is the only way a Christian can be motivated to forgive. On the level of conscious awareness my primary experience of encounter with God might be of God's deep and abiding love for me and desire that I draw into communion with God in Christ. To be sure, the actual process of doing so will involve confrontation with Sin and sin in my life; that will occur whether I reflexively thematize the confrontation in those terms or not. The process will also require what Volf and Jones speak of as "repentance," but what I think can also be named "ongoing conversion." But on the conscious level what shapes my motivation to forgive others may simply be awareness of God's love for me and my own responsive, loving desire to labor with God's Son to make the Kingdom of God present and known in my world.

If the religious/theological matrix of meanings from within which I experience harm and the pain it causes is primarily shaped by the affirmation of the love of God for us in Christ (rather than my own sinfulness before God), then I might well seek to forgive so as to heal the hurt. But that healing will be the proximate goal. Its further *telos*, whether explicit or implicit, will be to liberate me from the constraints of the pain so that I can be freer to love others—even by forgiving the unrepentant—as God has loved me. Certainly, God's forgiveness is "contained" in that love God has shown me, but that does not mean that my forgiven-ness is the driving force in my motivation to forgive others. From this perspective it appears that Smedes's account of forgiveness from below might have more profoundly Christian foundations than his critics allow.

The point here is that Volf's and Jones's presentations reflect the shared matrices of meanings of their particular Christian ecclesial communities. Those communities apparently emphasize the sinfulness of humanity as the central premise of the narrative, particularly insofar as it touches on the question of forgiveness. This is a familiar approach; it has a long history. But it is not the only one.[51] One can affirm the reality of Sin and of sins—as I do—without having that affirmation exercise the role in the narrative and its grounding of distinctively Christian practice of forgiveness that it does for writers like Volf and Jones. More to the point, it is not at all clear that such writers really do speak for the experience of all Christians. There is no evidence that all Christians who have sought to undertake to practice forgiveness because of their faith have done so on the basis of the motivation that Volf and Jones maintain must be present for that forgiveness to be Christian. The claim might be theologically coherent within a particular shared Christian matrix, but it does not necessarily hold for all. Christians whose ecclesially mediated telling of the narrative places greater emphasis on the love of God than on human sinful depravity might well find such renderings of Christian forgiveness as represented in Volf and Jones alien to their own experience and to their understanding of the Gospel.

This draws our attention to a profound lacuna in theological formulations that rely exclusively on this singular motivation as decisive for a distinctively Christian forgiveness. They are not sufficiently attentive to the range of Christian experiences of God to account for the varied motivations that move Christians to forgive. This lacuna therefore makes claims about a distinctively Christian forgiveness unstable. It does so in a manner that echoes a misstep identified in some of the secular discussions of forgiveness. It excludes on an *a priori* basis expressions of forgiveness that do not fit within its defining conditions. In other words, the argument is circular. As such it encodes instability into its account of distinctively Christian forgiveness.

---

[51] Fraser Watts lends support to this point in his observations on positive and negative readings of the terms used to translate into English the original Greek of the New Testament. As he observes: "The New Testament was first translated into English in a guilt culture, and that seems to have distorted the way in which it was translated. Modern translations have become more intelligible, but have not always corrected these initial conceptual distortions that came from the guilt culture of the Reformation period" (Watts, "Christian Theology," 54). In his analysis the excessively moralistic understanding of forgiveness as a response to sin in our present day obscures the broader meaning of *aphesis* (forgiveness) as "about liberation at the deepest personal level; it is not about exoneration from moral shortcomings" (ibid., 54–55).

## In Search of Stable Ground

To make the account of the relationship of the Christian narrative to distinctively Christian forgiveness more stable we need a different theological framework. We need a rendering of the Christian narrative that can make sense of the broad range of possible motivations that can—and I believe do—come into play when Christians undertake to enact Christian forgiveness. Moreover, this rendering must be able to account for motivations that are present in our reflexive awareness and also those that operate below the level of our conscious awareness; it must account for the range and multiplicity of motivations we now know, on the basis of psychological research, to be simultaneously at work in any human decision or action.

This cursory sketch of elements of the matrices of meanings operating in presentations such as Volf's and Jones's offers a preliminary insight into why they do not, and perhaps cannot, explore other motivations to forgive as legitimately a part of Christian forgiveness. These elements operate in the basement level of their theorizing.

That is, first, both authors identify influences in the surrounding culture that have undermined or distorted a proper appreciation of Christian forgiveness. These influences are presented as having a causative relationship to the inadequate understanding and practice of forgiveness. The influences named are real. On the ground-floor level they do appear to be causes. What Volf and Jones do not contend with is the extent to which the power of the ground-level shifts in meaning reflects deeper displacements taking place on the basement level. Viewed from the basement, the causative influences on the ground floor take on the status of symptoms.[52] Without attending to those deeper forces (the displacement of meanings within the personal and cultural matrices of meanings as they operate within the construction of the sense of self of the individual Christian) their proffered responses to Christian failures to forgive will be akin to using aspirin to treat appendicitis.

[52] Volf and Jones do not claim that these cultural influences are *exclusive* causes. Jones also points explicitly to the decline in ecclesial practices that could cultivate the embodiment of forgiveness. But beneath both cultural influences and the decline of ecclesial practices lies a shift in matrices of meanings. Both Volf and Jones are attempting to overcome precisely this shift, but since they do not identify the shift as such or as the underlying problem, and they do not analyze the dynamics of its operation, their proposed measures do not address the deeper problem directly.

Second, when we refocus our attention on this deeper level of meanings it becomes clear that the accounts do not give adequate attention to the human side of the dynamics of forgiveness. Specifically, they fail to attend to forgiving as a human act of meaning in response to a disruption in one's sense of self. Instead, they focus on the moral and religious obligation to forgive (and its origins in God's action toward us) as that obligation is conveyed by a normative telling of the foundational Christian story.[53] This reflects the preference for the "from above" approach to the question of Christian forgiveness, and with it a particular way of construing the theological importance of human experience itself. It is viewed under the rubric of sin as primary in the God/human relationship, or at least in our theologizing about it. A closer examination of what human beings are doing and what is taking place interiorly when we undertake to forgive would have opened the door to engaging the theological significance of this human experience. Alternatively, a different understanding of what is theologically significant (perhaps one that does not privilege the "from above" approach or give theological priority to sin) would open a space for a theological consideration of the interior dynamics of forgiveness as a human enactment.

Third, by not attending to these internal dynamics and their theological significance Volf and Jones miss the opportunity to explore how, especially in the postmodern context, the experience of grace as setting one free from the pain of not forgiving might be precisely the encounter with meaning that can effect the conversion called for. In other words, the desire to be saved from the pain of not forgiving (or not being able to move oneself to undertake forgiveness) might be the human experience that God uses to draw us into relationship and thereby to help us to grow in forgiving others. Indeed, throughout the gospels the desire for healing is a commonly identified motivation for people to seek out Jesus. That experience of healing then becomes the basis for telling others of the goodness of God—potentially also the basis for extending that goodness, including forgiveness, to others. The experience of healing is one of the most powerful ways in which the general message of salvation in the gospels becomes recognized as truth *for me* (for the one being healed), a

---

[53] This emphasis on the moral obligation to forgive is similar to that in the Anglo-American philosophical discussion. However, that discussion does give explicit attention to the sense of self under the rubric of "self-respect" in a manner that does not show up in Volf and Jones.

truth that can reorient my personal matrix of meanings even to the point of motivating me to undertake forgiveness of those who have harmed me.

Finally, these aspects of Volf's and Jones's presentations of forgiveness arise from basement-level valuations in their theologizing: theological prioritizing they do not subject to critical analysis, but that is problematic in the postmodern era. The operative conviction that recognizing oneself as forgiven sinner is essential if the forgiving we extend is to be Christian, the nagging tendency to see "the world" exclusively as the "other" and as a threat to Christian self-understanding, the failure to recognize that Christians might be motivated to forgive out of an experience of the love of God that has not been understood reflexively in relationship to the forgiveness of one's sins, and the preference for a theological artic-ulation of Christian forgiveness that privileges the "from above" mode of thought—these theological inclinations are all interrelated in the matrices that undergird their accounts of forgiveness. These theological moves arise from and contribute to a fundamental valuation of humanity as "deserving the wrath of God."[54]

We have here the outlines of a theological matrix of meanings that possesses its own coherence. Stand within it and it makes sense. But call any of its major elements into question and it begins to crumble. Unfor-tunately, the postmodern ethos does challenge many of those elements. Moreover, the heavy stress laid on fundamental human depravity (all are deserving of the wrath of God) in Volf's and Jones's presentations (and others like them) appears to prevent them from acknowledging that Christians experience their relationship with God in other ways that might be equally (or even more powerfully) motivating toward un-dertaking forgiveness. Thus for the Christian living in a context shaped by postmodern sensibilities such accounts of Christian forgiveness will be inadequate.

A more penetrating analysis of the dynamics of human forgiveness, if integrated into an appropriately theological framework (or conversely,

---

[54] Volf, drawing on Luther's formulation, is perhaps more explicit than Jones in this formulation, but the theme of God's wrath occupies a prominent place in their theologies of God's forgiveness of us. It is the counterpart to the "judgment of grace" language men-tioned above. Both authors are of the mind that, in Jones's formulation, "God's judgment and even God's wrath are oriented toward grace and reconciliation" (Jones, *Embodying Forgiveness*, 255). See also, Volf, *The End of Memory*, 115; idem, *Exclusion and Embrace*, 298; idem, *Free of Charge*, 138. The theme of the wrath of God also runs through Brauns, *Unpacking Forgiveness*, 45–48, 125.

a theological framework that takes those dynamics seriously in its theologizing) could provide an account of Christian forgiveness that would more stably (coherently, persuasively) press its claims on the practice of faith of Christians living in the postmodern context. It could also open inquiry into potentially more effective pastoral strategies both for promoting forgiveness within the ecclesial context and for proclaiming it credibly in the wider world. Such an analysis *could* serve a maieutic function—midwifing the forgiving-resistant individual into embracing the grace of forgiveness and undertaking to forgive others—by imbuing the enactment of forgiveness with greater gravity within the constellation of meanings constituting the sense of self of the postmodern Christian.

To make this more explicit: if the preceding analyses of the deeper causes of resistance to forgiving and of lacunae in traditional accounts of Christian forgiveness hold, it becomes clear that in our postmodern context of meanings those accounts can no longer presume that the ground on which they rest is stable. The contextual reality of the postmodern ethos calls for a different rendering of the story, one that can be correlated with the experience of present-day Christians as that experience is appropriated within the postmodern ethos.

It has become apparent that the contemporary contexts of meaning in which we find ourselves have destabilized the ground on which authors like Volf and Jones stand when articulating Christian forgiveness. There is cause enough in this for a call to rethink Christian forgiveness. But before turning to that task of rethinking, we will need to look more closely at the adequacy of the theological contents of the traditional narrative and the particular variations on it represented by Volf and Jones. We must ask the question of theological coherence.

# Chapter 9

# Theologically Shaky Ground

## Preliminaries

The previous chapter uncovered some limitations in Volf's and Jones's diagnoses of and responses to contemporary obstacles to Christian forgiveness. It also pointed toward a connection between those limitations and their theological methods. In general terms we can say that thinking about Christian forgiveness "from above" has occluded insight into the theological significance of the human dynamics involved in any act of forgiveness.

But what of the theological contents presented in their accounts? Do they hold up? Can they bear the weight they are intended to? How stable are they? These questions will find their answers at the intersection of the Christian narrative and the motivations it is supposed to engender. Indeed, a closer look at the traditional theological account of Christian forgiveness, as represented in both Volf and Jones, exposes three additional places of instability. The first shows up in the narrative of the saving work of Christ that has become most prominent in Western Christianity: substitutionary atonement. The second and third lie in the realm of theological anthropology. The second locus of instability involves the account of the human transformation that is supposed to lead to acts of forgiveness, while the third is implicated in the theological language used to account for resistance to forgiving.

## Atonement Theory and the Violence of God

The language of atonement has occupied a prominent place in Christian reflection on the saving work of Christ (soteriology) since the earliest days of Christian history. The faith of the early community and the writings of Paul reflect the idea that Christ has saved humankind from the power of sin and death. His death on the cross has brought about our salvation. Atonement is the most common overarching metaphor used to explain the saving efficacy of Christ's passion, death, and resurrection.[1] In recent times, however, despite its presence in Christian scriptures, this way of naming the saving work of Christ has come under critical scrutiny.[2]

Stephen Finlan has made an important contribution to the critical analysis of atonement theories by carefully examining the various strands of diverse cultural practices represented in the New Testament uses of atonement-related metaphors. He has drawn attention to the fact that the language(s) and the cultic practice(s) behind what has developed into Christian understandings of atonement are of different kinds. When Paul appropriates the language of atonement, far from presenting a systematic, conceptually integrated theory, he employs multiple metaphors drawn from different cultic and cultural histories (Jewish and Hellenic) in order to communicate the message of salvation.[3]

Finlan identifies several strands of thought behind Paul's various formulations and metaphors. Two that have left their imprint most strongly in Paul's writings are evident in the language of sacrifice and in metaphors connected to expulsion rituals (the scapegoat).[4] Sacrificial imagery is of various kinds, but in relationship to sin, sacrifice refers to human efforts to appease and placate a God who is legitimately angry over one's conduct.[5] Expulsion rituals, by contrast, involve transferring the sin of the

---

[1] For a clear articulation of the pre-Christian cultic history of atonement in Judaism and its reception into Christian reflection on the saving work of Christ, see Stephen Finlan, *Problems with Atonement: The Origins of, and Controversy about the Atonement Doctrine* (Collegeville, MN: Liturgical Press, 2005).

[2] See, for example, S. Mark Heim, *Saved from Sacrifice: A Theology of the Cross* (Grand Rapids and Cambridge: Eerdmans, 2006); Robert J. Daly, "Images of God and the Imitation of God: Problems with Atonement," *Theological Studies* 68 (2007): 36–51; J. Denny Weaver, "Forgiveness and (Non)Violence: The Atonement Connections," *Mennonite Quarterly Review* 83 (April 2009): 319–47; Hans Boersma, "Being Reconciled: Atonement as the Ecclesio-Christological Practice of Forgiveness in John Milbank," 183–202, in *Radical Orthodoxy and the Reformed Tradition* (Grand Rapids, MI: Baker Academic, 2005); J. Denny Weaver, "Response to Hans Boersma," 73–79, in *Atonement and Violence: A Theological Conversation*, ed. John Sanders (Nashville: Abingdon Press, 2006).

[3] Finlan, *Problems with Atonement*, 39–62.

[4] See ibid., 31–38, 50–52, for discussion of expulsion rituals and their relationship to Paul's thought.

[5] Ibid., 17–18.

community onto an innocent party (scapegoat) that is then driven outside the community, carrying the sin with it.[6]

One understanding of atonement derived from these mixed metaphors in Paul's writings achieved virtually canonical status in the Middle Ages. Anselm's *Cur Deus Homo?* integrated the elements of sacrifice and expulsion of sin with aspects of feudal social norms in order to explain the saving work of Christ.[7] Humankind, in sinning against God, had committed an infinite offense. (The measure of the offense is not the deed but the dignity of the one offended.) This requires payment of satisfaction. But since humankind owes everything it has to the one offended, we have nothing to offer to make satisfaction. Moreover, even if we did have something of our own to offer, it would be finite, and so incapable of offsetting the infinite offense. Consequently, it was necessary that one of infinite dignity who was guilty of no offense should make satisfaction for us. Thus God had to become human to make the necessary sacrifice to save humanity from permanent alienation from God.[8]

This basic framework, later picked up and adapted by Aquinas, then became standard teaching in Western Christian soteriology (theory of salvation), ultimately finding its way into the theologies of Martin Luther, John Calvin, and subsequent Reformers, while also retaining a prominent place in Roman Catholic thinking.[9] But despite its status in the history

---

[6] Ibid., 32–38.

[7] Anselm, *Basic Writings: Proslogium, Monologium, Cur Deus Homo, Gaunilo's In Behalf of the Fool,* trans. Sidney Norton Deane (La Salle, IL: Open Court, 1962). In other words, Anselm theologized from within the shared matrix of meanings he inhabited in medieval Europe, drawing on his own culture's basement-level convictions to theorize on the second story about the ground-level conviction that Christ effects our salvation. A contemporary response to the critique of Anselm argues that his theology should not be interpreted against the horizon of the feudal culture in which it was written but that Anselm exhibits an "aneconomic" (non-exchange-based) understanding of the dynamics of salvation. Daniel M. Bell, Jr., "Forgiveness and the End of Economy," *Studies in Christian Ethics* 20, no. 3 (2007): 325–44. Whether Bell is correct or not, the common reception of Anselm that has shaped Christian understanding of Christ's saving work in Western Christianity does see this economic exchange as integral to Anselm's argument; hence the many critiques.

[8] This position is well summarized in Joseph Ratzinger, *Introduction to Christianity* (orig. New York: Herder & Herder, 1970; repr. San Francisco: Ignatius Press, 1990), 172–74.

[9] See Daly, "Images of God," 45. The language and motif of atonement permeate the works of Hans Urs von Balthasar, for example. See Hans Urs von Balthasar, *A Short Primer*

of Western theology, contemporary theologians have begun to criticize the deeper implications of atonement theories of salvation.

Two theologically neuralgic points stand at the center of the criticism. The first is that these theories are pervaded by violence. That Jesus suffered a violent death is undeniable. The criticism is that the versions of atonement theory that have taken hold in the West make the claim that God *required* the violent death of Jesus in order to grant forgiveness.[10] Moreover, since—*ex supposito*—Christ is innocent, God required the death of an innocent to compensate for the offense of the guilty. This makes God a moral monster![11] It also renders conceptually incoherent the claim that God's forgiveness of us serves as the foundation and pattern of the forgiveness we are called to extend to others. God imposes on us the obligation to forgive others without cost, yet God demands payment in order to forgive. To borrow language from Derrida, God's forgiveness operates on an economy of exchange, paid in violence. Why may Christian forgiveness not do so? In theories of substitutionary atonement the dynamic of God's relationship to us in the face of sin would not serve as a model for our own forgiving. Our forgiving is reduced to a response to an extrinsic (and seemingly arbitrary) command: "do as I say, not as I do." The claim that Christian practice is grounded in God's self-revelation in Christ begins to sound hollow.

---

*for Unsettled Laymen* (San Francisco: Ignatius Press, 1985), 77; idem, *Convergences to the Source of the Christian Mystery* (San Francisco: Ignatius Press, 1983), 55; idem, *The Christian State of Life* (San Francisco: Ignatius Press, 1983), 191. Von Balthasar critiques the critics of Anselm's theory in his *Theo-Drama: Theological Dramatic Theory*, vol. 3, *Dramatis Personae: Persons in Christ* (San Francisco: Ignatius Press, 1992), 240.

[10] See Heim, *Saved from Sacrifice*, 25–26; Daly, "Images of God," 45–46; Robert J. Daly, *Sacrifice Unveiled: The True Meaning of Christian Sacrifice* (London and New York: T & T Clark International, 2009), 110–13. René Girard has sharpened the discussion of the place of violence in the structuring of social relations and in religious beliefs through his penetrating analysis of mimetic rivalry and the mechanism of the scapegoat. René Girard, *Violence and the Sacred*, trans. Patrick Gregory (Baltimore, MD: Johns Hopkins University Press, 1977); René Girard, *Things Hidden Since the Foundation of the World*, trans. Stephen Bann and Michael Metteer (Stanford, CA: Stanford University Press, 1987); idem, *The Scapegoat*, trans. Yvonne Freccero (Baltimore: Johns Hopkins University Press, 1986). Heim's work on the theology of the cross employs this analysis to reexamine the significance of Christ's death as a sacrifice to end sacrifice. There are many natural points of intersection between Girard's work and the questions raised in the present study.

[11] See Heim, *Saved from Sacrifice*, 25.

Contemporary advocates of atonement theories attempt to soften the harshness of this inconsistency. As Finlan points out, these efforts pursue diverse strategies, from redefining the terms of the discussion to spiritualizing the doctrine or criticizing it overtly while still trying to retain its essentials,[12] but they still fail to contend with violence as an essential component of the dynamics.

Miroslav Volf is aware of this tension. In his own account he addresses this by arguing that the violence is the result of human choice enacted against God. God makes God's self the willing victim in Jesus.[13] This appears to be something of a theological shell game. "God isn't really punishing someone *other* than God because Jesus is the Incarnate Word of God." But the fact remains that, even in this version, God requires the violence. Even if it is foreknown as a contingent act of human freedom, God chooses it (in the common understanding of this theory) in order to effect the sacrifice. Violence remains essential to God's forgiveness.[14] As J. Denny Weaver observes, "Volf's understanding of God's forgiveness actually depends on prior divine punishment and a God who sanctions and employs violence."[15] Weaver makes a similar observation regarding L. Gregory Jones's proposal. That is, "his [Jones's] presentation of how God in Christ makes forgiveness possible follows the logic of a satisfaction atonement motif—namely, that the death of Jesus satisfies an attribute or need in the divine economy."[16] God somehow requires violence to set the world back on its intended course.

---

[12] Finlan, *Problems with Atonement*, 84–105.

[13] See Miroslav Volf, *Free of Charge: Giving and Forgiving in a Culture Stripped of Grace* (Grand Rapids, MI: Zondervan, 2005), 145. See also the discussion in J. Denny Weaver, "Forgiveness and (Non)Violence," 336–38. Heim takes a similar approach in the closing pages of *Saved from Sacrifice*, 321–29. However, Heim distances himself from claims about God's wrath or God's justice requiring repayment, locating the need for violence (à lá Girard!) in the dynamics of human mimetic rivalry and of scapegoating. Violence then becomes what God agrees to endure in Christ because *we* require it.

[14] Volf, *Free of Charge*, 144–45.

[15] Weaver, "Forgiveness and (Non)Violence," 335.

[16] Ibid., 333. My own reading is that Jones is ambiguous on this point. His emphasis on the Just Judge who is himself judged by us and then raised is not as obviously committed to the necessity of violence as Volf's account. However, his approving citation of Barth's language: "[Jesus'] decisive work and word has to be His suffering and dying" (citing *Church Dogmatics* IV/1, p. 257) at L. Gregory Jones, *Embodying Forgiveness: A Theological Analysis* (Grand Rapids, MI: Eerdmans, 1995), 124, and Rowan Williams's language of the "pure victim" (citing *Resurrection*, p. 15) at *Embodying Forgiveness*, 125,

A second reason satisfaction theories of substitutionary atonement have come under fire is that they diminish the theological importance of the Incarnation.[17] This doctrine, so central to the Christian proclamation, is commonly reduced in such theories to an ancillary status.[18] It serves only (or primarily) to make possible the eventual violent death and the subsequent resurrection, but it has little theological import in its own right within atonement theories. The manner in which the Incarnation itself might contribute to salvation, enact forgiveness, or promote reconciliation with God—apart from the atoning death—is neglected. Similarly, the whole of the public life of Jesus before the passion can serve as moral guidance, but in atonement theories its integral relationship to effecting salvation and the forgiveness of our sins is also obscured. Jones attempts to vitiate this problem via his emphasis on the trinitarian dynamics of salvation as revealed in time. But his response remains largely at the level of the (re)assertion of basic Christian beliefs. He does not explain how the Word become Flesh *by that fact* relates to God's forgiveness of humankind other than to pave the way for the passion.[19]

These two theological problems (the place of violence in accounts of atonement and the theological marginalization of the Incarnation) render the most common atonement theories problematic. They are theologically

---

give evidence that he might indeed see violence as a requirement of the divine economy. It should be noted, however, that Rowan Williams explicitly rejects any hint of a divine requirement of violence. Indeed, as he argues, "If God's love is shown in the pure victim, it is shown (as we have seen) as opposition to violence: so it is impossible to conceive of the Christian God identified with the oppressor in any relationship of violence." Rowan Williams, *Resurrection: Interpreting the Easter Gospel* (Cleveland: The Pilgrim Press, 2002), 9–10. Whether this is fully appreciated in Jones's appropriation of the phrase "pure victim" from Williams is a matter for further exploration.

[17] Finlan sketches the difficulties and distortions that can occur in this regard in *Problems with Atonement*, 117–20.

[18] As Daly argues, drawing on Finlan, the Incarnation is actually central to Christianity; without it, Christianity falls apart. Atonement theories, on the other hand, are "derivative," of secondary importance, yet in some (many) articulations of Christian self-understanding atonement has become foundational. See Daly, "Images of God," 40–43. It is not clear to me that Heim's Girardian articulation of a theology of the cross overcomes this difficulty.

[19] If the Incarnation is integrally related to the dynamics of God's own forgiving, and if God's way of forgiving is to be relevant to human dynamics of forgiving, it will be important to draw the connection between the becoming flesh of the Word of God in Jesus and the dynamics of human becoming in general. This will establish a more integral connection between the forgiveness revealed in Jesus and the forgiveness Christians are called to practice.

unstable; when pressed on these points they lose their coherence. They are thus shaky foundations for articulating and promoting a distinctive Christian forgiveness. We therefore have reason to rethink those theological foundations, but we need to do so in a way that reflects sensitivity to the theological problems just raised.

We need to consider, first, whether Christian forgiveness can be articulated in a manner that does not suggest that God requires violence in order to forgive humankind. This can then provide a stable basis for arguing that Christian enactment of forgiveness is an expression of the disposition of God toward the humanity with whom God desires communion. By implication this also entails that the Christian motivation to forgive will have to eschew appeals to violence (including the soft violence entailed in the threat of damnation by an angry God) as a means of coercing forgiving practice. (Both Volf and Jones already point in this direction by shifting the locus of decision leading to damnation away from God to the sinful exercise of freedom. We choose to reject God and to stay bound in alienation.[20] God respects that choice.) *That* one might be moved to undertake forgiving another on the basis of fear of damnation cannot be denied. But to incorporate such a threat into a Christian understanding of forgiveness would be to retain violence (in the form of coercion) as an integral motive force within the Christian proclamation itself.[21]

With respect to the Incarnation, in rethinking Christian forgiveness it will be important to explain how this central event in Christian faith is itself integrally related to the dynamics of Christian forgiveness, both God's forgiveness of us and our forgiveness of others. How does the Word becoming flesh stand with respect to God's enactment of forgiveness toward humankind? What role does it play in the forgiveness Christians are called to extend to those who "trespass against us"?

### Forgiveness and Personal Transformation

A second locus of theological instability in accounts of Christian forgiveness based on traditional atonement theories lies at the intersection of two complexes of issues as these confront contemporary postmodern horizons of understanding. How do we name the transformation the sinner undergoes in faith? Specifically, how does that transformation

---

[20] See Jones, *Embodying Forgiveness*, 121, 128.

[21] Volf and Jones have already made gestures in the direction of separating the threat of damnation from the idea that God acts so as to punish.

stand in relationship to our enactment of forgiveness? and how do we characterize the resistance to forgiving? These issues are interrelated in Volf's and Jones's presentations. In both cases, on both sets of issues, the presentations they provide teeter on the edge of a slide into mythology—that is, a story that relies on religious language that is not well correlated with the horizons of meaning by which we make sense of the rest of our lives.

### Naming the Transformation

Although they use different terms, both Volf and Jones write about a transformation the sinner must undergo in order to receive the forgiveness offered by God. Volf prefers the language of grace while Jones emphasizes the action of the Holy Spirit. In both approaches it is divine initiative that transforms us and thereby enables us to forgive. But what is this transformation? In what does it consist? How is it related to God's forgiveness of *me*? How does it relate to the forgiveness I am called to extend to others?

Volf approaches the question of forgiveness from within the framework set out by Martin Luther. Cautious to avoid the notion that we can initiate or earn our own salvation (Pelagianism), he elaborates his understanding of transformation by drawing on the language of the indwelling of Christ. The (unmerited) gift of faith opens us to receive the judgment of grace that we are sinners yet forgiven because of Christ. Through this faith we are united to Christ, receiving the benefits of forgiveness through the grace of repentance. This establishes us in a new life. As Volf explains, commenting on two passages from the letter to the Romans,

> The connection between these two rather different metaphors—the metaphor of passage to new life and the metaphor of putting on a new outfit—is this: Because we have died to our old selves and live as new selves indwelled by Christ, we should take off the old and clothe ourselves with the new. The unspoken assumption is that the old self is not quite yet dead and the new self is not yet fully alive. Taking off the old and putting on the new is an ongoing process of dying and rising.[22]

---

[22] Volf, *Free of Charge*, 59. The metaphor of the old self dying and the new self rising comes from Rom 6:1-11. The image of taking off the old self and putting on the new is from Rom 4:22-24.

By the grace of faith we undergo a transformation into a new life, but we also are set upon a path of ongoing transformation. This ongoing transformation is a result of the indwelling of Christ, that is, Christ living within us. This indwelling is the reason why God does not "count our sins to us but instead counts to us Christ's righteousness."[23] We are thus, in the language of Luther, "*simul iustus et peccator*"—at the same time justified and sinner.

The transformation involved at this point is in our relationship to God and our sense of self. God has established us in faith by grace. This faith unites us with Christ; we look to him alone for our justification. Knowing ourselves to be sinners, yet accepted by God on account of the righteousness of Christ and therefore justified, Volf argues, we should be grateful.[24] Thus we experience the transformation as a change of attitude, toward ourselves and toward God. But Volf also argues that it grounds a change of motivation, for this gratitude should then issue in generosity to others by forgiving them for their sins.[25] In this transformation several elements come together: the recognition that we are sinners, that we are judged for our sinfulness, and that we are forgiven; the indwelling of Christ; and gratitude for the gift of forgiveness. By these elements the relationship with God, the sinner's self-awareness, and the sinner's disposition toward others are transformed. So far, so good.

There are two loci of instability in this account. First, it is incomplete. Volf insists that the experience of ourselves as forgiven sinners *should* result in gratitude and then lead to generosity in forgiving others. In point of fact, it does not always do so. This is implicit in the recognition that the transformation is not complete but ongoing. But how this ongoing transformation works, what it changes within us, and how the indwelling of Christ beyond the initial experience of faith effects that transformation, or what we experience or recognize of the experience, and how that leads to an increase in the practice of forgiveness: these are left vague.

The second locus of instability appears in Volf's treatment of resistance to forgiving. It hinges, in part, on a disjunctive description of the life of Christ within us. This new life within us, granted as grace in the gift of faith, is the transformation that grounds our ability to forgive others. The sinful person gifted with the grace of faith, according to Volf's analysis, should be moved by the recognition that she has been forgiven by God

[23] Volf, *Free of Charge*, 150.
[24] See ibid., 45–46, 110.
[25] Ibid., 130.

to forgive generously those who offend her. If she forgives, it is the life of Christ within her that moves her to forgive. If she withdraws from forgiving, it is the presence of sin within her that convicts her of not receiving the grace of forgiveness from God. "For us to hold any offender captive to sin by refusing to forgive is to reject the reality of God's forgiving grace."[26]

There is a problem here. Volf addresses the non-forgiveness of others as a matter of *refusal* to forgive. This suggests the sinful exercise of human freedom. Moreover, he casts any such putative refusal in terms of a rejection of "God's forgiving grace." Within the logic of his theological matrix this comes perilously close to claiming that any instance of non-forgiveness of another indicates that we have not received the grace of faith that saves!

I do not believe that this is Volf's intent. However, the disjunction Volf's language introduces into his presentation of these dynamics makes his narration ambiguous. Moreover, it renders his account of the transformation unstable in two ways. First, it makes the language of "ongoing process" of transformation obscure, if not incoherent. Either we are transformed by faith so that we forgive others, in which case ongoing transformation is irrelevant to our forgiving others (does this mean that it touches some other dimension of our human experience?), or we demonstrate that we are not transformed and therefore that we have rejected God's forgiving grace. Volf traces out no middle ground that would make his language about transformation as an ongoing process meaningful.

Second, by only adverting to the "refusal" to forgive, Volf completely overlooks the implications of contemporary psychological research.[27] As we have already explored in chapters 3, 4, and 5, there are many forces at work within us that can impede our *ability* to forgive. We are internally divided in our motivations. Yet it is precisely the realm of motivations that needs to be transformed, and this will come about by means of a *conversion* as discussed in chapters 5 and 6 and as mentioned above. It can begin at one moment (for example, the graced moment of recognizing oneself as a sinner, but forgiven), but its implications may take a lifetime to work their way through a person's matrix of meanings. This would be the natural point to elaborate how the grace of faith initiates an ongoing process of transformation in our motivations, but to do so would require

---

[26] Ibid., 180.

[27] This is surprising, given his scholarly engagement with the thought of Freud and the problematic memory in Volf, *The End of Memory*, esp. 153–58.

delving more deeply than Volf has done into the struggle to forgive from the human perspective ("forgiveness from below").

An additional tension in Volf's presentation bears mentioning. It touches on the question of the human contribution to the process of transformation *as an ongoing process.* Do we contribute anything? Where does human freedom come into play? These questions arise in those instances in which Volf writes as though it *is* we who act in forgiving, as though our freedom *is* positively engaged, making a contribution to the graced movement of forgiveness as we labor to forgive others.[28] In keeping with Luther's teaching (also affirmed by the Catholic Church and other Christian denominations) that we cannot initiate any positive acts that can effect our salvation—or, better said, that our salvation is a gift we cannot earn and that we receive as grace—and in keeping with the "forgiveness from above" account he has presented, Volf devotes little attention to the human enactment other than to emphasize what we *should* do.

What he does not explore is how, in the ongoing transformation, our enactment of forgiveness toward others stands in relationship to the ongoing transformation itself. Certainly, he holds that the transformation of grace empowers us to forgive. But does our acting on that empowerment relate to our personal, ongoing transformation? If so, how? And how do we provide a theological account of the struggle to forgive in this process of transformation? Is there any theological way of discussing the struggle to forgive other than appealing to the language of sin? Is there no room here for talking about development and growth without lodging blame for its absence?

In fairness to Volf, it must be acknowledged that the issues raised here are at a different level of discourse than that of his intended readership. He is writing for the first floor. The questions I have raised are directed toward the basement level and their implications for the theorizing that takes place on the second floor. But they remain questions appropriate to the articulation of Christian forgiveness, an elaboration of the dynamics of its enactment, and claims about its distinctiveness.

L. Gregory Jones provides an alternative approach to understanding the transformation that takes place through faith. In many respects it is quite similar to Volf's, but Jones explores the question of transformation in a way that emphasizes the trinitarian dynamics of the process and the role of ecclesial pedagogy in promoting practices of forgiveness. Like

---

[28] See Volf, *Free of Charge*, 162, 165.

Volf, he sees the transformation in question as a matter of Christ living in the believer,[29] but his presentation places greater emphasis than Volf's on three other elements: the operation of the Holy Spirit in bringing about the transformation, the fact that the transformation occurs within an intentional process, and therefore, implicitly, the importance of human freedom in choosing to exercise ourselves in practices that will promote the transformation within us. On this basis he is then able to advocate practices that discipline Christians in the embodiment of forgiveness.

In the terms Jones uses, God reveals in the life, death, and resurrection of Jesus God's own judgment of grace on humankind. This judgment of grace confronts us with the reality of sin and our sin-distorted judgment. It discloses the pervasiveness of this sinfulness in human history. This is a universal judgment on humanity, but it is accompanied by the forgiving love of God who does not abandon us to sin, death, and destruction. Thus Christ is the revelation of both God's judgment on humankind and God's forgiving love.

It is the work of the Holy Spirit to make this universal truth particular in the life of the believer. The Holy Spirit works the transformation by which the sinner recognizes that she is judged for her sins, but nonetheless forgiven.[30] In the face of that judgment of grace, the sinner can then repent. The transformation and the recognition go together. Without the recognition and its consequent repentance, there is no transformation. Without the transformation there is no repentance in the recognition; instead, the recognition issues only in denial and redounds to condemnation. With the transformation, the recognition becomes endurable as a moment of grace. Forgiveness is not offered "in general"; it is being given to *me*. It is personal and particular.

This is what Jones refers to as the experience of "forgiven-ness."[31] I experience myself as having been forgiven. I have been liberated from the weight of past sin and can orient myself toward the future as one who has been forgiven.[32]

---

[29] Jones makes reference to the process of learning to appropriate and embody Christ (see Jones, *Embodying Forgiveness*, 128), and again, to the need to learn how to discern how to appropriate and re-present Christ (see ibid., 136).

[30] Ibid.

[31] See, for example, ibid., 66–67, 105, 121. The concept of "forgiven-ness" as a way of life for those who know that they have first been forgiven runs as a consistent theme through Jones's work.

[32] Ibid., 148.

Up to this point the transformation Jones describes is very similar to that of Volf. But Jones goes beyond Volf in elaborating the ongoing transformation that follows.

> As St. Paul reminds us, the Spirit transforms our past (and the world's past) for the sake of new life in the future (see in particular Romans 8). Further, because our forgiveness involves a recovery and redemption of the past, not its obliteration, we face the *ongoing task* of cultivating habits and practices that enable us to discern, in the Spirit, how we should appropriate Christ's forgiveness—and understand our ongoing call to daily repentance—in our particular lives and situations.[33]

As Jones argues, this appropriation is not a matter of passive receptivity of God's action,[34] nor is it a privatized and individualistic undertaking. It requires our active participation and cooperation as members of the Body of Christ, of the web of social relations called "church."[35] Initially we enter into the church via baptism. But the significance of baptism extends well beyond the moment of its occurrence. Baptism initiates a process of transformation into which we must live and that, as we are transformed by this "living into," enables us to continue the work of the Kingdom. That is,

> Through baptism, Christians are inducted into God's eschatological Kingdom through the pattern of Christ's death and resurrection (see

---

[33] Ibid., 157–58; see also 179.

[34] He observes (ibid., 163): "forgiveness is a habit that must be practiced over time within the disciplines of Christian community: This is so because, as I have been suggesting, in the face of sin and evil God's love moves toward reconciliation by means of forgiveness. Forgiveness aims to restore communion on the part of humans with God, with one another, and with the whole Creation. This forgiveness is costly, since it involves acknowledging and experiencing the painful truth of human sin and evil at its worst. In the midst of such brokenness, God's forgiveness aims at healing people's lives and re-creating communion in God's eschatological Kingdom.

"Even so, such healing and re-creating is not God acting wholly without us. They also invite, and require, our practices, which—by the guiding, judging, and consoling work of the Holy Spirit—enable us to witness to God's forgiving, re-creating work and to be transformed into holy people. To be involved in such practices is to engage the narrative of the Triune God's creative and re-creative work as Father, Son, and Spirit; likewise, to believe faithfully in the Triune God is to have our lives formed and transformed through participation in Christian practices."

[35] Ibid., 167.

Romans 6:1-11). As such, the resurrection of the Crucified One calls people to a baptismal repentance, a daily living into our baptism that occasions the transformation of relationships. Such transformed relationships break the cycles of violence and vengeance. The risen Christ—the Judge judged for us, the pure Victim sacrificed for us—returns to us his judges with a judgment that does not condemn but calls us to new life.[36]

The practices of the church are to promote this ongoing transformation into living the life of the Kingdom by forming us to live ongoing lives of repentance under the guidance of the Holy Spirit. This is a life lived out under the sign of forgiveness received and further extended to those we encounter. Other ecclesial practices also contribute to the promotion of forgiveness. Eucharist is chief among them. It provides a basis for understanding the context of Christian forgiveness by locating us within the story of Christ's ongoing redemptive work. Confession of sins, repentance, and the possibility of excommunication of the unrepentant pertain more directly to the ecclesial exercise of forgiveness.

In a more attenuated sense Jones also sees a relationship between forgiveness and practices of prayer and healing.[37] These practices help the Christian to experience herself as living within the ongoing Christian story. Drawing on the philosophical paradigm of an Aristotelian-Thomist virtue ethics, Jones argues that these practices, properly understood, can cultivate habits within us that can transform us into the forgiving holiness to which we (Christians) are called.[38] Presupposed, of course, is that it is the work of the Holy Spirit that guides us into these practices and effects the transformation in cooperation with our exercise of intentional acts (freedom). Through this transformation, effected at the intersection of the work of the Holy Spirit and our freedom by means of these intentional ecclesial practices, we then develop the capacity to discern what it would mean to enact forgiveness in the diverse particular circumstances that confront our daily lives. Thus, Jones summarizes,

---

[36] Ibid., 125; see also 167, 168, 184.

[37] This is summarized in ibid., 165–66. Specific treatment of the individual themes can be found as follows: Eucharist and forgiveness at pp. 175–82; the dynamics of confession, reconciliation, and excommunication within the context of a community committed to reconciling forgiveness at pp. 182–97; the relationship of forgiveness to practices of prayer and healing at pp. 197–204.

[38] See ibid., 218.

We learn to attend to the particular as we learn to become people of character, or, more precisely, as we learn to become holy. In the craft of forgiveness, this involves attending to the work of the Spirit as we seek—paradigmatically, in the context of Christian community—to discern what forgiveness entails in specific contexts and specific lives. Being initiated into the craft of forgiveness involves us in a twofold process: On the one hand, we are learning what it is about ourselves that needs to be transformed if we are to become holy people; on the other hand, we are learning how to diagnose and discern the craft of forgiveness in the situations and contexts that we and others face in the world around us. These two dimensions of our learning are distinct though inextricably interrelated.[39]

This formulation contrasts with Volf's account. Jones affirms and develops the importance of human freedom in cooperating with the work of the Holy Spirit. At the same time, by affirming that the work is from first to last under the guidance and influence of the Holy Spirit he avoids any hint of Pelagianism. Jones's presentation contrasts with Volf's further in that it provides a more detailed account of the transformation that occurs. Shifting the locus of the discussion from the indwelling of Christ who does or does not live in me to the action of the Holy Spirit who effects a communion with the triune God while leading us into holiness (a temporally extended process), Jones avoids the ambiguity and tension present in Volf's sometimes disjunctive language. Moreover, the emphasis on the Holy Spirit's work with and in us (and with and in the Christian community) recognizes the importance of human freedom in responding to the movement of the Spirit. We do positively cooperate with the movement of the Spirit, although the gift of the Spirit enables that cooperation. In drawing us to holiness the Spirit transforms our freedom so that it can exercise itself in ways increasingly reflective of God's own way of loving and forgiving. The transformation involved is therefore unambiguously dynamic, historically situated, and personally distinctive; it is interwoven with the dynamics of personal becoming.

Nevertheless, something is missing in this account. Jones does provide a theological description of how the transformation takes place (under the influence of the Holy Spirit and via the exercise of human freedom) *when* it does in fact take place. But it does not always occur. When it does occur, we do not always experience the transformation as straight-line

---

[39] Ibid., 227.

progress; it can come in fits and starts. This reality lies beneath Jones's desire to retrieve the "arcane disciplines."

Jones demonstrates great sensitivity to this complexity when he elaborates on the ways in which practices of forgiveness should be promoted. He consistently returns to the language of discernment. We need to discern the context in which the forgiving is to take place. We need to discern how forgiving is to be enacted in those conditions. We need to discern the particularity of what the Spirit is asking of us in forgiving.[40] This emphasis on discernment, and on growing in discernment, is critical to his emphasis on forgiving as a "craft" that must be developed. It also stands in relationship to his advocacy of finding "exemplars of the craft of forgiveness" who can serve as mentors in the development of the craft.[41]

There is much practical wisdom in Jones's discerning, pedagogical approach. It makes sense for any religious group to specify practices for the formation of its members in accord with the ideals it espouses. But something in this account leaves me uneasy. The promotion of practices does not necessarily lead to the *change in motivation* that would make the forgiving a specifically Christian practice. If full acceptance in a group requires the demonstration of certain practices, the motivation to enact those practices might simply be conformity for the sake of social belonging. A formation will certainly occur, but will it be the trans-formation of motivation that coheres with the Christian narrative as spelled out by Jones? Jones himself is aware that one can appear to be enacting forgiveness when not actually doing so. The same would be true of Christian forgiveness, given the schema he has articulated.[42]

---

[40] "My alternative presumes the necessity of ongoing discernment of what constitutes authentic forgiveness in the irreducibly diverse traditions and situations in which people find themselves." Jones, *Embodying Forgiveness*, 209.

[41] Ibid., 228.

[42] See Jones, *Embodying Forgiveness*, 262, where he observes, "However, Christians have tended to deny or repress either of these judgments (that we define our lives by what we hate and that we are tempted to create enemies in order to maintain our identities). We have wanted to deny the reality of such hatred (or desires for revenge), believing that the call to forgive *requires* us to deny that reality in the name of love and forgiveness. This results in cheap grace with untransformed passions, thoughts, and actions. Hence, through a curious irony, which Nietzsche was quick to note, too many Christians (and others) have linked together a repressed hatred and an ideology of forgiveness. The results, unsurprisingly, are devastating for everybody concerned: for those who inflict suffering and those who suffer, and more broadly, for our communities and our politics."

If the decisive element in distinctly Christian forgiveness is its motivation—an intentional engagement with the practice of forgiveness *because* one has recognized that the good news of God's forgiveness in Christ is offered to me personally (the acceptance of the judgment of grace)—then the theological justification for disciplinary practices will depend on demonstrating that they, in fact, produce *that* specific change in motivation as the basis for a change in behavior. But while Jones has provided an argument for the promotion of changes in behavior and has elaborated on the care with which they must be employed, the intrinsic connection between the theological narrative, the practices prescribed for promoting forgiving behaviors, and the internal transformation of the *motivations* necessary to produce specifically Christian forgiveness has not been presented. It has been assumed.

This raises the question whether Jones is overly sanguine about the positive outcomes of the processes for cultivating the embodiment of forgiveness he prescribes. Supposedly, retrieving those practices and explicating them from within the context of a more robust understanding of the trinitarian dynamics of the faith will foster the transformation of motivations (presupposing the action of the Holy Spirit, of course). But this claim, as reasonable as it sounds, is questionable. Is there any evidence to suggest that, when practiced in the past, those arcane disciplines actually made Christians—individually or collectively—more forgiving? Or, perhaps more to the point, is there any indication that these practices have effected change in motivations in the terms Jones's narrative specifies? The historical record on Christian practice does not immediately appear to support an affirmative response.

Moreover, even if the historical record were to support Jones's hopes, we have reason to question whether resurrecting those practices would be effective for the transformation of Christians living in our contemporary postmodern culture. In our present context those practices might not have the desired effect. Given the basement-level shifts in meaning identified in the previous chapter, it is also possible that a member of an ecclesial community will experience the renewal of such practices as alienating, demeaning, or irrelevant to the "real world."[43] Indeed, the perceived lack of relevance might have played a pivotal role in why the practices declined in the first place. Reinstating them or developing others without attention to the deeper level of meanings whose displacement charac-

---

[43] See the discussion of the shifts of meaning above.

terizes our present context could well create a situation in which the practices intended to foster the enactment of forgiveness are experienced as themselves coercive or violent.[44] Being forced to undergo some of the practices Jones prescribes, far from producing a greater transformation into the life of Christ, could simply inflict wounds. For the meaning of these practices is not determined exclusively by the stated intentions of those promoting them; it will always also be a function of the matrix of meanings from within which they are interpreted by the one who is pressed to undergo them.

Jones does not explore the possibility that promoting practices of repentance and forgiveness could go awry, and yet this is pivotal to his presentation, for, as with Volf, the issue is not just transformation of behavior; it is transformation of our motivations so that we will want to enact forgiveness *because* we have first been forgiven by God in Christ. Such a transformation will need to take place in the matrix of meanings that shapes our recognition of meaning in and response to harm,[45] but it will also require conversion at a deep level, in the alignment of meanings that are not directly accessible to our conscious life and that nonetheless still shape our behaviors. While it is true that the cultivation of good habits can effect changes in spontaneous inclinations shaping our behavior, it is not clear that such behavioral changes effect the change in motivation they are intended to produce. It might be that one is merely conforming to the standards of behavior required in order to remain in good standing in the group. According to Jones's premises, these would not be Christian motivations.

At this point it is important to note that I am sympathetic to Jones's project. He is attempting to mediate between the "from above" approach to the narrative of forgiveness and the "from below" on the level of the promotion of practice. This is a vital undertaking (although it is not my project). But Jones has approached it by merging two kinds of rationale. From above, he has taken a theological rationale for presenting the importance of forgiving. From below, he has adopted practices on the basis

---

[44] Jones is aware that disciplinary practices can have effects counter to those intended. This emerges in his discussion of punishment in *Embodying Forgiveness*, 272–73.

[45] Jones agrees with the point I am making here, but in a different context, when he observes that people internalize harm in different ways (*Embodying Forgiveness*, 72). His intent is to argue against the validity of using harm as an excuse to escape responsibility for one's own life. But the personal dynamics of recognition implied in his comments support the point I am making here.

of expediency toward attaining an end: cultivation of character in the practice of the virtue of forgiveness. The connection between the narrative and the specific practice(s) being promoted is extrinsic: a command to forgive. Particular practices are embraced on the basis of pragmatics. The theological warrant for these particular practices is missing. The link between such practices and changes in motivation needs to be more clearly drawn.

In part this discontinuity in the realms of discourse appears to be a function of a basement-level presupposition operating in Jones's personal theological matrix. It is the assumption that there is a discontinuity between the dynamics of divine forgiveness and reconciliation on the one hand, and the human dynamics of transformation on the other. They are not only understood to be of different orders (divine/human: grace/sin), but also of different kinds (self-emptying and forgiving/repentance). This makes weaving the two realms together into a coherent theological account of Christian forgiveness difficult. An alternative telling of the Christian narrative might overcome this problem, but if it is to advocate for promotion of specific disciplinary practices in a theologically coherent way that overcomes the gap between "from above" and "from below" approaches to forgiveness it will also need to provide a theological account for the loci—not just social, but also individual—of resistance to forgiving and the *meanings* that sustain that resistance. These are the places where transformation needs to occur.

### Naming the Loci of Resistance to Forgiving

This brings us to a third theological stumbling block in the accounts presented by Volf and Jones, one rooted in theological anthropology: the origin(s) within the person of her resistance to forgiving. Volf and Jones both recognize that we do experience resistance to forgiving; this reality is the provocation for writing their books. But their explorations into the origins of that resistance are limited. In part the resistance can be attributed to the influences of culture that undermine the extent to which we value forgiveness or imagine it as a viable response to experiences of harm (sin). Volf goes further by making the claim that our resistance is a reflection of our rejection of God's forgiveness. This is an expression of the power of Sin within us. Jones is ambiguous on this point. However, the limited attention to human dynamics of forgiveness in both authors does not provide us with alternative ways of understanding this resistance other than "sin."

However, it is questionable whether "sin" is a fully adequate way of accounting for this experience of resistance. As the analysis of human resistance to forgiving in chapter 5 brought to light, we are not as free to determine our course of action as we might want to think. Some of this unfreedom is simply a function of our humanity. As human—as body-spirit realities who are in the process of personal becoming over time—we are unable to completely dispose of ourselves in any finite act of willing or choosing. We live (and become) with a built-in resistance to any individual exercise of freedom (hence the temporal duration of the process of becoming).[46] Even if we do choose to affirm the call to forgive in this instant, our forgiving will not be complete; resistance to that choice and its implications can emerge at a later time. The completeness of our acts of forgiveness comes only with time and with continual reaffirmation of the commitment.

---

[46] The point being made here follows the elaboration of concupiscence in Karl Rahner, "The Theological Concept of Concupiscencia," *Theological Investigations 1*, trans. Cornelius Ernst (New York: Crossroad, 1982), 347–82. Although our individual acts of freedom intend fullness and completeness, they do not attain it. Rahner presents this as a function of the tension between nature and person, but his argument supports the formulation here presented in terms of personal becoming. He observes, "The free act does indeed dispose of the whole subject, in so far as it is as free act an act of man's personal centre, and so, by the root as it were, draws the whole subject in sympathy with it. And yet man's concrete being is not throughout its whole extent and according to all its powers and their actualization the pure expression and the unambiguous revelation of the personal active centre which is its own master. In the course of self-determination, the person undergoes the resistance of the nature given prior to freedom, and never wholly succeeds in making all that man is into the reality and the expression of all that he comprehends himself to be in the core of his person. There is much in man which always remains in concrete fact somehow impersonal; impenetrable and unilluminated for his existential decision; merely endured and not freely acted out. It is this dualism between person and nature, insofar as it arises from the dualism of matter and spirit and not from man's finitude, the dualism of essence and existence and the real distinction of his powers given with it, that we call concupiscence in the theological sense" (369). It is important to note, however, that this understanding of concupiscence is not rejecting the traditional Catholic understanding of mortal sin. One could still, in principle, consciously commit oneself to a serious course of action which one knows to be serious and counter to the will of God with such a resoluteness that one rejects the grace of salvation. The articulation of concupiscence accounts for the possibility within our nature of repentance (grace being presupposed). Further elaboration on the doctrine of mortal sin is beyond the scope of the present inquiry.

It is true that we can willfully and actively oppose God's call to forgive. This is a realistic possibility and would, from a Christian perspective, be an expression of sin. But even in that refusal to forgive, it is not certain that all the forces within us (or even *any* of them) that resist the call are oriented as they are because of sin, nor is it clear that sin is the only theologically relevant category for understanding resistance. It is certainly questionable whether from the standpoint of helping people to grow in their disposition to and practice of forgiveness it is the most illuminating.[47]

There are dynamics at work in any of our choices that are beyond our direct volitional control and are not necessarily functioning as they do because of sin. Indeed, the insights of modern psychology have drawn our attention to the many layers of psychic processes at work in each of us. Some of them are accessible to conscious reflection; some are not. Some may be directly aligned in relationship to a particular intention by an act of will; others may not. We simply are not fully at our own disposal in any decision. Some of our resistance to any possible course of action is merely an expression of what it means to be the human persons we are. The exclusive attribution of this resistance to "sin" (whether Sin in the world as the state of "fallenness" that has embedded itself in the structures and dynamics of human relationships or individual sins) is no longer adequate to the nuances of understanding now available to us. To rely exclusively on sin as the only way to explain our resistance to forgiving when we live in a world characterized by the dislocations of meaning identified above is to render the Christian account of forgiveness increasingly mythological in this postmodern age.

### A Broader Landscape of Christian Forgiveness?

Both Volf and Jones are aware of a broader landscape of psychological literature on forgiveness. Why do they not draw on those insights to elaborate on the resistance to forgiving? In part this may be a reflection of deficiency in the shared Christian matrix of meanings itself. Within the Christian narrative, forgiveness is discussed only as directed to sin. But is this a necessary restriction?

We observed a parallel issue in the moral philosophical and psychological discussions insofar as they sought to restrict the language of for-

---

[47] It can, in fact, function in a way analogous to blaming victims for the crimes they have suffered. See Jones, *Embodying Forgiveness*, 118.

giveness to specifically moral harms. In chapter 5 our analysis of the dynamics of forgiveness led to the conclusion that we can, and often do, enact the same dynamics in relationship to non-moral harms that we enact in relationship to moral harms. Forgiveness is not just for moral offenses. So also, in a Christian context, forgiveness might be intended for more than just sin.

Does the parallel hold for Christian forgiveness? Volf and Jones have not argued against the idea of forgiving what is not sin; it appears that the notion never occurred to them.[48] Whether an understanding of forgiveness for experiences other than sin can be articulated appropriately within a Christian matrix of meanings is an open question. However, two considerations do point in that direction. The first has to do with the understanding of "sin." As Fraser Watts points out, the way we presently read scriptural texts on forgiveness through a moralistic lens reflects a very different understanding of sin than was operative at the time the texts were written.

> The key difference is that forgiveness is now understood much more moralistically than it is in either the Old or New Testaments. Christianity is much less concerned with morality, as it is conventionally understood, than is normally assumed. Moralism is not necessarily a virtue or a blessing; on the contrary, it can be a problem. As Pelz and Pelz (1963) say, it can be our "subtlest camouflage, for it keeps us preoccupied with a few symptoms while the rot spreads" (p. 116). As the New Testament sees it, moral failings are simply not the main issue, whereas forgiveness addresses our real needs and deepest problems.[49]

While forgiveness is addressed to "sin" in the New Testament, "sin" entails the full range of realities not ordered according to God's desires for us and our world. It need not entail moral culpability as currently understood, although it often does. A contemporary approach to approximating the distinction implied by Watts is to distinguish "Sin," as a condition of the world that arises from past sinful choices and exerts pressure to recapitulation of such choices, from "sins" as individual morally culpable

---

[48] Jones does appear to draw near to this possibility when he writes (*Embodying Forgiveness*, 235–36) about forgiving injuries of minor importance.

[49] Fraser Watts, "Christian Theology," 50–68, in *Forgiveness in Context: Theology and Psychology in Creative Dialogue*, ed. Fraser Watts and Liz Gulliford (London and New York: T & T Clark, 2004), at 54, citing Werner and Lotte Pelz, *God Is No More* (Philadelphia and New York: J. B. Lippincott Company, 1964), 120.

decisions or actions.[50] Volf and Jones employ this schema. But the question remains whether there is more to forgiveness—God's forgiveness of us and the forgiveness Christians are called to extend to others—than simply responding to morally culpable actions.

Second, in chapter 6 we noted that, on the purely human level, people enact in relationship to non-moral harms the same dynamics involved in forgiving moral harms. On the basis of the phenomenon of this enactment we concluded that forgiveness can be directed toward non-moral harms. Presumably Christians operate in the same way. The question, then, is whether when Christians enact forgiveness toward non-moral harms it would be, properly speaking, an enactment of *Christian* forgiveness. According to the analyses of Volf and Jones, as long as the enactment is motivated by gratitude arising from the recognition that one has been forgiven by God, it would seem that Christian forgiveness of non-moral harms would be possible.

We shall return to the question of Christian forgiveness of non-moral harms in the next chapter. The present point is simply that the question of Christian forgiveness may take us onto a broader landscape than is commonly envisioned. Indeed, it leads us into a realm where the insights arising from our phenomenological description of forgiveness must be integrated into the telling of the Christian narrative itself. We will need to weave together our understanding of the Divine action in forgiving us, the transformation that occurs within us in forgiving, the place of both dynamics in the unfolding of God's Kingdom in time, and the dynamics of human personal becoming as they relate to the question of human enactment of forgiveness. In other words, we will need to rethink Christian forgiveness.

## The Challenge of this Broader Landscape

To bring about this integration of Christian forgiveness with the description of forgiveness as a basic human enactment presented in chapter 6 should be relatively simple. But there is a catch. Integrating insights drawn from secular disciplines into Christian self-understanding can

---

[50] See the discussion in Roger Haight, "Sin and Grace," 375–430, in *Systematic Theology: Roman Catholic Perspectives*, ed. Francis Schüssler Fiorenza and John P. Galvin (Minneapolis: Fortress Press, 2011), esp. 396–98. Pope John Paul II, *On Social Concern* (*Sollicitudo Rei Socialis*), Encyclical Letter (Boston: St. Paul Books and Media, 1984), nos. 36–38, develops this same line of thought.

challenge articulations of Christian self-understanding. Christians of the second and third centuries wrestled with the extent to which pagan philosophy could be used to explicate Christian doctrine. The same issue resurfaced when Aquinas appropriated Aristotle into his theology (a move Martin Luther roundly condemned during the Reformation).[51] And it lives on today.

Jones exhibits a present-day sensitivity to this concern when he discusses the use of philosophy and other disciplines in Christian theology. But unlike Luther in his invective against Aristotle, Jones is quite open to the possibility that Christian understanding and practice of forgiveness can be enriched by dialogue with these other disciplines.

> Philosophical investigations, as well as psychological, social, political, and other forms of inquiry, are crucial to our craft of continually clarifying and deepening our understandings and practices of forgiveness. For example, such investigations are important when philosophers carefully distinguish between, say, forgiveness and condoning, when psychologists investigate patterns of individuation and connection and the diverse problems that often diminish and destroy people's abilities to foster and sustain relationships, and when social and political theorists analyze the ways in which economies and structural systems produce and replicate patterns and practices that undermine people's capacity for communion with one another.[52]

Nevertheless, Jones argues, the appropriation and integration of these disciplines into a Christian understanding of forgiveness must take account of the fact that their findings are embedded in "traditions" (I would say "matrices of meanings") that might conflict with preexisting articulations of fundamental Christian convictions.[53] Therefore they must be measured

---

[51] "[Luther] fiercely resented Aquinas precisely because he blamed him for introducing Aristotle into Christian theology. And of Aristotle, Luther wrote: 'This defunct pagan has attained supremacy; impeded, and almost suppressed, the Scriptures of the living God. When I think of this lamentable state of affairs, I cannot avoid believing that the Evil One introduced the study of Aristotle.'" Roger Haight, *The Experience and Language of Grace* (New York: Paulist Press, 1979), 82. Haight is quoting Luther from "An Appeal to the Ruling Class of German Nationality as to the Amelioration of the State of Christendom," in *Martin Luther: Selections from His Writings*, ed. John Dillenberger (Garden City, NY: Doubleday Anchor, 1961), 470–71.

[52] Jones, *Embodying Forgiveness*, 224.

[53] Ibid., 225.

against their coherence with the life of communion to which we are called by the Triune God.[54]

This brings us back to a tension mentioned above, between the clarity of Christian identity, preserved from distortion, and the surrounding world (or culture). The caution Jones raises is legitimate; we have an imperative to sift and discern the insights we appropriate from non-Christian sources into our self-articulation as Christians. However, if the Christian message is to find a hearing among those who inhabit worlds shaped by multiple, competing matrices of meanings, then the presentation of the Christian message must credibly engage with and potentially *learn from* those other matrices of meanings, those non-Christian sources, whether the traditions they are embedded in cohere with the understanding of the Triune God or not.[55] This is particularly true when those disciplines give us greater understanding of the human condition. Such traditions can challenge us to dig more deeply into the Christian terrain on which we stand. This might lead to a more deeply held conviction regarding the rightness of our current way of naming what it means to be Christian, but it might also challenge us to purify the way we think about, name, and embody the Spirit of Christ. Both results are possible. Both have occurred in the past. It is reasonable to expect that both will occur again in the future. The question is how we are to proceed.

### Next Steps in the Christian Landscape

We began this chapter with the question whether the traditional account of Christian forgiveness, as represented by Volf and Jones, is sufficiently stable to make sense of the language of Christian forgiveness. Our exploration has brought into focus problems in the traditional narrative of substitutionary atonement as well as limitations in the understanding of the ways both Volf and Jones attempt to name the experience of transformation the Christian undergoes in being moved to enact forgiveness toward others. We also uncovered limitations in their theological frameworks both for naming the encounter with resistance to forgiving and for identifying the loci of that resistance.

Two persistent lacunae repeatedly surfaced in our explorations: an overemphasis on approaching Christian forgiveness "from above" and

[54] Ibid.

[55] Fraser Watts discusses Jones's lack of interest in dialogue between theology and psychology. See Watts, "Christian Theology," 5.

a corresponding neglect of theological attention to the human dynamics of enacting forgiveness. These two lacunae, seen in relationship to basement-level shifts in meaning in the present (postmodern) cultural shared matrix of meanings, lend these theological accounts of Christian forgiveness and its distinctiveness a mythological character. The narrative of why one should forgive has little connection with what one is actually undertaking when forgiving. Thus the meanings embedded in the narrative appear to exist in a different realm from that in which we live the rest of our lives.

The course of this chapter suggests that we do indeed need to rethink Christian forgiveness. We need to find a way to present the Christian narrative that can justify the language of a distinctive Christian enactment of forgiveness, that is theologically coherent, that makes sense within the contemporary postmodern horizon of meanings, thereby avoiding a deterioration into mythology, and that addresses the lacunae just named. That is the task of the next chapter.

# Chapter 10

# Reorienting in the Landscape of Christian Forgiveness

## Preliminaries

The preceding two chapters have drawn our attention to what I have called unstable ground in the land of Christian forgiveness. They have called into question the adequacy of traditional approaches to naming Christian forgiveness and thereby indicated the need to rethink Christian forgiveness itself. In the process, chapters 8 and 9 highlighted for our inquiry some of the criteria that will be essential to this rethinking. To put it succinctly, a more adequate account of Christian forgiveness must: (1) be grounded in the Christian narrative, (2) be responsive to the basement-level shifts in meaning brought about by the emergence of the postmodern ethos, (3) be theologically coherent, and (4) correlate with human experience as that is currently understood.

Beyond those basic criteria there is one more that is essential to this investigation. We need an account of Christian forgiveness that can help us to resolve whether there is something distinctive about it. Is there a distinctive Christian forgiveness? The approaches presented by Miroslav Volf and L. Gregory Jones suggest that there is. It resides in the motivation to forgive. But the way they have articulated the motivational dimension of Christian forgiveness has raised its own questions. It does not correlate well with the broad range of Christian experience, nor does it clearly indicate whether Christian enactments of forgiveness involve *doing* anything distinctive. Is the only difference between Christian forgiveness and other expressions of forgiveness located in the motivation?

This question has been the guiding star of our path across the distinctive landscapes of forgiveness. We shall take it up directly in the next chapter, but to do so we will need a theological account of forgiveness that meets the criteria of adequacy just named. Providing such an account is the task of this chapter, but to arrive at such an account will require that we reorient ourselves in the landscape of Christian forgiveness. Many of the landmarks will remain the same as in the traditional telling of the narrative, but by viewing them from a different position we will discover resources for addressing our question that had previously lain hidden. Two distinct shifts in focus define the reorientation that will take us forward. They are interrelated.

## Two Shifts in Perspective

The first shift is in the kinds of questions we will be asking. In the traditional accounts of Christian forgiveness as presented in Volf and Jones, the fundamental link between the Christian narrative and the forgiveness Christians are to practice resides in the distinctive Christian motivation to forgive. Both Volf and Jones employ the narrative (and their own retelling of it) in order to indicate the proper Christian motivation. That motivation is directly linked to the explicit content of the narrative itself. The answers their accounts provide revolve around God forgiving us in Christ by his death on the cross.

Some of the problems with these approaches have already been identified in the previous chapter, but there is a further issue that impinges on the shift in the kinds of questions we need to ask. The traditional accounts of Christian forgiveness presuppose that the meaning of "forgiving" is clear. If we take the "forgiveness" described in substitutionary atonement accounts as our norm, then forgiving means exacting a price to satisfy our offended honor in order to allow relationships to resume. But this is precisely what Jesus—the incarnate Word of God, the revelation of God in human form—did *not* do. So what does it mean to forgive? What are we *doing* (what is God doing) when we (or God) undertake(s) to forgive? Therefore the first shift in focus will not ask about the fact of God's forgiveness, nor will it initially ask about the "how" of God's forgiveness (although this will be addressed), nor will it emphasize whether, why, or under what conditions we should (or should not) forgive.

The questions we shall pursue will parallel those posed to the philosophical and psychological discussions in part 2. We shall ask about the formal characteristics of the enactment. What is God doing in relationship to us when God enacts forgiveness? This question is intimately related with another that provides the basis for the content of our answer to the first. What is Jesus doing when Jesus forgives? We will be asking about God's *enactment* of forgiveness toward us as that is revealed in Jesus' *enactments* of forgiveness. This will provide us with insight into the forgiveness Christians are called to enact toward others.

Changing the focus of our questions, however, will not be enough. We will also need to refocus our theological starting point. The traditional account views the story of Christian forgiveness, understandably enough, through the lens of Sin: the human experience of alienation from God, neighbor, and creation itself. This draws our attention to the forgiveness we need and receive from God. This is then taken as foundational to the forgiveness we are to extend to others, yet it is precisely this starting-point that can so easily reduce the Incarnation to a necessary precursor to the passion.

An alternative account, preserved in the Christian East and retrieved for the West by such theologians as Karl Rahner, urges us to start instead with God's desire to give God's self to us in love.[1] This is the reason for creation itself. It is important to note in this context that substitutionary atonement theories are not essential to the Christian narrative. As S. Mark Heim points out, "Such a view [substitutionary atonement] has never been prominent in the Eastern Christian church, and it was not the dominant view in the Western church for the first half of its history."[2] Eastern Christian theologians hold that God would have become

---

[1] Karl Rahner, *Foundations of Christian Faith: An Introduction to the Idea of Christianity* (New York: Seabury, 1978), 120. As Rahner writes (p. 123): "The spiritual essence of man is established by God in creation from the outset because God wants to communicate himself: God's creation through efficient causality takes place because God wants to give himself in love. In the concrete order man's transcendence is willed to begin with as the realm of God's self-communication, and only in him does this transcendence find its absolute fulfillment. In the only order which is real, the emptiness of the transcendental creature exists because the fullness of God creates this emptiness in order to communicate himself to it."

[2] S. Mark Heim, "Cross Purposes: Rethinking the Death of Jesus," *Christian Century* (22 March 2005): 20–25, at 20, 22. The issue is at the heart of a current debate about the proper meaning of sacrifice in a Christian context. For further information, see S. Mark Heim, "Christ Crucified: Why Does Jesus' Death Matter?" *Christian Century* (7 March 2001): 12–17; idem, "No More Scapegoats: How Jesus Put an End to Sacrifice," *Christian Century* (5 September 2006): 22–29; idem, *Saved from Sacrifice: A Theology of the Cross* (Grand Rapids and Cambridge: Eerdmans, 2006); and Robert J. Daly, "Images of God and the Imitation of God: Problems with Atonement," *Theological Studies* 68 (2007): 36–51; idem, "New Developments in the Theology of Sacrifice," *Liturgical Ministry* 18 (Spring

incarnate even if there had never been sin.[3] Incarnation, in Eastern theological matrices, is seen as the culmination of creation itself and the fullest expression of God's desire for communion with humankind. From the human perspective the reality of sin changes the significance of the Incarnation for us, but the *logos* (order, plan, intention) of the created order always included the Incarnation, independently of human sinfulness.

If we reorient ourselves on the theological landscape in accord with these two shifts in perspective we can formulate a theological postulate to guide our further exploration. The God who created us in order to be able to give God's self to us in love also made created reality so that it could be the bearer or medium of this divine self-gift. Finite reality— creation—has been made in such a way that God can use it (and does!) to communicate a humanly transformative, saving encounter with the absolutely transcendent Creator. To put this into a Catholic idiom, God has made created reality such that it can be *sacramental*.

Two cautionary notes are in order here. First, the word "sacramental" can be problematic. It can, by association with the sacramental rituals of Christian communities, suggest the idea of a "special" experience, set apart from the daily order. Sacraments, after all, are celebrated in sacred rituals in spaces that are set apart from the ordinary, profane world (churches). Their specialness is, to some extent, a function of their having been distinguished from ordinary life. This is precisely *not* what the present use of "sacramental" intends. It points in the opposite direction. As the exposition below will clarify, the everyday, ordinary stuff of life *is* sacramental—is the medium of encounter with God—even though it

---

2009): 49–58; idem, "Sacrifice Unveiled or Sacrifice Revisited: Trinitarian and Liturgical Perspectives," *Theological Studies* 64 (2003): 24–42; idem, *Sacrifice Unveiled: The True Meaning of Christian Sacrifice* (London and New York: T & T Clark International, 2009).

[3] This line of thought receives an early articulation in Irenaeus of Lyons's theology of the Incarnation as a "recapitulation of creation" and its fulfillment. It is correlated with an understanding of salvation "primarily as communication of and participation in divine life (2 Peter 1:3-4), not primarily as forgiveness of sins. Salvation is the perfection of Creation" (John P. Galvin, "Jesus Christ" 255–314, in *Systematic Theology: Roman Catholic Perspectives*, ed. Francis Schüssler Fiorenza and John P. Galvin [Minneapolis: Fortress Press, 2011], at 275). It resurfaced as a fundamental difference of soteriological orientation between the Thomists and the Scotists in the Late Middle Ages. "The Scotists hold the opposite [to the Thomists] position: the Word would have become flesh even if Adam had not sinned. The motive of the incarnation is the perfection of creation. While not denying that Christ in fact overcame sin, the Scotists see this as a subordinate effect, accomplished in the process of fulfilling God's original design" (Galvin, "Jesus Christ," 278).

does *not* seem particularly religious or special. This is one of the fundamental implications of the doctrine of the Incarnation: God enters into
the reality of human experience, even in its most tawdry ordinariness.

Second, the approach taken here has implications touching on approaches to many branches of theology—Christology, Soteriology, Grace,
Ecclesiology, and Eschatology prominent among them. To do justice
to these implications would require several additional volumes. What
follows will therefore necessarily be in the form of a sketch, touching on
these various theological disciplines insofar as it is helpful toward addressing our ultimate question regarding the distinctiveness of Christian
forgiveness.

## A Sacramental Cosmos, A World of Grace

Understood in relationship to our first shift in focus—the different
kinds of questions to be asked—the idea of a sacramental cosmos can
provide us with a way to approach the question of Christian forgiveness
that is profoundly different from (but not necessarily in conflict with)
that elaborated in the traditional accounts. It will focus our attention on
a dynamic, mediated encounter and its distinguishing characteristics.
Here we will be asking about what God and Jesus are mediating to us in
forgiving and what we are mediating to others when enacting Christian
forgiveness. This line of inquiry will, in its turn, clarify for us what "forgiving" means in this context. As a next step in this line of inquiry we
shall dig more deeply into this notion of "sacramentality."

### Sacraments and Sacramentality

To contemporary theologians the concept of sacramentality invoked
here is fairly self-evident. It has not always been so. Indeed, for the popular imagination sacramentality has to do with the ecclesial sacraments
(the number varies according to the ecclesial group). It refers to the effect
of grace that the sacramental action is intended to signify (and bring
about) for the person of faith.[4] For Catholic Christians in the period

---

[4] There are important variations in the theologies of sacraments among the distinctive
Christian denominations. The understanding of the relationship between the signification
and the effect associated with it varies significantly from the Catholic to the Lutheran
to the Reformed traditions. The basic point indicated here is the association of an effect
of grace with the celebration of the sacrament in the ritual.

before the Second Vatican Council the church was popularly understood to be sacramental because it "had" the sacraments. The sacramentality of the church was derived from the fact of the sacramental enactments.

## FUNDAMENTAL REVERSALS IN THE THEOLOGY OF GRACE

In the decades before Vatican II, penetrating theological research brought about a reversal in this commonplace understanding. Ground-breaking studies by Yves Congar, Henri de Lubac, Otto Semmelroth, and Karl Rahner led to the realization, enshrined in Vatican II's *Lumen Gentium,* that the fundamental nature of the church itself is sacrament.[5] Edward Schillebeeckx further developed this insight, using the theology of Thomas Aquinas to affirm the sacramentality of Christ himself.[6] Further, the individual sacraments are sacramental—have their graced effects—because they are expressions of the self-realization of the church's own nature.[7]

This reversal in the understanding of the relationship between sacraments and the sacramentality of the church rests in turn on a revolution in theological thinking about grace itself. Earlier generations of theologians had focused attention on the created effects of grace, thought of in terms of discrete irruptions of divine power into the "natural" realm.[8] Particularly

---

[5] See, for example, Yves Congar, *The Mystery of the Church* (Baltimore: Helicon Press, 1960); Henri de Lubac, *The Splendour of the Church,* trans. Michael Mason (London and New York: Sheed and Ward, 1956); Otto Semmelroth, *Die Kirche als Ursakrament* (Frankfurt: Josef Knecht, 1953); Karl Rahner, *The Church and the Sacraments,* QD 9 (New York: Herder and Herder, 1963). Josef Meyer zu Schlochtern, *Sakrament Kirche: Wirken Gottes im Handeln der Menschen* (Freiburg: Herder, 1992) provides a penetrating analysis of the emergence and development in the concept of the church as sacrament from preconciliar discussions up to the mid-1980s.

[6] Edward Schillebeeckx, *Christ the Sacrament of the Encounter with God* (Kansas City, MO: Sheed and Ward, 1963).

[7] See, for example, Karl Rahner, "Understanding the Priestly Office," 208–13, in idem, *Theological Investigations* 22 (New York: Crossroad, 1991), 210. The status of "because" in this statement requires nuance. The faith conviction is that the graced effect results from God's fidelity to God's own action in and through the church. Thus the grace to which the church witnesses and that comes to effective expression in and through the church is not a function of human manipulation of God, but of God's own freely bestowed self-gift in the church as the ongoing, historical sign and instrument of that self-gift.

[8] This revolution in thinking, itself a retrieval of neglected aspects of a fuller tradition, runs throughout Karl Rahner's understanding of grace as attested, for example, in Karl Rahner, "The Concept of Mystery in Catholic Theology," 36–73, in idem, *Theological In-*

in a Catholic context, the association of distinctive effects with specific sacraments may have contributed to a popular sensibility in which grace was to be encountered primarily, if not exclusively, in discrete, usually ritual events. The grace of the sacraments was understood in terms of its ability to outfit the faithful to confront the (presumably graceless) rest of life.[9] Sacraments functioned in the imagination in a manner analogous to batteries, providing power that had to be frequently recharged.[10] This, in turn, reinforced the idea that "grace" referred to a created entity other than God, something that could be used.

In the mid-twentieth century serious theological reflection called the underlying assumptions of this worldview into question, on two fronts. First, theologians began to direct their attention away from emphasis on what has been called "created grace." This expression refers to the created effects arising from the enactment of the sacraments (as well as other

---

*vestigations* 4, trans. Kevin Smyth (London: Darton, Longman & Todd, 1966), at 65–67; Karl Rahner, "Remarks on the Dogmatic Treatise '*De Trinitate,*'" 77–102, in *Theological Investigations* 4, at 81. He names the prevailing theological attitude this revolution in thinking addresses when he observes: "In a word, the relationship between nature and grace is conceived in such a way that they appear as two layers so carefully placed that they penetrate each other as little as possible." Karl Rahner, "Nature and Grace," 165–88, in idem, *Theological Investigations* 4, at 167.

[9] "How does the average Catholic Christian feel about a sacrament as he customarily receives it? We might describe this act of receiving (though of course with the provisos already mentioned) as follows: the Christian feels that he lives in a secular world. He is aware that his life in this world is subject to commandments of God which are difficult to fulfil. He is aware of being summoned by God and set upon a course which leads him out of this present life through the gates of death and beyond into the eternity of God. He has to maintain union with God, his true future and the law-giver presiding over his life even in the present. He passes to and fro from this secular world into a sacral sphere, a 'fanum' or 'temple.' It is only here (and in a true sense exclusively here, so far as his personal feelings are concerned, whatever his head may tell him from its stock of theological knowledge) that it is possible to achieve any real encounter with God in which this God meets him not merely as making moral demands upon him but as sanctifying him and bestowing grace and strength upon him. This is achieved precisely in the sacraments and above all by holy Mass in the Eucharist. In these sacraments God's actions upon humanity touch the individual as it were from without, penetrate him, sanctify him, and transform him (at least carrying these processes a stage further, although for the most part the effects are experienced as very transitory and in a sense peripheral)." Karl Rahner, "Considerations on the Active Role of the Person in the Sacramental Event," 161–84, in *Theological Investigations* 14 (London: Darton, Longman & Todd, 1976), at 162.

[10] See, for example, ibid., 162–65.

"graces" one might experience in particular moments of life).[11] But these created effects are so only because of the prior "uncreated grace"—God's own gift of self in the sacramental encounter. The mid-century rethinking of grace led to the conviction that, fundamentally, "grace" refers to "uncreated grace," God's completely unmerited, free offer of God's self to us in love for our salvation. Other experiences identified as grace are so in a derivative or dependent sense.

As this emphasis on uncreated grace emerged, theology of grace shifted on another front. It began to recognize that the encounter with grace is not as rare as previous generations had imagined. God's offer of God's self to us in love for our salvation need not be conceived as intermittent or punctual (occurring only at certain points). It is a perpetual offer, by God's own choosing and in accord with God's will to create beings with whom God could share a communion of life and love. This offer is a consistent, if largely unrecognized, co-conditioning element of every aspect of human existence.

Rahner therefore termed grace understood as this co-conditioning element a "supernatural existential."[12] As an existential of human existence it is ever present in our experience, but it is also not directly graspable as such. Just as freedom, self-presence, and our situatedness in history are all necessary co-conditioning aspects of our personal histories of becoming but can never be directly grasped in any individual act, so too with God's offer of self. It is an existential of our human existence, but as supernatural it is different from other existentials. It is not intrinsic to our human nature and therefore necessary to our existence that God make such an offer, yet God does, in fact, make the offer, at all times and in all places.

---

[11] Particularly in scholastic theologies preoccupied with the conditions for "causing" grace to be effected in the performance of the sacramental ritual, the understanding of grace to which "created grace" refers leaves one with the impression that grace itself is an entity over which we exercise control. This is counter to the beliefs and intentions of scholastic theology, but one can understand how the emphasis on created grace could foster such a misinterpretation. Thomas Aquinas noted that in his own day, the language of grace had already undergone a shift in emphasis from "God's very mercy itself" to a created, "entitative" condition understood as a *habitus*. See the discussion in Stephen J. Duffy, *The Dynamics of Grace: Perspectives in Theological Anthropology* (Collegeville, MN: Liturgical Press, 1993), 127.

[12] See Rahner, *Foundations*, 126–33; idem, "Concerning the Relationship between Nature and Grace," 297–317, in *Theological Investigations* 1, trans. Cornelius Ernst (New York: Crossroad, 1982), esp. 312–13.

This line of thinking undergirds the reversal in understanding of the sacramentality of the church and of the sacraments. It also leads to the conviction that all creation is sacramental, at least *in potentia*. The whole of creation and all its parts are capable of being used by God to mediate a transformative, saving encounter between God and the creature. Indeed, God is constantly making the appeal to give God's self to humankind in and through the daily exercise of our capacity for self-transcendence in love and freedom—that is, in and through the media by which we enact our free, intentional participation in our own processes of personal becoming.[13] The Second Vatican Council gave substantial support to this line of thinking when it affirmed that

> Those who, through no fault of their own, do not know the Gospel of Christ or his Church, but who nevertheless seek God with a sincere heart, and, moved by grace, try in their actions to do his will as they know it through the dictates of their conscience—those too may achieve eternal salvation. Nor shall divine providence deny the assistance necessary for salvation to those who, without any fault of theirs, have not yet arrived at an explicit knowledge of God, and who, not without grace, strive to lead a good life.[14]

---

[13] This approach to grace as an existential of human experience—an existential in the mode of God's offer of self to us for our fulfillment and salvation—is the basis for Rahner's affirmation of salvation for non-Christians and even atheists. The phrase "anonymous Christian" is a shorthand way of naming this reality. Unfortunately, though the theological insight into the dynamics of grace has gained significant acceptance in the broader Christian theological landscape, the phrase "anonymous Christian" has evoked critical reaction from a variety of quarters. See, for example, Karl Rahner, "Anonymous Christianity and the Missionary Task of the Church," 161–78, in *Theological Investigations* 12 (London: Darton, Longman & Todd, 1974); idem, "Observations on the Problem of the 'Anonymous Christian,'" 280–94, in *Theological Investigations* 14 (London: Darton, Longman & Todd, 1976). The concept of the anonymous Christian received a scathing critique in Hans Urs von Balthasar, *The Moment of Christian Witness* (San Francisco: Ignatius Press, 1969). For an insightful assessment of this dispute between Rahner and von Balthasar see Eamonn Conway, *The Anonymous Christian—a Relativised Christianity? An Evaluation of Hans Urs von Balthasar's Criticisms of Karl Rahner's Theory of the Anonymous Christian*, Europäische Hochschulschriften XXIII, Theologie, vol. 485 (Frankfurt and New York: Peter Lang, 1993).

[14] *Lumen Gentium* (Dogmatic Constitution on the Church) 16, in *Vatican Council II: The Conciliar and Post Conciliar Documents*, ed. Austin Flannery, OP, rev. ed. (Northport, NY: Costello, 1996), 367–68.

And further, "since Christ died for all, and since all men [*sic*] are in fact called to one and the same destiny, which is divine, we must hold that the Holy Spirit offers to all the possibility of being made partners, in a way known to God, in the paschal mystery."[15]

These affirmations reflect the theological reorientation that had oc-curred in the years before the council. God is generous in offering the grace of salvation. This suggests that God is also much more generous in forgiving than previous generations might have imagined.

We are dealing here with a fundamental shift in the center of gravity of a theological matrix of meanings. This becomes most evident when we contrast these shifts in thinking with the idea that "all are deserving of the wrath of God." When this affirmation (desert of wrath) is deeply embedded within the basement-level foundations of a theological per-spective it makes sense to think of grace as a limited, punctual insertion of the supernatural into the human realm. If we understand God's rela-tionship to us primarily from the standpoint of the impact of Sin on our lives and our world—our alienation from God—and if we emphasize the divine transcendence and the need for divine justice to be satisfied for reconciliation to occur, then we can understand why God might be sparing in bestowing the grace of forgiveness.

But if the more fundamental reality (basement-level conviction) is the desire of the Triune God to bestow God's own self in love on what is other than God, then the offer of God's self to us as a constant, co-con-ditioning element of human existence from first to last makes more sense. Then Sin does not possess the greatest weight in our theological matrix (it is not our primary point of theological orientation), but God's own graciousness does. Our emphasis will not be on explaining God's (limited) mercy to us in the face of the overwhelming reality of Sin, but rather accounting for the theological significance of Sin from within the framework of the good creation to which God constantly offers God's self. That is, we will need to name how Sin functions within the finite reality established by God's creative activity. We shall return to this point shortly.

## Between Grace and the Holy Spirit

The shifts in the understanding of grace, from emphasis on "created grace" to thinking in terms of "uncreated grace" and from grace as rare,

---

[15] *Gaudium et Spes* 22 (Pastoral Constitution on the Church in the Modern World), in ibid., 924.

punctual event to grace as co-conditioning dimension of human existence, matured at about the same time that another theological shift began to emerge: the revitalization of the theology of the Holy Spirit. For centuries in the Western church the Holy Spirit had been the forgotten member of the Trinity in all but name.[16] This may well have been a consequence of the ascendancy of the language of grace in Western scholasticism. For, as Yves Congar observed,

> The Spirit, then, is the principle realizing the "Christian mystery," which is the mystery of the Son of God who was made man and who enables us to be born as sons [*sic*] of God. Catholic theologians speak of "grace." In so doing, they run the risk of objectivizing it and separating it from the activity of the Spirit, who is uncreated grace and from whom it [grace] cannot be separated. Only God is holy, and only he can make us holy, in and through his incarnate Son and in and through his Spirit. . . .[17]

Whatever the cause(s) of this neglect of the Holy Spirit, the latter part of the twentieth century witnessed a retrieval and renewal of theological reflection on the action of the Holy Spirit in the life of the church and in the world at large. The created grace identified with the sacraments has, as a function of this renewal, come to be understood as the personal effect of the Holy Spirit drawing the believer into relationship with God in Christ.[18] That is, renewed emphasis on the role of the Holy Spirit has helped to shift the understanding of the dynamics of sacramental grace away from a kind of mechanistic, created effect into the realm of a vital, personal, relational encounter with the Living God through the mediation of created realities, effected by the action of the Holy Spirit.

---

[16] See Yves Congar, *The Holy Spirit in the "Economy" Revelation and the Experience of the Spirit*, vol. 1 of *I Believe in the Holy Spirit*, trans. David Smith (New York: Crossroad, 1997), 159–64, where Congar also indicates some prominent substitutes for the Holy Spirit in piety and theology.

[17] Yves Congar, *"He Is the Lord and Giver of Life,"* vol. 2 of *I Believe in the Holy Spirit*, trans. David Smith (New York: Crossroad, 1997), 68–69.

[18] This would be expressed differently depending on the specific sacrament under discussion. Congar examines the implications of the invocation of the Holy Spirit (*epiclesis*) and the significance of the Holy Spirit specifically in relationship to the theology of Confirmation and the theology of Eucharist in Yves Congar, *The River of the Water of Life (Rev 22:1) Flows in the East and in the West*, vol. 3 of *I Believe in the Holy Spirit*, trans. David Smith (New York: Crossroad, 1997), 217–74.

We can summarize the elements of this theological matrix of meanings in three statements. First, God has made creation so that it can bear the divine self-communication to humanity in a mode that can transform us into holiness in communion with God. Second, in view of God's abiding will to bring about this communion, God can and does freely extend this self-communication (uncreated grace, the Holy Spirit) universally in the mode of an appeal to human freedom. Third, this appeal is mediated to us in and through our engagement with the created reality to which God desires to give God's self. Simply put, we inhabit a sacramental cosmos, a world of grace.

## SACRAMENTAL COSMOS AND THE DYNAMICS OF RECOGNITION

This claim about a sacramental cosmos can be misleading. It can sound like an ontological assertion: a statement about being, about *what* things are. It is certainly that, but it is more. To claim that the cosmos is fundamentally sacramental is also to make a theological statement about *how* the cosmos operates (its dynamics) and about its significance (its fundamental meaning). These three aspects (being, dynamics, and meaning) are interrelated. The cosmos exists only in and through its dynamic process of mediation, the process that also grounds the possibility of its being known (and hence being recognized as meaningful). The real expresses itself in what is other than itself so as to attain its own actuality.[19] The Christian belief that God created finite reality in order to give God's self to it in loving communion provides the theological underpinning of this understanding of the sacramental cosmos.

As a theological affirmation and a religious conviction, the idea of a sacramental cosmos may be easy to affirm. But when measured against our observations of the world around us this conviction can find itself confronted by serious questions. Two are particularly important for the progress of the present inquiry. First, we are affirming that the whole of the created world really is imbued with God's offer of self (the active presence of the Holy Spirit offering God's self to us as grace). Yet it is not always recognized as such. What are we to make of this lack of recognition? Or conversely, what is happening when it is recognized?

---

[19] Karl Rahner analyzes this dimension of finite being and its relationship to infinite being in his discussion of the "real symbol." See Karl Rahner, "The Theology of the Symbol," 221–52, in *Theological Investigations* 4, trans. Kevin Smyth (London: Darton, Longman & Todd, 1966), at 224–35.

Second, even when it is recognized and affirmed at the level of the Christian narrative, what role does this recognition play in the efficacy of the Spirit's action? After all, the Second Vatican Council has affirmed that even those with no knowledge of the Christian narrative can be saved. So why is it important to be able to recognize the action of the Holy Spirit/the event of grace for what it is?

In response to the first question it is essential to note the character of the claim we are making about the world we inhabit. Certainly it is a truth claim. But it is a truth claim expressing a matter of belief, grounded in an act of faith.[20] It is a claim that cannot be directly verified in any un-ambiguous, empirical sense. Any affirmation of the existence of the Holy Spirit or of grace as a supernatural experience of encounter with God necessarily presupposes that one believes in God, grace, and the Holy Spirit. Such affirmations arise from a fundamental orientation toward the utterly transcendent (but also utterly immanent) Other, God. Any affirmation that I have encountered that transcendent God in a particular experience rests on the foundation of that faith and on the fact that that faith has come to reflexive awareness from within a matrix of meanings that can understand God as acting in that way.

The understanding of God entailed in such an affirmation is that expressed in Christian shared matrices of meanings. "God" is the God of Jesus Christ, the one he addressed as "Abba," Father. From within this matrix of meanings Christians understand that our ability to affirm this belief in words and to live from it is a consequence of a gift, faith, bestowed on us by God through the Holy Spirit. This Spirit draws us into communion with God in Christ. Over the course of our individual histories of personal becoming we grow into this communion (or not) through our free responses to the promptings of the Holy Spirit (grace).

Viewed from the human side of the experience, Christian recognition of the action of the Holy Spirit (recognition of grace) in any particular aspect of our lives rests on this faith, understood in the light of the Christian narrative. Any act of recognition, as we saw in chapter 5, is a matter of grasping significance in the data of experience. Grasping significance

---

[20] This formulation draws on the work of Roger Haight in chaps. 1 and 2 of his *Dynamics of Theology* (New York: Paulist Press, 1990). Haight, for his part, is building on insights from the work of Paul Tillich on the distinction between faith and beliefs. In this distinction faith is the orientation toward an object of ultimate concern. That orientation comes to expression in beliefs that arise from reflection on the deepest orientations within us that shape our actions. The beliefs then provide us with a means to intentionally orient our further actions.

is intrinsically a process of interpretation. We make this interpretation from within and in relation to the matrices of meanings (personal and shared) that we inhabit as we interact with the world around us. That is, we recognize God's activity in and through the "stuff" of our world (people, events, nature, our thoughts and feelings, ecclesial worship, workplace environment, and so on) when we are moved to interpret that "stuff" from within the matrix of the Christian narrative.

Approaching this experience of recognition from the side of God's initiative, what we affirm in faith is that our interpretation is not merely a subjective insight; rather, it is a result of God's activity, filling the quotidian events of our lives with a meaning, importance, and effect they would not otherwise have by making them the locus of a personal encounter between us and God *and* by opening our minds and hearts to recognize them as such. Thus the movement to recognition of God's active presence in finite experience is itself sustained and guided by God's initiative, both in offering God's self *and* in opening the person to recognize that she is dealing (or has been/was dealing) with God in this moment. God's initiative leads her to recognize God's action in the light of the Christian narrative *and* to see herself in relationship to that narrative as it continues to unfold. That is, by the working of the Holy Spirit she comes to recognize herself as participating in what we are here calling "a sacramental cosmos," a world of grace. The Christian narrative provides her with the key to interpreting that world and her place in it. It provides a complex of meanings that shapes her sense of self and her self-world relations.

Nevertheless, even if we do affirm the Christian narrative and have been moved to do so by an act of personal faith beyond the custom of socially supported habits, there is no guarantee that we will recognize the action of the Holy Spirit or the movement of grace in any given event. If, as Rahner has argued, grace—God's offer of self to us by the Holy Spirit—is present to every moment of our lives, and if grace is—as Christian faith claims—a matter of encounter with the utterly transcendent God, its presence is not accessible to our normal powers of observation. We cannot say "This portion of the experience is 'grace' and that is not." The presence and action of the divine in any human experience must be disclosed to our reflective awareness if it is to be grasped as such. That is, our reflective awareness of God's presence and action in our experience presupposes that God reveals that presence and action to us in a personal encounter.[21]

---

[21] This understanding is evident in the accounts of forgiveness presented by Volf and Jones. Where we differ is on the question whether reflexive awareness of God's action and

If the movement of grace has not been revealed—disclosed to our reflective consciousness—what then? Does it remain an impotent co-conditioning element? Not necessarily. The ubiquity of the offer of God's own self to us, making its appeal to our freedom and sustaining our freedom in action, occurs, and we respond to it, whether we are reflexively aware of it or not. It occurs via the interaction of this offer (grace, the action of the Holy Spirit) with our human freedom as we move beyond our current attainment of self into the self we are becoming.[22] In the movement of self-transcendence toward self-giving love of neighbor as the preeminent example of grace at work we implicitly affirm the invitation of God into the life of communion in Christ through the Holy Spirit, or, conversely, when we refuse such an invitation we engage a process of becoming that is counter to the movement of grace and the prompting of the Holy Spirit. This is occurring, Rahner maintains, whether we are reflecting on it as such or not. Further, it is occurring whether one is Christian or not.[23]

---

my response to it are essential or whether the grace can operate, and still be Christian, even when I am not reflexively aware of it as such. We differ further on whether there are other legitimately Christian ways of thematizing the encounter with God that would/could still be appropriate motivation for our enactments of forgiveness to be properly Christian.

[22] "Because the subject's response in freedom is itself really and truly for the subject himself something given to him, without it losing thereby the character of the subject's own responsible and accountable action, a good decision along with everything which it presupposes as its mediation correctly has the character of an intervention of God, even though this takes place in and through human freedom, and hence can be explained functionally to the degree that the history of freedom can be explained, namely, insofar as it is based on elements objectified in time and space" (Rahner, *Foundations*, 89).

[23] Both Volf and Jones make gestures in the direction of this common dynamic when allowing for the possibility of salvation for non-Christians. Volf accounts for non-Christians forgiving by referring both to the "seeds of the Word" that are present in other religious traditions and to the fact that "Christ does not need to be confessed, honored, or named to be present and to shape people's convictions and practices." Miroslav Volf, *Free of Charge: Giving and Forgiving in a Culture Stripped of Grace* (Grand Rapids: Zondervan, 2005), 222–24, at 223. This, of course, raises the question about what distinguishes forgiveness as Christian. It would seem to be the explicit awareness of oneself as having been forgiven by God in Christ and the function of that awareness in motivating one's own enactments of forgiveness. See also L. Gregory Jones, *Embodying Forgiveness: A Theological Analysis* (Grand Rapids: Eerdmans, 1995), 251–62, for a discussion of some of the theological issues underlying this question. Jones is primarily concerned in this section with the possibility of ultimate damnation of anyone.

Recognition, however, can play an important role in this dynamic of offer and response.[24] The Christian narrative points toward this experience of grace (engagement with God through the action of the Holy Spirit). It provides a conceptual framework for understanding the properly theological significance of human experience. On a notional level, Christians can affirm the idea of grace reaching out to invite us at each moment, but the movement from notional affirmation to *personal recognition* of the truth of this dynamism of God's engagement with us is itself an event of grace.[25] In that movement we are set free to align our individual acts of freedom with the trajectory of God's own action more intentionally. That is, recognition—the movement from notional affirmation of the Christian narrative to personal embrace of its truth as *my* truth, itself an event of grace—enables us to orient our process of personal becoming in a trajectory that moves toward the Kingdom of God, the communion of love with God and with neighbor.

It should be noted that the effective presence of the Holy Spirit in any given event of one's life is sometimes (perhaps most often) only recognized long after the event, by a process of looking back. That is, God's active presence is often confirmed retrospectively, via a reinterpretation of events that were not recognized as imbued with God's presence at the time. This is a common theme in the Christian scriptures. God tells Moses that the proof of what God says will occur when Moses has accomplished the task assigned and has brought the Israelites back to the holy mountain to worship (Exod 3:11-13). The flash of recognition at the table in Emmaus led the disciples to identify that it was in fact the Risen Lord who had accompanied them on the journey (Luke 24:13-35). At a later point in time a graced realignment of our grasp of meaning in the events of our histories may issue in an experience of recognition. This new awareness of the presence of God along the way in our past

---

[24] This is the reason that Volf, Jones, and other writers devote such attention to these themes. They do so out of the conviction that awareness of how God works in the world can contribute to our cooperation with God's desires for us as revealed in Christ.

[25] This seems to be the point behind the distinction between "becoming a Christian" and "becoming Christian" in Brian Zahnd, *Unconditional?* (Lake Mary, FL: Charisma House, 2010), 56–57, a point underscored by the experience of Dietrich Bonhoeffer as recounted in Jones, *Embodying Forgiveness*, 10, 33. It likewise appears to be implicated in the connection between practices of Christian virtue, including the "arcane disciplines" of penance, and growth in holiness, which underlies Jones's project. See Jones, *Embodying Forgiveness*, 227.

can then orient the path of our future becoming, for then the notional meaning we affirm as a matter of belief becomes aligned in a personally vital way with the ultimate concern living in our hearts. But all of this occurs by means of our (always-already graced) engagement with the world, via the mediation of immediacy to God. It thereby confirms that we inhabit a sacramental cosmos.

### Sin in the Sacramental Cosmos

Although God has created a world other than God's self to be able to share God's self in love and communion with what is other, the history of this world has been marked by rejection of that offer. Not always. Not uniformly. But pervasively and persistently. Our world is shaped by Sin—the refusal of the offer of God's self in and through the media of this world and our neighbor. As both Volf and Jones (and so many others) have pointed out, the history of sin is not merely one of individual acts. It is also, and more deeply, a pervasive force arising from the history of human sinful choices, a force that has become embedded in the structures of relationships in our world. These structures of relationships, affected by histories of sin, perpetuate themselves by promoting values and behaviors that incline toward further sinful acts. Thus one can distinguish—as Jones does—"Sin" as a pervasive force conditioning our acts of freedom from "sins" as those individual acts.[26]

We can therefore think of Sin as a kind of "counter-sacramental" tendency or impulse co-conditioning our individual exercises of freedom. Rather than fostering an inclination toward exercises of freedom that issue in communion of life and love it sets us in opposition to one another and, even more perniciously, leads us to regard our oppositional relationships as righteous and justified.[27] As counter-sacramental, Sin

---

[26] Jones, *Embodying Forgiveness*, 62. See also Roger Haight, "Sin and Grace," 375–430, in Schüssler Fiorenza and Galvin, *Systematic Theology*, at 396, where Haight affirms: "Sin is both a structure prior to the exercise of freedom and one that is actualized by freedom itself." This articulation aligns with Jones's characterization of the distinction.

[27] The dynamics of this process are examined in great detail under the rubric of "mimetic rivalry" in the works of René Girard; see his *Violence and the Sacred*, trans. Patrick Gregory (Baltimore: Johns Hopkins University Press, 1977), 143–68; idem, *Things Hidden Since the Foundation of the World*, trans. Stephen Bann and Michael Metteer (Stanford, CA: Stanford University Press, 1987), 283–98; idem, *The Scapegoat*, trans. Yvonne Freccero (Baltimore: Johns Hopkins University Press, 1986). Girard's foundational insights have found their way into contemporary theological reflection on sin and redemption in James

moves us to resist and undo the trajectory of development that God intended in establishing creation, the movement toward communion in God's own life. Individual sins occur when we exercise our freedom in cooperation with those impulses to "counter-sacramentality," impulses that set us against the trajectory God has intended from the start.

When characterizing "Sin" and "sins" in this way it is important to observe two caveats. First, on the experiential level "Sin" does operate as a counter-sacramental force, but this is not to suggest that it has some sort of reality independent of creation itself. No gnostic dualism is implied here. In keeping with the insights of the two creation accounts in Genesis, we can affirm that God created the world and saw that it was good; Sin entered the world through misuse of human freedom.[28] Over the centuries of human social existence, Sin has become embedded in our structures of relating, thinking, feeling, and choosing. It co-conditions our freedom, not by "nature" but by historical fact.

Second, to suggest that "Sin" functions counter-sacramentally could leave us with the impression that everything is either sacramental or counter-sacramental, either grace or Sin. This makes sense in a worldview that sees creation as having been completed "on the sixth day." But it is important in our present-day matrix of meanings to at least raise the question whether the story contained in the first Genesis creation story does not lead us to overlook an important third designation: becoming. The phenomenology of the human person articulated in chapter 5 and based on empirical and existential insights affirmed in contemporary psychology reflects the experience that our selves are in the process of becoming. Chapter 8 challenged the assumption that all resistance to movements of grace can simply be reducible to Sin or sinful choices. Resistance might also be a function of our finitude and our temporally situated process of becoming. We become ourselves over time. We are never sufficiently in command of ourselves that we can, in a single choice, make an irreversible decision with respect to God's offer of self, so long as we continue to have freedom. We always have the possibility of choosing to alter the trajectory of future becoming that we set by prior decisions. The same inability to commit ourselves fully in any one decision comes to expression even when we affirm the invitation of grace. Our yes to

Alison, *The Joy of Being Wrong: Original Sin through Easter Eyes*, foreword by Sebastian Moore (New York: Crossroad, 1998); Raymund Schwager, *Der Wunderbare Tausch: Zur Geschichte und Deutung der Erlösungslehre* (Munich: Kösel, 1986).

[28] Genesis 1:1–3:24.

the promptings of the Holy Spirit is never complete. This need not be a function of Sin; it can just as well be a function of our finitude.[29]

This perspective gains further support when we recognize that the capacities we have as adults are far greater than those we had as children. So, too, in the case of spiritual development as that comes to expression in our freedom. As we grow, and especially as we grow under the influence of grace/the Holy Spirit's movement in our lives, our capacities expand and change. As the Spirit invites us beyond levels of previous attainment, the lack of attainment up to that point may be experienced as resistance; it is a struggle to grow. This resistance is different from setting ourselves in active opposition to the requirements of living the Gospel.

To be sure, it is entirely possible in either case that Sin is operative. But, in a manner analogous to our inability to distinguish with absolute clarity what is of grace and what is not in any individual experience, it is difficult to indicate in any finite experience of resistance to the invitation of the Spirit whether that resistance is a function of Sin (and therefore possibly a matter of culpable misuse of freedom) or a function of non-culpable, developmental immaturity or of the finitude of our acts of freedom. At the very least the implications of contemporary understandings of psychological development caution us to avoid the assumption in traditional accounts of Christian forgiveness that reduces all resistance to forgiving to the culpable rejection of grace, thereby equating it with sin. The disconnect that arises between the traditional narrative and the resources now available to human self-understanding can contribute to a marginalization of this part of the Christian narrative as myth.

This point is important for the understanding of the sacramental cosmos being presented here. If creation really was "completed" on the sixth day, as the first Genesis creation account tells us, the introduction of Sin into the world by human choice makes a simple disjunction of Sin and grace an understandable way of reading our human situation. From this it is not a great step to concluding that "all are deserving of the wrath of

---

[29] The Carmelite author Ruth Burrows addresses this point succinctly at the beginning of her *Guidelines for Mystical Prayer* when she writes: "Think of your soul as a castle, St Teresa tells us. God dwells in the innermost room. You, as yet, do not and you must learn to go within, from room to room until you reach the innermost centre where he is. The rooms are there, it is just that you haven't learned to enter them. But nowadays we see things differently. The rooms are *not* there! We grasp that we are gradually coming into being; the potentiality which we are—unique in each instance—is slowly 'realised.'" Ruth Burrows, *Guidelines for Mystical Prayer* (London: Sheed and Ward, 1976), 10.

God." But if the cosmos itself is still in the process of becoming—that is, still being created through its unfolding, developmental process—and if the human person is likewise not complete, but throughout the course of a lifetime growing into capacities for freely responding to God that, in their emergence, have yet to be determined in their orientation toward or away from the inclinations of grace, then the understanding of God's grace (the offer of God's self to us through the Holy Spirit) takes on a distinctive nuance. The encounter with God's grace not only draws us out of the power of sin and death but also draws us into the persons we *are being created* to be! That is, from the standpoint of human personal becoming, our affirmative response to the invitation of the Holy Spirit into communion with God is not only redemptive, it is also creative. We are co-participants with God in our own ongoing creation. The internal resistance we experience in response to the invitation of the Spirit might be a consequence of Sin, but it might also be the "growing pains" of persons in the process of becoming.[30]

### From God's Forgiveness to Christian Forgiveness

The traditional account of Christian forgiveness situates our forgiveness of others in relationship to God's forgiveness of us in Christ. This makes good sense. However, the question still needs to be asked, "what is God doing in relationship to us when God forgives us?" or perhaps more trenchantly, "what is it about what God does in Christ and through the Holy Spirit that makes it to be forgiveness?" That is, we need to ask the question about the divine enactment of forgiveness *as forgiving.* This will establish a way for us to approach the question of what Christians are called to enact and, further, how that might be distinctive from forgiveness as a basic human enactment.

### *The Dynamics of God's Forgiveness*

Taking up the question of God's forgiveness presents us with a methodological problem that must be acknowledged at the outset. Our understanding of God's forgiveness comes to us through the revelation of God in Christ under the illumination of the Holy Spirit. In the order of

---

[30] We are touching on a fundamental challenge to theological anthropologies that have taken on a quasi-canonical status in Western Christianity. Here we are only naming the issue. The question requires further investigation than can be undertaken in this context.

exposition that follows it will be necessary to presuppose some of what we will ultimately be arguing. That is, there will be a kind of circularity to the argument. However, this is the kind of circularity that is unavoidable in the presentation of any matrix of meanings. From within this matrix it should have the appearance of coherence. In any case, drawing on elements already presented in the standard accounts, we can make some preliminary statements about what God is doing when forgiving.

## Opening a Relational Space for Reconciliation

At a minimum we can claim that, in forgiving, God (re)opens (or keeps open) a relational space in which communion can be (re)established. This is the practical presupposition of the claim that God sent Christ to effect reconciliation. Indeed, it is an intrinsic moment of both Volf's and Jones's presentations that God's forgiving decision is always antecedent to our repentance.[31] Divine forgiveness sets the stage. This is implicit in the divine offer of self to the sinner. "But God proves his love for us in that while we were still sinners Christ died for us" (Rom 5:8).

But as Volf and Jones maintain, the gift of grace—the encounter with the God who forgives even in the judging—is what makes the repentance itself possible. At the level of divine engagement with the human, God's forgiveness is more than antecedent. It is also proactive. If we accept the theological claim that God is always at work reaching out to offer God's own self to humankind to draw us into communion, then the forgiveness of God that grounds the possibility of reconciliation cannot be separated from the offer itself. God takes the initiative—acts proactively—in and through forgiving to bring about reconciliation and communion. From another angle, God's proactive pursuit of reconciliation with humankind presupposes that God has already forgiven us.[32]

Although God's forgiveness is antecedent to our repentance and acceptance of it, our acceptance, itself sustained by God's grace, is what makes it actual in our personal histories.[33] The grace offered becomes

---

[31] Volf, *Free of Charge*, 179. Jones nuances his discussion of the priority of God's forgiveness in critical dialogue with Richard Swinburn's presentation in *Responsibility and Atonement* (Oxford: Clarendon Press, 1989) in Jones, *Embodying Forgiveness*, 150–60.

[32] See the discussion of the parables in Luke 15 below.

[33] The point being made here parallels the scholastic sacramental teaching that the sacraments are effective *ex opere operato* but that their subjective efficacy is dependent on the receptivity of the recipient. As the maxim goes, *quid quid recipitur secundum modum*

the actual grace that shapes my trajectory of personal becoming, either in its acceptance (describing a reconciled and reconciling trajectory) or in its rejection (describing a trajectory of prolonged alienation from communion with God).

## THE INTERPERSONAL RELATIONAL CHARACTER OF DIVINE FORGIVENESS

Thus God's offer of forgiveness is always in the mode of an offer of God's own *self* to us for communion with God in Christ by the working of the Holy Spirit. That is, God's forgiveness is the offer of personal relationship with God. Christians recognize this offer to be mediated by our union in faith with the person of Christ. Faith, for its part, is a gift from God (grace), effected within us by the action of the Holy Spirit in whose ambit we live and who draws us—in freedom—to respond. To put this in other terms, the forgiveness God offers is an invitation into personal relationship with God, an invitation to participation in the Triune life itself, but in a mode appropriate to our own created reality. Our participation shows itself insofar as our processes of personal becoming, by our grace-sustained free choices, reflect ever more deeply the dynamics of that Triune life.[34]

Christians have come to identify those trinitarian dynamics in terms of self-donation in love. As theologians have argued for centuries, this

---

*recipientis recipitur est* (what is received is received according to the mode of the recipient). This parallels the point Volf is getting at about the reception of a gift and the judgment of God. Volf, *The End of Memory*, 121–74. See Jones, *Embodying Forgiveness*, 147, where he elaborates on the significance of Ruby Turpin's experience of revelation in Flannery O'Connor's short story, "Revelation."

[34] Not all Christian thinkers embrace the idea that we should measure our forgiving against the standard set by God. "In a similar way, I suggest that caution needs to be exercised over the idea that human forgiveness should be modelled on God's forgiveness. We do not have, and cannot hope to have, the resources of grace that God brings to forgiveness. Also, there is a degree of asymmetry in the relationship of God to each human being that is not paralleled in the relationships between human beings." Fraser Watts, "Christian Theology," 50–68, in *Forgiveness in Context: Theology and Psychology in Creative Dialogue*, ed. Fraser Watts and Liz Gulliford (London and New York: T & T Clark, 2004), at 55. Volf, by contrast, is committed to the idea that God's forgiveness is the model for our practice; see Volf, *Free of Charge*, 48, 179; idem, *Exclusion and Embrace: A Theological Exploration of Identity, Otherness, and Reconciliation* (Nashville: Abingdon Press, 1996), 30–32, 100. This basic commitment also underlies Jones's interest in a better understanding of the trinitarian basis of Christian life and the promotion of imitative practices of repentance and forgiveness.

absolute, mutual self-bestowal is what characterizes the life of the Triune God *ad intra*.[35] The Triune life is characterized by an absolute self-giving/ self-emptying of the Divine Persons to one another in love, a *kenosis*. This dynamism of divine self-emptying comes to expression in finite reality in Christ. As the letter to the Philippians puts it, "[Christ] emptied himself . . ." (Phil 2:7). The sinner is invited to embrace an analogous self-emptying in the movement toward reconciliation with God. This self-emptying is at the heart of repentance. The act of repentance involves letting go of the personal matrix of meanings in which we see our harmful actions as righteous. By doing so we reorient the trajectory of our future becoming. In other words, repentance involves conversion. This conversion has *kenosis* at its core. By this *kenosis* through repentance, our personal becoming echoes the self-donation we have come to identify as characterizing the three persons of the Trinity in relationship to one another and to created reality. This self-emptying into the other "opens the space" *within* us by which we can enter into reconciliation with God. It does so within the space God's antecedent forgiveness has already opened *for* us.[36]

[35] Recent scholarship has called into question the extent to which it is meaningful to speak of the inner divine relations. See, for example, the theses of Piet Schoonenberg, SJ, as presented in Catherine M. LaCugna, *God for Us: The Trinity and Christian Life* (San Francisco: HarperSanFrancisco, 1991), 217–20. LaCugna's larger project argues that speculation on the inner divine relations has contributed to the separation of *theologia* from *oikonomia*, of reflection on God from reflection on God's self-disclosure in the economy of salvation. She writes (*God for Us*, 221): "We can incorporate the essential concerns of both the economic-immanent and the essence-energies distinctions, with the biblical, creedal, ante-Nicene vision of the economy, in the following principle: *theologia* is fully revealed and bestowed in *oikonomia*, and *oikonomia* truly expresses the ineffable mystery of *theologia*." Apart from the merits of the argument LaCugna is making, the element that is important for the present discussion is that the *kenosis* observed in the economy is truly reflective of God's self.

[36] Volf employs the same metaphor of opening a space when he describes the dynamics of reconciliation in *Exclusion and Embrace*, 126, 142–43. The point I am making here about God opening a space as one of the formal characteristics of God's forgiveness gains support when Volf observes: "Building on statements like these, some theologians have suggested that the world was created so that it would be redeemed and finally glorified. Redemption, they maintained, was not a solution God thought up after human beings botched up God's first attempt. Instead it was the purpose of creation. This view may or may not be right. But it does seem that God decided to redeem the world of sin before the Creator could lay down its foundations. Each of us exists because the gift of life rests on the gift of forgiveness." Volf, *Free of Charge*, 136.

Thus the repentant sinner empties herself of the sense of self identified with (and justifying) the offense. She undergoes a *kenosis* that makes it possible for her to enter into the opening created by the antecedent forgiveness. In the process she "becomes other." She recognizes in the embraced repentance under the judgment of the offense she is turning away from a distorted, sin-bound self toward a truer self. She recognizes in the possibilities opened by the space of forgiveness the opportunity to affirm her own better future self by renouncing her past self. *"Whoever would save her life will lose it, but whoever loses her life for my sake and for the Gospel will save it."*[37] The movement by which she repents is the same movement by which she embodies, in a fuller degree, the Triune dynamics of self-emptying love and, in the process, the actualization of the Kingdom of God in her life. Embrace of forgiveness, affirmation of new trajectory of personal becoming, self-emptying of old sense of self—all occur simultaneously in the acceptance of the offer of God's self in the moment of grace. The dynamism is, from first to last, personal, and this in two ways: first, because it is relational; by this dynamism we enter into a relational space that forgiveness has already opened. But second, this dynamism is personal because it is the expression of our own personal becoming. The *kenosis* at the heart of our repentance sets out the trajectory of our future personal becoming in relation to God, self, and neighbor.

## Explicit and Hidden Dynamics

If we read this account of God's enactment of forgiveness in relationship to the presentation on grace and the Holy Spirit above it becomes immediately clear that the dynamics of God's forgiveness reaching out to touch the sinner and the sinner's acceptance of the offer of forgiveness in the relationship may or may not be explicitly recognized as such but may still be effective in transforming the sinner.[38] That is, there is a dynamic interplay between the offer and the acceptance of forgiveness that takes place, to some degree, on the level of conscious, intentional life. But it might also occur in ways that are not directly accessible to conscious

[37] See Matthew 10:39; 16:25; Mark 8:35; Luke 9:24.

[38] This is the conviction that underlies Rahner's discussion of "anonymous Christians" and the Second Vatican Council's affirmation of the possibility of salvation for those who do not share Christian faith. Fraser Watts articulates the same point using the distinction between objective and subjective aspects of Christian forgiveness in "Christian Theology," 56.

reflection, at least at the time of occurrence. These dynamics operate whether one is professedly Christian or not, but in distinctive ways.

For the Christian, the narrative of God's engagement with humankind for our salvation provides an interpretive matrix that can allow us to identify this or that event as a moment of grace. Whether our identification of the action of grace at a particular moment is, in fact, correct can only be assessed on the basis of a faith commitment that interprets itself and the world from within the matrix set out by the understanding of the narrative itself. But the Christian narrative matrix posits both that God is at work to draw us into communion *and* that our response to God's initiative is important. Christians can then look upon the events of life and seek (and find) within them opportunities for their own affirmation of their commitment to relationship with God. That is, the narrative provides a way for Christians to interpret their experience and orient their intentionality so as to align their future becoming with the highest values of their religious matrix of meanings. They can intentionally orient their exercise of freedom to cooperate with the movement of the Holy Spirit (grace) as they understand it.[39]

However, the faith that affirms the Christian narrative does not liberate the believer from the vicissitudes of being human. Christians, too, are moved and shaped in our actions by psychic forces that are not directly accessible to our conscious reflection or the dictates of our intentional choices.[40] Those psychic forces within us, insofar as they pull against the invitation of grace, still require the kind of realignment called "conversion." To some extent the grace-sustained intentional alignment of our conscious decisions can reverberate within our personal matrices of meanings so as to reorient those forces not yet converted. But that may be a gradual, unrecognized conversion, only seen at a later time when in our conscious reflection we come to recognize a freedom for the trajectory of grace where earlier we found resistance. In that newly recognized freedom the Christian can also recognize the *vestigia Dei*, the footprints of God.

Those not of a Christian self-understanding, including atheists, will not have the benefit of faith in the Christian narrative to orient their

---

[39] This conviction underlies both Volf's and Jones's presentations, but Jones's emphasis on embodiment of a correct understanding (revised understanding of the doctrine of the Trinity) through the disciplines of repentance illustrates the connection he sees between reflective awareness and the promotion of practice.

[40] This fact is underdeveloped in Volf's and Jones's presentations. The inadequacy of their presentations to address the questions I am posing in this study can, in part, be traced to their neglect of this issue.

intentional lives, but the understanding of grace articulated above indicates that they, too, are recipients of God's offer of self. For these people the experience can be thought of as analogous to that of the Christian's struggle with unconscious forces. Grace works unrecognized, but it is still operative. As Vatican II suggested, it shows itself in people responding to the call of conscience, a call that beckons beyond what is convenient or self-interested in order to serve one's neighbor, even at the price of personal sacrifice.[41] The same dynamics of grace (responding to the Spirit-borne offer of God's gift of self) as are at work in the experience of Christians also operate in the lives of non-Christians and atheists. The difference is that, by grace, Christians recognize that our shared Christian interpretive matrix names the deeper truth of the meaning of our own existence.

## The Sacramental Mediation of God's Forgiveness

The preceding observations on the dynamics of God's forgiveness draw the sacramental character of its mediation into focus. God's forgiveness is already present prior to any act of repentance. It is borne to the person by God's offer of self as our fulfillment in communion with God. This offer is, to use Rahner's terms, an abiding existential of human experience; it co-conditions every moment of human life. But we cannot directly identify this abiding offer to distinguish it from the ordinary experiences of our world. Indeed, these ordinary experiences are precisely the normal media that bear God's offer to us. They are the media of the divine self-offer, even when we do not recognize them as such.

Thus, even though I might not recognize it at the time, when I respond to an irascible colleague by choosing to listen respectfully (even though I might disagree strongly) and trying to understand his perspective, resisting the impulse to strike back and overpower, this is evidence of an affirmative response to the movement of grace. When a parent foregoes a long-hoped-for luxury in order to provide better opportunities for the education of her child this self-giving love bears the marks of an affirmative response to grace. When a man, long estranged from a former friend or a relative over a now-half-forgotten offense reaches out to reopen communication, resisting the impulse to reproach, the *vestigia dei* are present.

These are the ordinary ways in which we respond to God's offer of self, with its intrinsic offer of forgiveness. And these acts, even though they

---

[41] See the revised understanding of sacrifice proposed in Daly, "New Developments," esp. 55–58; idem, "Sacrifice Unveiled or Revisited," esp. 40–42.

do not necessarily involve matters of sin, do imply God's forgiveness. As events of grace they point to the acceptance of God's offer of self in a manner that works against the resistant impulses in our motivations—impulses toward resentment, self-interest, and posturing our own righteousness. Viewed from the perspective of Sin (not necessarily sins), these events of grace may involve repentance of the impulses that run counter to the affirmation of God's invitation as that has been articulated in the Christian narrative. Viewed in relationship to human personal becoming they might also be expressions of confrontations with the limits of our current attainments of freedom, and therefore inertia, or lack of development, rather than sin. In the process of reorienting our trajectories of personal becoming in accord with that grace of repentance these events of grace deepen our reconciliation with God and advance the Kingdom of God proclaimed by Jesus. But this happens only in and through our grace-sustained, free engagement with the media of our lives—the people, the histories, the meanings by which we appropriate our selves. That is, our encounters with God's forgiveness are sacramentally mediated, borne to us by our engagement with a world of grace.

### The Dynamics of Divine Forgiveness in Jesus Christ

At the heart of the Christian proclamation lies the claim that the God who desires to enter into a communion of love with us has, in fact, entered into the human experience in the person of Jesus. In him we encounter the fullness of the presence of God in human form. That is, he is *the* fundamental sacrament of encounter with God (as Schillebeeckx put it). Every dimension of his human reality, we believe, expresses God's way of being human. His human reality both makes God present and reveals God's way of being toward us. It also reveals the quality of relationship God desires to have with us. In his becoming human, in his personal process of becoming as Jesus of Nazareth, in his ministry, his suffering, his death and resurrection, he made God's offer of self present to humankind. He thus embodied the dynamics of God's forgiveness into the world.

### THE INCARNATION AS SACRAMENTAL MEDIATION AND REVELATION OF GOD'S FORGIVENESS

Viewing the person of Jesus in this light helps us to understand how the Incarnation is much more than a necessary prerequisite for the death of Jesus; it is the sacramental expression in time of God's desire for communion with us—and *therefore* of God's forgiveness. To put it in somewhat mechanistic terms, the incarnation of the Logos in Jesus is the "sign and instrument . . . of communion with God and of unity among all."[42] Christ is the sacrament of reconciliation with God because he embodies, enacts, incarnates the forgiveness of God.

In this perspective it is important to recognize that the Incarnation is not limited—as popular imagination might have it—to the moment when Jesus was conceived by the Holy Spirit in Mary's womb. Rather, the Incarnation can legitimately be understood as having an initiation, but also an extension in time. We can find scriptural grounding for this perspective if we consider the deeper significance of the prologue to John's Gospel. There we read that "the Word (Logos) became flesh" (John 1:14). God spoke the Word that was "in the beginning with God" and "was God" (John 1:1) and that Word came and "lived among us" (John 1:14). But this Word was not spoken in our time in a single instant; it "became flesh"—that is, became the fullness of what it means to be human—over the course of a human lifetime. God's "speaking" of the Word took the form of a personal becoming, one that embodied God's *Logos*: God's hopes, order, desires for human flourishing with one another and in relationship with God.

Over the course of a whole lifetime of "taking flesh" Jesus expressed God's disposition toward us and God's desires and hopes for us. This "speaking" included as its inner *logos* the forgiveness of God that always already precedes the possibility of our repentance, where Sin is at issue. But this speaking also invites us beyond our current attainments of personal becoming, into ever greater freedom to share in God's love. It makes known in the flesh of Jesus God's desire for reconciliation and for intimate communion with us. It thereby also makes known God's ongoing creative work in calling us into personal becoming in communion with God. It proclaims God's desire to liberate us from the power of Sin and from our current limitations, and to transform us into the holiness of the Kingdom of God.

God's entry into the human condition in Christ makes present a forgiveness that already exists. In the person of Jesus, God's forgiveness becomes concretely present, accessible, and palpable for those whom Jesus encounters. He offers the possibility of renewed relationship with God because he opens up a space of relationship in which reconciliation can occur.

---

[42] *Lumen Gentium* 1.

The incarnation of Jesus—over the course of a lifetime—is the sacramental *mediation* of God's forgiving love. But it is also its *revelation*. Although this is not always recognized in the moment, and frequently protested against when made explicit, Jesus revealed that God's primary disposition toward us is characterized by forgiveness. The Christian community communicates this in its narrative. But this narrative is itself the result of reflection on the experiences that gave rise to it. Most especially, the Christian narrative is shaped by the experience of encounter with the Risen Lord, an encounter that sheds light backward on the events surrounding the person of Jesus, reinterpreting them in the light of his risen presence, and forward on the mission and purpose of the community that proclaims his Gospel.

Enshrined in the scriptural texts, the revelation of God's forgiving love in Jesus, when heard and received in grace (under the influence of the Holy Spirit), effects a revelatory experience of recognition for the believer. This is one of the ways in which the sacramental mediation of the Incarnation continues to exercise its effect in time as both sacrament and revelation.

## THE MINISTRY OF JESUS

We can make this general description of the sacramental character of the Incarnation more concrete when we turn to the ministry of Jesus as recounted in the gospels. As Mark indicates (and Matthew and Luke echo), the message with which Jesus began his public ministry was the advent of the Kingdom (or Reign) of God (Mark 1:15; Matt 4:17; Luke 4:43). As the incarnate Word of God, Jesus did more than proclaim the Kingdom; he made it present in his person. In his preaching he called those alienated from God to repentance (conversion) toward the order of life in relationship that God desires for us: communion of persons in love. In his actions he reached out to all, but especially to those who were publicly ostracized, those marginalized for their "sinfulness."

Yet despite his embodiment of the Kingdom there is tension in its realization between the "already" and the "not yet." This tension shows up in the varied reactions Jesus receives. Some embrace the message; others hold back from it; still others fight against it. The Kingdom, therefore, is unfailingly present in Jesus, but its realization for those who encounter Jesus occurs only in their acceptance of it. Only when they repent of a trajectory of personal becoming opposed to or not yet ready to receive the Kingdom can they experience the Kingdom as having come.[43]

---

[43] Both Volf and Jones draw on this dynamic tension between the already and the not-yet dimensions of the Kingdom in their presentations on the dynamics of repentance,

To render this in terms of forgiveness, when Jesus proclaims the Kingdom he is already embodying-forth the opening of a space within which reconciliation with God and neighbor can occur according to the *logos* of God. He is bringing forgiveness. By his interactions with those he meets, Jesus invites a response. That invitation itself is a manifestation of forgiveness. But the forgiveness, which anticipates the repentance and makes it possible, only attains its fruitfulness when it is accepted by the one who believes. This acceptance of the offer of forgiveness is not separate from but is enacted within the hearer through the movement to believing the Good News. It is the act of faith that effects repentance. Thus the Kingdom Jesus proclaimed and made present in his person is the sacramental actualization of God's anticipatory forgiveness when it comes to fruition in reconciliation.

This line of reasoning suggests that seeing the Incarnation as the sacramental expression of God's forgiveness extended over a lifetime can provide an integrative hermeneutic for understanding the whole of the public ministry of Jesus and its relationship to the forgiveness his followers are called to practice: his teachings, his miracles, his interaction with sinners, even his confrontation with the religious authorities. All are sacramental mediations, in word or in deed, of the forgiveness of God, inviting all to repent of what does not accord with the Kingdom. We can therefore find in the ministry of Jesus the foundation for the understanding of God's forgiveness sketched in the previous section. In the ministry of Jesus we can see that he opens a space into which all people, but especially those who have been excluded as "sinners" and "unclean," are welcomed into relationship. This opened space comes in advance of any indication of repentance, for God's forgiveness is proactive, seeking the "lost sheep"(Luke 15:1-7). It provides the relational environment within which repentance makes sense and can take place without being imposed or coerced.

Those who enter the relational space Jesus opens, if they remain, are already undergoing the repentance—the Greek is *metanoia*, turning around, conversion—that makes reconciliation possible. In and through relationship with the Incarnate Word of God, those who have been alienated undergo a graced realignment of the meanings out of which they have lived. They reorient themselves, under the influence of the grace mediated by Jesus in that opened space, toward a new trajectory of personal becoming.

---

but they do not explore its implications from the perspective of the human (but grace-sustained) process of human personal becoming, except under the category of Sin or sins.

This reading of Jesus' ministry finds confirmation in the account Jesus gives of his own actions. In all of the Synoptic Gospels, Jesus names the reason for his table fellowship with "tax collectors and sinners" (Matt 9:10; Mark 2:16; Luke 15:1-2). In Matthew and Mark he explains that "those who are well have no need of a physician, but those who are sick; I have come to call not the righteous but sinners" (Mark 2:17). Jesus has come to restore those who are entangled in disorder so that they may live the order of life (*logos*) of the Kingdom of God. He does so in and through the medium of his personal engagement with them. The forgiveness of God is already present, in him, opening the possibility of reconciliation.

Perhaps the most illuminating apologia for Jesus' actions, the one that most clearly illustrates the dynamics of divine forgiveness, appears in Luke. When Jesus responds to the grumbling of the Pharisees and scribes over his table fellowship with sinners, he tells three parables. The first two—the parables of the lost sheep and of the lost coin—emphasize God's proactive stance toward seeking out and saving what had been lost (Luke 15:4-7 and 8-10). But for the Pharisees the most shocking dimension of God's forgiveness, the one exhibited in Jesus' table fellowship practices, is God's willingness to lavish forgiveness even on those who might not repent.

This is the fundamental point of the parable commonly called the Prodigal Son. Although it is often interpreted as a story of repentance, such a reading completely misses the point![44] Jesus is explaining why he associates with those who are publicly identified as sinners. There is nothing to indicate that they have repented at the time the story is told. In the story, the younger of two sons asks for his share of the inheritance that would come to him upon his father's death. Essentially he is communicating his impatience that his father has not yet died and showing that he is more interested in how he can profit from the death than he is in the relationship with his father. He then demonstrates further contempt for his father by "squander[ing] his property in dissolute living" (Luke 15:13). When a local famine finds him without further resources, he works for a farmer by tending pigs. He is in dire straits.

---

[44] Jones appears to incline to such a reading in *Embodying Forgiveness*, 58–59. Henri Nouwen's meditation on Rembrandt's painting, "The Return of the Prodigal Son," exhibits a similar tendency. Henri J. M. Nouwen, *The Return of the Prodigal Son: A Story of a Homecoming* (New York: Doubleday, 1992), 45–58. Both authors read into the story motivations that are not explicit in the text itself.

Here is the point at which, I believe, many interpreters of this parable go wrong. Luke tells us that, in his hunger and dereliction, he "came to himself" (other translations say "he came to his senses").[45] He decides to return to his father. But notice: Luke does not say that the young man "repents." He does not use any form of the word *metanoia*—turning around in the sense of a conversion or repentance. This is crucial for understanding the story. When the young man thinks about returning to his father's house, Luke makes very explicit that he is still selfish, self-interested, willing to exploit the goodness of his father. "How many of my father's hired hands have bread enough to spare, but here I am dying of hunger!" (Luke 15:17). Even in his return to his father the young man shows himself to be reprobate. He has not repented of anything but his hunger.

This is the heart of Jesus' response to the Pharisees and the scribes. The love of the father for the wayward son, a love that comes to expression in forgiveness, does not depend on the son's repentance. The forgiving love of God is prodigal. It is impelled by its own inner *logos* to reach out proactively to embrace the sinner, for that is the only way in which the sinner can have any hope of repenting, not under condemnation but in the context of a love that welcomes even before one is ready to respond fully to its implications.[46] The forgiving love of God is prodigal. It is willing to squander itself even on those who might never respond to its invitation. Jesus, the Incarnate Word of God, by his table fellowship with sinners embodies and sacramentally mediates this forgiveness in the welcome he extends even to the most heinous of sinners.

But there is a further point to this parable. When the father goes out to try to bring in the elder son we see that forgiveness is not just extended to the sinful younger son. The father also forgives the elder son of his righteousness—the righteousness by which he allows himself to undo the *logos* of the Kingdom to which God calls us. The righteous elder son needs to repent of the use to which he puts his righteousness, making it a foundation for hatred and ostracism of the sinner, even of the unrepentant sinner. The father forgives the elder son of his righteousness and opens up a relational space that invites him, too, to repentance![47]

[45] The New American Bible uses the translation "came to his senses."

[46] Both Volf and Jones get at this dynamism in their discussions of the judgment of grace and the response of repentance.

[47] Jones approaches this understanding in his discussion of the elder son in *Embodying Forgiveness*, 59.

## Sacramental Dynamics in the Passion, Death, and Resurrection

How does this sacramental cosmology cohere with the events of the passion and death of Jesus? Does its rendering of forgiveness not founder on the shoals of rejection? Reading these events in the light of this sacramental, incarnational cosmology suggests a conclusion that is much the reverse. The passion demonstrates God's unswerving fidelity to God's own self-emptying, self-bestowing, forgiving love in Jesus and to God's abiding desire for communion with us creatures. As the incarnate sacramental presence of God's forgiving love, Jesus effects the encounter between that divine love and humankind in the form of forgiveness. Faithful to the mission received from his Father, in his passion and death Jesus brings the offer of God's forgiving love to its unsurpassable actualization—beyond the limits of total rejection. He demonstrates God's offer of forgiveness to humankind to be without conditions. Even as he takes his last breath, he prays that God's forgiveness may continue to reach out to those who brought about his death. His death on the cross thus becomes the sign of the irrevocable character of God's love and forgiveness, but also the instrument by which that love and forgiveness achieve their unsurpassable expression in human history.

Although Christians can now recognize this meaning in the death of Jesus, it took the resurrection to make it known. Without the encounter with the Risen Lord, the death on the cross is only a sign of defeat. In the light of the revelation that Christ has been raised from the dead, the utter rejection of God's forgiving love incarnated in the crucifixion is changed. It becomes, for those who believe, the sign of the triumph of forgiveness over rejection. It reveals the lengths to which God will go to hold open a space within which reconciliation in love can occur. That revelatory sign—insofar as it is revelatory—works a sacramental effect in those who believe. Drawn by the Holy Spirit, those who look upon the cross and receive the grace of faith in God's saving work in Christ come to believe. The sign, when recognized as such in the moment of grace, draws forth a transformative faith. But we can also read this in the other direction. The faith the Spirit brings to birth within us recognizes its proper object and comes to explicit awareness of itself in the encounter with the sign.[48]

---

[48] "Sign" in this context need not be understood primarily in terms of a physical cross but can be taken as the meaning contained in the story of Jesus that one comes to rec-

From within this way of reading the events of Jesus' death it does make sense to speak of Jesus paying a price. But it is not a price paid to God in order to compensate God's offended honor. The price is not about setting the scales of justice in balance. It is a price paid to a blind humanity ("they do not know what they are doing," Luke 23:34). By paying this price Jesus incarnates the fullness of God's forgiveness. He embodies God's fidelity to God's own purpose, seeking to draw a blind, bent, and sinful humanity into a communion of love. The price Jesus pays on the cross mediates both the full enactment (embodiment, incarnation) of God's offer of self to us in forgiving love *and* the revelation of that offer. Jesus pays to us the price we demanded and, in so doing, demonstrates and makes historically actual the full extent of God's prodigal love.

The price paid by the death on the cross is both sign and instrument of God's forgiveness. The Spirit Jesus breathes out in his death, the Spirit who animates the church at Pentecost, opens the eyes of believers to recognize this sign—the cross—as the sign of God's forgiveness and God's offer of reconciliation. The Spirit turns our hearts (repentance, conversion) to receive this forgiving love for what it is, thereby making this sacramental sign fruitful in the life of the believer (reconciliation).

In this sense we can thus claim that the death on the cross, when seen through the lens of the resurrection, reveals both the fact and the irrevocable nature of God's forgiveness. *That* Jesus suffered a violent death and *that* this death has come to be recognized by believers as the sign of God's forgiveness and the pivotal moment in the reconciliation of humankind with God is, for Christians, beyond dispute. But understood from within the dynamics of God's relation to created reality—a relationship that operates according to sacramental dynamics—one need not maintain that God actually *required* the violent death of Jesus in order to balance the scales of divine justice.[49] We can, instead, read the story of Jesus in terms of God's ongoing desire to share God's own life with us in the most intimate of ways.[50]

---

ognize as the truth of God's self-giving love for us. Thus faith comes from hearing and responding, in grace, to the proclamation of the good news.

[49] This conviction runs through the critical engagement with atonement theories in Heim, *Saved from Sacrifice*; and Daly, *Sacrifice Unveiled*.

[50] I believe this approach opens the door to a more integral reading of the relationships among the doctrines of creation, incarnation, grace, and redemption than the standard narrative can sustain. A fuller elaboration of these connections is beyond the scope of the present work.

*Discipleship, Ecclesial Life, and Ongoing Incarnation*

Of course, there is more to the Christian story. During his earthly ministry the sacramental sign of encounter with God's forgiving love in Jesus was limited to Jesus' own localized presence, the words he spoke, his actions, and the message of the Kingdom his disciples carried forth from those localized expressions. Before the resurrection that mediation of encounter with God appeared to have been shattered by the death on the cross. But in the resurrection the irrevocability of God's forgiving love overcomes its utter rejection. The Risen Lord reveals that God's forgiveness is greater than our ability to reject it; reconciliation remains possible.

The resurrection transforms the localized sacramental experience of encounter with God's forgiveness in Jesus into the revelation of a forgiveness that is not bounded by that time and space. The community of believers bears the message, in a reciprocal relationship with other believers and, beyond that, to a world not yet moved to faith. As Paul so insistently reminds the communities to which he writes, they have been called to, and baptized into, a new life in Christ. They have become the Body of Christ. This is the work of the Holy Spirit, transforming the believer into faith and into communion in love. The ways Christians act toward each other and toward the larger world are to reflect and embody the life of the Kingdom of God that Jesus himself proclaimed and embodied.

But as Paul's writings attest, living this new life is challenging. The members of the Christian communities remain disciples—learners—of the new Way. Their reading of scripture, their prayers, and their sharing in the breaking of the bread are to build them up as the Body of Christ. The Spirit of Christ living within them, and within which they live, is to guide their interactions. They are to stretch themselves in reaching out to live this new life ever more fully. In relationship to one another and to those outside the community they are to embody the mode of relationship with others that God has shown to be God's way of relating to us in Christ. Thus, individually and communally, Christians are to be both signs and instruments of the Kingdom of God, effecting its progress in the world under the guidance of the Holy Spirit.

Christian life—Christian discipleship—is thus fundamentally sacramental. It arises from mediated encounter and becomes the mediation of encounter with the God who saves us in Christ through the working of the Holy Spirit. This sacramental life—this (trans)formation in discipleship—occurs at the intersection of the processes of becoming of the individual person and the ecclesial community as these are lived out in the world. These processes operate according to the dynamics of personal becoming explored earlier. They are always situated within and mediated by matrices of meanings that themselves are always in the process of transformation. The ecclesial community bears the proclamation of its narrative and attempts to form the believer to see herself in relationship to that narrative.[51] Practices of prayer, communal worship, responses to the needy, reflection on the foundational narrative: these shape the individual Christian's sense of self as a participant in the community's shared matrix of meanings.

At the same time the individual Christian, as she grows in freedom and self-possession in relationship to the shared matrix, if she appropriates that shared matrix as her own, will inevitably do so by filtering it through her own interpretive lens. Her life in the community will then impress itself on the manner in which the community bears its narrative into the future. She will shape the future becoming of her ecclesial home even as it shapes hers. Insofar as these processes of becoming—individual and ecclesial—are under the guidance of the Holy Spirit they embody a reciprocal sacramental relationship between the believer and the ecclesial community.

The dynamism of divine forgiveness we have been exploring is crucial to the unfolding of this sacramentally mediated process of becoming for both the individual disciple and the ecclesial community. It is the foundation of the communion to which the *ecclesia* and the individual Christian bear witness even as they seek to enact it and embody it ever more fully. The *ecclesia* opens a relational space prior to any act of repentance. That relational space derives its shape and character from the narrative that names the faith of the community—the shared matrix of meanings. The *ecclesia* mediates that space to those drawn to it by the working of the Holy Spirit (grace) in the concrete circumstances in which the *ecclesia* itself exists. It offers a space of welcome in the mode of forgiveness. The forgiveness, if it is true to its source, is unconditional. That forgiveness is only actualized—the sacrament is only made effective—when it is received (act of faith, grace), when the one drawn to faith enters into

---

[51] Jones devotes a great deal of his work to precisely this point. This is evident especially when he draws on Bonhoeffer to emphasize the importance of formation in the "arcane discipline" of penitential existence and practices of forgiveness within the community, but the point has broader implications. The Christian community has an explicit responsibility to form its members in the life of discipleship of which the "arcane discipline" is a part. See Jones, *Embodying Forgiveness*, 28–32, 192, 228.

the transformation to which forgiveness invites (ongoing conversion, repentance, the life of discipleship).

The evidence of that transformation, at least in part, is the increasing degree to which the one who receives forgiveness grows in the capacity to extend the same forgiveness to others, prior to their repentance, without conditions. That is, the evidence of the transformation is the degree to which the Christian disciple becomes a sacramental bearer of God's mode of forgiveness to others.[52] But her cooperation with the movement of grace in being a sacramental bearer of God's forgiveness for others is also the grace-sustained process by which she freely embraces her own transformation. In her own person, as she engages with the world around her, she mediates God's offer of self in the mode of forgiveness to those she encounters. She embraces God's ongoing creative, redemptive work as the truth of her own personal becoming, and in so doing she actualizes the ecclesial reality of the Body of Christ. She becomes a sign and instrument of communion with God and neighbor. She incarnates the Kingdom of God.

To state this slightly differently, the disciple, in the same process of enacting God's forgiveness toward others—always by means of the Holy Spirit/grace—also actualizes her own transformation into the Body of Christ. In the Spirit she becomes a sacramental "incarnation" of the offer of God's forgiveness to others by her free embrace of this forgiving trajectory of personal becoming as her own deepest truth. The disciple becomes a disciple by living the teaching—and thereby becoming the teaching herself.

We have returned here to the difficult question of the personal transformation in grace raised in the previous chapter. Whereas the traditional accounts affirm *that* a transformation occurs, their ability to explain that transformation as a process is hampered by an overemphasis on a "from above" approach to forgiveness, neglect of the dynamics of human personal becoming, and a tendency to disjunctive reasoning (either faith or no faith, either sin or grace). Resituating the discussion within the dynamics of sacramental mediation of encounter with God in the context of human becoming allows us to be more articulate about the transformation: to affirm that a transformation does occur, that it takes place over time, that

---

[52] This seems to be the existential point toward which Volf points when he argues that refusal to forgive is evidence that one has not accepted the grace of forgiveness from God. The valid point behind his claim, however, is hampered by the disjunctive conceptual framework (either/or), which does not adequately name the experience of transformation as a process.

it is a matter of grace/the action of the Holy Spirit, *and* that it works in and through the freedom of the person over the course of a lifetime. The transformation can therefore be understood as a continuously unfolding, dynamic process at the intersection of grace and human freedom.

Further, this approach suggests that the locus of transformation is something other than the change in one's motivation to forgive others (or not). The change in motivation identified by Volf and Jones can be understood as the evidence of a deeper change, a reorientation in the trajectory of one's personal becoming that *consequently* comes to expression in different motivations. Naming the transformation in these terms makes it possible to see how motivations such as love for God or desire to be more strongly identified with Jesus could also be properly Christian motivations. So, too, could the desire to be healed of the pain one carries from holding onto resentment. Each of these could be the locus of a transformative encounter that liberates one to embrace the effort to forgive others.

In other words, approaching the discussion of the transformative impact of God's forgiveness of us from within the framework of sacramental dynamics allows us to affirm that transformation does take place in grace, but it also opens up a broader way of accounting for *how* that transformation is experienced by Christians. However, affirming that explanation requires that one step within a distinctive Christian matrix of meanings, that sketched above. Once that step has been taken, our affirmations about that transformation can be verified in faith on the basis of personal experience. This sacramental approach to the question of transformation in faith thus opens up the possibility of integrating the "from above" and the "from below" approaches to Christian forgiveness.

## Conclusion

We began this chapter with the task of reorienting ourselves in the landscape of Christian forgiveness. The purpose of this reorientation has been to provide a more adequate account of such forgiveness, measured against the concerns raised in chapters 8 and 9. Our approach has placed the story of Christ within the larger narrative of God's desire to give God's self in love to what is other than God. Rethinking the Christian narrative within this framework has allowed us to identify what God is doing when God forgives, to identify a continuity between the dynamism of God's creative action and God's redemptive action, to ground our understanding of God's forgiveness in the revelation of Christ as the Incarnation of God's enactment of forgiveness, and to indicate how God's way of forgiving, as revealed in Christ, impinges on the life of the Christian both as recipient of forgiveness and as one called to extend that same forgiveness to others.

The course of our exploration has embraced the conviction that Christian forgiveness is *distinguishable* on the basis of its connection to the Christian narrative, but we have suggested that the locus of the Christian-ness cannot simply be identified with the transformation of motivation identified by Volf and by Jones. Beneath the change in motivation a more fundamental transformation is taking place, one that grounds any changes in motivation. This is the transformation of one's trajectory of personal becoming because of a realignment of the meanings constituting the sense of self. Thus at least one aspect of distinctive Christian forgiveness derives from the meanings the narrative offers for the enactment.

Locating the transformation at level of meanings constituting the sense of self has opened up possibilities not available to traditional accounts of Christian forgiveness. First, it implies that one may have different consciously thematized motivations when undertaking to forgive and still be enacting Christian forgiveness. It has thus broadened the landscape of Christian forgiveness.

Second, understanding the transformation in terms of the sacramental dynamics described above—weaving together "from above" and "from below" approaches—provides a theoretical framework from within which to account for one's own particular struggles to forgive, experiences of liberation for extending forgiveness, and the ongoing development of one's capacities for forgiving as distinct-but-related movements in the life of grace. This allows the postmodern skeptic to correlate the narrative of Christian faith with her own experience of reality in a way not easily supported by one-sidedly "from above" accounts. It can thus act against impulses to dismiss the Christian narrative as myth. And third, seeing the transformation in terms of an ongoing interpersonal developmental movement in our growth in the Spirit as disciples of Christ can illuminate the connection between our intra-mundane experiences of salvation and their fulfillment in the eschatological Kingdom of God.

No telling of the Christian story can guarantee that it will be received in a transformative way. Ultimately, any transformation will take place in the inscrutable intimacy where human freedom encounters God's invitation. But the presentation in this chapter suggests an approach that allows additional (and different) points of access—places of contact between human experience as it is commonly understood today and the Christian narrative—than those found in the traditional narrative. It offers possibilities to the postmodern context of meanings that the traditional narrative does not.

# Chapter 11

# The Distinctive Terrain
# of Christian Forgiveness

## Preliminaries

The previous chapter articulated theological foundations for rethinking the Christian narrative. It transposed the story of God's redemptive work in Christ into the larger horizon of God's desire to give Godself in love to what is other than God as our salvation and fulfillment. This reoriented perspective allowed us to view God's forgiveness of us as in continuity with the dynamism of God's creative action in the cosmos. It also allowed us to see a greater continuity between creation, incarnation, and redemption by rethinking them in terms of sacramentality. The framework of sacramentality, for its part, opens the door to recognizing the forgiveness Christians are called to embody (incarnate) as in continuity with and as an extension of God's creative action.

This way of rethinking the Christian narrative brings about a shift in the function of the narrative in relationship to our own enactments of forgiveness. As with the traditional narrative, the reorientation proposed here still provides a matrix of meanings by which the ecclesial community can orient its members in their religious formation, but in this revised telling the admonition to enact forgiveness, even of our enemies, although still an integral part of the narrative, operates differently. No longer a merely extrinsically imposed obligation, often inculcated coercively, in this narrative the intrinsic relation between our enactment of forgiveness and our own ongoing transformation and fulfillment in relationship with God comes more clearly into focus.

The retelling of the narrative presented here places the emphasis not on the ability of the narrative (under the influence of grace/the Holy

Spirit) to change conscious motivations but rather on the realignment of the trajectory of personal becoming of the Christian in accord with the purpose and fulfillment of Christian life as articulated in the Christian narrative. The conscious motivations that cause one to undertake to forgive can, therefore, be diverse. Not just gratitude for the recognition that God's forgiveness is for me personally (not merely in general), but also the desire to be more like Jesus, hunger for justice, commitment to the mission of advancing the Kingdom of God, and even the desire to be healed of the pain arising from the harm one has suffered—all of these (and more) can be motivations proper to distinctively Christian forgiveness, for all of them can arise in their particularity from the deep realignment of one's sense of self—and consequent realignment of the trajectory of one's personal becoming—through encounter with God in the Spirit.

The theological reorientation of the previous chapter has thus opened for us a much wider landscape of Christian forgiveness than the traditional narrative envisions. The time has come for us now to draw together what has emerged thus far and, on the basis of this reorientation, to name Christian forgiveness in its distinctiveness, both as a specific actualization of a way of life grounded in the Christian narrative and in the particular characteristics of its enactment.

## Naming a Distinctive Christian Forgiveness

In one way we have already signaled the distinctiveness of Christian forgiveness by emphasizing its relationship to the Christian narrative. But rather than resolving our questions, the content of that narrative poses its own challenges, for the forgiveness Christians are to practice is at the same time both a human enactment and a participation in the dynamics of God's own way of forgiving. The human enactment—the forgiveness Christians are to extend to others—takes on new meaning when understood in the light of God's forgiveness as revealed in Christ. To name Christian forgiveness in its distinctiveness we must therefore first recall the characteristics of God's forgiveness and then use them as a lens through which to interpret the characteristics of forgiveness as a basic human enactment.

### Characteristics of God's Way of Forgiving

Up to this point we have spoken of God's way of forgiving in terms of the opening of a relational space in the wake of an experience of harm, an experience that produces relational rupture. Forgiveness, by means of the space it opens, makes possible the repentance and reconciliation that in their turn provide the basis for the communion in love that God intends for creation. When we view it in these terms we can begin to see that there is a common, unifying element in God's relationship to what is other than God. Whether in the initial act of creation or in the restoration of right relationship through grace-mediated reconciliation, God is consistently appealing to humankind to embrace the relationship God offers. There is thus a greater dynamic continuity between God's creative and redemptive action in the world than is commonly recognized when these are both seen in relationship to what God does in forgiving.

For Christians, the way we come to understand God's forgiveness is by looking at the life, ministry, death, and resurrection of Jesus: the whole course of the Incarnation. In the previous chapter we identified five characteristics of God's way of forgiving. These are different aspects of one unified dynamism; they are interrelated in God's forgiving.

First, God's forgiveness is *proactive*. It is an expression of God's openness to and desire for restored relationship with us even before our repentance. In the face of human histories of ruptured relationship it goes forth in love to create the space that makes repentance possible. It thus precedes our response.

Second, God's forgiveness is *freely given*. God exacts no repayment or restitution before forgiving. It is, rather, God who pays the price, the price of self-emptying in love in order to give Godself to us. God absorbs the offense.

Third, it is *sacramental*. God's forgiveness is mediated to us through our engagement with the world around us. This world is the medium through which God appeals to our freedom, inviting us to repent of what alienates us from God.

Fourth, God's forgiveness has a *preferential option for those most in need of receiving it*. As Jesus puts it, "I have come to seek out and save what was lost."

Fifth, God's offer of forgiveness exhibits a *missionary impulse*. In the face of alienation and sin, yet still desiring that we be reconciled, God enters into what is other than God. God makes incarnate in the world the eschatological communion of the Kingdom of God in Jesus through his enactment of forgiveness.

These characteristics of God's forgiveness—the forgiveness exhibited in Jesus—establish benchmarks for a distinctively Christian enactment. Christians, as disciples of Jesus, are called to carry forth the mission of

Jesus, a mission still at work in the world under the guidance of the Holy Spirit, by opening a relational space within which reconciliation moving toward communion becomes possible. Christians are to labor in the Spirit to make the Kingdom present. Thus Christian forgiveness is to be a proactive, freely given sacramental mediation of transforming encounter with God (grace, Holy Spirit). It is especially concerned to reach those most in need of it and is therefore directed by a consciousness that the Christian has been sent on mission to actualize this forgiveness as the expression of the Kingdom of God in time.

### Transforming the Characteristics of Human Forgiveness

Where the Spirit of God is at work in the life of the believer, leading her to extend forgiveness to others, we can expect that the characteristics of the human enactment of forgiveness mentioned earlier will be transformed. They will take on the form of Christ's own enactment of God's forgiveness. They will acquire a new significance that the believer can recognize. (This does not imply that the new significance will always be reflexively present in the consciousness of the individual Christian when she is undertaking to forgive, but it will be recognizable on later reflection.)

The *act of freedom in personal becoming* that characterizes any human enactment of forgiveness becomes a faith-filled *participation in God's creative and redemptive work*. It transforms the harm that ruptured the relationship into an occasion of grace. By its freely chosen enactment this act of forgiveness cooperates with the movement of the Spirit to liberate the one wounded from the power of retributive impulses. Grace sets the wounded one free to choose a non-retributive trajectory of personal becoming—a trajectory that reflects God's own response to our ruptures of relationship. It enables the one harmed to see in the event of harm an occasion in which a redemptive response is possible, a response that turns the harm into a sacramental event. For the one harmed, the meaning of the event changes. It is not simply a harm now understood as forgiven but rather a harm that has become an opportunity in which she can grow into deeper communion with God in Christ by responding to the Spirit's invitation to embody God's way of forgiving. The harm is being redeemed for the one who undertakes to forgive. The one undertaking to forgive becomes thereby ever more fully an incarnational expression of the Body of Christ.

Further, embracing a commitment to forgive a harm redeems the harm for the offender even as it redeems the one harmed. If the offender comes to recognize the forgiveness and repent of the harm, that harm, as forgiven, becomes the sign that the offender is not bound to the initial meaning of a past offense. Forgiveness, if accepted, sets the offender free to embrace a different trajectory of future becoming. She has the possibility of entry into communion with the one harmed—if not now, then sometime in the future. Her personal becoming into the future is unfettered by the alienation initially arising from the harmful act. Both the wounded party and the offender are redeemed from the way the history of offense could have constrained the future of their relationships—to each other and to the larger world.

This act of freedom in personal becoming is simultaneously a participation in God's creative action in the world. As creatures always in the process of becoming, we have not yet been fully created. Aspects of ourselves are continually undergoing development and change—sometimes for good, sometimes for ill. When, under the influence of God's offer of self, we choose a trajectory of personal becoming that embodies God's way of forgiving, we are cooperating with God in that creative process—a creative act that is not yet complete. Insofar as we do so we are also cooperating with God in the grace-borne creative process at work in the one who has offended, laboring to open a space in which her repentance and conversion can flourish and she can grow in communion with God and us in grace. Thus, to return to an earlier question, every act of forgiveness performed by a Christian *is* Christian forgiveness *to the extent that* it is aligned with the trajectory of personal becoming in accord with God's creative and redemptive action in the world, whether it is reflexively grasped as such or not.

Our *commitment* not to use the harm as an occasion for retribution likewise undergoes a change. It becomes our *consecration* of the history of the harm and its place in our lives into God's care. That history is no longer mine to dispose of or respond to as I wish. It is now part of God's story—the story of God's transformative action in the world. As such, both the history and the memory of it *as consecrated to God's care* become potentially sacramental, for the one harmed and for the offender. The one harmed can find in that memory the (re)affirmation of God's active presence in setting her free to forgive and to shape a new trajectory of personal becoming. The one who offended, when he recognizes the forgiveness and repents of the offense, can find in that memory the encouragement to stay true to the trajectory spelled out by his repentance.

The *conversion* at the heart of the human enactment of forgiveness takes on its own distinctive meaning when embraced within the

Christian matrix of meanings. It becomes more than merely the re-alignment of meanings to overcome impulses toward retribution. It is, instead, the expression of an ongoing process of increasing conformity to the life of Christ within us through the working of the Holy Spirit. It is our ongoing transformation into clearer incarnation of the presence of Christ healing our world. It comes to expression in a realigned trajectory of personal becoming, in accord with the gospels. This conversion—an ongoing transformation—is our *life as disciples of Christ.*

Finally, the *eschatological orientation* of human enactments of forgiveness, when undertaken as an expression of Christian faith, does more than point toward an unspecified future. It actually *makes that hoped-for future real in the present moment.* It anticipates the Kingdom of God in the here and now. The Kingdom of God, as the incarnate life of Christ, becomes actual *in* the one who forgives and *for* the one who receives that forgiveness. The sacramental (grace-bearing and grace-revealing) dimension of the enactment of forgiveness thus make present the way of relating hoped for in the eschatological Kingdom in the moment it becomes active. The Kingdom comes to expression in our world when we undertake to enact forgiveness.

### Transformation of Meaning, and Recognition

It is important to note a caveat when speaking of a transformation of the meaning of the human enactment. A Christian will have been schooled in some version of the Christian story. She is therefore able to anticipate future experiences of harm as occasions for reaffirming her own identification with that story. It is from within her Christian matrix of shared meanings that she can do so, but this does not mean that the transformed meaning is operative in a reflexively identifiable way at the moment she is confronted with a real harm in the present, nor does it mean that she is specifically thinking about the relationship of this harm to the context of meanings from which her sense of self is constituted. It also does not mean that her efforts to undertake forgiveness (or not) are consciously correlated with the Christian narrative. Any or all of these conditions might be operative, but they also might not.

When we talk about God's way of forgiving as revealed in Christ as transforming the meaning of forgiving as a basic human enactment we are making a different kind of claim. We are saying that the Christian, looking at her effort to enact forgiveness, and doing so with an awareness of her own relationship with God in Christ, will be able to recognize the coherence (or not) of her enactment with the transformed significance described above. She will be able to recognize that her forgiving has a deeper significance because of its participation in and alignment with God's own way of forgiving as revealed in Christ, and in her own resistance to forgiving she will recognize the disparity between the trajectory of personal becoming to which she has been called and her current state of progress along that trajectory.

### Distinctiveness at the Intersection of Meaning and Enactment

This approach to naming Christian forgiveness draws together the "from above" and "from below" approaches by disclosing the continuity of dynamism in God's way of forgiving as revealed in Christ and the forgiveness Christians are called to enact. God does not impose an extrinsic burden upon us, but rather empowers us to participate in God's work by disclosing a deeper possibility for the merely human enactment of forgiveness. Whether we recognize it or not, undertaking to enact forgiveness is an expression of the purpose for which God created the world: the movement toward reconciled communion with God in love.

But recognizing and affirming this meaning within the Christian context carries with it further implications for the distinctiveness of Christian forgiveness. These emerge at the intersection of meaning and enactment. The meanings constituting the Christian matrix impel Christians to enact forgiveness in identifiably distinctive ways. Without exhausting all of the loci of distinctiveness, we can nonetheless illustrate this point by considering three aspects of the forgiveness Christians are called to enact.

## ABSORBING THE COST

A first distinguishing characteristic can be expressed in terms of absorbing the offense or "paying the price." Pamela Hieronymi is unique among the philosophers discussed in chapter 2 for her acknowledgment of this element of forgiveness.[1] One could extend her point by arguing that there is a twofold cost to be absorbed in forgiving: the offense itself and the energy expended in restraining one's retributive impulses. But whereas Hieronymi maintains the necessity that the offender repent before forgiveness is extended, Christian forgiveness does not.

---

[1] Pamela Hieronymi, "Articulating an Uncompromising Forgiveness," *Philosophy and Phenomenological Research* 62, no. 3 (May 2001): 529–55, at 551.

This points to a fundamental cleavage between philosophical approaches and the Christian approach presented here. In most of the philosophical approaches, evidence of repentance is, in a sense, the price to be paid for receiving forgiveness. Hieronymi recognizes that even when this price has been paid there is still a cost that the one harmed must absorb, although this is not elaborated. Further, although Hieronymi correctly recognizes that the one harmed must absorb the cost, she does not provide any reasons why one would be motivated to do so, beyond the (conditional) moral imperative that one forgive.

The Christian matrix of meanings, by contrast, does not require repentance, but provides a way of revaluing the significance of absorbing the offense. Doing so is no longer merely a loss. The Christian can come to recognize it as participation in the life of God, in the mission of incarnating the Kingdom of God, in the graced transformation of oneself and of the event for the sake of the benefit of the offender, and in the possibility of communion in love that comes on the far side of reconciliation. The Christian affirms that these possibilities are of higher value than her pursuit of retribution, and so undertakes to forgive. She therefore commits to wrestling with her own resistance to ongoing conversion as she consecrates the history of the harm to God in the incarnation of her own discipleship.

This is not to suggest that the Christian condones the offensive behavior. The very act of undertaking to forgive implies negative judgment on the offensive act. Indeed, in view of the mission to proclaim and incarnate the Kingdom, the Christian can and must oppose what is counter to the Kingdom.[2] But this does not prevent the Christian from

---

[2] This point is made in different language in each of the three Christian authors we have profiled. Smedes emphasizes that we must name the truth of what has harmed us (Lewis B. Smedes, *The Art of Forgiving: When You Need to Forgive and Don't Know How* [New York: Ballantine Books, 1996], 62). He writes: "You will forgive only when you dare look at people eyeball to eyeball and tell them that they are responsible for what they did. Forgiving is fair to wrongdoers because it holds them to the incriminating touchstone of their own free humanity" (Smedes, *Forgive and Forget: Healing the Hurts We Don't Deserve* [New York: HarperCollins, 1984], 130). Miroslav Volf devotes considerable attention to the topic under the rubric of "remembering rightly" throughout his *The End of Memory: Remembering Rightly in a Violent World* (Grand Rapids, MI: Eerdmans, 2006); idem, *Exclusion and Embrace: A Theological Exploration of Identity, Otherness, and Reconciliation* (Nashville: Abingdon Press, 1996), 131–32; and idem, *Free of Charge: Giving and Forgiving in a Culture Stripped of Grace* (Grand Rapids, MI: Zondervan, 2005), 175. L. Gregory Jones explores the importance of eliciting the truth in confession if we are to reestablish communion, and the necessity of a community in helping us to "narrate the

proactively forgiving the person who commits the offensive action. It is precisely in view of advancing the sacramental actualization of the Kingdom that she absorbs the cost and dares to forgive even before the offender's repentance.

### THIRD-PARTY FORGIVENESS

A second aspect of a distinctive Christian forgiveness is its scope. It is not just that Christians are to forgive those who offend them; they are also to bring forgiveness to those who offend others, even when they themselves have not been directly touched by the harm. This is represented in the text on "the Keys" (Matt 16:19; cf. 18:18) as well as in the resurrection appearances and commissioning the disciples to forgive (John 20:22-23). It is surprising that this aspect of Christian forgiveness—perhaps its most radical characteristic—is passed over in silence in the traditional accounts. We will need to touch on the philosophical objections to this concept before clarifying its Christian distinctiveness.

In the philosophical literature the extension of forgiveness for harms one has not directly suffered oneself is sometimes referred to as "third-party forgiveness."[3] We can distinguish two variants on the issue of

---

truth of our lives" (Jones, *Embodying Forgiveness: A Theological Analysis* [Grand Rapids, MI: Eerdmans, 1995], 199, 187, respectively).

[3] See, for example, Charles Griswold, "Debating Forgiveness: A Reply to My Critics," *Philosophia* 38 (2010): 457–73, at 467, where the author distinguishes third-party forgiveness (forgiveness on behalf of another for an offense done to the other) from forgiveness for a harm done to oneself by the infliction of harm on another (for example, the forgiveness parents give to a killer for the death of their child). The former case raises the issue of "standing," the same issue raised by Simon Wiesenthal in *The Sunflower* (New York: Schocken Books, 1976). If we understand forgiving as somehow abrogating someone's responsibility—absolving of guilt—with respect to the offense, then the issue of standing is problematic. And as Griswold's interlocutor, Adam Morton, charged, "If we allow the pain and grief caused by knowledge of the offence to establish victim-hood, then any wrong doing will have as victims all those who are offended by its wrongness." (Adam Morton, "Central and Marginal Forgiveness: Comments on Charles Griswold's 'Forgiveness: A Philosophical Exploration,'" *Philosophia: Philosophical Quarterly of Israel* 38, no. 3 (2010): 439–44, 442.) This raises two questions: first, do we not, in fact, take offense at things done to others in such a way that we must engage the dynamics of forgiveness? I believe we do. This may not please moral philosophers who want to determine who is right to forgive and who is not, but judged by the dynamics engaged when forgiving and when dealing with such situations we are dealing with the same reality. The exclusion of this case as not appropriately forgiving is a matter of circular reasoning. Second, I have to

forgiving a harm one has not directly suffered. One variant is forgiveness on behalf of another. This is one of the issues raised by Simon Wiesenthal in *The Sunflower*. Did he have the standing to forgive on behalf of those whom the SS officer had killed? Moral philosophers roundly reject this kind of enactment unless some specific authorization has been given. The common conviction is that only the one who has been harmed has the authority to forgive. But what if the victim has authorized another to forgive on her behalf? What then? We shall return to this case shortly.

The second variant in third-party forgiveness is forgiving another on one's own behalf for a harm done to a third party. For example, someone murders my cousin. I am not the victim; do I therefore have anything to forgive? And if so, what would this forgiveness mean?

On this variant the philosophical responses are ambiguous. On the one hand, some argue that one does not have moral standing to resent and forgive someone for a harm one has not suffered oneself.[4] Impulses to retribution in such cases would, presumably, be ruled out of bounds, themselves immoral. Therefore, since forgiveness is only for moral harms one has directly suffered, forgiveness is not applicable in third-party situations. But the fact is that retributive impulses do arise in such cases and people do undertake to enact forgiveness (or withhold it) in response to them. Therefore, on the other hand, some philosophers allow (concede?) that the offense done to another might be a moral harm to a third party for which the third party might offer forgiveness.[5] This second case, however, is not heavily explored in the literature.

--------------------

wonder precisely who "we" is. "If *we* allow . . . ." Who, precisely gave Morton (and Griswold) and their companions the "standing" to make such exclusions? Charles Griswold, "Debating Forgiveness," 467; see also Charles L. Griswold, *Forgiveness: A Philosophical Exploration* (Cambridge: Cambridge University Press, 2007), 117–19; see also William R. Neblett, "Forgiveness and Ideals," *Mind* 83, no. 330 (April 1974): 269–75, at 271.

[4] See, for example, Jeffrey G. Murphy and Jean Hampton, *Forgiveness and Mercy*, 21, where Murphy states, "To use a legal term, I do not have *standing* to resent or forgive you unless I have myself been the victim of your wrongdoing. I may forgive you for embezzling my funds; but it would be ludicrous for me, for example, to claim that I had decided to forgive Hitler for what he did to the Jews. I lack the proper standing for this. Thus, I may legitimately resent (and hence consider forgiving) only wrong done *to me*." Griswold makes a similar point when he states that "in the paradigmatic case the victim alone owns the moral right to forgiveness." Griswold, *Forgiveness: A Philosophical Exploration*, 48. However, Griswold does allow for the possibility of third-party forgiveness under certain restrictions. See ibid., 117–20.

[5] Griswold acknowledges the existential experience but excludes this as a case of third-party forgiveness because it involves forgiving someone, not for the offense directly

What may constitute a lacuna in the philosophical discussions becomes deeply disturbing by its relative absence in the Christian literature on forgiveness.[6] Third-party forgiveness in both variants is integrally related to the mission entrusted to Christians. Yet the Christian literature does not engage the questions raised about third-party forgiveness by the philosophers. This needs to be addressed, but how? The philosophical concerns do impinge on Christian practice. Ideally, the response to those philosophical concerns should be acceptable without appeal to religious data. On the other hand, we are attempting to clarify the distinctiveness of the Christian enactment of forgiveness. We will therefore need to address the matter of third-party forgiveness in a way that highlights that distinctiveness in relation to the Christian matrix of meanings we have been articulating.

Weaving together the Christian narrative with the phenomenology of human experience of forgiveness provides us with the resources we need to address both concerns. In the phenomenology we clarified that the kind of harm that evokes forgiveness as a potential response is an event of meaning. It is a meaning that disrupts the sense of self and of the self-world relationship. When someone other than myself has been harmed it can have a harmful impact on me, precisely because I can recognize in the harmful act a threat or wound inflicted on the meaning-world I inhabit, the one that underlies my sense of self. I may therefore recognize it as harmful and experience it as a harm to me.[7]

In the face of such a recognized meaning, a retributive impulse is quite natural and may even be appropriate. My response is directed at the offender for the event of harm *because I recognize that it also harms me*

---

done to the victim, but for one's own experience of loss or harm occasioned by one's recognition of the harm done to the victim. See Griswold, *Forgiveness: A Philosophical Exploration*, 117. It is thus a moral harm, that the "third party" may undertake to forgive, but the forgiveness undertaken does not forgive on behalf of the victim for the harm she suffered. It is therefore, in Griswold's understanding, not really third-party forgiveness. He reserves this term for forgiveness bestowed on behalf of the victim.

[6] Jones does affirm the possibility and even the obligation of third-party forgiveness in his response to the question posed by Wiesenthal's *The Sunflower*. Jones, *Embodying Forgiveness*, 288. However, the point is made in passing, without further development.

[7] Hieronymi gets at this idea when she identifies in the harm a present and future threat to the victim. I would argue that such a threat directed specifically to the victim can also have the impact of a threat to others and can therefore be experienced as a harm one might need to forgive. Hieronymi, "Articulating an Uncompromising Forgiveness," 546, 550.

*and my self-world relations.*[8] It disrupts my personal and shared matrices of meanings. Moreover, that the process by which I would overcome that retributive impulse functions according to the same dynamics as what I must engage when responding to harms that touch me directly. I must undertake to forgive. Thus, looking at the question of third-party forgiveness from the perspective of the human enactment of forgiveness suggests that this is a real human possibility, but in making this affirmation it is important to recognize what this kind of forgiveness does and does not do.

Forgiveness enacted in this way does not undo the history of the harm. It does not remove the offender's responsibility for having offended or the obligation to try to rectify the offense. It most certainly does not substitute for the necessary process of repentance and seeking to effect reconciliation with the one harmed, if that is still possible. But it does do something very important. It invites the offender, through interpersonal relationship, into a space in which her own trajectory of personal becoming can be transformed and reoriented in a prosocial manner. It invites the offender into a space of conversion. The meaning and power of the harmful event in the life of the offender can change. In that third-party forgiveness I commit myself not to use the harm done to another as a justification to harm the offender in return. That history of harm takes on a new meaning for me. Extending that forgiveness to the offender also opens up to the one harmed, insofar as she is still present, a context in which to see the offender in relationship to a larger horizon of meanings. This has the potential to help her in the process of restabilizing her sense of self and self-world relations and may open the door to her willingness to engage forgiveness and work toward reconciliation.

---

[8] The point being made here highlights a limitation in some of the philosophical discussions. These tend to try to isolate the meaning of the harm within limited bounds. Essentially, in affirming its moral meaning they abstract it from the very relational context (matrix of meanings) that gives it that moral weight. But the meaning does not exist apart from those who recognize it, and that recognition depends on the matrix of meanings that underlies the recognition. My point is that the isolation of a "meaning" for an event apart from the matrix that gives it its meaning, and therefore makes possible that others in the shared matrix might also need to forgive the harm, is simply a fiction. It purchases theoretical clarity at the price of disregard for human experience. Hieronymi, by contrast, notes the social setting of the enduring threat that evokes the protest of resentment, confirming the approach to harming self and self-world relations being made here. Hieronymi, "Articulating an Uncompromising Forgiveness," 550.

This kind of forgiveness is possible on a purely human level, but the very limited attention and support given to it in the moral philosophical discussions helps to underscore why third-party forgiveness is a distinctive element of Christian forgiveness. For the moral philosophers this is a possibility. For Christians this kind of forgiveness is integral to the narrative that grounds the shared matrix of Christianity.

Christian forgiveness can find positive meaning in extending such forgiveness because doing so is an expression of the Christian mission to actualize the Kingdom of God in the world. The self-implication of the becoming-self in the Christian narrative provides a rationale for and a meaningfulness to undertaking this kind of forgiveness—a meaningfulness not provided in the moral philosophical discussions. Extending such forgiveness is integral to the narrative that gives Christian discipleship its shape and direction.

Undertaking to forgive the affront to the matrix of meanings that constitutes my sense of self and my self-world relations is an expression of the sacramentally mediated grace that effects my own transformation into an incarnation of the Kingdom in the present, even as it makes of my forgiveness a sacramental offering of redemption to the one who has committed the harm. By opening this space in which the offender can reweave relationship with a larger human community I invite the offender into a context of meanings that does not approve of the offensive action but that also does not bind her meaning to it. I allow and encourage her, in a relationship marked by proactive forgiveness, to find her way to another trajectory of personal becoming in which the memory of the harm as forgiven can provide support to her own efforts to embrace the grace of repentance.

But what about forgiving on behalf of another, the unanswered question mentioned above? Can someone entrust to a third party the capacity to forgive on their behalf? Christians hold that God has already done so. God has entrusted to disciples of Jesus the ability to forgive on God's behalf. We have, in fact, been charged with the mission to bring God's forgiveness to the world. But that's God. What about people? Can human beings entrust to another the right to forgive on their behalf?

This is a real issue for those Christian communities that recognize and celebrate a sacramental practice of confession and penance. The understanding of Christian forgiveness laid out in this chapter provides a way of understanding this distinctive practice. As indicated above, third-party forgiveness does not obviate the need for repentance or for seeking to effect personal reconciliation with the one offended, but as an expression of God's forgiveness it does welcome the offender back into the Body of Christ. It embraces the individual as a member of the community of disciples and sets him free to grow more deeply into the repentance that has already been presupposed and expressed by entering into the sacramental practice.

The one who has offended is thus reconciled with the community, but the individual reconciliation with the person directly harmed may still require further work. This is the point Jones pursues with such eloquence in his critique of "cheap grace."[9] The one harmed—assuming she is a member of the ecclesial community—has given an implicit affirmation to the representatives of the community to actualize sacramental forgiveness *on the community's behalf.* This is part of the shared matrix of meanings she herself inhabits. But the forgiveness given on behalf of the community does not substitute for her own. She may need more time to grow into the possibility of forgiving the harm done, let alone facing the prospect of an interpersonal reconciliation. This is part of the journey of her own discipleship.

## DISCIPLESHIP AND PERSONAL DEVELOPMENT

This brings us to a third aspect of a distinctive Christian forgiveness, one that is underdeveloped in the literature on Christian forgiveness.[10] Implicit in the language of discipleship is the notion that we do grow and develop as Christians. Our free response to the invitation of grace—a response itself supported by grace—is the means by which we cooperate in our own growth in communion with God in Christ through the working of the Holy Spirit. Jones, Volf, and other Christian writers wrestle with different languages to name this phenomenon. We are transforming from "being a Christian" to "being Christian."[11] The idea is that the externally

---

[9] Jones, *Embodying Forgiveness.* "Cheap grace" is a constant point of concern throughout the text.

[10] This is a central concern of Jones's project. It corresponds to the "from below" aspects of his efforts to promote practices that will lead us to embody forgiveness. Although I am sympathetic to the aims of his project, I believe it needs to take greater account of the resources of developmental psychology.

[11] The contrasting phrases are from Brian Zahnd, *Unconditional?* (Lake Mary, FL: Charisma House, 2010), 56–57. The point he is making is addressed in Jones, *Embodying Forgiveness,* 10 (with reference to Bonhoeffer's self-assessment as a theologian), and 45, 167, 173, 175, and 207, among other places, under the heading of "becoming holy." In

communicated Word becomes the inner reality of our own selves. This notion, it seems to me, is what Volf is also getting at in the language I have criticized above as excessively disjunctive and what Jones is attempting to address with his emphasis on "embodying" forgiveness.

This process of growth and development in Christian-ness is at work in our enactments of forgiveness. Forgiving is not an all-or-nothing phenomenon; it is something into which we grow as a dimension of our personal becoming. We do so in our struggles to embrace grace while eschewing Sin and its influences in our lives, but we also do so in and through the process and according to the dynamics of personal becoming that are natural to us as humans, for these are always already undertaken from within the ambit and invitation of grace itself (Rahner's supernatural existential). Consequently, as indicated earlier, we need not view our struggles to forgive exclusively under the rubric of Sin. They may also be the sign of the not-yet-attained freedom to forgive that God is still creating within us.

The recognition, implicit and underdeveloped in many Christian writers, that we grow into our capacity to forgive, has no counterpart in the moral philosophical discussions explored for this study. They do advert to the idea that forgiving takes time. They might even acknowledge that it is a process.[12] But the assumption is that the capacity for forgiving is already present and that it is the same for one moral agent as for another. Further, forgiving is treated as an "either/or" proposition. Either it is moral to forgive or it is not. Thus one who forgives—assuming the conditions for the moral enactment are in place—is engaged in moral behavior. In some philosophers the one who withholds forgiveness in those conditions is not acting morally. The lynchpin to this argument is the assumption that all have the same moral capacity. The idea that one grows into the *capacity* for forgiveness has a better footing among psychologists who read forgiving as a process.[13]

---

Volf, the idea is implicit in the disjunctive language he uses to name the phenomenon of transformation in faith. (See chap. 7.)

[12] See, for example, Griswold, *Forgiveness: A Philosophical Exploration*, 42, 98, 114; Norvin Richards, "Forgiveness," *Ethics* 99, no. 1 (October 1988): 77–97; Haber, *Forgiveness*, 18, 22.

[13] See, for example, Mona Gustafson Affinito, "Forgiveness in Counseling: Caution, Definition, and Application," 88–111, in *Before Forgiving: Cautionary Views of Forgiveness in Psychotherapy*, ed. Sharon Lamb and Jeffrie G. Murphy (New York: Oxford University Press, 2002) at 93, 98.

The Christian matrix of meanings, by contrast, provides something that distinguishes Christian forgiveness from both the moral philosophical discussions and those psychological approaches that avoid explicit (and, more often, implicit) reliance on assumptions derived from Christianity. It provides a narrative that can make sense of this growth and development in the *capacity* to forgive. It does so under the rubric of discipleship. This narrative involves the one facing the challenges of forgiveness in a larger context of meanings that can both support and challenge her growth. For the Christian narrative is not merely a personal story, such that the growth into forgiveness would be the journey of an isolated individual in conjunction with the assistance of a therapist (although a therapist might be involved). It is the story of a people, a community called "church." It is the story of the Body of Christ, in which all members together are called to confront the challenge of incarnating the Kingdom of God in all their relations.

This is not to suggest that the distinctiveness of Christian forgiveness on this point has been as sharply drawn by Christians as might currently be warranted, nor is it to suggest that Christians have all that is needful to articulate and explicitly support the promotion of Christian forgiveness as a dimension of discipleship into which we must grow. Indeed, Christians have much to learn from psychology about the dynamic processes involved in developing the capacity to forgive. This present study is, in part, an initial effort at conceptualizing how to integrate some of the findings of psychology into a theologically coherent, more holistic understanding of Christian forgiveness. But it is to suggest that Christianity has the resources for articulating the integral relation of this developmental dimension to the distinctiveness of Christian forgiveness. These resources have been inchoate in Christian self-understanding from the beginning. Further, the Christian narrative provides a context for making sense of both the developmental dimensions of undertaking the task of forgiving and the value of even attempting to do so. It does this in a manner not currently available to non-religious approaches to philosophy and psychology.

These three aspects of the enactment of forgiveness to which Christians are called illustrate the distinctiveness arising at the intersection of meaning and enactment within the Christian matrix of meanings. It is not that other traditions or approaches cannot or could not elaborate forgiveness in a way that might include analogous aspects. Rather, the Christian approach to forgiveness presented here, by the matrix of meanings expressed in its narrative, both affirms the positive value of these aspects and clarifies their integral place within the narrative itself. These are not options within Christian forgiveness; they are essential to Christian forgiveness *as Christian*.

## Implications of this Way of Naming Christian Forgiveness

This way of naming Christian forgiveness in its distinctiveness both emerges from and gives its own specificity to a Christian matrix of meanings. It therefore has implications for how we approach other articulations of Christian forgiveness, and Christian self-understanding more generally. Here it will be helpful to indicate in a preliminary way how this rethought Christian forgiveness stands in relationship to issues that have already surfaced.

### Gospel Hermeneutics

We have already touched on how the present approach to understanding Christian forgiveness can serve as a hermeneutic for reading the gospels. God's antecedent, proactive forgiveness has been mediated to us and revealed for us in the Incarnation (life, ministry, death, and resurrection of Jesus). The whole of Jesus' life makes present God's forgiving love as the advent of the Kingdom of God to which all are called. Thus whether healing a leper, casting out a demon, forgiving an adulteress, or admonishing the scribes and Pharisees, Jesus is making (sacramentally) present the dynamics of divine forgiveness that make reconciliation with God in the Kingdom possible.

Two parables on forgiveness (the Prodigal Son, the Merciless Servant) have already been discussed. Their relationship to this reading of the Christian narrative should be sufficiently clear. But two other passages bear special attention. The first is in the Sermon on the Mount. It is the instruction that Jesus' followers are to "turn the other cheek." Curiously, this passage received little explicit attention from either Volf or Jones, yet it is a direct statement about the practice of forgiveness. Unfortunately, it is also easily misunderstood. Taken as a command in isolation from any hermeneutic context, this teaching can become (and has been) an occasion for perpetuating abusive conduct. It can be read as a minimum, absolute standard of conduct. Not turning the other cheek can be taken as a rejection of what it means to be a Christian. Being Christian, therefore, would require that we remain in abusive situations. The history of this way of reading the passage has been written in the blood of its victims.

If we read this teaching from within the matrix of the Christian narrative presented in the previous chapter and the understanding of distinctively Christian forgiveness presented above, however, the teaching is no longer an isolated command. It becomes, instead, a sacramental mediation (by means of concept and language) of the eschatological Kingdom of God toward which Christians are oriented in their (our) trajectories of personal becoming. No longer a minimum standard of practice, it is an eschatological hope that, nonetheless, becomes present in us when, under the influence of the Holy Spirit, we are liberated for the ability to enact it here and now. But as a sacramental enactment of the Kingdom—by means of incarnating God's own way of responding to offenses—it has a twofold importance for disciples. On the one hand it manifests a freedom for the Kingdom into which we are called to grow. It is therefore a concrete orientation point for our growth in communion with God in Christ as disciples. We must grow and develop into the capacity to turn the other cheek.

On the other hand, as a sacramental enactment of the Kingdom it is part of the mission entrusted to Christians for the actualization of that Kingdom in our world. In this respect turning the other cheek requires the discernment of disciples seeking to *bear witness*. Simply submitting to abuse does not of itself witness to the Kingdom. The disciple on mission to advance the Kingdom must discern whether and under what conditions turning the other cheek will be effective in the advancement of the Kingdom or whether in the present context it will merely serve as capitulation to and perpetuation of evil. Both the capacity to discern and the capacity to enact the turning of the other cheek are realities into which we can only grow over time, in grace, as the Holy Spirit sets us free for the life of the Kingdom.

The second passage to consider is the parable of the Good Samaritan. This is not commonly taken as a story of forgiveness, but when it is read through the hermeneutic of the Christian matrix we have been elaborating and through the lens of distinctively Christian forgiveness articulated above, the connections begin to emerge. The Samaritan sees the need for healing. He opens a relational space within his own life to receive the person in need (as the priest and the Levite did not) and proactively commits himself to absorb the cost. The story illustrates the transformative love of the Samaritan; he turns a stranger into a neighbor and thereby becomes a neighbor to the stranger.

On one level this is a story of extraordinary hospitality. (In its unconditional character it moves in the direction of the hospitality envisioned by

Derrida.) As such, it points toward an eschatological fullness of relational openness that Christians identify with the Kingdom of God. Boundaries of kinship, identity, tribal rivalries, and social status fall away as we move through reconciliation to communion. But on another level, precisely because those boundaries—adverted to in the story, but set aside—do not impede becoming neighbor, this is a story of forgiveness. The Samaritan, by his enactment of hospitality, forgives the victim his otherness. Indeed, even the boundaries between hospitality and forgiveness begin to fade.

### Forgiving Non-moral Harm

This brings us back to the question of forgiving non-moral harms. If forgiving really is a matter of (re)opening a relational space within which relationship moving toward communion can be established or restored, then what obstructed the relationship need not be a moral harm. Indeed, it need only be a meaning that, in its recognition, occasions alienation by its position within one's personal matrix of meanings.

The examples indicated in chapter 6—a decision not to pursue a romantic relationship with someone who wants one, being let go from one's job because of economic reasons, and being challenged about one's addiction or self-destructive behaviors—would certainly fit here. Similarly, the realignment of one's trajectory of personal becoming so as to overcome ingrained racial, ethnic, or social prejudice, for example, although not necessarily a response to a specific harmful event, would still be a response to the meaning of a harm embedded in a socially mediated shared matrix of meanings. The fear and hostility, even resentment such prejudices carry are overcome by the same dynamics described in the human enactment of forgiveness. But the proactive, missionary dimensions of Christian forgiveness and the call to enact forgiveness in response to harms one has not directly experienced oneself can lead a Christian to activate the dynamics of Christian forgiveness in ways that do begin to look like hospitality. They draw the Christian into a much broader landscape of forgiveness than is commonly imagined, in order to make the Kingdom present.

### Forgiving and Reconciling

The Kingdom of God, as it has been presented, comes to expression when the quality and character of our relationships with one another are suffused by the life of Christ in the Holy Spirit. When that happens, barriers and sources of alienation have been surpassed and we are reconciled with one another. Forgiving is the response Christians are called to make to those conditions and events that occasion and perpetuate alienation. It opens the door to the possibility of reconciliation. But to reconcile requires that one accept the offer of forgiveness, with its naming and judgment of the situation that occasioned the relational rupture.

Forgiving and reconciling are thus two distinct enactments. Forgiving aims at reconciling. Reconciling presupposes forgiving. This is true whether one is speaking of forgiving and reconciling as basic human enactments or considering them as distinctly Christian. But the Christian articulation of forgiveness presented above also points toward further ways of naming the distinction. Forgiving differs from reconciling in that it is proactive, freely given, absorbs the cost of the offense, reaches out to those most in need of it, and is expressive of a missionary impulse. It is enacted unilaterally. Reconciling, on the other hand, multilateral. Two or more parties come together to actually reconstitute their relationship.[14]

Even though they are distinct in what they enact, forgiving and reconciling share some qualities in common in this Christian account. Both are sacramental mediations of encounter with God. Through the incarnation of forgiveness—opening the space for a possible reconciliation following an offense—the offended party makes sacramentally present in her own person the offer of God's own way of being toward the offender. This offer is itself an expression of the ongoing transformation of the offended party under the influence of the Holy Spirit into the presence of Christ for the offender (whether that is recognized as such or not). By his repentance, itself a movement of the Holy Spirit in union with the offender's freedom, the offender receives the forgiveness, with its judgment of the rupture, and mediates his own graced encounter with God back to the one who forgives.

But in neither case is the sacramental mediation a punctual event (occurring at only one point in time). Both forgiving and reconciling may have identifiable initiations in time, but they must be lived out *over* time. Their sacramentality is mediated in and through the ongoing process of the personal becoming of the participants as their responses to the harm come to expression in the alignment of their trajectories

---

[14] Griswold offers a valuable account of how this might work. The parties involved work to a common understanding of the event and its significance. Whereas Griswold sees this process as integral to forgiveness itself, I see it as the distinct enactment of reconciling. Griswold, *Forgiveness: A Philosophical Exploration*, 98–110.

of becoming with the advancement of the Kingdom of God. They are actual as sacramental expressions of the Kingdom in those moments when they shape the relating of those who seek to incarnate them, or, conversely, the eschatological Kingdom becomes actual at those times and in those places when we enact, and live from the enactment of, the dynamics of forgiving and reconciling. Thus, neither forgiving nor reconciling is an end in itself. Both derive their importance for Christianity from the invitation into *communion* of life and love with God and one another that we refer to as the Kingdom. In their enactments they are sacraments of the Kingdom.

### The Question of Soft Violence

One of the issues that surfaced in the philosophical discussions of forgiveness and again in our examination of traditional approaches to Christian forgiveness is the way in which violence has been inscribed into different approaches to forgiveness. We noted that coercion, whether through the threat of judgment or ostracism or some other means, frequently seeps into the understanding of the conditions for forgiveness. In the moral philosophical accounts we noted that one is threatened with moral censure in some cases if one does forgive (because the requisite conditions of moral forgiveness have not been fulfilled) or if one does not (because the conditions have been fulfilled).

We have noted in the preceding chapters that traditional Christian approaches to forgiveness are not above reproach in this regard. The traditional Christian narrative encodes violence into the story of divine forgiveness; God requires violent sacrifice in order to be able to forgive. From the standpoint of the Christian *enactment* of forgiveness of others, a kind of soft violence also can play a role. The threat of condemnation for not forgiving others has had a long history in the Christian spiritual imagination.

Both Volf and Jones attempt to ameliorate this problem in their presentations. They both hold that those who deny forgiveness to others place *themselves* in opposition to grace; this is their act of freedom, not God's. Volf further distances himself from retributive violence in his reading of the parable of the Merciless Servant in Matthew 18. Jones treads a narrow line between love of enemies and his support for the legitimacy of punishing offenders in certain circumstances. In the case of the unrepentant he also advocates excluding people from community, but always with a view toward their reform.

While their intentions are admirable, it is not clear that these authors are fully successful in removing violence from their theological explanations of Christian forgiveness. In part this may be a function of some ambiguity in the way they distinguish forgiving from reconciling. When the two become conflated, as they often do in the philosophical discussions, forgiving requires that one "pay the price of repentance" in order to be forgiven, and that one reconcile (as the completion of forgiveness) when the proper conditions of repentance have been fulfilled. Those who do not forgive are under the threat of moral condemnation. (Volf and Jones incline to the position that they condemn themselves.) This threat functions as a coercive pressure to exact conformity of behavior. It is a kind of soft violence.

The rethought approach to Christian forgiveness presented above attempts to eliminate the presence of soft violence from its understanding of forgiveness. First, its narrative recognizes that violence has occurred in Christ's sacramental incarnation of God's forgiveness, but violence as such was not a requirement on God's part. Second, the present account recognizes that forgiving is an ongoing process that we undertake from within our personal matrices of meanings as an expression and a specification of our trajectories of personal becoming. It might be that forgiving a particular harm or reconciling with a particular offender at this moment is beyond our capacity. Our yearning to be the forgiving and reconciling people we are called to be, even when we are not yet capable of this, may itself testify to the redemptive power of the Spirit, calling us to further and deeper transformation. But focusing the narrative on God's desire to give Godself to us in love as our fulfillment and salvation, rather than on our wretchedness and God's just wrath, shifts the deeper foundations of the narrative away from the coercive threat of punishment toward the invitation to relationship. This is a basement-level shift in meaning that runs counter to the ethos of the traditional narrative.

Of course, there might well be pain in coming to forgive and in enacting reconciliation, but this pain does not arise from the external imposition of a threat of punishment, coercing me into undertaking an enactment I would otherwise refuse. It is, rather, the pain that comes with conversion—with any struggle to grow and to realign our sense of self by appropriating challenging new meanings. For the one forgiving, it may be the pain of absorbing the offense or of recognizing that I am not as free for loving others as I thought I was. It might be the growing pains of a freedom for forgiving struggling to be born. For the one reconciling, it might be the pain of recognizing that I have harmed another and the struggle to repent of the harm I have done, so as to heal the relationship.

It is the struggle of realigning the trajectory of my future becoming. This is not the pain of a violence imposed but of a trajectory of transformative growth embraced at the intersection of freedom and grace.

## Diversity of Christian Motivations

The issue of soft violence brings us back to one of the themes common to Volf's and Jones's presentations: transformation of motivations. Both of their accounts emphasized the recognition that one is a sinner, has been judged, but has nonetheless been offered mercy. Repentance is the acceptance of this "judgment of grace." In that repentance the forgiven sinner is supposed to be moved by gratitude to become generous toward those who have sinned against her. This is the motivation that, in their accounts, makes forgiveness to be Christian.

In previous chapters I have taken issue with this position, essentially on two grounds. First, it lodges the distinctively Christian element in a singular, consciously appropriated interpretation of one's relationship with God as the exclusive motivation for forgiving. This conscious motivation presupposes that one accepts the specific narrative of salvation, based on the substitutionary atonement foundation, as the definitive interpretation of what it means to be Christian and in relationship with God. In point of fact, however, this is not the only Christian narrative available, nor is it as central to Christian self-understanding as the Incarnation, which this narrative marginalizes. So the claim that *this* understanding of one's relationship to God is definitive of Christian forgiveness is misplaced.

Second, this account of Christian motivation overlooks the fact that Christians, like any other human beings, can undertake to forgive for many possible reasons. Further, in any human act multiple motivations will be at work. So, too, with Christians. The understanding of a distinctive Christian forgiveness presented here allows for a variety of possible Christian motivations. One might be moved to forgive for the reasons identified by Volf and Jones, but one might also be moved by the desire to more closely imitate Jesus, or to continue his work to advance the Kingdom, or because of the desire to labor for transformative justice in accord with the teachings of Jesus; one might even desire to find healing for one's angry heart so as to be more loving. There are many distinctively Christian ways in which one might thematize the motivation to forgive. Any of these, and many others, could be the graced impetus that would render the motivation to forgive distinctly Christian.

**Forgiving and Remembering**

One of the themes running through Miroslav Volf's theology of forgiveness is the notion of forgetting. He maintains that the fulfillment of forgiveness occurs when the memory of the event is allowed to slip into oblivion.[15] This, he argues, is only fitting, for even God forgets our offenses.[16] Two aspects of his position deserve mention here. The first is his reading of the scriptural testimony. He observes:

> Scripture explicitly states that God doesn't even remember our sins.
> They don't come to God's mind (Jeremiah 31:34; Hebrews 8:12;
> 10:17). So it's not just that we're innocent at the moment we are
> forgiven. In God's memory, we've been made innocent across the
> entire span of our lives. God looks at us and doesn't superimpose on
> us our former transgressions. Our transgressions don't exist anywhere
> anymore. They don't stick to us as guilt, and they don't stick to God's
> memory of us. We were sinners, but we are no longer sinners—in a
> sense, not even sinners past![17]

The second aspect is eschatological. The fulfillment of the eschaton, for Volf, requires that the forgetting occur.

> If we remembered wrongs suffered in the world to come, we would
> not only defer to the wishes of evildoers, we would also pay too much
> respect to evil itself. What incredible power evil would have if once
> you had wronged someone, you, the person you had wronged, and
> God would remain permanently marked by it! Would there not in
> the eternal memory of wrongs suffered resound a hellish laughter
> of the seemingly defeated and yet strangely triumphant underworld,
> triumphant because it has succeeded in casting eternally its dark
> shadow over the world to come? To be fully overcome, evildoing
> must be consigned to its proper place—nothingness.[18]

From the perspective on Christian forgiveness presented above, Volf's insistence on forgetting is not only unnecessary, it is also theologically objectionable. It is unnecessary because it is based on a misunderstanding regarding events and their meanings. It presupposes that our forgiving of

---

[15] Volf, *Free of Charge*, 173–74, 177, 182.

[16] Volf, *Exclusion and Embrace*, 136; *Free of Charge*, 173–74, 177.

[17] Volf, *Free of Charge*, 173–74.

[18] Volf, *The End of Memory*, 214.

a wrong makes no difference to the meaning of the historical event that is being forgiven. A wrong that has been forgiven would be remembered *as forgiven*. It would be remembered as the occasion of a sacramental irruption of the Kingdom of God into the life of the one harmed and into the life of the one who received the forgiveness. Far from paying respect to evil, this memory would be an exaltation of the Glory of God triumphing over evil. Thus one of the implications of the rethought Christian forgiveness proposed here is that forgetting the offense is not necessary.

Such forgetting is also theologically problematic. Apart from Volf's inclination to read the metaphorical language of the scriptural texts as literal statements regarding God's mind, the position Volf is espousing renders our histories of personal becoming irrelevant to our identities and to the eschatological fullness of our relationship with God in the Kingdom. Who will I be before God except the one whom God's grace has transformed over the course of a history of personal becoming? For God to "forget" this would be for God to regard me apart from the reality of our history of relationship. Such an account seems to me to seek reassurance through the cultivation of a myth. It is a rendering both a-historical and counter-incarnational. Remembering the sins of the past, whether my own or those that have been committed against me, as having been overcome by grace and transformed thereby into sacramental encounters with God, it seems to me, is not the occasion for reproach that Volf seems to fear, but is the occasion for rejoicing in God's goodness.

### Dialogue with Secular Discussions of Forgiveness

The rethinking of Christian forgiveness presented here has implications for many of the issues raised in our explorations of the secular landscapes of forgiveness. As with the Christian approaches, so here too, the present approach reorients the basis for considering the questions raised in the secular discussions. We can see this by briefly revisiting three issues from within the matrix of Christian forgiveness: impossible forgiveness, the separation of the offender from the act, and the self-worth of the one forgiving.

#### Impossible Forgiveness

Jacques Derrida challenged the commonly held conviction that there is any such thing as forgiveness. Forgiveness is impossible. But if it were to be possible it would only be in the case of the unforgivable. In chapter

4 we explored the merits and limits of Derrida's provocation. Then, in the phenomenology of the human enactment of forgiveness presented in chapter 6, we made something of a *rapprochement* with Derrida's claims about the impossibility of forgiveness. Reading forgiveness through the lens of a human enactment that must be carried out in time and that implicates the depths of our personal matrices of meanings, including those complexes of meanings that operate beneath our consciousness, we recognized that we could only make a pronouncement on the completeness of an enactment of forgiveness at that moment when our personal becoming no longer has a future. In other words, only at the moment of death does our forgiving (or not) of another reach a point of irreversibility.

This suggests that, even without appealing to any theological frame of reference, forgiveness has an intrinsically "eschatological" orientation. It aims at an irreversibility that can never be fully assured so long as our personal becoming is in process. The forgiveness we seek to enact toward others—forgiveness as a completed state—is therefore, in this sense, "impossible." We are dealing here with a different sense of impossibility than Derrida had in mind. It does not derive from a deconstruction of the concept of forgiveness; rather, it is an "impossibility" that is intrinsic to the dynamics of the enactment human beings attempt when we seek to forgive.

The distinctive Christian forgiveness articulated here provides a theological account of this human experience. Understanding forgiveness as the foundation of the reconciliation of the eschatological Kingdom of God, we can render this impossibility of forgiveness as the tension between the "already" and the "not yet" of the Kingdom. Forgiveness has not yet permeated the course of human history, either as a whole or as a response to particular harms, as we hope for it to do in the fullness of the Kingdom. But at each moment when we undertake to forgive under the impulse of the Holy Spirit, however imperfectly we may do so, the Kingdom becomes actual, becomes sacramentally actual in and through our enactment of it. The impossible becomes actual by the transformation God's Spirit works in us as we incarnate the form of God's own forgiveness that has been revealed in Christ.

### Separating the Offender from the Offense

A persistent theme in forgiveness literature is the importance of separating the offender from the offense. As we have seen in our progress across the different forgiveness landscapes in this study, the separation called for can be problematized in different ways. In the moral philosophical discussions the separation is necessary if the forgiveness is to be a moral enactment. But Jeffrie G. Murphy believes there are multiple reasons for the forgiver to make such a separation, while Joram Graf Haber, Charles Griswold, and Pamela Hieronymi require that the offender repent. Derrida, for his part, argues that if one has repented there is no need to forgive because we are dealing with a different person. The separation brought about by the repentance has rendered the one who initially offended an inappropriate subject for forgiveness.

The writings of Miroslav Volf take a different approach. Forgiveness is possible independently of such a separation. The forgiving itself removes the guilt of the offender.[19] As indicated above, Volf maintains that forgiving reestablishes innocence. The obliteration of the offense he has in mind here comes very close to the kind of forgetting advocated by Derrida. The separation of the offender from the offense is actually a dimension of reconciliation. To receive the forgiveness offered, the offender must separate himself from the meaning of the harm and, to use L. Gregory Jones's language, accept the judgment of grace.

The theological difficulties with the idea of forgetting have already been identified above. The basis for the objections presented above also applies here. On the one hand, to forgive another we do need to be able to recognize that the offender is more—has greater and other meaning—than the meaning associated with the offense. We need to be able to recognize a distinction. But on the other hand, if forgiving does change the meaning of the offense for us—from mere offense to offense *as forgiven*, that is, from mere offense to sacramental event of transforming grace—then neither forgetting nor separating seems to be warranted. Retaining the association between the one who occasioned the harm and the harm, now transformed in meaning by grace, becomes part of the ongoing sacramentality of the event, both for the one forgiving and for the one forgiven (if and when he is able to receive it). Thus reading Christian forgiveness from within the dynamics of sacramental mediation of encounter with God offers an entirely different approach to the question of separating the offender from the offense.

[19] This is an important part of his account of forgiveness and of the rightness of forgetting the offense. See Volf, *Free of Charge*, 131, 173–74; Volf, *The End of Memory*, 119, 127, 137, 178.

*Self-Worth and Forgiveness*

One of the places where this Christian account (and many others) comes into conflict with secular discussions is on the importance of preserving the self-worth or self-respect of the one who has been harmed. The desire to preserve self-respect is invoked as a justification for withholding forgiveness until the offender has repented. The phenomenology of forgiveness as a human enactment of meaning has already challenged this assumption. It suggests that our self-respect is not lodged in any one response to any one event, but rather has its basis in a whole range of interrelated meanings and complexes of meanings within our sense of self and our self-world relations. The restabilization of the sense of self that occurs following an experience of harm is in part a process of reweaving the matrices relevant to our self-respect into a stable whole in the face of the history of the offense.

Depending on the other meanings involved and the nature of the offense, it is possible that one's sense of self and one's self-respect are most integrally expressed and affirmed by forgiving even before the offender has repented. For one who has embraced Christianity and its shared matrix of meanings, forgiving before the repentance of the offender could very legitimately be an affirmation of respect for one's own worth *as a Christian*. If one's sense of self is shaped by a faith commitment to advancing the Kingdom of God proclaimed by and incarnated by Jesus, she might well find her greatest worth in engaging the struggle to forgive. In the account of Christian forgiveness presented here, doing so would be the affirmation of a trajectory of personal becoming for the sacramental incarnation of the Kingdom in one's own life.

## Conclusion

Is there a distinctive Christian forgiveness? This is the question that has driven our inquiry. Our exploration of the various landscapes of forgiveness has led to an affirmative response. There is, indeed, a distinctive Christian forgiveness. It is not totally different from forgiveness as a basic human enactment; in that case it would be something else entirely. But Christian forgiveness, when compared with the phenomenology of forgiveness as a human enactment and when compared with the secular approaches examined along our journey of exploration, does have distinguishing features.

We can summarize these features briefly. Christian forgiveness finds its rationale in a narrative drawn from the events surrounding Jesus of Nazareth. That narrative arises from the faith of believers that Jesus is the

Christ, the anointed of God, the unique incarnation of God, the Risen Lord. The Christian narrative expresses a shared matrix of meanings Christians are called to internalize and embody in their lives, including through the enactment of forgiveness according to the manner of God's own forgiveness as revealed in Christ. It tells the believer that she is more than the recipient of the narrative; she is also the embodiment of its continuation to the extent that she is transformed by it.

Thus the Christian narrative gives distinctive meaning to the enactment of forgiveness: it is a transformative participation in the life and work of Christ. It is transformative for the one who forgives, for the one who is forgiven and receives that forgiveness, and for the larger range of relationships intersected by those involved in the forgiveness. The narrative, therefore, provides a way of specifying the desired trajectory of personal becoming of the Christian and the place of forgiveness in that trajectory, but its language of the Kingdom of God also indicates an eschatological orientation or purpose for undertaking to forgive.

The rethinking of Christian forgiveness presented here allows us to go beyond these basic affirmations and to articulate in a theologically coherent way how the narrative, the action of the Holy Spirit, and the trajectory of personal becoming intersect in the construction of the matrix of meanings of the individual Christian. It provides a framework for understanding multiple motivations (besides the gratitude for having been forgiven) as appropriately Christian for the individual enacting forgiveness, and, from within the understanding of creation as fundamentally sacramental, the rethinking of Christian forgiveness establishes a way of understanding the mission to bring forgiveness to those who have not repented and even to those who have not harmed us directly, thereby further underscoring the distinctiveness of Christian forgiveness.

Indeed, our rethought approach to Christian forgiveness makes it possible to articulate the coherence between God's way of forgiving, the Incarnation, the order of creation, the dynamics of redemption, the particular details of the life, ministry, death, and resurrection of Jesus, and our own participation in the advancement of the Kingdom of God. Affirming this coherence and the distinctiveness of Christian forgiveness as presented in this rethought form presupposes, of course, the disciple's commitment to this rendering of the Christian narrative. This commitment is expressed most fully not through conceptual affirmation, but through a life of ongoing conversion under the guidance of the Holy Spirit into the incarnation of the Kingdom of God.

# $\mathcal{A}$fterword

# Questions
# for Further Consideration

Our exploration of the landscapes of forgiveness, both secular and Christian, has touched on many more issues than we can satisfactorily address. The complexity of the question of forgiveness itself implies that our journey will never be complete; new questions will continually arise and old answers will be challenged by emerging, unforeseen insights. But the course we have followed in these pages has already pointed out places in this landscape of rethought Christian forgiveness that might well prove fruitful for further investigation.

## Developmental Processes

A first area for investigation is at the intersection of developmental psychological research and the understanding of Christian discipleship. It is not uncommon in the literature to discuss forgiving as a process. It has a beginning; it points toward a fulfillment. The account of personal becoming in terms of the construction of personal matrices of meanings provides a possible framework for exploring in greater detail the particularities of the development confronted by individuals in their own journeys of personal becoming. This is a line of inquiry worth pursuing.

In addition, there is a further developmental issue that invites investigation. Is forgiving the same enactment for a four-year-old as it is for an adolescent or for a middle-aged woman or man or for an elderly person? We have provided in these pages a general phenomenology of forgiving that would seem to have application to all ages. However, even assuming this general description to be accurate, we must still confront the question, within the Christian context, of the growth in transformation into the incarnation of the life of the Kingdom and how that might change the forgiveness enacted in different situations. How might the growth in the capacity to forgive also express itself in different enactments?

For example, what would it look like for a child suffering continual parental abuse to attempt to forgive, given the nature of the harm *and* the limited range of meanings available to the construction of the child's sense of self? Can the invitation of the Kingdom really expect as much of this child as it would call for from an adult in an abusive relationship? I think not. But how do we learn to discern and articulate the development required? The resources of developmental psychology and research into faith development are important here, but they need to be brought to bear particularly on the question of the development of the *capacity* to forgive, not only as a psychological issue but as a theological question.

### Self-Forgiveness

A second theme that has surfaced from time to time on our journey has been the question of self-forgiveness. This carries with it its own complexities. When we have done something that has harmed another we might well repent of it. We might even have begun the process of reconciliation with the one harmed. But we can still carry within us an internalized self-reproach that hampers a stable reweaving of our personal matrices of meanings. That non-integration can thwart our ability to flourish. It can skew our own processes of personal becoming just as much as clinging to resentments for the offenses of others can do. In the process it can hamper our ability to grow into the sacramental incarnation of the Kingdom we are called to be.

Self-forgiveness is the way we name the process of stabilizing our sense of self in the face of such self-reproach. But "self-forgiveness" is something of a misnomer. True, we do need to realign the internal meanings we use to attack ourselves, but the process of accomplishing this will not be purely an internal matter. It seems to me that, as with our sense of self and our self-world relations generally, so also in the case of self-forgiveness the reforming of meanings will be integrally related to the broader context of meanings we inhabit. In a mode analogous to the hope for transformation behind the forgiveness we offer to the not-yet-repentant and to third parties, as presented above, self-forgiveness must be co-mediated to us through our engagements with others. Others will communicate, through their acceptance and love for us, that we are not reducible to or definable by the events in our past that we use to punish ourselves.

This, too, deserves further exploration.

## The Question of Justice

Finally, it is important to mention the theme of justice. This has run as a background concern throughout most of the secular debates and has an important place within the Christian discussions as well. We have not devoted much explicit attention to justice in this study. Our concern has been to identify the dynamics involved when one undertakes to forgive as a human enactment and then to consider whether Christian forgiveness is in any way distinctive.

When the question of justice arises in moral philosophical discussions of forgiveness, the concern is commonly to identify what is morally right. This is often correlated with reestablishing a balance in relationship by means of retribution. This kind of justice is implicated in the traditional rendering of substitutionary atonement. God is in a dilemma, caught between God's absolute justice and God's absolute mercy. The atonement satisfies God's demand for justice and allows God to extend mercy.

This understanding of justice in relationship to a theology of Christian forgiveness is a problem. It reads into God's actions our own standards of justice. It makes it appear that God's absolute justice requires equalizing the "amount" of offense God has suffered with a payment to God's honor. In human affairs we do often act as though equalizing the balance is our normative standard of justice. This is implied in our retributive impulses.

But the revelation of God's forgiveness as incarnated in Jesus and as expressed in his teachings gives us a different picture. This is evident in the parable of the Prodigal Son. God's justice shows itself not in equalizing the balance but in going above and beyond equalizing, in pouring out God's own self in order to restore right relationship. God's justice—God's Righteousness—is marked by a superabundance of generosity that seeks to restore the order of life, the *logos* of life for which God created us. God's justice shows itself in redeeming what has been distorted by sin and by transforming it into an occasion for the sacramental expression of God's own Kingdom in the present moment. It shows itself in its incarnation. Far from being the counterweight to God's justice, God's forgiveness—the forgiveness Christians are called to enact as the sacramental incarnation of the Kingdom—is the expression of that justice.

This reading of God's justice through the lens of the present account of Christian forgiveness is only a preliminary step. It points out a direction deserving of further theological exploration.

# Bibliography

Abbey, Ruth. "Charles Taylor, Sources of the Self: The Making of the Modern Identity," 268–90, in *Central Works of Philosophy, Volume 5: Quine and After*, edited by John Shand. Durham: Acumen, 2006.

Affinito, Mona Gustafson. "Forgiveness in Counseling: Caution, Definition, and Application," 88–111, in *Before Forgiving: Cautionary Views of Forgiveness in Psychotherapy*, edited by Sharon Lamb and Jeffrie G. Murphy. New York: Oxford University Press, 2002.

Ahn, Ilsup. "The Genealogy of Debt and the Phenomenology of Forgiveness: Nietzsche, Marion, and Derrida on the Meaning of the Peculiar Phenomenon." *The Heythrop Journal* 51 (2010): 454–70.

Alison, James. *The Joy of Being Wrong: Original Sin Through Easter Eyes.* Foreword by Sebastian Moore. New York: Crossroad, 1998.

Anselm. *Basic Writings: Proslogium, Monologium, Cur Deus Homo, Gaunilo's In Behalf of the Fool.* Translated by Sidney Norton Deane. La Salle, IL: Open Court, 1962.

Aponte, Harry J. "Love, the Spiritual Wellspring of Forgiveness: An Example of Spirituality in Therapy." *Association for Family Therapy and Systemic Practice* 20 (1998): 37–58.

Atkins, Kim. "Friendship, Trust, and Forgiveness." *Philosophia: Philosophical Quarterly of Israel* 29, nos. 1–4 (May 2002): 111–32.

Badiou, Alain. "The Subject Supposed to Be a Christian: On Paul Ricoeur's Memory, History, Forgetting." Review of *Memory, History, Forgetting. The Bible and Critical Theory* 2, no. 3 (2006): 27.1–27.9.

Baker, Marjorie E. "Self-Forgiveness: An Empowering and Therapeutic Tool for Working with Women in Recovery," 61–74, in *Women's Reflections on the Complexities of Forgiveness*, edited by Wanda Malcolm, Nancy DeCourville, and Kathryn Belicki. New York: Routledge, 2008.

Balthasar, Hans Urs von. *The Moment of Christian Witness.* San Francisco: Ignatius Press, 1969.

———. *The Christian State of Life.* San Francisco: Ignatius Press, 1983.

————. *Convergences: To the Source of the Christian Mystery*. San Francisco: Ignatius Press, 1983.

————. *A Short Primer for Unsettled Laymen*. San Francisco: Ignatius Press, 1985.

————. *Theo-Drama: Theological Dramatic Theory*. Vol. 3, *Dramatis Personae: Persons in Christ*. San Francisco: Ignatius Press, 1992.

————. *Geschichte des eschatologischen Problems in der modernen deutschen Literatur*. Einsiedeln and Freiburg: Johannes Verlag, 1998.

Baumeister, Roy F., Julie Juola Exline, and Kristin L. Sommer. "The Victim Role, Grudge Theory, and Two Dimensions of Forgiveness," 79–104, in *Dimensions of Forgiveness: Psychological Research and Theological Perspectives*. Laws of Life Symposia. Philadelphia and London: Templeton Foundation, 1998.

Baynes, Kenneth. "Self, Narrative, and Self-Constitution: Revisiting Taylor's 'Self-Interpreting Animals.'" *Philosophical Forum* 41, no. 4 (2010): 441–57.

Bell, Daniel M., Jr. "Forgiveness and the End of Economy." *Studies in Christian Ethics* 20, no. 3 (2007): 325–44.

Blomberg, Craig L. "On Building and Breaking Barriers: Forgiveness, Salvation and Christian Counseling with Special Reference to Matthew 18:15-35." *Journal of Psychology and Christianity* 25, no. 2 (2006): 137–54.

Boersma, Hans. "Being Reconciled: Atonement as the Ecclesio-Christological Practice of Forgiveness in John Milbank," 183–202, in *Radical Orthodoxy and the Reformed Tradition*. Grand Rapids, MI: Baker Academic, 2005.

Boeve, Lieven. "Bearing Witness to the Differend: A Model for Theologizing in the Postmodern Context." *Louvain Studies* 20, no. 4 (Winter 1995): 362–79.

————. "Critical Consciousness in the Postmodern Condition: New Opportunities for Theology?" *Philosophy and Theology* 10, no. 2 (1997): 449–68.

————. *Interrupting Tradition: An Essay on Christian Faith in a Postmodern Context*. Louvain Theological & Pastoral Monographs 30. Louvain: Peeters, 2003.

Bonhoeffer, Dietrich. *The Cost of Discipleship*. Translated by R. H. Fuller. New York: Macmillan, 1963.

Bovensiepen, Gustav. "Attachment-Dissociation Network: Some Thoughts about Modern Complex Theory." *Journal of Analytic Psychology* 51 (2006): 451–66.

Brandsma, Jeffrey M. "Forgiveness: A Dynamic, Theological and Therapeutic Analysis." *Pastoral Psychology* 31, no. 1 (Fall 1982): 40–50.

Brauns, Chris. *Unpacking Forgiveness: Biblical Answers for Complex Questions and Deep Wounds*. Wheaton, IL: Crossway, 2008.

Burrows, Ruth. *Guidelines for Mystical Prayer*. London: Sheed and Ward, 1976.

Butler, Joseph. "Upon Forgiveness of Injuries." In *Sermons*. New York: Robert Carter & Brothers, 1729.

————. "Upon Resentment." In *Sermons*. New York: Robert Carter & Brothers, 1729.

Cantens, Bernardo. "Why Forgive? A Christian Response." *Proceedings of the American Catholic Philosophical Association* 82 (2009): 217–28.

Caputo, John D., and Michael J. Scanlon, eds. *God, the Gift, and Postmodernism*. Bloomington and Indianapolis: Indiana University Press, 1999.

Caputo, John D., Mark P. Dooley, and Michael J. Scanlon, eds. *Questioning God*. Bloomington: Indiana University Press, 2001.

Care, Norman S. "Forgiveness and Effective Agency," 215–31, in *Before Forgiving: Cautionary Views of Forgiveness in Psychotherapy*, edited by Sharon Lamb and Jeffrie G. Murphy. New York: Oxford University Press, 2002.

Chagigiorgis, Helen, and Sandra Paivio. "Forgiveness as an Outcome in Emotion-Focused Trauma Therapy," 121–41, in *Women's Reflections on the Complexities of Forgiveness*, edited by Wanda Malcolm, Nancy DeCourville, and Kathryn Belicki. New York: Routledge, 2008.

Christman, John. "Narrative Unity as a Condition of Personhood." *Metaphilosophy* 35, no. 5 (October 2004): 695–713.

Cioni, Patrick F. "Forgiveness, Cognitive Restructuring and Object Transformation." *Journal of Religion and Health* 46, no. 3 (September 2007): 385–97.

Coleman, Paul W. "The Process of Forgiveness in Marriage and the Family," 75–94, in *Exploring Forgiveness*, edited by Robert D. Enright and Joanna North. Madison: University of Wisconsin Press, 1998.

Congar, Yves. *The Mystery of the Church*. Baltimore: Helicon Press, 1960.

————. *The Holy Spirit in the "Economy": Revelation and the Experience of the Spirit*. Vol. 1 of *I Believe in the Holy Spirit*. Translated by David Smith. New York: Crossroad, 1997.

————. *"He Is the Lord and Giver of Life."* Vol. 2 of *I Believe in the Holy Spirit*. Translated by David Smith. New York: Crossroad, 1997.

————. *The River of the Water of Life (Rev 22:1) Flows in the East and in the West*. Vol. 3 of *I Believe in the Holy Spirit*. Translated by David Smith. New York: Crossroad, 1997.

Conway, Eamonn. *The Anonymous Christian—A Relativised Christianity? An Evaluation of Hans Urs von Balthasar's Criticisms of Karl Rahner's Theory of the Anonymous Christian*. Europäische Hochschulschriften 23, Theologie, Vol. 485. Frankfurt am Main and New York: Peter Lang, 1993.

Daly, Robert J. "Sacrifice Unveiled or Sacrifice Revisited: Trinitarian and Liturgical Perspectives." *Theological Studies* 64 (2003): 24–42.

————. "Images of God and the Imitation of God: Problems with Atonement." *Theological Studies* 68 (2007): 36–51.

————. "New Developments in the Theology of Sacrifice." *Liturgical Ministry* 18 (Spring 2009): 49–58.

————. *Sacrifice Unveiled: The True Meaning of Christian Sacrifice*. London and New York: T & T Clark International, 2009.

Dawkins, Richard. *The Blind Watchmaker: Why the Evidence of Evolution Reveals a Universe without Design*. New York: Norton, 1996.

————. *A Devil's Chaplain: Reflections on Hope, Lies, Science, and Love*. Boston: Houghton Mifflin, 2003.

————. *The God Delusion*. Boston: Houghton Mifflin, 2008.

DeCourville, Nancy, Kathryn Belicki, and Michelle M. Green. "Subjective Experiences of Forgiveness in a Community Sample: Implications for Understanding Forgiveness and Its Consequences," 1–20, in *Women's Reflections on the Complexities of Forgiveness*, edited by Wanda Malcolm, Nancy DeCourville, and Kathryn Belicki. New York: Routledge, 2008.

De Lubac, Henri. *The Splendour of the Church*. Translated by Michael Mason. London and New York: Sheed and Ward, 1956.

Denham, Susanne A., et al. "Emotional Development and Forgiveness in Children: Emerging Evidence" 127–42, in *Handbook of Forgiveness*, edited by Everett L. Worthington, Jr. New York: Routledge, 2005.

Dennett, Daniel C. *Darwin's Dangerous Idea: Evolution and the Meanings of Life*. New York: Simon & Schuster, 1995.

————. *Breaking the Spell: Religion as a Natural Phenomenon*. New York: Viking, 2006.

————, and Alvin Plantinga. *Science and Religion: Are They Compatible?* Point/Counterpoint Series. New York: Oxford University Press, 2011.

Derrida, Jacques. *Given Time: 1. Counterfeit Money*. Translated by Peggy Kamuf. Chicago: University of Chicago Press, 1992.

————. *Adieu to Emmanuel Levinas*. Translated by Pascale-Anne Brault and Michael Naas. Stanford, CA: Stanford University Press, 1999.

————. "Foreigner Question," 3–74, in Jacques Derrida and Anne Dufourmantelle, *Of Hospitality: Anne Dufourmantelle Invites Jacques Derrida to Respond*. Stanford, CA: Stanford University Press, 2000.

————. *On Cosmopolitanism and Forgiveness*. London: Routledge, 2001.

DiBlasio, Frederick A. "The Use of a Decision-Based Forgiveness Intervention Within Intergenerational Family Therapy." *Journal of Family Therapy* 20 (1998): 77–94.

Dickey, Walter J. "Forgiveness and Crime: The Possibilities of Restorative Justice," 106–20, in *Exploring Forgiveness*, edited by Robert D. Enright and Joanna North. Madison: University of Wisconsin Press, 1998.

Duffy, Stephen J. *The Dynamics of Grace: Perspectives in Theological Anthropology*. Collegeville, MN: Liturgical Press, 1993.

Duska, Ronald, and Mariellen Whelan. *Moral Development: A Guide to Piaget and Kohlberg*. New York: Paulist Press, 1975.

Enright, Robert D. "Counseling within the Forgiveness Triad: On Forgiving, Receiving Forgiveness, and Self-Forgiveness." *Counseling & Values* 40, no. 2 (1996): 107–27.

———, and Moral Development Study Group. "Piaget on the Moral Development of Forgiveness: Identity or Reciprocity?" *Human Development* 37, no. 2 (March–April 1994): 63–80.

———, and Joanna North, eds. *Exploring Forgiveness*. Madison: University of Wisconsin Press, 1998.

———, Suzanne Freedman, and Julio Rique. "The Psychology of Interpersonal Forgiveness," 46–62, in *Exploring Forgiveness*, edited by Robert D. Enright and Joanna North. Madison: University of Wisconsin Press, 1998.

Exline, Julie Juola, and Roy F. Baumeister. "Expressing Forgiveness and Repentance: Benefits and Barriers," 133–55, in *Forgiveness: Theory, Research, and Practice*, edited by Michael E. McCullough, Kenneth I. Pargament, and Carl E. Thoresen. New York: Guilford Press, 2000.

———, and Anne L. Zell. "Does a Humble Attitude Promote Forgiveness? Challenges, Caveats, and Sex Differences," 235–51 in *Women's Reflections on the Complexities of Forgiveness*, edited by Wanda Malcolm, Nancy DeCourville, and Kathryn Belicki. New York: Routledge, 2008.

Finlan, Stephen. *Problems with Atonement: The Origins of, and Controversy about, the Atonement Doctrine*. Collegeville, MN: Liturgical Press, 2005.

Fitzgibbons, Richard. "Anger and the Healing Power of Forgiveness: A Psychiatrist's View," 63–74, in *Exploring Forgiveness*, edited by Robert D. Enright and Joanna North. Madison: University of Wisconsin Press, 1998.

Flanigan, Beverly. "Forgivers and the Unforgivable," 95–105, in *Exploring Forgiveness*, edited by Robert D. Enright and Joanna North. Madison: University of Wisconsin Press, 1998.

Flannery, Austin, ed. *Vatican Council II: Constitutions, Decrees, Declarations*. Northport, NY: Costello, 1996.

Freedman, Suzanne, Robert D. Enright, and Jeanette Knutson. "A Progress Report on the Process Model of Forgiveness," 393–406, in *Handbook of Forgiveness*, edited by Everett L. Worthington, Jr. New York: Routledge, 2005.

Frie, Roger. "Identity, Narrative, and Lived Experience after Postmodernity: Between Multiplicity and Continuity." *Journal of Phenomenological Psychology* 42 (2011): 46–60.

Frise, Nathan R., and Mark R. McMinn. "Forgiveness and Reconciliation: The Differing Perspectives of Psychologists and Christian Theologians (Survey)." *Journal of Psychology and Theology* 38, no. 2 (Summer 2010): 83–90.

Galvin, John P. "Jesus Christ," 255–314, in *Systematic Theology: Roman Catholic Perspectives*, edited by Francis Schüssler Fiorenza and John P. Galvin. Minneapolis: Fortress Press, 2011.

Gartner, John. "The Capacity to Forgive: An Object Relations Perspective." *Journal of Religion and Health* 27, no. 4 (Winter 1988): 313–20.

Giddens, Anthony. *Modernity and Self-Identity: Self and Society in the Late Modern Age*. Stanford, CA: Stanford University Press, 1991.

Girard, René. *Violence and the Sacred*. Translated by Patrick Gregory. Baltimore, MD: Johns Hopkins University Press, 1977.

———. *The Scapegoat*. Translated by Yvonne Freccero. Baltimore, MD: Johns Hopkins University Press, 1986.

———. *Things Hidden Since the Foundation of the World*. Translated by Stephen Bann and Michael Metteer. Stanford, CA: Stanford University Press, 1987.

Grenz, Stanley J. *A Primer on Postmodernism*. Grand Rapids, MI: Eerdmans, 1996.

———, and John R. Franke. *Beyond Foundationalism: Shaping Theology in a Postmodern Context*. Louisville: Westminster John Knox, 2001.

Griswold, Charles L. *Forgiveness: A Philosophical Exploration*. Cambridge: Cambridge University Press, 2007.

———. "Forgiveness, Secular and Religious: A Reply to My Critics." *Proceedings of the American Catholic Philosophical Association* 82 (2009): 303–13.

———. "Debating Forgiveness: A Reply to My Critics." *Philosophia* 38 (2010): 457–73.

Haaken, Janice. "The Good, the Bad, and the Ugly: Psychoanalytic and Cultural Perspectives on Forgiveness," 172–91, in *Before Forgiving: Cautionary Views of Forgiveness in Psychotherapy*, edited by Sharon Lamb and Jeffrie G. Murphy. New York: Oxford University Press, 2002.

Haber, Joram Graf. *Forgiveness*. Savage, MD: Rowman & Littlefield, 1991.

Haight, Roger. "The 'Established' Church as Mission: The Relation of the Church to the Modern World." *The Jurist* 39, no. 1/2 (1979): 4–39.

———. *The Experience and Language of Grace*. New York: Paulist Press, 1979.

———. *Dynamics of Theology*. New York: Paulist Press, 1990.

———. "Sin and Grace," 375–430, in *Systematic Theology: Roman Catholic Perspectives*, edited by Francis Schüssler Fiorenza and John P. Galvin. Minneapolis: Fortress Press, 2011.

Hamilton, Kelly. "'Hate the Sin but not the Sinner': Forgiveness and Condemnation." *South African Journal of Philosophy* 28, no. 2 (2009): 114–23.

Heim, S. Mark. "Christ Crucified: Why Does Jesus' Death Matter?" *Christian Century* (7 March 2001), 12–17.

———. "Cross Purposes: Rethinking the Death of Jesus." *Christian Century* (22 March 2005), 20–25.

————. "No More Scapegoats: How Jesus Put an End to Sacrifice." *Christian Century* (5 September 2006), 22–29.

————. *Saved from Sacrifice: A Theology of the Cross*. Grand Rapids, MI, and Cambridge: Eerdmans, 2006.

Hieronymi, Pamela. "Articulating an Uncompromising Forgiveness." *Philosophy and Phenomenological Research* 62, no. 3 (May 2001): 529–55.

Hitchens, Christopher. *God Is not Great: How Religion Poisons Everything*. New York: Twelve, 2007.

————, ed. *The Portable Atheist: Essential Readings for the Nonbeliever*. Philadelphia: Da Capo, 2007.

————, and Douglas Wilson. *Is Christianity Good for the World?* Moscow, ID: Canon Press, 2009.

Hoffman, Karen D. "Forgiveness without Apology: Defending Unconditional Forgiveness." *Proceedings of the American Catholic Philosophical Association* 82 (2009): 135–51.

Holmgren, Margaret R. "Forgiveness and the Intrinsic Value of Persons." *American Philosophical Quarterly* 30, no. 4 (October 1993): 341–52.

————. "Forgiveness and Self-Forgiveness in Psychotherapy," 112–35, in *Before Forgiving: Cautionary Views of Forgiveness in Psychotherapy*, edited by Sharon Lamb and Jeffrie G. Murphy. New York: Oxford University Press, 2002.

Horner, Robyn. *Rethinking God as Gift: Marion, Derrida, and the Limits of Phenomenology*. New York: Fordham University Press, 2001.

Jankélévitch, Vladimir. "Should We Pardon Them?" Translated by Ann Hobart. *Critical Inquiry* 22, no. 3 (Spring 1996): 552–72.

————. *Forgiveness*. Translated by Andrew Kelly. Chicago: University of Chicago Press, 2005.

John Paul II, Pope. Encyclical Letter *On Social Concern* (*Sollicitudo Rei Socialis*). Boston: St. Paul Books and Media, 1984.

Jones, L. Gregory. "Crafting Communities of Forgiveness." *Interpretation* 54, no. 2 (April 2000): 121–34.

————. *Embodying Forgiveness: A Theological Analysis*. Grand Rapids, MI: Eerdmans, 1995.

————, and Célestin Musekura. *Forgiving as We've Been Forgiven: Community Practices for Making Peace*. Downers Grove, IL: InterVarsity Press, 2010.

Kaminer, Debra, Dan J. Stein, Irene Mbanga, and Nompumelelo Zungu-Dirwayi. "Forgiveness: Toward an Integration of Theoretical Models." *Psychiatry* 63, no. 4 (Winter 2000): 344–57.

Karen, Robert. *The Forgiving Self: The Road from Resentment to Connection*. New York: Doubleday Anchor Books, 2001.

Kasper, Walter. *The God of Jesus Christ*. New York: Crossroad, 1986.

Katongole, Emmanuel, and Chris Rice. *Reconciling All Things: A Christian Vision for Justice, Peace and Healing*. Downers Grove, IL: InterVarsity Press, 2008.

Kearney, Richard. "Forgiveness at the Limit: Impossible or Possible?" *Proceedings of the American Catholic Philosophical Association* 82 (2009): 85–97.

Kohlberg, Lawrence. *The Meaning and Measurement of Moral Development*. The Heinz Werner Lectures 13. Worcester, MA: Clark University Press, 1981.

———. *The Philosophy of Moral Development: Moral Stages and the Idea of Justice*. Essays on Moral Development 1. San Francisco: Harper & Row, 1981.

———. *The Psychology of Moral Development: The Nature and Validity of Moral Stages*. Essays on Moral Development 2. San Francisco: Harper & Row, 1984.

———, Charles Levine, and Alexandra Hewer. *Moral Stages: A Current Formulation and a Response to Critics*. Contributions to Human Development 10. Basel and New York: Karger, 1983.

Konstam, Varda, et al. "Forgiveness in Practice: What Mental Health Counselors Are Telling Us," 54–71, in *Before Forgiving: Cautionary Views of Forgiveness in Psychotherapy*, edited by Sharon Lamb and Jeffrie G. Murphy. New York: Oxford University Press, 2002.

Kremer, Alexander. "Richard Rorty's Interpretation of Selfhood," 191–99, in *Self and Society*. Central European Pragmatist Forum 4, edited by Alexander Kremer and John Ryder. New York: Rodopi, 2009.

Kristeva, Julia. "Hatred and Forgiveness; or, From Abjection to Paranoia," 183–94 in *Hatred and Forgiveness*, translated by Jeanine Herman. European Perspectives: A Series in Social Thought and Cultural Criticism. New York: Columbia University Press, 2010.

———. "The Passion According to Motherhood," 79–94, in *Hatred and Forgiveness*, translated by Jeanine Herman. European Perspectives: A Series in Social Thought and Cultural Criticism. New York: Columbia University Press, 2010.

———. "The Triple Uprooting of Israel," 213–21, in *Hatred and Forgiveness*, translated by Jeanine Herman. European Perspectives: A Series in Social Thought and Cultural Criticism. New York: Columbia University Press, 2010.

Kuhn, Thomas S. *The Structure of Scientific Revolutions*. Chicago: University of Chicago Press, 1962.

LaCugna, Catherine Mowry. *God for Us: The Trinity and Christian Life*. San Francisco: HarperSanFrancisco, 1991.

Lakeland, Paul. *Postmodernity: Christian Identity in a Fragmented Age*. Minneapolis: Fortress Press, 1997.

Lamb, Sharon. "Introduction: Reasons to Be Cautious about the Use of Forgiveness in Psychotherapy," 3–14, in *Before Forgiving: Cautionary Views of Forgiveness in Psychotherapy*, edited by Sharon Lamb and Jeffrie G. Murphy. New York: Oxford University Press, 2002.

———. "Women, Abuse, and Forgiveness: A Special Case," 155–71, in *Before Forgiving: Cautionary Views of Forgiveness in Psychotherapy*, edited by Sharon Lamb and Jeffrie G. Murphy. New York: Oxford University Press, 2002.

———, and Jeffrie G. Murphy, eds. *Before Forgiving: Cautionary Views of Forgiveness in Psychotherapy*. New York: Oxford University Press, 2002.

Leisegang, Hans. *Denkformen*. Berlin: Walter de Gruyter, 1928, new ed. 1951.

Lonergan, Bernard J. F. *Insight: A Study of Human Understanding*. London: Darton, Longman and Todd, 1957.

———. "Cognitional Structure," 205–21, in *Collection*, edited by Frederick E. Crowe and Robert M. Doran. London: Darton, Longman & Todd, 1967; repr. in Collected Works of Bernard Longergan. Toronto: University of Toronto Press, 1988.

———. "Natural Knowledge of God," 117–34, in *A Second Collection*, edited by William J. F. Ryan and Bernard J. Tyrrell. Philadelphia: Westminster, 1975; repr. in Collected Works of Bernard Lonergan. Toronto: University of Toronto Press, 1974.

———. "The Transition from a Classicist World-View to Historical-Mindedness," 1–10, in *A Second Collection*, edited by William F. J. Ryan and Bernard J. Tyrrell. Collected Works of Bernard Lonergan. Toronto: University of Toronto Press, 1974.

———. *Method in Theology*. New York: Seabury Press, 1979.

———. "The Form of Inference," 3–16, in *Collection*, edited by Frederick E. Crowe and Robert M. Doran. Collected Works of Bernard Lonergan. Toronto: University of Toronto Press, 1988.

———. "A Definition of Metaphysics," 181–99, in *Understanding and Being: The Halifax Lectures on* Insight, edited by Elizabeth A. Morelli and Mark D. Morelli. Collected Works of Bernard Lonergan. Toronto: University of Toronto Press, 1990.

———. "Common Sense," 84–108, in *Understanding and Being: The Halifax Lectures on* Insight, edited by Elizabeth A. Morelli and Mark D. Morelli. Collected Works of Bernard Lonergan. Toronto: University of Toronto Press, 1990.

———. "Elements of Understanding," 33–58, in *Understanding and Being: The Halifax Lectures on* Insight, edited by Elizabeth A. Morelli and Mark D. Morelli. Collected Works of Bernard Lonergan. Toronto: University of Toronto Press, 1990.

————. "Ethics and God," 225–51, in *Understanding and Being: The Halifax Lectures on* Insight, edited by Elizabeth A. Morelli and Mark D. Morelli. Collected Works of Bernard Lonergan. Toronto: University of Toronto Press, 1990.

————. "Judgment," 109–32, in *Understanding and Being: The Halifax Lectures on* Insight, edited by Elizabeth A. Morelli and Mark D. Morelli. Collected Works of Bernard Lonergan, 109–32. Toronto: University of Toronto Press, 1990.

————. "Knowing and Being," 133–55, in *Understanding and Being: The Halifax Lectures on* Insight, edited by Elizabeth A. Morelli and Mark D. Morelli. Collected Works of Bernard Lonergan. Toronto: University of Toronto Press, 1990.

————. "Metaphysical Analysis and Metaphysical Integration," 200–24, in *Understanding and Being: The Halifax Lectures on* Insight, edited by Elizabeth A. Morelli and Mark D. Morelli. Collected Works of Bernard Lonergan. Toronto: University of Toronto Press, 1990.

————. "Self-Appropriation and Insight," 3–32, in *Understanding and Being: The Halifax Lectures on* Insight, edited by Elizabeth A. Morelli and Mark D. Morelli. Collected Works of Bernard Lonergan. Toronto: University of Toronto Press, 1990.

————. "The Analogy of Meaning," 183–213, in *Philosophical and Theological Papers 1958–1964*, edited by Robert C. Croken, Frederick E. Crowe, and Robert M. Doran. Collected Works of Bernard Lonergan. Toronto: University of Toronto Press, 1996.

————. "The Mediation of Christ in Prayer," 160–82, in *Philosophical and Theological Papers 1958–1964*, edited by Robert C. Croken, Frederick E. Crowe, and Robert M. Doran. Collected Works of Bernard Lonergan. Toronto: University of Toronto Press, 1996.

————. "Method in Catholic Theology," 27–53, in *Philosophical and Theological Papers 1958–1964*, edited by Robert C. Croken, Frederick E. Crowe, and Robert M. Doran. Collected Works of Bernard Lonergan. Toronto: University of Toronto Press, 1996.

————. "Philosophical Positions with Regard to Knowing," 214–43, in *Philosophical and Theological Papers 1958–1964*, edited by Robert C. Croken, Frederick E. Crowe, and Robert M. Doran. Collected Works of Bernard Lonergan. Toronto: University of Toronto Press, 1996.

————. "The Philosophy of History," 54–79, in *Philosophical and Theological Papers 1958–1964*, edited by Robert C. Croken, Frederick E. Crowe, and Robert M. Doran. Collected Works of Bernard Lonergan. Toronto: University of Toronto Press, 1996.

————. "Time and Meaning," 94–121, in *Philosophical and Theological Papers 1958–1964*, edited by Robert C. Croken, Frederick E. Crowe, and Robert M. Doran. Collected Works of Bernard Lonergan. Toronto: University of Toronto Press, 1996.

Lowe, Walter. "Christ and Salvation," 235–51, in *The Cambridge Companion to Postmodern Theology*, edited by Kevin J. Vanhoozer. Cambridge: Cambridge University Press, 2003.

Lyotard, Jean-François. *The Postmodern Condition: A Report on Knowledge*. Translated by Geoff Bennington and Brian Massumi. Theory and History of Literature. Minneapolis: University of Minnesota Press, 1979.

————. *The Differend: Phrases in Dispute*. Translated by Georges Van Den Abbeele. Theory and History of Literature. Minneapolis: University of Minnesota Press, 1988.

Macaskill, Ann. "Just-World Beliefs and Forgiveness in Men and Women," 39–59, in *Women's Reflections on the Complexities of Forgiveness*, edited by Wanda Malcolm, Nancy DeCourville, and Kathryn Belicki. New York: Routledge, 2008.

McCullough, Michael E. "The Psychology of Forgiveness: History, Conceptual Issues, and Overview," 1–14, in *Forgiveness: Theory, Research, and Practice*, edited by Michael E. McCullough, Kenneth I. Pargament, and Carl E. Thoresen. New York: Guilford Press, 2000.

————, et al. "Interpersonal Forgiving in Close Relationships: II. Theoretical Elaboration and Measurement." *Journal of Personality and Social Psychology* 75, no. 6 (1998): 1586–1603.

————, and Everett L. Worthington Jr. "Religion and the Forgiving Personality." *Journal of Personality* 67, no. 6 (1999): 1141–64.

————, Kenneth I. Pargament, and Carl E. Thoresen, eds. *Forgiveness: Theory, Research, and Practice*. New York: Guilford Press, 2000.

Metz, Johannes Baptist. *Christliche Anthropozentrik: Über die Denkform des Thomas von Aquin*. Munich: Kösel, 1962.

Moody-Adams, Michele. "Reply to Griswold, *Forgiveness: A Philosophical Exploration*." *Philosophia* 38 (2010): 429–37.

Mullet, Étienne, and Michèle Girard. "Developmental and Cognitive Points of View on Forgiveness," 111–32, in *Forgiveness: Theory, Research, and Practice*, edited by Michael E. McCullough, Kenneth I. Pargament, and Carl E. Thoresen. New York: Guilford Press, 2000.

Murphy, Jeffrie G. "Forgiveness in Counseling: A Philosophical Perspective," 41–53, in *Before Forgiving: Cautionary Views of Forgiveness in Psychotherapy*, edited by Sharon Lamb and Jeffrie G. Murphy. New York: Oxford University Press, 2002.

————. *Getting Even: Forgiveness and Its Limits.* New York: Oxford University Press, 2003.

————, and Jean Hampton. *Forgiveness and Mercy.* Cambridge Studies in Philosophy and Law. Cambridge: Cambridge University Press, 1988.

Murray, Lynne. "Intersubjectivity, Object Relations Theory, and Empirical Evidence from Mother-Infant Interactions." *Infant Mental Health Journal* 12, no. 3 (Fall 1991): 219–32.

Neblett, William R. "Forgiveness and Ideals." *Mind* 83, no. 330 (April 1974): 269–75.

Neu, Jerome. "To Understand All Is to Forgive All—Or Is It?" 17–38, in *Before Forgiving: Cautionary Views of Forgiveness in Psychotherapy,* edited by Sharon Lamb and Jeffrie G. Murphy. New York: Oxford University Press, 2002.

————. "Rehabilitating Resentment and Choosing What We Feel." *Criminal Justice Ethics* 27, no. 2 (Summer/Fall 2008): 31–37.

Newberg, Andrew B., Eugene G. d'Aquili, Stephanie K. Newberg, and Verushka deMarici. "The Neuropsychological Correlates of Forgiveness, 91–110, in *Forgiveness: Theory, Research, and Practice,* edited by Michael E. McCullough, Kenneth I. Pargament, and Carl E. Thoresen. New York: Guilford Press, 2000.

Niebuhr, H. Richard. *Christ and Culture.* New York: Harper & Row, 1951.

Noll, Jennie G. "Forgiveness in People Experiencing Trauma," 363–75, in *Handbook of Forgiveness,* edited by Everett L. Worthington, Jr. New York: Routledge, 2005.

Nouwen, Henri J. M. *The Return of the Prodigal Son: A Story of a Homecoming.* New York: Doubleday, 1992.

Piaget, Jean. *Genetic Epistemology.* Translated by Eleanor Duckworth. New York: Columbia University Press, 1970.

Prusak, Bernard G. "What Are the 'Right Reasons' to Forgive? Critical Reflections on Charles Griswold's *Forgiveness: A Philosophical Exploration.*" *Proceedings of the American Catholic Philosophical Association* 82 (2009): 287–95.

Puka, Bill. "Forgoing Forgiveness," 136–52, in *Before Forgiving: Cautionary Views of Forgiveness in Psychotherapy,* edited by Sharon Lamb and Jeffrie G. Murphy. New York: Oxford University Press, 2002.

Pulaski, Mary Ann Spencer. *Understanding Piaget: An Introduction to Children's Cognitive Development.* New York: Harper & Row, 1971.

Raffoul, François. "Derrida and the Ethics of the Im-Possible." *Research in Phenomenology* 38 (2008): 270–90.

Rafman, Sandra. "Restoration of a Moral Universe: Children's Perspectives on Forgiveness and Justice," 215–34, in *Women's Reflections on the Complexities of Forgiveness,* edited by Wanda Malcolm, Nancy DeCourville, and Kathryn Belicki. New York: Routledge, 2008.

Rahner, Karl. "Concerning the Relationship Between Nature and Grace," 297–317, in *Theological Investigations* 1, translated by Cornelius Ernst. New York: Seabury Press, 1961.

———. *The Church and the Sacraments*. Quaestiones Disputatae 9. New York: Herder and Herder, 1963.

———. "The Concept of Mystery in Catholic Theology," 36–73, in *Theological Investigations* 4, translated by Kevin Smyth. London: Darton, Longman & Todd, 1966.

———. "Nature and Grace," 165–88, in *Theological Investigations* 4, translated by Kevin Smyth. London: Darton, Longman & Todd, 1966.

———. "Remarks on the Dogmatic Treatise '*De Trinitate*,'" 77–102, in *Theological Investigations* 4, translated by Kevin Smyth. London: Darton, Longman & Todd, 1966.

———. "The Theology of the Symbol," 221–52, in *Theological Investigations* 4, translated by Kevin Smyth. London: Darton, Longman & Todd, 1966.

———. "Anonymous Christianity and the Missionary Task of the Church," 161–78, in *Theological Investigations* 12. London: Darton, Longman & Todd, 1974.

———. "Considerations on the Active Role of the Person in the Sacramental Event," 161–84, in *Theological Investigations* 14. London: Darton, Longman & Todd, 1976.

———. "Observations on the Problem of the 'Anonymous Christian,'" 280–94, in *Theological Investigations* 14. London: Darton, Longman & Todd, 1976.

———. *Foundations of Christian Faith: An Introduction to the Idea of Christianity*. New York: Seabury, 1978.

———. "Understanding the Priestly Office," 208–13, in *Theological Investigations* 22. New York: Crossroad, 1991.

Ratzinger, Joseph. *Introduction to Christianity*. New York: Herder & Herder, 1970; repr. San Francisco: Ignatius Press, 1990.

Richards, Norvin. "Forgiveness." *Ethics* 99, no. 1 (October 1988): 77–97.

———. "Forgiveness as Therapy," 72–87, in *Before Forgiving: Cautionary Views of Forgiveness in Psychotherapy*, edited by Sharon Lamb and Jeffrie G. Murphy. New York: Oxford University Press, 2002.

Ricoeur, Paul. *Memory, History, Forgetting*. Translated by Kathleen Blamey and David Pellauer. Chicago: University of Chicago Press, 2004.

Rudd, Anthony. "In Defence of Narrative." *European Journal of Philosophy* 17, no. 1 (2007): 60–75.

Rye, Mark S., et al. "Religious Perspectives on Forgiveness," 17–40, in *Forgiveness: Theory, Research, and Practice*, edited by Michael E. McCullough, Kenneth I. Pargament, and Carl E. Thoresen. New York: Guilford Press, 2000.

Sampson, Edward E. "Deconstructing Psychology's Subject." *The Journal of Mind and Behavior* 4, no. 2 (Spring 1983): 135–64.

Sandage, Steven J., and Ian Williamson. "Forgiveness in Cultural Context," 41–55, in *Handbook of Forgiveness*, edited by Everett L. Worthington, Jr. New York: Routledge, 2005.

Sandford, John Loren, Paula Sandford, and Lee Bowman. *Choosing Forgiveness: Turning from Guilt, Bitterness and Resentment Towards a Life of Wholeness and Peace.* Lake Mary, FL: Charisma House, 2007.

Sandler, Joseph. "Fantasy, Defense, and the Representational World." *Infant Mental Health Journal* 15, no. 1 (Spring 1994): 26–35.

Schillebeeckx, Edward. *Christ the Sacrament of the Encounter with God.* Kansas City, MO: Sheed and Ward, 1963.

Schlochtern, Josef Meyer zu. *Sakrament Kirche: Wirken Gottes im Handeln der Menschen.* Freiburg: Herder, 1992.

Schwager, Raymund. *Der Wunderbare Tausch: Zur Geschichte und Deutung der Erlösungslehre.* Munich: Kösel, 1986.

Sells, James N., and Terry D. Hargrave. "Forgiveness: A Review of the Theoretical and Empirical Literature." *Journal of Family Therapy* 20 (1998): 21–36.

Semmelroth, Otto. *Die Kirche als Ursakrament.* Frankfurt: Josef Knecht, 1953.

Smedes, Lewis B. *Forgive and Forget: Healing the Hurts We Don't Deserve.* New York: HarperCollins, 1984.

———. *The Art of Forgiving: When You Need to Forgive and Don't Know How.* New York: Ballantine Books, 1996.

Swidler, Ann. "Saving the Self: Endowment Versus Depletion in American Institutions," 41–55, in *Meaning and Modernity: Religion, Polity and Self.* Berkeley: University of California Press, 2002.

Tangney, June Price, Angela L. Boone, and Ronda Dearing. "Forgiving the Self: Conceptual Issues and Empirical Findings," 143–58, in *Handbook of Forgiveness*, edited by Everett L. Worthington, Jr. New York: Routledge, 2005.

Taylor, Charles. *Sources of the Self: The Making of the Modern Identity.* Cambridge, MA: Harvard University Press, 1989.

———. *A Secular Age.* Cambridge, MA: Belknap Press of Harvard University Press, 2007.

Thomas, Joshua M., and Andrew Garrod. "Forgiveness after Genocide? Perspectives from Bosnian Youth," 192–211, in *Before Forgiving: Cautionary Views of Forgiveness in Psychotherapy*, edited by Sharon Lamb and Jeffrie G. Murphy. New York: Oxford University Press, 2002.

Verdeja, Ernesto. "Derrida and the Impossibility of Forgiveness." *Contemporary Political Theory* 30, no. 1 (April 2004): 23–47.

Voiss, James K. "Thought Forms and Theological Constructs: Toward Grounding the Appeal to Experience in Contemporary Theological Discourse," 241–56, in *Encountering Transcendence*, edited by Lieven Boeve, Hans Beybels, and Stijn van den Bossche. Leuven: Peters, 2005.

Volf, Miroslav. *Exclusion and Embrace: A Theological Exploration of Identity, Otherness, and Reconciliation*. Nashville: Abingdon Press, 1996.

————. *Free of Charge: Giving and Forgiving in a Culture Stripped of Grace*. Grand Rapids, MI: Zondervan, 2005.

————. *The End of Memory: Remembering Rightly in a Violent World*. Grand Rapids, MI: Eerdmans, 2006.

Vollmer, Fred. "The Narrative Self." *Journal for the Theory of Social Behavior* 35, no. 2 (2005): 189–205.

Wadsworth, Barry J. *Piaget's Theory of Cognitive Development: An Introduction for Students of Psychology and Education*. New York: David McKay, 1971.

Walrond-Skinner, Sue. "The Function and Role of Forgiveness in Working with Couples and Families: Clearing the Ground." *Journal of Family Therapy* 20 (1998): 3–19.

Watts, Fraser. "Christian Theology," 50–68, in *Forgiveness in Context: Theology and Psychology in Creative Dialogue*, edited by Fraser Watts and Liz Gulliford. London and New York: T & T Clark, 2004.

Weaver, J. Denny. "Response to Hans Boersma," 73–79, in *Atonement and Violence: A Theological Conversation*, edited by John Sanders. Nashville: Abingdon Press, 2006.

————. "Forgiveness and (Non)Violence: The Atonement Connections." *Mennonite Quarterly Review* 83 (April 2009): 319–47.

Webster, John. "The Human Person," 219–34, in *The Cambridge Companion to Postmodern Theology*, edited by Kevin J. Vanhoozer. Cambridge: Cambridge University Press, 2003.

Worthington, Everett L. *Forgiveness: Psychological Theory, Research, and Practice*. New York: Routledge, 2006.

————, ed. *Handbook of Forgiveness*. New York: Routledge, 2005.

————. "Initial Questions about the Art and Science of Forgiving," 1–13, in *Handbook of Forgiveness*, edited by Everett L. Worthington, Jr. New York: Routledge, 2005.

————. "More Questions about Forgiveness: Research Agenda for 2005–2015," 557–73, in *Handbook of Forgiveness*, edited by Everett L. Worthington, Jr. New York: Routledge, 2005.

Yancey, Philip. *What's So Amazing about Grace?* Grand Rapids, MI: Zondervan, 1997.

Yandell, Keith E. "The Metaphysics and Morality of Forgiveness," 35–45, in *Exploring Forgiveness*, edited by Robert D. Enright and Joanna North. Madison: University of Wisconsin Press, 1998.

Zahavi, Dan. "Is the Self a Social Construct?" *Inquiry* 52, no. 6 (December 2009): 551–73.

Zahnd, Brian. *Unconditional?* Lake Mary, FL: Charisma House, 2010.

Zeuthen, Katrine, Signe Holm Pedersen, and Judy Gammelgaard. "Attachment and the Driving Force of Development: A Critical Discussion of Empirical Infant Research." *International Forum of Psychoanalysis* 19 (2010): 230–39.

# Index

409